Rising from the Mailroom to the Boardroom

Internal Audit and IT Audit

Series Editor: Dan Swanson, Dan Swanson and Associates, Ltd.,
Winnipeg, Manitoba, Canada

The Internal Audit and IT Audit series publishes leading-edge books on critical subjects facing audit executives as well as internal and IT audit practitioners. Key topics include Audit Leadership, Cybersecurity, Strategic Risk Management, Auditing Various IT Activities and Processes, Audit Management, and Operational Auditing.

Corporate Governance: A Pragmatic Guide for Auditors, Directors, Investors, and Accountants
Vasant Raval

The Audit Value Factor
Daniel Samson

Managing IoT Systems for Institutions and Cities
Chuck Benson

Fraud Auditing Using CAATT: A Manual for Auditors and Forensic Accountants to Detect Organizational Fraud
Shaun Aghili

For more information about this series, please visit: https://www.routledge.com/Internal-Audit-and-IT-Audit/book-series/CRCINTAUDITA

Rising from the Mailroom to the Boardroom

Unique Insights for Governance, Risk, Compliance, and Audit Leaders

Bruce R Turner, AM, CRMA, CISA, CFE, MAICD

CRC Press
Taylor & Francis Group
Boca Raton London New York

CRC Press is an imprint of the
Taylor & Francis Group, an **informa** business

First edition published 2021
by CRC Press
6000 Broken Sound Parkway NW, Suite 300, Boca Raton, FL 33487-2742

and by CRC Press
2 Park Square, Milton Park, Abingdon, Oxon, OX14 4RN

ISBN: 9780367559991 (hbk)
ISBN: 9781032042909 (pbk)
ISBN: 9781003096047 (ebk)

Typeset in Times LT Std
by KnowledgeWorks Global Ltd

Dedicated to my family for their unconditional love, inspiration, and support. To our children, Nicole, Jacqueline, and Glen, and their partners Robert, Brendan, and Sally. To our grandchildren, Elina, Elijah, Lucinda, Zachary, Ashton, and Shauntelle. And especially to my loving wife and best mate, Bea, for her unwavering care, encouragement, and devotion throughout our more than 40 years together.

Contents

PART 4 Postface

Other Recent Books by the Author

- *New Auditor's Guide to Internal Auditing* (Internal Audit Foundation, 2019)
- *Team Leader's Guide to Internal Audit Leadership* (Internal Audit Foundation, 2020)
- *Powering Audit Committee Outcomes* (Internal Audit Foundation, 2020)

Epigraph

"You can listen to what everybody says, but the fact remains that you've got to get out there and do the thing yourself."

Dame Joan Sutherland
Australian opera singer and actress (1926–2010)

Disclaimer

Firstly, an alert for any Aboriginal or Torres Strait Islander readers. There is reference to and images of people who have passed away.

Most of the stories in this book are informed by true-life events. However, the sequencing has been rearranged so stories do not always correspond to the entity cited at the start of the chapter. Personal and organizational identifiers have been removed or deliberately left vague, other than those listed in the dedication and acknowledgements, or as captions of photographs.

Accordingly, names, characters, businesses, events, and incidents other than those explicitly cited should be viewed as either products of the author's imagination or applied in a fictitious manner. Any resemblance to organizations or actual persons, living or dead, is purely coincidental.

Monetary values used in the book are quoted in Australian dollars (AUD). To facilitate comparison to other currencies, in mid-2020 the value of AUD1,000 equaled USD685, EUR612, or GBP552.

Acknowledgments

To CRC Press (Taylor & Francis Group) for their commitment to educative storytelling across the globe. Special thanks to Gabriella Williams and Daniel Kershaw of the Taylor and Francis Group for their exemplary publishing support and encouragement throughout the project; to Dan Swanson for his ongoing mentoring and support; to Manisha Singh and Kyle Meyer for their professional efforts in editing the manuscript; and to the subject matter expert reviewers for providing invaluable advice and ideas.

Foreword

This book will support aspiring professionals, business leaders, and board members in becoming fit for the future. It collates fresh ideas and strategies to help people address daily workplace challenges and ultimately develop in their careers.

The author, Bruce Turner, is a well-respected transformational leader who has extensive experience on audit committees and boards, coupled with deep and broad professional governance, risk, compliance, and audit experience, across the government, health, manufacturing, and financial services industries. As such, he is positioned to see things through the eyes of an audit committee chairman and board director, so that he clearly reconciles audit committee and board needs with what should be provided.

Bruce shares his insights on holistically managing and advancing a career across five decades through storytelling, case studies, practical examples, illustrations, and photographs. The visuals are amazing! These insights will inspire the adoption of better practices. He has not shied away from reflecting on both the ups and the downs of the journey to show that even though a career does not always follow a smooth and uneventful trajectory, a significant legacy for the wider community sits at the end of the rainbow. The cautionary tales about challenges that can test one's resolve help to open one's eyes to the challenges.

The original *Four-I Framework for Career Development* (intuition, ideas, intent, and impact) reflects on the different stages of a professional career from learning the ropes for a firm career foundation, through helping others succeed, and embracing executive challenges, to ultimately shaping high-level boardroom and C-suite agendas. The takeaways are drawn together into 101 building blocks, each one providing crucial career-long learnings.

The book is fresh, well-written, relevant, and generates insights that help readers to optimize their impact and outcomes. It will help business leaders, governance, risk, compliance, and audit leaders to look beyond the known, enabling them to rewire their inherent thinking processes to accommodate the expectation that they deliver value through relevant insights and foresight, and ultimately meaningful outcomes.

Bruce captures the essence of change in the executive summary when he espouses, "Governance, risk management, compliance and assurance professionals have evolved from simply sharing a hindsight perspective to delivering fresh insights, and are increasingly expected to demonstrate foresight. In delivering insights and foresight it is crucial to understand the dynamics of conversations in the boardroom and around the audit committee table. This book provides those unique perspectives."

The insights immersed throughout this book will aid boards and audit committees to embrace world class oversight practices to their performance and conformance activities, by inspiring improvements in the secretariat and others that support them. That will, in turn, help close the gap between what boards and audit committees expect and what is being delivered from business leaders and governance, risk management, compliance, and assurance specialists reporting to them.

Dan Swanson CIA, CISA, CAP
President and CEO
Dan Swanson and Associates
Winnipeg, Canada

What Others Are Saying

"When I was a young receptionist, the idea that I would one day have a 'career' and become a Non-Executive Director and Chair of Audit and Risk Committees was completely alien to me! The 'how' I got there was very challenging and on reflection the 'thing' I lacked the most was a mentor who could show me the picture of what may lay ahead and how to manage it. I wish I had Bruce's incredible experience and expertise, that he has captured so well in this book, as my guide. His genuine love of developing and supporting others shines through and we are all the 'more-wise' and 'well-armed' through this book!"

Dianne Hill
Non-executive Company Director Australia

"Readers will find this a wonderful journey with real life experiences. The format is very good, and Bruce's explanations make it an easy process to follow. I particularly like the guide to learning and reading."

Bob McDonald OAM
Business Leader and Past Chairman of the USA-based IIA Global Board of Directors

"Bruce is a prolific author in his field and is well-known as a luminary of the internal audit profession in Australia and internationally. His professional reputation is first class. I haven't seen a book on the market that specifically compares to this. It will be of specific interest to the internal auditing community, other audit professionals, governance, risk and compliance professionals, practitioners, researchers, and students. The book will also be of relevance to boards and audit committees."

Andrew Cox
Audit Committee Chairman Australia

"Bruce inspired me to seriously pursue an internal audit career and rise to the chief audit executive level. His reputation in the industry speaks for itself based on his many audit and risk management achievements within the financial services and government sectors in Australia. In this book Bruce has distilled many lessons learned from his rich career into a pragmatic and structured approach to career management. I highly recommend it to any professional wanting to better understand the mindset and skills needed to advance through leadership roles up to and including board membership."

Glen Howard
Chief Audit Executive Canada

Executive Summary

When people first join the workforce they have a natural intuition, and this is one of the single most important attributes that differentiates individuals with high potential from those that will inevitably fall into an "average" performance level. It's important to recognize the wisdom of Dame Anita Roddick who said, "Whatever you do, be different. If you're different, you will stand out."

As people develop through different stages of their career, they glean ideas from others or develop new ones themselves. Inspiration can be drawn from the incredibly talented and visionary Walt Disney who said, "It's kind of fun to do the impossible." This is vitally important when businesses strive to differentiate themselves through innovative products and services; talented individuals ultimately make a difference!

Once they reach an executive level (or a role that is sufficiently influential within an organization, profession, or as a scrutineer), individuals need to operate with intent so that others follow them in the march towards realizing the values, vision, objectives, and goals of the entity. Jack Welch sagely observed, "Before you become a leader, success is all about growing yourself. After you become a leader, success is about growing others."

Once people reach the pinnacle of their career sitting around the boardroom table (or in another influential role), they can have a profound impact not just on their entities but on their broader communities. The wisdom of Dr Stephen Covey helps to shape the thinking of these people, "To achieve goals you've never achieved before, you need to start doing things you've never done before."

The journey from the "mailroom to the boardroom" follows the story of a young professional who initially moved into the internal auditing profession as part of the "new breed," then rose through the ranks into senior leadership and chief audit executive roles, before assuming audit committee and board roles that had an immense influence on governance, risk, compliance, and audit professionals. **Exhibit 0.1** illustrates the four-I framework for career development from the mailroom to the boardroom.

The storytelling provides insights to people at all levels on the importance of positioning oneself to step into leadership roles, help them understand how to evaluate and pursue potential career growth opportunities, and provide tips on how to holistically manage and advance their career.

Success does not always follow a smooth and uneventful trajectory, and this story reflects insights from both the ups and the downs of the journey. Each chapter shares insights, better practices, case studies, practical examples, and real-life challenges. Irrespective of the reader's professional

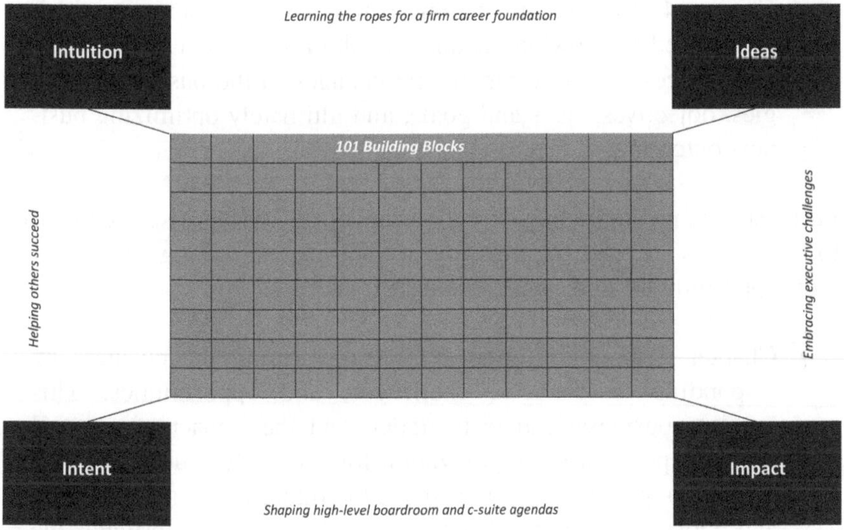

EXHIBIT 0.1 The four-I framework for career development – from the mailroom to the boardroom.

level and aspirations, these stories and accompanying tips will inspire higher-level thinking and deliver practical solutions aimed at enhancing organization-wide governance, risk, compliance, and assurance practices.

Part 1 of the book focuses on the need for establishing a firm career foundation by learning the ropes. It reflects on the importance of realizing your potential by choosing to act in ways that drive your success.

- Chapter 1 kicks off by reflecting on techniques for inspiring staff to perform at the optimal level, and introduces functions of business leaders that help to nurture a reputation as an employer of choice.
- Chapter 2 delves into delivering optimal customer service, which requires business leaders to develop a clear direction, motivate staff to deliver sustained success, embed a customer-centric culture, and align customer service delivery to business strategies, objectives, risks and goals.
- Chapter 3 works its way through approaches for sustaining a nimble and well-controlled business environment that requires business leaders to maintain a robust control environment, respond to evolving business opportunities, and inspire the people and equip them to succeed, which ultimately translates into growing the business and periodically refreshing the business strategies, objectives, risks and goals.

- Chapter 4 leads us into shaping better business outcomes which is achieved by growing the talent pool, making the hard decisions when necessary, accommodating changes to the business strategies, objectives, risks and goals, and ultimately optimizing business outcomes.

Part 2 shifts into embracing executive challenges. It impresses on the need to help others succeed by investing in their growth, taking an interest in their opportunities, and caring about their success.

- Chapter 5 identifies options for transforming the business by responding to changes, challenges, and opportunities. This requires business leaders to understand the impact of external changes, position the organization for successful business transformation, pursue action to reshape the future business landscape, and boost the strength of the team to deliver. It encapsulates the sentiment attributable to Jack Welch that, "Before you become a leader, success is all about growing yourself. After you become a leader, success is about growing others."
- Chapter 6 focuses on translating corporate values and business changes into sustained success, which is founded on living the corporate values, maintaining credibility with staff, gaining business efficiencies, and translating business changes into success.
- Chapter 7 identifies working within the business as a critical success factor for governance, risk, compliance, and assurance specialists, as it helps them to deliver what boards and business leaders truly need.
- Chapter 8 rounds out this part by taking a deep dive into the challenges of leading a transformational agenda, a common requirement for contemporary business leaders and those that support them. It emphasizes the need to stay focused on the stakeholders, deliver upon stakeholder expectations by nurturing a performance culture and customer-centric mindset, maintain a continuous improvement philosophy, and navigate the inevitable challenges and changes.

Part 3 reflects on opportunities for shaping the high-level agenda in the boardroom and the C-suite. It emphasizes that success comes from keeping the big vision in sight, fueling your vision with perseverance, then embracing your unique talents.

- Chapter 9 addresses the challenges of securing board roles and meaningfulness in retirement. This involves maintaining meaningful conversations, understanding the role, responsibilities and dynamics of boards, striving to make a difference, and keeping fit and focused on the end game.

- Chapter 10 emphasizes the importance of leveraging your personal brand to shape capability and champion causes. It explores two key themes – shaping the capability of emerging leaders and championing causes that help to make the world a better place.
- Chapter 11 considers the importance of shaping a strong audit committee performance, achieved by maintaining a continued focus on the responsibilities assigned by the board, establishing a credible oversight function, aligning the skills to the needs of the function, and driving an outcomes-focused approach.
- Chapter 12 closes out part three by addressing the essential ingredients for the board's oversight of business performance and conformance, including providing clarity of direction, establishing the fundamentals for sustained success, driving a values-based culture, and knowing how the business is really operating.

Part 4 provides a postface (i.e. additional information at the end of a book about the people and events that put the earlier chapters into perspective). This helps to draw the threads together by emphasizing the importance of remembering where you came from and to learn from the past, while focusing on where you need to go, how you'll get there, and being mindful of the legacy you'll leave.

- Chapter 13 outlines the steps for realizing your full potential and emphasizes the need for establishing firm foundations for continued success, providing the nourishment for your career to take shape, nurturing a professional personal brand and polished image, and maintaining an eye on the future while leaving your footsteps in the sand.
- Chapter 14 draws on more recent events to emphasize the ongoing need to respond to changes in the global business environment, which results in leveraging fresh ways of operating, maintaining longer-term business sustainability, staying connected and attuned to opportunities, and ultimately safeguarding the business, its people, and the brand.
- Chapter 15 takes a glance into the future given there are many new technology developments that will reshape the way businesses operate in the future through innovative methods, systems, and devices, which, in turn, will result in a huge increase in the number of cybercrimes and hackers that organizations will need to combat.

Governance, risk management, compliance, and assurance professionals have evolved from simply sharing a hindsight perspective to delivering fresh insights, and are increasingly expected to demonstrate foresight. In delivering insights and foresight it is crucial to understand the dynamics of conversations in the boardroom and around the audit committee table.

The book provides unique perspectives that help business leaders shape governance, risk management, compliance, and assurance efforts that reflect world-leading practice. In doing so, it ultimately helps boards, audit committees, and business leaders enhance and protect business value and achieve business objectives and strategies.

The book will inspire people from all levels, and will especially appeal to those who enjoy the insights gained from storytelling, case studies, and practical examples. Readers will gain value from reading and embracing the building blocks. How they derive value will depend on their role and responsibilities. In some cases, they can implement building blocks themselves or direct or influence others to do so. Notably:

- Boards will gain insights on how to better control the organization while balancing the sometimes-conflicting demands of their conformance and performance obligations. They will be well-placed to champion the building blocks attributable to business leaders, auditors, and GRC specialists by encouraging them to embrace fresh ideas.
- Audit committees and other board committees can champion the building blocks that shape good governance and boost effective financial reporting, risk management, internal control, compliance, and assurance activities, including external audit and internal audit. They can also directly embrace the range of practices that enhance the value they deliver to the board and to business leaders.
- The CEO can gain ideas (or reminders) that aid in optimizing shareholder value and/or delivering services. They can also challenge governance, risk, compliance, and assurance specialists to adopt leading practices that help the organization to realize its vision, mission, business objectives, and strategies in line with organizational values.
- Business leaders (including members of the C-suite) will gain ideas on strategic thinking, inspiring employees to embrace the organization's vision, build teams, develop talent, make decisions, and ultimately grow the organization.
- The chief audit executive and internal auditors will be better-placed to independently undertake audits that add value, improve the organization's operations, and help it to achieve its objectives.
- Governance, risk management, compliance, and other assurance functions will gain ideas that boost the meaningfulness and outcomes of second line of defense functions.

This is an essential read for any business professional – across different stages of their career – who is seeking to understand the core skills and experiences required to plan an effective career and achieve incremental steps up the ladder of success. It is of equal interest to educators and career counsellors. The book provides a unique contribution through 101 discrete building blocks that cover the whole career life-cycle up to and including the board level.

About the Author

Bruce R Turner AM, CRMA, CGAP, CISA, CFE, MAICD, FFIN, FIPA, FFA, FIML, PFIIA, JP

Bruce is a well-respected transformational leader who has extensive experience on audit committees and boards, coupled with deep and broad professional governance, risk, compliance, and audit experience. He established an exemplary record as a chief audit executive (CAE).

He was appointed a Member (AM) in the Queen's Birthday Honours of 2015 in recognition of his significant service to public administration through governance and risk management practices and to the profession of internal auditing. His global certifications in risk management assurance, government auditing, information systems auditing, and as a fraud examiner are complemented by him achieving fellow status with the Financial Services Institute of Australasia, Institute of Public Accountants, Institute of Management and Leaders, and Institute of Internal Auditors Australia; he has also achieved professional membership with the Australian Institute of Company Directors.

Bruce has held board and independent audit committee roles over the last 15 years in 30 diverse organizations, including central government, construction, customer service, environment, finance, for-purpose, health, infrastructure management, local government, natural resources, parklands, parliamentary services, regulatory authorities, state revenues, supreme audit institution, telecommunications, and transport. He is a past international chair of the Global Public Sector Committee of the Institute of Internal Auditors (IIA) 2014–2015, spent six years on the IIA–Australia Board to mid-2018, and remains an active executive coach, mentor, and White Ribbon Ambassador.

He has more than five decades of practitioner and leadership experience across the globe, traversing the energy, financial services (commercial, merchant, and central banking), government, manufacturing, and transport sectors. He has mentored, supported, nurtured, and led professionals, audit committee members, CEOs, and board chairs. He is well-positioned to share his wisdom in this book.

Bruce was the 2008 recipient of the Bob McDonald Award, which is the highest honor that can be conferred by IIA–Australia. In the same year, he was a Penrith City Wall of Achievement recipient in his hometown (one of Australia's top 20 cities by population), recognizing his success in influencing the efficient, effective, and ethical operation of organizations critical to the local community.

Bruce retired from fulltime work in 2012 after five years as chief internal auditor at the Australian Taxation Office, one of the largest public sector organizations in Australia. He previously held CAE roles at commercial service delivery organizations, Integral Energy Australia, and StateRail. Under his stewardship, StateRail was just one of two Australian recipients ever of IIA–Global's Commitment to Quality Improvement Award. He has presented papers at conferences across the world and is an accomplished author, and was awarded an IIA–Global Outstanding Contributor Award in 2014.

He continues to pursue his passion for inspiring the development of others and advancing the profession through storytelling. In his first decade of retirement, he authored more than 40 publications, co-authored an additional 15, and reviewed and edited another 40. He lives in Australia at the Blue Mountains, west of Sydney, with his wife of more than 40 years, Bea; their children and grandchildren live close by.

Preface

KEY FEATURES OF THE BOOK

1. Has broad global application, especially for developed nations across the five populated continents, and is equally relevant across myriad industries and the private, government, and not-for-profit sectors.
2. Provides governance, risk, compliance, and audit professionals with fresh insights that enable them to deliver to key stakeholders to a higher standard by gaining a unique perspective of the conversational dynamics in the boardroom and around the audit committee table.
3. Shares insights on how to holistically manage and advance a career across five decades, through to audit committee and board roles.
4. Tells the story from a board and audit committee perspective with the aim of helping governance, risk, compliance, and audit leaders to look beyond the known. That way they will be equipped to close the gap between what they provide to boards and audit committees and what those functions expect.
5. Includes takeaways, resources, useful references, and a study guide.

OVERALL CONSTRUCT

The book is structured in four parts as follows. A page at the start of each part will provide high-level insights about that element aimed at whetting the appetite and reflect the central character's *rising* knowledge and awareness. Then 12 primary chapters are evenly spread through the three main parts of the book, and closes out with a postface to draw in the formative years and more recent global events.

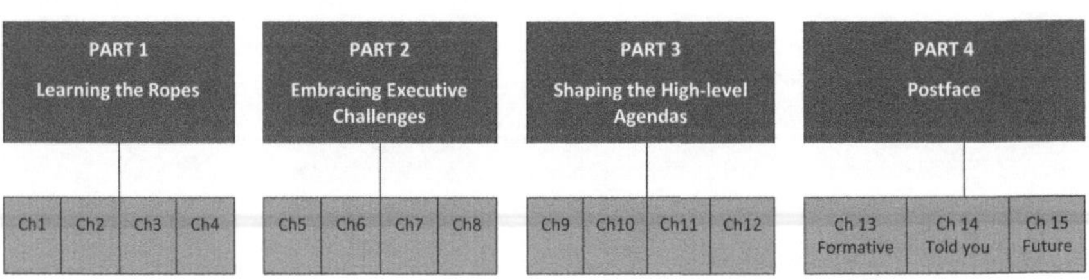

CHAPTER CONSTRUCT

Each chapter has a consistent construct as illustrated below.

Personal story charting the career from the mailroom to the boardroom. This is the 'central character' and flows through from chapter to chapter and gradually builds.	
Short sharp commentary on the role that was held, together with a profile of the entity (e.g. nature, dimensions, breadth of operations, total assets, equity, profit, staffing numbers).	
Key takeaways and Deep Dives	Highlight the key takeaways, lessons learned, and challenges (personal, professional, career-wise).
	Deep dive through case studies into a number of themes related to the elements of leadership, business acumen, governance, risk, compliance, and auditing.
	Practical 'how to' examples and templates associated with the above elements.
	Each of the personal stories translates into broader influences which are implicit in the takeaways.
	Each chapter wraps-up with *Ten Closing Reflections* to help the reader digest the insights, by summarizing key lessons to be learned and messages or actions for the reader.

TIMEFRAMES

Throughout the book, reference is made to different decades throughout my working career. These descriptors are related to the following indicative timeframes. The decades are not intended to align precisely with the different stages of growth.

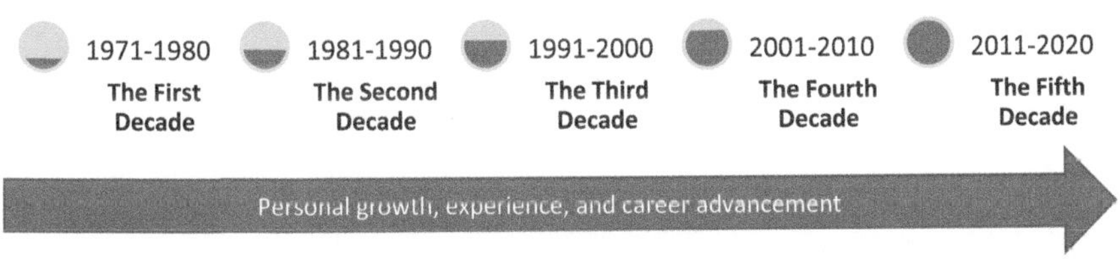

PHOTOS

Collage representing the 1st stage of growth	Collage representing the 2nd stage of growth	Collage representing the 3rd stage of growth	Mixed collage - the career bookends

Each photo includes a caption that links to a story in the book. The collage reflects the story and insights that underpin each part, and run through the chapters.

THE 101 BUILDING BLOCKS FOR SUCCESS

Building a new home requires many skills, from design and architecture, through to bricklaying, carpentry, electrical, and plumbing, and finished off with painting, fittings, and flooring. All of the diverse trades play different roles in getting the home ready for occupation. Building a career has similar parallels.

The book showcases 101 different building blocks for crafting a career, and these are summarized on the next page. The takeaways are drawn from four different phases (or parts) of a successful career and are designed to equip people with unique, powerful, and practical ideas to build excellence in leadership. Each building block should be embraced regularly for sustained success in the longer-term. The building blocks provide a useful study list and reflect all the skills I recommend readers acquire as they move into more senior leadership and oversight roles.

101 Building Blocks – The Key Takeaways

Ch							
Part 1 – Learning the Ropes							
1	Onboard younger employees thoughtfully	Create a learning environment	Maintain a fun business environment	You reap what you sow	Leverage emotional intelligence	Apply the risk appetite	Shape the control environment
2	Embrace the vision and values	Understand the culture	Grasp key business drivers	Develop business acumen	Evolve product knowledge and customer service imperatives	Understand the purpose of business	Nurture a reputation as an employer of choice
3	Understand the changing business environment	Assess new product risks	Meet stakeholder expectations	Develop capability	Evolve the business assurance arrangements	Develop an assurance map	Maintain resilience
4	Identify talent	Maintain professional development	Deal with poor performance	Balance internal alignment and external focus	Manage business restructuring	Drive excellence in leadership	Learn from the international scene
Part 2 – Embracing Executive Challenges							
5	Lead the change agenda	Build capacity and capability	Address professional blind spots	Shape business transformation	Inspire others	Respond to once-in-a-lifetime events	Consider competition pressures
6	Step-up the internal audit vision	Monitor outcomes from shared services and outsourcing	Establish key performance indicators	Manage whistleblowers meaningfully	Maintain effective communication with staff	Maintain behavioral standards	Manage mergers and acquisitions

7	Work within the business	Shape good investigations governance	Inspire a culture of integrity	Apply risk management across the business	Maintain effective compliance	Ensure business continuity	Monitor insurance arrangements
8	Lead a transformation agenda	Establish meaningful stakeholder communications	Inspire innovation and improvement	Recognize good performance outcomes	Manage customer complaints well	Maintain focus when under attack	Prepare for "life's third act"
Part 3 – Shaping the High-level Agendas							
9	Work well with the board	Find the right board	Make the transition	Stay connected	Maintain health and wellbeing	Pay it forward	Reflect on the journey periodically
10	Understand your personal brand	Shine the light on domestic violence	Focus on mental health	Deliver mentoring and coaching	Improve Indigenous health and wellbeing	Provide storytelling that is meaningful	Volunteer to help others
11	Drive the capability and diversity of audit committees	Leverage the company secretary	Deliver meaningful audit committee reporting	Focus on the fundamentals	Shape audit committee performance	Nurture GRC better practices and coordination	Oversight digitization
12	Maintain a skills-based board	Embed the corporate values	Shape the organizational strategy	Understand the lived culture	Oversight business performance and conformance	Optimize communication between the board and board committees	Manage CEO succession planning

Part 4 - Postface								
The Formative Years								
13	Leverage your curiosity	Evaluate and pursue potential career growth opportunities	Remain motivated	Present oneself professionally	Invest in personal professional growth	Stay mates for life	Fix it if it's broken	Leave a legacy
And We Told You So … the 2020s								
14	Embrace crisis management	Maintain a pandemic plan	Pursue red tape reduction	Sustain the supply chain long-term	Consider risks to sovereignty	Maintain professional connections	Watch out for others in need	Position yourself to step from one level of leadership to another
A Glance into the Future …								
15	Leverage the insights of IT auditors							

There are supplemental summaries in the back of the book that provide more context on its content, including 101 Key Insights, Listing of Exhibits, and Further Reading.

AUDIENCE

Rising from the Mailroom to the Boardroom provides essential insights for boards, audit committees, business leaders, auditors, and GRC specialists. Within the context of this book, these descriptors have the following meanings.

Description	Meaning
Boards	The governing body, being the persons or officers having ultimate control of an organization. In the private and for-purpose sectors this is usually the board of directors, whereas in the public sector this could be the board for a government trading enterprise, department head where there is no board (e.g. secretary, director general, chief executive), or the local council (local government).
Audit committees	A committee of the board with its objectives defined and documented in its charter, and its efficiency and effectiveness measured against its objectives. An independent audit committee is fundamental to good governance, and typically (i) focuses on financial reporting integrity; (ii) oversees risk and assurance activities including external audit, internal audit, risk management, internal control, and compliance; and (iii) liaises with the board, auditors and management. The internal audit activity typically reports functionally to the audit committee.
CEO (chief executive officer)	The CEO is charged with overseeing the entire operation of an organization with a view to realizing its vision, mission, business objectives and strategies in line with organizational values. The CEO typically reports to the board, with responsibilities spanning effective operating, marketing, financial, cultural and legal strategies that optimize shareholder value or deliver services within the public sector.
Business leaders	People at the highest level within an organization who provide strategic thinking, inspire employees to embrace the organization's vision, build teams, develop talent, make decisions, and ultimately grow the organization. They include members of the c-suite. The c-suite refers to the executive-level managers within an organization, such as the CEO, chief financial officer (CFO), chief operating officer (COO), and chief information officer (CIO).
Auditors	*Internal auditors* - People within the organization whose job it is to independently undertake internal auditing, aimed at adding value and improving an organization's operations and helping to achieve its objectives. *Chief audit executive* - the head of internal audit; the person in a senior position responsible for effectively managing the internal audit activity in accordance with the internal audit charter and the mandatory elements of the International Professional Practices Framework. *External auditors* – Persons who are external to and independent of the organization who undertake an external audit of the financial statements in accordance with laws and external auditing standards.
GRC specialists	*Governance, risk management, and compliance* - people who specialize in the second line of defense functions. *Assurance* encompasses the work of auditors.

EXHIBIT 0.2 Meaning of boards, audit committees, business leaders, auditors, and GRC specialists.

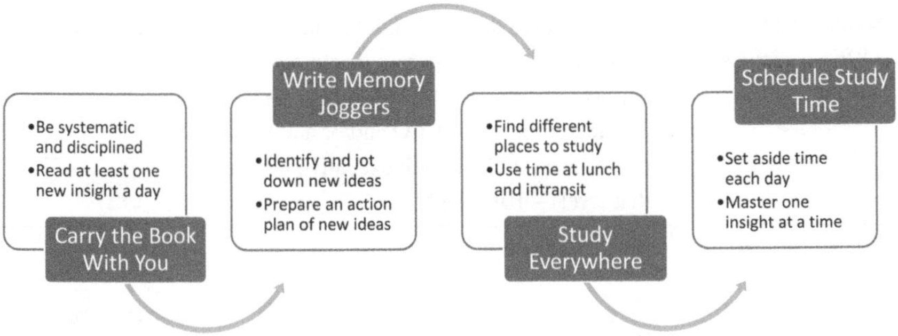

EXHIBIT 0.3 How to best learn the insights from this book.

STUDY GUIDE

The book contains an extensive range of insights for people to digest, and some will benefit from a structured "study plan" to help them learn and apply the ideas. **Exhibit 0.3** shows how this could be constructed. Each of the primary chapters concludes with "Closing Reflections" to aid the study (145 in all). The reflections that focus on the "board" or "audit committee" are equally relevant for business leaders and governance, risk, compliance, and assurance specialists who can champion the concepts.

A proven technique is to embrace a 100-day improvement plan, where individuals read through one of the insights (and the related closing reflections) each day for just over three months. They then document and implement those ideas that resonate with them as opportunities to enhance current governance, risk management, compliance, and assurance arrangements. Shorter study plans can be pursued by board and audit committee members or those aspiring to those roles as they will be building on their base learning.

Your Role	Areas of Focus	Study Plan Length
Board and audit committees	• Read in-depth chapters 9, 10, 11, 12, and Postface 2020s (36 insights) • Browse through other takeouts and delve deeper into areas of interest	50-day study plan
Business leaders	• Read in-depth chapters 4, 5, 8, 9, 10, and Postface (51 insights) • Delve into chapters 9, 11, and 12 to understand stakeholder needs • Browse and recap chapters 1 to 3 and refresh relevant activities • Scan chapters 6 and 7 if mature governance, risk, compliance, and assurance arrangements are in place (otherwise delve more deeply to drive change)	75-day study plan

Auditors and GRC specialists	• Read in-depth the whole book, study new concepts, identify opportunities to be applied, and develop an action plan for consideration by the CEO and/or audit committee (or chief audit executive if below that level) – 101 insights	100-day study plan

Part 1

Learning the Ropes

Key message: It's important to realize your potential by choosing to act in ways that drive your success.

"Bruce Turner is one of the most capable officers I have had the pleasure to work with. The potential for him is unlimited because with his knowledge and ability he would be able to undertake without difficulty any position.

Mr Turner has been a tower of strength at this office and everything asked of him has been done with speed and accuracy. His cooperation with other staff including me has been unbeatable."

Clive Morley
Bank Manager
State Bank of New South Wales
June 1983

1 Packing a Pistol in the Mailroom

Business skills are vital to the success of governance, risk, compliance, and assurance professionals in the modern business world. Learning an industry from the ground up can help to launch a successful career through well-rounded grassroots experience, though an untrained teenager carrying a pistol is unlikely to fit within contemporary risk tolerance levels. This chapter highlights emotional intelligence, passion for learning, risk comprehension, and an innovative mindset as crucial levers in forging a pathway to success ... and it also signals the value of heeding life lessons, like punctuality, given a career was almost extinguished on "day one" upon arriving late to an induction session. It highlights the importance of the message from Walt Disney (1901–1966), "It's kind of fun to do the impossible."

Entity Profile and Role

Sector:	Financial services sector – retail banking
Entity:	Rural Bank of New South Wales
Entity description:	The Rural Bank operated as a state-owned limited-scope financial institution that primarily lent to and dealt with farmers during its early years. It operated from 1933 until 1982 when its mandate was extended to a standard commercial bank, and its name was changed to the State Bank of NSW. Because of its limitations on operating as a savings bank, the Rural Bank established a relationship with the Tamworth Building and Investment Society (TBIS) in November 1976. The TBIS changed its name to the Rural Building and Investment Society (RBIS) with transactions accepted throughout the Rural Bank network. The RBIS ultimately transferred its engagements to the State Building Society in October 1982 For entity metrics, see Chapter 4
Primary role:	Clerical, accounting, and customer services
Main responsibilities:	Entry-level (junior) clerical and ledger-keeping roles. Steady rise into customer service, telling (cashier) then examining and supervisory roles
Timeframe:	The First Decade. (Descriptors for the timeframe are provided at the beginning of the book to reference the different decades throughout my working career. These descriptors are indicative and are not intended to align precisely with the different stages of growth)
Purpose of Table (relevant to all chapters):	The content in this table is included at the start of each chapter to provide context to the storytelling in terms of the role and responsibilities I held at that time, and the nature of the organizations where I was working

PERSONAL STORY

I entered the workforce during a time when great change was gaining momentum.

- Gough Whitlam was a transformational political leader who was elected Australian Prime Minister in 1972. One of his early decisions was to abolish conscription and end Australia's involvement in the Vietnam war. This was personally significant, as I was nearing an age where I could well have been compelled to enter military service.
- The banking industry was on the cusp of computerization which made many of the manual processes obsolete. I am glad though that I learnt the bank's back-office operations from the ground up as it gave me "street cred" through my later banking roles.
- Importantly, banks had traditionally used "seniority" as the sole basis of promotion, but this was transitioning to a "performance-based" regime. As I had been identified as a high performer, this aided my career trajectory.

As a result of a school competency assessment, the school's career advisor mentioned to me that I would be well-suited to banking, and there was a job on offer at the Rural Bank in my hometown of Penrith. I was given a phone number to call, which I did about a week later; in hindsight, I was a bit casual about it.

I ultimately met the bank manager and was given some forms to fill out which had to be completed in traditional fountain pen and ink. As I had been using a ballpoint pen for several years, I ended up splattering ink all over the forms and was reluctant to hand them in. But I did so after some "gentle parental persuasion." My chances of securing the job were slim, but I was unconcerned as I was not actively looking for a job and the six weeks of vacation before senior high school was quite appealing.

To my surprise, I was one of 6 junior bankers appointed to the Rural Bank's Penrith branch in the summer of 1971, joining a local staff of around 40. My starting salary was a modest $1,636 per annum (equivalent to $10,426 in 2020). This was one of the largest Rural Bank branches in the state outside the Sydney CBD and was designated as a "super grade" branch. I started a few days after I finished high school. In retrospect, a break would have been nice.

There I was in the Rural Bank mailroom in Penrith using an old typewriter to address correspondence and using a wet sponge to affix the postage stamps. It was late-1971 and I had left secondary (high) school to start my first full-time job. I had turned 16 the month before. It was prior to *any* computerization and the modern technologies that would emerge over the ensuing decades.

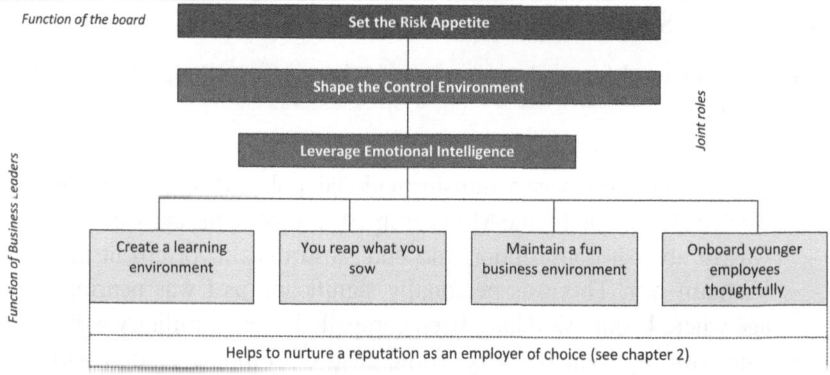

EXHIBIT 1.1 Inspiring staff to perform at the optimal level – board and business leader roles.

The key insights from this phase of my story are:

- Onboard younger employees thoughtfully.
- Create a learning environment.
- Maintain a fun business environment.
- You reap what you sow.
- Leverage emotional intelligence.
- Apply the risk appetite.
- Shape the control environment.

CONTEXT

Many business leaders attribute the success of the business to their staff. There are many factors that inspire staff to perform at an optimal level to help the business achieve its strategies, objectives, and goals. Some of these elements are discussed in this chapter and illustrated in **Exhibit 1.1**; underpinning these efforts are the risk appetite established by the board, and the control environment maintained by the business leaders.

KEY TAKEAWAYS AND DEEP DIVES

Onboard Entry-Level Employees Thoughtfully

Setting the Scene

My first day in the workforce involved an induction session conducted face-to-face at the bank's corporate headquarters in Martin Place Sydney. Beginning my first fulltime job and spending the first day in Sydney was a bit daunting for a 16-year-old kid (involving train trips totaling nearly two hours, across a distance of 40 miles). One of the other new appointees was Stephen McDonald (who went onto acting fame after a few years in the bank); Stephen and I agreed to travel together, as he was confident, an experienced train traveler, was a couple of years older, and knew his way around the city. Or so we thought!

We managed to get ourselves lost, and finally made our way into the induction session nearly an hour late. At the time, the facilitator was stressing the importance of punctuality. It was an uncomfortable start to my working career. It was a good lesson though, and I made a point thereafter of always being on time. I took personal responsibility for my movements, and was attuned to travel logistics and had a Plan B in case there was an unexpected disruptive event.

The bank had a structured development program for its junior bankers and that experience impressed upon me the importance of creating a learning environment (discussed in the next section). I had learnt from day one that punctuality is paramount and demonstrates respect to others. But there were many idiosyncrasies of fulltime work compared to school that I needed to learn.

In the last century, bankers were promoted based on seniority, and performance was not a factor. While that changed over time (to my benefit), one of the early lessons was that "rank has its privileges." All senior positions were held by males, and it was customary to call them "Mr <surname>." You were never permitted to call them by their first name. There was a clear pecking order.

While I started my first job straight from high school, now-a-days entry-level employees for "white collar" roles at large entities (e.g., financial institutions, government departments, and professional firms) usually come through established entry-level employment programs tailored for graduates, cadets, and scholars. An overview of these programs is contained in **Exhibit 1.2**.

As I rose into more senior roles, I recognized the value of supporting entry-level employment programs. While it is essential to have a core of experienced veterans on the team, graduates often bring a fresh energy, enthusiasm, and a thirst for learning. A critical success factor was building a relationship with the manager of the entry-level employment programs and extolling the benefits of attaching people from all disciplines into a governance, risk, compliance, or assurance functions. We steadily built a reputation as a "go to" place and gained further momentum when people from non-financial areas like marketing, HR, and communications reflected on the benefits of their experience.

By way of example, we were quite successful in engaging in the graduate program when I was at the Australian Tax Office and at one stage had

EXHIBIT 1.2
Examples of common entry-level employment programs

Program Type	Overview	Requirements
Graduate program	A two-year fulltime development program, consisting of four 6-month rotations. (Some programs are shorter, e.g., three rotations over eighteen-months).	Must have completed or be completing final year of an undergraduate degree at university.
Cadet program	A one- to two-year development program with cadets placed in business areas related to their undergraduate qualification. Work for a minimum of 14 hours a week during the university semester and 35 hours a week during university breaks.	Must be entering their penultimate or final year of an undergraduate degree at university. (Note: May have the opportunity to stream into the graduate program.)
Scholar program	A three- to five-year program with scholars having the option to work 14 hours a week during the university semester and must work 35 hours a week during the university break. University fees are reimbursed at the end of each semester with a credit average to be maintained to remain on the program.	Must be entering the first or second year of an undergraduate degree at university. (Note: May have the opportunity to stream into the graduate program.)
Cadet program for other vocational educational and training	A two-year development program, for people from diverse backgrounds, looking to gain paid work experience whilst they undertake a comprehensive non-university tertiary course in a related discipline (e.g., business, marketing, IT, project management).	Studying for a vocational qualification with a registered training organization or government tertiary training entity. (Note: Will have an opportunity to apply for roles within the entity at the completion of the program.)

six graduates in our team. While I was based interstate, each month or so when I visited the Canberra and outer-Melbourne offices, I would allocate an hour or so to meet with the graduates and have an informal conversation. I would respond to their questions or a topic they suggested, or I would select a topic that was relevant to their stage of development and we would talk through that. Graduates in other parts of the business would reflect that they had never even seen their senior executive in charge.

The graduates would usually spend a 6-month rotation and about half would ultimately select our area for their permanent placement at the conclusion of the program. The others went on to become strong ambassadors for the role that we play within the organization.

What It Means for Business

Entry-level employment programs within financial institutions, government entities, and professional organizations are well-developed (see examples in **Exhibit 1.2**). These programs often include:

- Tailored training and on-the-job development through a structured process.
- The opportunity to work on real projects with cutting-edge technology.
- The prospect of learning directly from experts in the field of their studies.
- Strong networking, through special monthly events and a Young Professionals Network.
- Flexible working arrangements to facilitate further study.
- A personal mentor and executive sponsor.

These programs will usually provide a competitive salary from day one and a high likelihood of a permanent (ongoing) role if they successfully complete the program.

Graduate programs, in particular, are highly competitive. They usually run for eighteen to twenty-four months with several rotations into diverse business areas of up to six months. The selection process is robust using behavioral and other indicators aimed at determining who has the capabilities, experience and knowledge best suited to the requirements of the business.

Business leaders should recognize the value of supporting entry-level employment programs as people on these programs often bring a fresh energy, enthusiasm, and a thirst for learning that often rubs off on the organization's core of experienced veterans on the team.

Create a Learning Environment

Setting the Scene

The Rural Bank had an impressive induction and training program for their probationary junior bankers that catered well for my style of learning. It combined on-the-job training with well-constructed training manuals that had self-testing questionnaires at the end of each topic. I immersed myself in the training programs and excelled.

The probationer training program consisted of eight modules covering the routine banking processes of cheques, dishonors, customer counter enquiries, lodgments, remittances, security, periodical dues, and postages. While some of my peers struggled with the tests, I achieved 100 percent in half the modules and an overall score of 790 out of 800 (98.75 percent).

Through an effective and well-constructed training regime, I found that I adapted very quickly and successfully to a banking career. It was probably not unexpected as my best subjects at school were mathematics, commerce, and English (and woodwork), and I had a strong work ethic. Whereas some of my supervisors and trainers would try to bluff their way through with limited knowledge, I had discovered a great capacity for learning … and to learn "the right way" of doing things. If I did not understand something, I would personally research the topic until I had developed a high level of expertise, well beyond that of some of my supervisors.

As an avid learner, I would quickly master a topic once I grasped the what, why, and how of the operation. I also learnt the "ins and outs" of the full range of the bank's products (discussed further in Chapter 2). Any young staff-member should strive to master the operation, services, and products if they have ambitions to rise into more senior and challenging roles. The aspiration to learning an industry from the ground up through well-rounded grassroots experience should be impressed upon them by business and specialist leaders.

There were many times throughout my career when I had to grasp opportunities that I wasn't really ready for and make the most of them. But in the end these experiences ultimately contributed to my success. Miranda Tapsell describes in her book *Top End Girl* how similar experiences helped to shape her award-winning acting career, "I was thrown in the deep end, but my experiences at NIDA (National Institute of Dramatic Art) had made me resilient and quick-thinking. Obviously, I was very green next to the actors I shared the stage with. Not inferior, but new. You know what I mean. But my career has been built on being given opportunities I wasn't ready for. I'm a seasoned actor because of it."

Effective training and development programs underpin personal and corporate success.

What It Means for Business

Each generation has been influenced by the world as it was during their formative years. Traditionalists experienced the Great Depression. Many baby boomers experienced an abundant, healthy, post-World War economy. Gen X watched as their parents sacrificed greatly for their companies. Millennials were raised during the boom times, often experiencing strong parental support. Generation Z came along after the Internet was created and are therefore highly technically competent, and the global coronavirus pandemic (COVID-19) in 2020 is likely to shape their future thinking.

There are differences in the learning preferences across the generations as illustrated in **Exhibit 1.3**. Business leaders need to establish effective training and development programs, and must recognize that a "one-size-fits-all" training, development, and communication style will not achieve optimal results. On-the-job learning delivery approaches for the respective generational audiences should be flexible and suitably tailored for their needs. Traditionalists and baby boomers prefer a traditional classroom style, whereas Gen X is more likely to gravitate towards a self-directed, self-paced approach, and Millennials prefer an integrated approach incorporating technology and media (such as webinars) into their learning.

Maintain a Fun Business Environment

Setting the Scene

One of my early administrative tasks involved the local cheque exchanges. All the local banks had a daily "local exchanges" process where every bank met at the National Bank and passed over all cheques drawn on the local branch of the other bank to either receive or pay the net equivalent through a bank warrant. This was intended to speed up the clearance of local cheques for customers to be able to utilize the funds. A centralized state-based approach was implemented by the end of the 1970s and local exchanges were discontinued.

The local exchanges allowed us to interact and have fun with our colleagues in other banks. It also enabled some silly but good-humored gags, with junior bankers asked to go to another bank with a variety of requests, like borrow the scales so we could balance the ledgers; obtain a verbal agreement form; borrow a left-handed screwdriver. It is unlikely under current bullying and harassment laws that these activities would be permitted or tolerated. But there was always a sense of fun.

Of course, fun can also be the result of the range of characters that businesses interact with. One of the Rural Bank customers was Jim Whiteman who ran a local business with his wife Dorothy. Jim was a practical joker who would often come into the bank with good-humored requests. He would front the enquiry counter and ask a new staff member for the balance of his account. Once delivered, he would say he wanted to withdraw all of the money then redeposit it just so he could verify that the bank still had all his money. It added to Jim's legend when workmates fell for his gags.

In my early days as chief audit executive at StateRail (see Chapter 6), I once thought the mood of the team was downcast and heading for a rut. So, I wore a long orange wig to an all-staff meeting; when there was little

EXHIBIT 1.3

Generational learning preferences[1]

Descriptor	Born	Age Range in 2021	Messages that Resonate	Preferred Learning Style
Traditionalists	1927–1945	76 through to 94	Your experience is respected	• Informational learning style • Traditional classroom setting using mainly lectures • Task-specific • One-on-one coaching • Excellent at mentoring
Baby Boomers	1946–1964	57 through to 75	You are needed and valued	• Transformational learning style • Traditional classroom learning extended to learning through participation, critical reflection, reflection, and feedback
Generation X (Gen X)	1965–1980	41 through to 56	Do it your way	• Self-directed or self-paced • Highly receptive to e-learning series of structured lectures • Requires integration of technology and media in learning • Make it easy to access the information and industry procedures
Generation Y (Millennials)	1981–2000	21 through to 40	You will work with other bright, creative people	• Informal, incidental learning • Requires integration of technology and media in learning (webinars, social networking, sites, Avatars) • Personalized learning through customized environment
Generation Z	After 2000	Under 21	You will have advancement opportunities	• Yet to be firmly established; likely to be substantially technology-based

Note: The descriptions and age ranges are intended to be indicative; they vary in different publications.

[1] Bruce Turner, *GREAT Ways to Motivate Your Staff: Shaping an Audit Team that Adds Value and Inspires Business Improvement* (Altamonte Springs, FL: The Institute of Internal Auditors Research Foundation, 2016), 13,22. Modified and consolidated.

to no reaction from the staff, I realized that some fresh resources were required to change the collective mindset, and when I recruited wisely things started to gradually change.

I contrast the StateRail experience with a totally different experience at the Australian Tax Office (see Chapter 8) when I wore an orange suit to an office harmony day event that I was hosting for the Penrith site. Later that day, I was in contact with the audit committee chair who was nearly two hundred miles away in Canberra. He mentioned quite jovially, that he had heard about me wearing the orange suit, and it was clear he liked the idea. The grapevine at the Tax Office was strong, and underpinned a highly professional workforce. This sort of interaction with the Tax Office's Penrith staff reflected their sense of fun and meaningfulness; when historian Leigh Edmonds was researching his book *Working for all Australians 1910-2010,* he visited the Penrith site and reflected that it had the "joy of life" in it. A thoughtfully considered and apt catchphrase.

*Each year, **harmony day** celebrates cultural diversity, and is about inclusiveness, respect, and a sense of belonging for everyone. Orange is the color chosen to represent harmony day, as the color traditionally signifies social communication and meaningful conversations, and relates to the freedom of ideas and encouragement of mutual respect.*

"Enjoying work should be our No. 1 priority," according to esteemed author, consultant, and trainer J. Michael Jacka. "If you are not having fun – if you cannot be excited about what you are doing – you cannot do your best work. In fact, you probably can't even do good work. Not every minute must be rainbows and unicorns. But every task, project, and opportunity should contain at least a glimmer of possibilities of excitement – of fun."[2]

Work should be fun, with people enticed by the joy of it. All business and specialist leaders should understand what drives performance excellence; I realized very early that a sense of fun is paramount to sustained success … even if it does take you out of your comfort zone! And it is one of the essential ingredients for becoming an employer of choice.

What It Means for Business

Strong staff engagement delivers business success. While staff engagement can seem intangible in nature, a high level of engagement will actually translate into positive financial contributions or optimal service levels

---

[2] J. Michael Jacka, "The Mind of Jacka: Three Rules to Audit By", *Internal Auditor* (April 2020): 63.

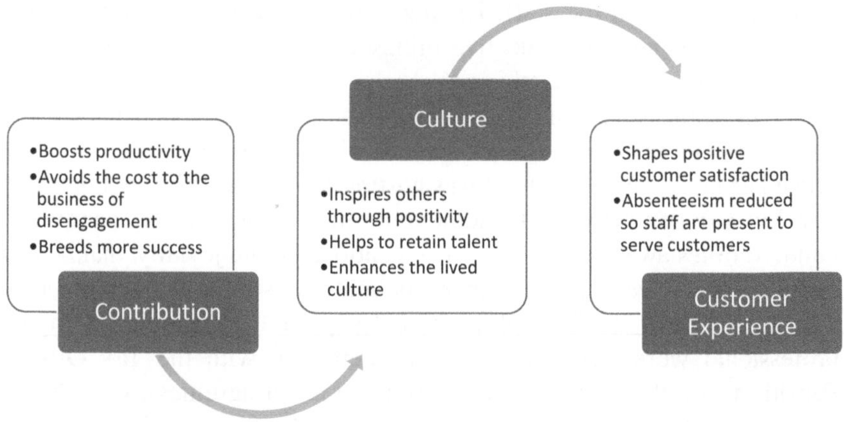

EXHIBIT 1.4 Benefits of staff engagement.

(e.g., within the private sector this can be reflected in profitability, and in the public sector the delivery of better services).

Staff engagement reflects the extent to which staff are committed to their employer, passionate about their work, and invested in the success of the organization. Staff who are engaged are intrinsically motivated, go the extra mile, use discretionary effort, and care about their work and not just their remuneration. They understand that an organization's long-term success and achievement of its objectives and goals (the purview of the board and CEO primarily) is reliant on how well they and their colleagues perform their day-to-day responsibilities and satisfy customers and other stakeholders.

The benefits of having an engaged workforce are illustrated in **Exhibit 1.4** through the three lenses of the organizational contribution, lived culture, and customer experience.

Effective staff engagement contributes to a strong lived culture (discussed in Chapter 2). One way of measuring the organization's lived culture against the desired culture is a periodic staff engagement survey. These surveys help to determine whether the staff feel valued, if they are committed, and whether they believe they are operating at an optimal level. It also assesses their commitment and understanding of the organization's vision, mission, objectives, values, and outcomes.

Business leaders should review the results of staff engagement surveys and identify clear and specific actions that are to be taken to address the perception of staff, when those perceptions are at odds with the organization's intended objectives and direction.

It is not unusual for employees to register their discontent when completing staff engagement surveys, especially in organizations that are undergoing significant change and disruption. Business leaders need to assess the results objectively, taking into account prior results, trends, and known disruptions across employee levels, locations, and business units. The action plan should focus on a small number of manageable themes rather than try to solve everything that is put to them.

Where there is disengaged staff, business leaders need to address the underlying reasons. Engagement can be strengthened where business leaders hire the right people, onboard new hires effectively, offer meaningful professional learning and development opportunities, and deal with the people who don't fit the desired culture (including poor performers, discussed in Chapter 4).

Improved engagement can be achieved through business leaders actually engaging with their people. Staff need to hear directly from their senior leaders, as messages are often diluted or miscommunicated when others are relied upon to share them. Business leaders have many potential touchpoints with employees, including entity-wide newsletters, executive briefings, team briefings, corporate events, and digital media (e.g., webinar, podcast, YouTube video, and internal social media channels such as Facebook, Twitter, Instagram, or Snapchat).

Having fun underpins staff engagement by helping to effectively manage and improve the emotions of employees. Having happy employees (balanced with productive workplace outcomes) results in improved teamwork, more trusting relationships, and stronger employee retention. The outcomes of a sense of fun at work are illustrated in **Exhibit 1.5**, with benefits for the business, the team and the individual.

You Reap What You Sow

Setting the Scene

I required references to support my job application and received glowing support from longstanding and highly respected Penrith residents, Albert Rickwood and Dorothy Whiteman.

Mr Rickwood was my elderly next-door neighbor who had long-suffered from the debilitating illness emphysema. He had a large houseblock on the corner. Because of his incapacity and immobility, I used to mow his lawns each week for several years as a teenager for the rather modest sum of $1 (equivalent to less than $7 in 2020) for several hours' work. As I mowed, he would often stand around and admire my work, with a smile on his face and a twinkle in his eye. It was so encouraging to see him there. He wrote in my reference that, "I would like to state that Bruce is polite and respectful in manner. His actions are obliging and thoughtful in every degree of consideration to others. The parental upbringing of this boy is shown in all respects to his manner. I can recommend his services to anyone who may require someone of trust and integrity." Mr Rickwood was a lovely man

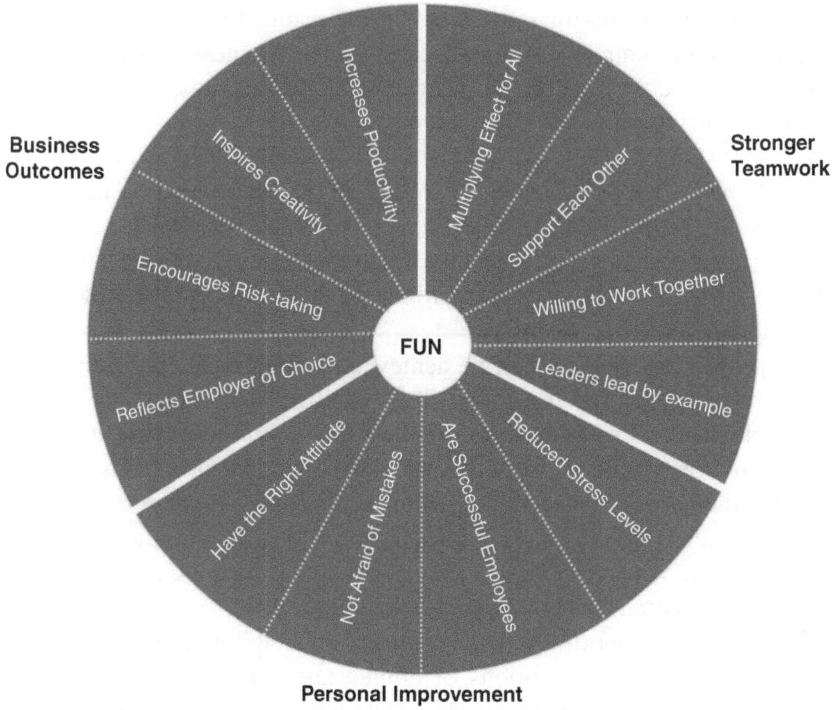

EXHIBIT 1.5 Benefits of inspiring a sense of fun at work.

and unfortunately, he did not survive for long after I had started my first job. He was a justice of the peace (JP) which I ultimately achieved in 1981 and have maintained since.

Mrs Whiteman ran a local retail business in the laneway just behind the Rural Bank. I did not know it at the time, but she was a customer of the bank and well-known to the branch manager Rupert Collins. Mrs Whiteman wrote in my reference that, "Bruce is a stable, pleasant young lad never having given his parents any trouble of any kind. He studies diligently, and I have no hesitation in recommending him to any position of trust." I found out later that Mrs Whiteman's reference was influential in my being offered appointment to the Rural Bank. I remained in close contact with Mrs Whiteman until her passing, bringing a smile of pride to her face every time I was in contact with her, especially when I reminisced at how she was the catalyst for my successful career in banking.

What It Means for Business

I learnt at a young age that you reap what you sow, where "sowing" is a metaphor for one's actions, and where you are ultimately "reaping" the results of those actions. I was genuinely being kind and helpful to Mr Rickwood and Mrs Whiteman, and expected nothing in return. But they were sincerely honored to proffer a reference for me.

The educator and author Dr Stephen Covey used the phrase "emotional bank account" to reflect the same thing in his best-selling book *The Seven Habits of Highly Effective People.* It was during an intensive training course on the *seven habits* many years later that I reflected on the importance of this concept and how it had influenced my career to that time.

Individuals need to recognize the power of their actions when dealing with other people, as the benefits of those actions can prove far greater in advancing one's career than they ever imagined.

Leverage Emotional Intelligence

Setting the Scene

I was an above-average student at secondary high school and achieved a school certificate result with credits for each of the six examinable subjects. While I should probably have achieved the higher grade of advanced for some subjects like commerce (in particular), I had not applied myself well enough. As a result, I did not fulfil my potential at school and I am sure that this frustrated my teachers and parents. But my home life was most difficult at that time, with my parents ultimately separating just prior to my final school exams.

Notwithstanding the family challenges, my school reference was quite positive. It reflected that my conduct was good; my attitude was willing and cooperative; and my neatness was very good. The school principal Jack Dillon commented, "Bruce was a pleasant, honest and reliable student whose best subjects were mathematics and science."

My talents and potential were recognized quickly by the bank manager and other senior staff in the branch. I was shifted out of the mailroom after just a few weeks and became a branch ledger-keeper. The bank maintained manual ledgers locally for its loan products which required a high degree of mathematical accuracy and speed. We did not have calculators, so every month we would have to manually calculate the interest on the home and farming loans, then post these transactions to the account, together with the borrower's monthly instalments (loan repayments) and any other transactions. It was essential to keep the ledgers up-to-date so the Loans Officers could identify any borrowers who fell into arrears, following which they would write to them or instigate other recovery action.

I transitioned from the loans ledger-keeper to interest bearing deposit (IBD) ledger-keeper. Due to its history, the Rural Bank was not authorized as a savings bank which meant that its deposit-taking was restricted to term deposits in the form of IBDs. This was a clumsy and costly way of managing deposits as interest had to be manually calculated (and checked by someone else) on every single deposit (which could be as low as $20) rather than on the overall balance of the account as was the case with traditional savings accounts. So, if someone had invested $20 per week and was withdrawing $1,000 there would be over fifty separate calculations, each with a different term.

Throughout this chapter (and some later chapters), I have cited the results of some of my work-related training courses and my tertiary academic results. I have done so to highlight that the academic results of young people at school can be inhibited by their personal and family circumstances at that time; their school results are not necessarily an indication of the heights they could well achieve during their career because of factors such as their work performance, natural wisdom, emotional quotient, and opportunities.

The concept of emotional intelligence (emotional quotient) emerged in the mid-1990s after first being mentioned in the 1960s. It is interesting to note that my ability and trait qualities commented upon by Mr Rickwood, Mrs Whiteman, and Mr Dillon align nicely to many of the recognized features of emotional intelligence. I understand now that my career was underpinned by a high level of emotional intelligence, and this was reflected in an independent professional assessment undertaken during the fourth decade of my career.

What It Means for Business

Emotional intelligence underpins a person's wellbeing and their success in the workplace. People with high emotional intelligence usually perform well, have better job satisfaction, and tend to demonstrate higher interpersonal functioning, leadership abilities, and stress management. Of course, it is ultimately the blend of both EQ (emotional quotient) and IQ (intelligence quotient) that determines how well a person does in their life and career.

A person's emotional quotient refers to their level of ability to understand other people, what motivates them, and how to work cooperatively with them. This becomes increasingly important as a person steps up into more senior leadership roles, as it is their EQ rather than their IQ that will inspire others to achieve optimal results. The five categories of emotional intelligence are illustrated in **Exhibit 1.6**.

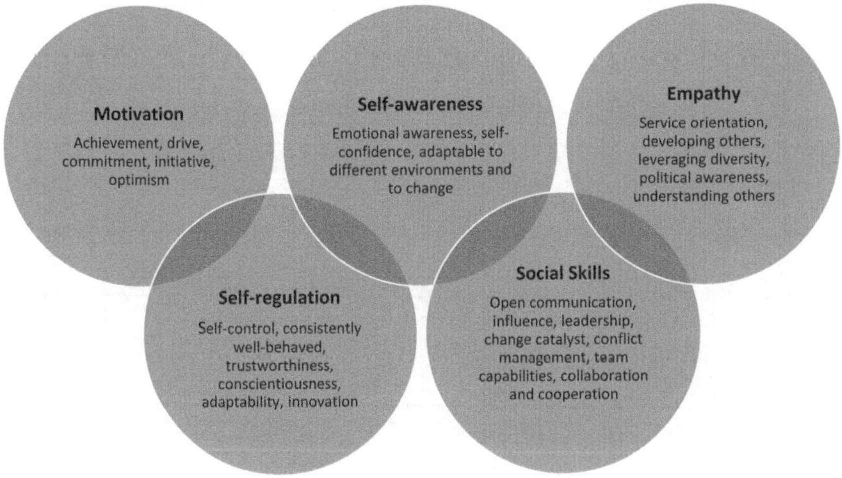

EXHIBIT 1.6 Five categories of emotional intelligence.

The ***Emotional and Social Intelligence Leadership Competency Model*** *is a unique framework developed by Daniel Goleman and Richard Boyatzis, identifying the specific, evidence-based competencies that are the building blocks of emotional and social intelligence in leadership. A useful resource is "Building Blocks of Emotional Intelligence: 12 Leadership Competency Primers," which is a 12-book series by Daniel Goleman (Author), Richard Boyatzis (Author), Richard J Davidson (Author), and 13 more.*

It is especially important for business leaders to master their emotional intelligence as their every move is being watched, scrutinized, and dissected by people at all levels of the organization. The tone at the top is entrusted to the way they behave.

All team members need to demonstrate positive emotional qualities regardless of their role and level of seniority. People with a high level of emotional intelligence are naturally empathetic to the feelings of others, and they therefore thrive in a team environment. They respond especially well to the emotional needs of their stakeholders as they are consistently attuned to whether the stakeholder feels valued, understood, remembered, reassured, important, in control, special, or good. They are effective communicators, build trust with others, and forge constructive relationships. Typically, they understand their personal strengths and weaknesses, so they welcome and address feedback offered to them. Common features of high and low emotional intelligence are illustrated in **Exhibit 1.7**.

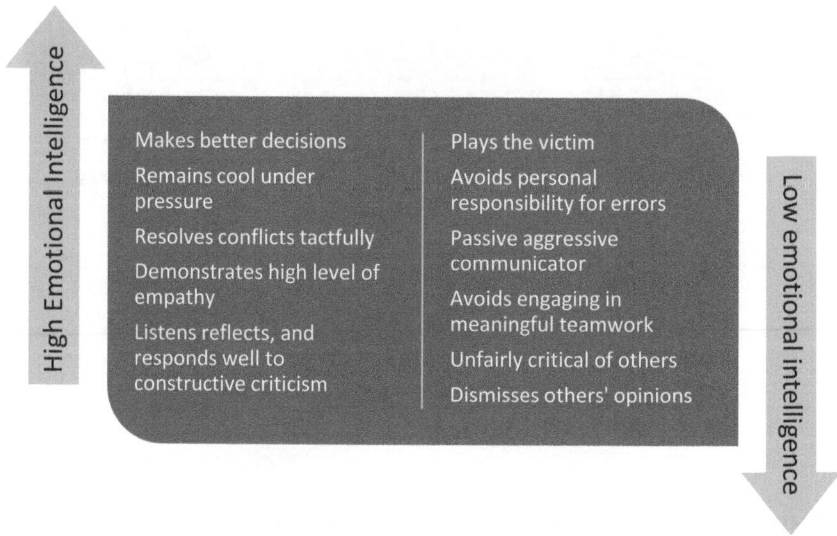

EXHIBIT 1.7 Features of high and low emotional intelligence.

Business leaders can assess the emotional intelligence of their team members and potential candidates by asking well-crafted questions, then listening to the responses, observing the body language, and watching for red flags contained in **Exhibit 1.7** (low emotional intelligence). Examples of questions include:

- What's the most challenging ethical dilemma you've faced at work and how did you deal with it? What was the outcome?
- How do you feel when someone criticizes your work? How do you respond? Do you consider what you have learned?
- Tell me about a time you had a conflict with a work colleague or a supervisor. How did you resolve the conflict?
- How would you handle a customer who called to complain that the price of a product or service was too high?

Apply the Risk Appetite

Setting the Context

My first job was as a mail (postages) clerk. Rather than working in a separate "mailroom" as such, it was actually a single desk (meant for one) that was shared by several of the junior bankers towards the front of the "back office." In addition to preparing and posting the mail, the job involved handling the customer enquiry counter which was consistently busy throughout the bank's opening hours.

There was also a range of administrative tasks, with one of these involving trekking to the post office each day to get cash for any mail orders and postal orders that had been banked (these transactions were not part of the financial industry settlement system). The value was never high (probably a few hundred dollars on average), yet we teenagers were required to carry a loaded pistol to the post office for security, which seemed ridiculous back then, but even more so now as I reflect upon it.

Security has evolved at banks since the 1970s. As a young teller, I always had a loaded pistol in my teller's box, as did my colleagues. Once or twice a year we attended a pistol range to practice our skills, which were at best mediocre. We also learnt how to carefully clean and load the pistols with limited success.

Each of the teller's boxes was connected to a common alarm (an ear-piercing siren) which you set off by pushing your foot down on a button on the floor. The system was rudimentary, and there was nothing to indicate which alarm had been activated. The alarm was deafening. On one occasion, we were operating with four tellers and someone inadvertently set off the alarm. No one knew who had done it, and it became quite comical (and somewhat distressing) as the tellers kept randomly pushing buttons to try to close it down, to no avail. Once the police arrived the power could be cut, and the situation was resolved.

The formalization of the risk appetite concept during the twenty-first century has been a welcome catalyst to changing practices and internal controls that had little rational basis other than "they'd always been done that way."

What It Means for Business

While all entities need to take risks to create value, the risk-taking must always be within acceptable parameters. An entity's risk appetite reflects the mutual understanding between the CEO and board of the drivers and boundaries for opportunity-seeking behavior and strategic decisions, specifically those related to growth, value preservation, innovation, transformation, and change. A risk appetite statement drives a balanced approach to value-creation so that acceptable risks are pursued only where the consequences can be reasonably managed.

The board has an important role in setting these parameters for the entity through a risk appetite statement (or similar); it then has to be satisfied that the CEO has established has a suitable risk management framework to identify and manage risk on an ongoing basis (Chapter 7 explores in more detail the application of risk management across the business).

For the purposes of determining the risk appetite across an entity, the board will typically define and apply several risk appetite descriptors and use these in determining risk appetite statements for to each of the entity's risk consequence categories (e.g., financial; reputation; legal, governance, and compliance; environmental; growth and commercialization; people, safety, and culture; operations and service delivery). The risk appetite statements translate each consequence category into a target risk level to represent the optimal level of risk that the board is willing to take for the category.

As an example, risk appetite descriptors might be as follows:

Eliminate – No appetite. Risks to be eliminated or controlled to lowest possible level within available resources and in accordance with legislative requirements

Minimize – Little or no appetite. Risks to be minimized to low level. Some small residual risk acceptable.

Manage – Some appetite. Risks to be managed within tolerance levels. Some elevated level of risk may be acceptable to achieve specified outcomes.

Maximize – Considerable appetite for risk. Pursue higher rewards despite higher levels of inherent risk. However, pursuit of objectives must not be at the expense of sound governance processes

When the residual risk falls outside of the target risk level during a risk assessment (for a particular decision or as part of the routine periodic update), management will be required to make a decision not to proceed without specific board approval, or will need to establish and report on the action to bring the risk within the defined risk appetite.

Situations may arise where a specific risk falls within the entity's risk appetite, but the risk owner wants to further reduce their residual risk exposure. This might be a result of:

- Importance of the activity being managed and its outcomes.
- Degree of control the entity has over the risk.
- Potential and actual losses that may arise.
- Benefits and opportunities presented by the risk (e.g., actions may be instituted by the risk owner to boost project management efficiency and effectiveness for a major project).

Exhibit 1.8 illustrates how several of the entity's risk consequence categories have been applied against the defined risk appetite to some stories

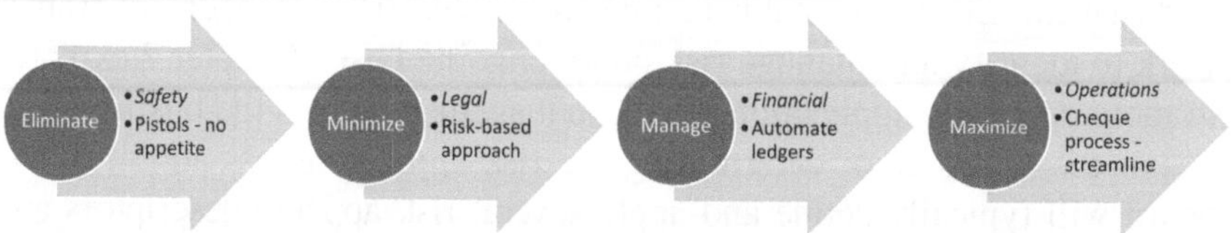

EXHIBIT 1.8 Examples of risk appetite in practice.

reflected in this chapter to reflect consideration of innovation, transformation, and change. These changes reflect initiatives that challenge the status quo.

Shape the Control Environment

Setting the Scene

In my early-20s, I was shifted from the telling role to the "back office" where I performed the role of branch examiner, initially covering long-term loan and personal loan ledgers, and term deposits.

As an examiner, I had to check that the ledger-keeper had posted all of the transactions and calculated the interest correctly for loans and term deposit accounts. Importantly, I had to oversee the monthly balancing of all of the ledgers to the general ledger which was time-consuming and stressful if a ledger-keeping error was missed and not corrected at the time of entry.

I attended an examiners training course in 1976. It was held over two weeks in Sydney, simultaneously with a ledger-keeper course (which my Penrith workmate, good friend, and future wife Bea was attending). The first activity every morning was to complete a difficult and challenging mental-arithmetic exercise which had a strict time limit. It involved a long series of exercises, involving addition, subtraction, multiplication, and division. I achieved the very rare feat of 100 percent accuracy and 100 percent completion rate every day across the ten days. At the end of the course, I received a very positive assessment with comments including, good appearance; good dress sense and grooming; friendly, likeable personality; good verbal expression; good judgment, would adopt a practical approach; and very good course participation, conscientious. With an overall rating of 92 percent for test results and positive feedback on my course participation, my overall assessment was "very good" and I was rated "equal first" in the course.

A significant early-career lesson was the importance of encouraging people to challenge the status quo, recognizing it helps to deliver innovative solutions that ultimately fuel the competitive edge of the business.

One of the daily examining tasks was to "read" all the many hundreds of cheques that were presented against the customer's current bank accounts. In addition, the examiners checked that the signatures were authorized and valid (by manually checking against the specimen signature until they became familiar with the signatures of the regular customers), examiners had to physically read the date, amount, and words on the cheques to ensure that they were correct (otherwise the cheques could be dishonored for things like amounts in words and figures not agreeing, or the cheque being stale or postdated).

An early innovation I experienced was a change in the process for reading cheques and other instruments in the mid-1970s. Someone had completed a cost/benefit analysis and found that if branch examiners concentrated on reading cheques greater than $300, it would reduce their workload appreciably, lower the processing cost, provide greater customer service capacity, and still maintain the risk of potential loss to an acceptable level. While there were legislative obligations under the *Bills of Exchange Act* and the *Cheques Act*, any variations to the bank's processes were unlikely to heighten compliance risks to an unacceptable level. This was a paradigm shift in thinking, and proved to be so successful that cheque reading limits were incrementally increased over the ensuing decade.

It was a great example of people challenging the status quo to deliver value to the business and its customers. I have found it to be a wonderful success story for innovative thinking that I have used throughout my career to inspire others to "think outside the box."

CHAPTER 1 – TEN CLOSING REFLECTIONS

- Business leaders should recognize the value of supporting entry-level employment programs as people on these programs often bring a fresh energy, enthusiasm, and a thirst for learning that often rubs off on the organization's core of experienced veterans on the team.
- Business leaders need to establish effective training and development programs; recognize that a "one-size-fits-all" training, development, and communication style will not achieve optimal results; and should tailor on-the-job learning delivery approaches to meet the needs and learning styles of the respective generational audiences.
- Business leaders should recognize that a fun work environment translates into happy and engaged employees, and ultimately strong staff engagement delivers business success.
- Business leaders will find staff engagement surveys useful in pinpointing when employee perceptions are at odds with the organization's intended objectives and direction.
- Individuals need to recognize the power of their actions when dealing with other people, as the benefits of those actions can prove far greater in advancing one's career than they ever imagined.
- Individual's need to develop and apply emotional intelligence as it underpins their wellbeing and success in the workplace, often reflected through their performance outcomes, job

satisfaction, interpersonal functioning, leadership abilities, and stress management.

- Business leaders should assess and leverage the emotional intelligence of their team members and potential candidates by asking well-crafted questions, listening to their responses, observing the body language, and watching for red flags.
- The board should establish a risk appetite statement and ensure the CEO establishes a suitable risk management framework to identify and manage risk on an ongoing basis.
- The CEO should ensure the risk appetite statement drives a balanced approach to value-creation – including growth, value preservation, innovation, transformation, and change – so that acceptable risks are pursued only where the consequences can be reasonably managed.
- Business leaders and employees should use the risk appetite to challenge the status quo, make changes to established practices and internal controls that had little rational basis other than "they'd always been done that way," and ultimately drive innovative solutions that fuel the competitive edge of the business.

2 Looking for Meaningfulness in Customer Service Mottos

In some parts of the world, the reputation of the financial services industry has been tarnished by scandals, poor practices, and shoddy self-serving cultures. As a consequence, the financial services industry and other businesses are refocusing their efforts on meaningful customer service practices. This chapter reflects on a time when a bank's motto was "we do more for you personally," and how those customer service imperatives helped to encourage innovation and shape contemporary professional governance, risk, compliance, and assurance practices. It explores recent changes to the "purpose of business" across the broader business environment; and it puts into perspective the wisdom of Sir Richard Branson who said, "If you look after your staff they'll look after your customers. It's that simple."

Entity Profile and Role

Sector:	Financial services sector – retail banking
Entity:	Rural then State Bank of New South Wales.
Entity description:	The State Bank of NSW started life in 1933 as the Rural Bank of NSW. In 1982, its name was changed to the State Bank as part of a corporatization process. The State Bank maintained the Rural Bank's long-standing motto, "We do more for you personally." For entity metrics, see Chapter 4
Primary role:	Customer services
Main responsibilities:	Various retail banking, lending and supervisory roles
Timeframe:	The Second Decade

PERSONAL STORY

The Rural Bank (and subsequently the State Bank) strived to put meaning to its customer service motto, "We do more for you personally." This was reflected in the corporate values and the extensive customer service training that was delivered at every stage of the banker's career.

"Personal service" meant that frontline banking staff were required to help the customer in every way possible, to maintain and enhance the level of customer satisfaction, and strive to exceed their expectations. We were expected to go the extra mile in making sure a customer was happy and satisfied with the bank's products or services.

If you were in a customer-facing role like a teller, you would be required to undertake a comprehensive weeklong training course devoted to the products, services, and operations that tellers were expected to fulfil. I remember one of my managers commenting that telling was one of the best customer service jobs I would ever hold. In retrospect, he was right. I learnt a great deal about how best to deal with people from all walks of life.

I attended an extensive weeklong teller's training course in Sydney in 1973, and achieved an excellent assessment with comments including appearance good, dresses well; bright and friendly personality; and, good customer relations, should prove popular. With an overall average of 92 percent for the results of the various tests, my overall assessment was "very good" which was towards the top of the class.

We were trained in communication and problem resolution skills to ensure that the needs of every customer were met in a manner that reflected positively on the bank and its values. We learnt that 87 percent of people share their stories of great customer service with others, and we were tasked with serving customers in an efficient, positive, polite, caring, timely, attentive, upbeat, and pleasant manner. These were the values and ideals that I maintained through my career.

In line with its motto, the bank's customers were put first at every stage. For instance, if a customer thought he or she had been charged a fee unfairly, the branch staff had the delegation to make an assessment and waive the fee if the circumstances warranted.

As the 1980s progressed, the State Bank's stewardship changed and the business transformation accelerated. The bank's balance sheet became more highly leveraged, profitability became a key driver, and customer service standards started to decline. Many of the branch staff were the same, but a new culture was being framed. Delegations for local staff to make local decisions were wound back (including delegations to waive and refund unfair fees and charges).

For the next few decades, restructures within the banking sector became commonplace and job security diminished. Many bankers were made redundant, with well-trained bankers having to find other ways to support their families.

Of course, the personal service diminished and disappeared and the State Bank looked like it was generating higher and higher profits. The sleeping giant had been awakened. Until the global market crashed in 1987.

Arguably, shorter-term profits were generated at the expense of maintaining longer-term customer service excellence and business sustainability. The State Bank was ultimately offloaded by its state government owner

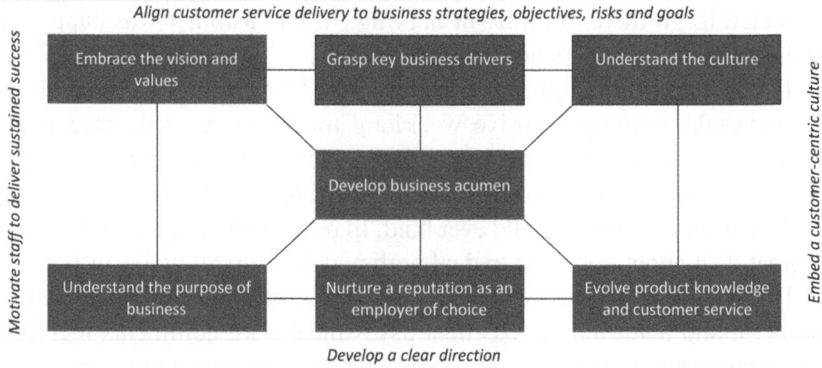

EXHIBIT 2.1 Delivering optimal customer service.

in 1994 through a trade sale. In recent years, independent enquiries into the practices of banks and other financial institutions have identified many instances of them behaving badly … and of putting the customer somewhere towards the back of the field.

The key insights from this phase of my story are:

- Embrace the vision and values.
- Understand the culture.
- Grasp key business drivers.
- Develop business acumen.
- Evolve product knowledge and customer service imperatives.
- Understand the purpose of business.
- Nurture a reputation as an employer of choice.

CONTEXT

Business leaders are taking a fresh look at the way they deliver goods and services to customers, with a view to having a more meaningful focus on their needs and expectations. There are many factors that underpin a customer-centric approach, with some of these elements discussed in this chapter and illustrated in **Exhibit 2.1**.

KEY TAKEAWAYS AND DEEP DIVES

Embrace the Vision and Values

Setting the Scene

I have always seen the usefulness in determining a vision that clearly and succinctly articulates a mental image of what the senior leaders want their business or defined activity to be in the future. A well-considered vision statement should capture the essence of the broader business objectives, goals, and aspirations and provide a clear focus that inspires the staff to head in the right direction.

When I joined the Australian Taxation Office as the chief audit executive (see Chapter 8), we determined a vision to transform the internal audit function so it was recognized as a world-class practice. The vision was determined in consultation with the audit committee and internal audit staff, and, once agreed, it was incorporated in the internal audit charter.

The internal audit staff at the Australian Taxation Office embraced the vision, and within a few years, an independent assessment confirmed that we had, indeed, achieved a world-class level. It meant a lot to me upon announcing my retirement that the internal audit staff presented me with a silver goblet thoughtfully engraved with my name, years of service, and the inscription "World Class Chief Internal Auditor." This small but salient gesture recognized that we had successfully translated the vision into reality.

The vision statement (your reason for being) should be explicitly aligned with the corporate values (discussed further in Chapter 12).

After a period of stability, one of my boards was undergoing a refresh as board directors were completing their staggered terms and new directors were being brought onto the board. Of course, in these situations part of the corporate history is lost and the original meaning of the corporate values can become misplaced, clouded, or diluted. I suggested that the board complete a "values refresh" exercise at the next scheduled board strategic planning retreat. The board chair and the CEO agreed, and the session went well.

Board members were challenged to think about a series of questions. What is this value and its underlying assumptions? What do we really mean by it? What ideas or mental images does the value encourage? Is it understood by staff, customers, suppliers, and other stakeholders?

The retiring board members had the opportunity to clarify the original drivers of the values and, in doing so, inspire an understanding of the true meaning of the corporate values into the next generation of senior leaders who would be championing them in the future.

What It Means for Business

A vision statement aligned to the purpose of the business should "live" within the organization, and inform its overarching strategies, risk mitigation efforts, strategic and business plans, and codes of conduct. The organization's progress and success in delivering upon the vision should be monitored objectively, and refreshed periodically.

When taken together, the key insights from this phase of my story are illustrated in **Exhibit 2.2**.

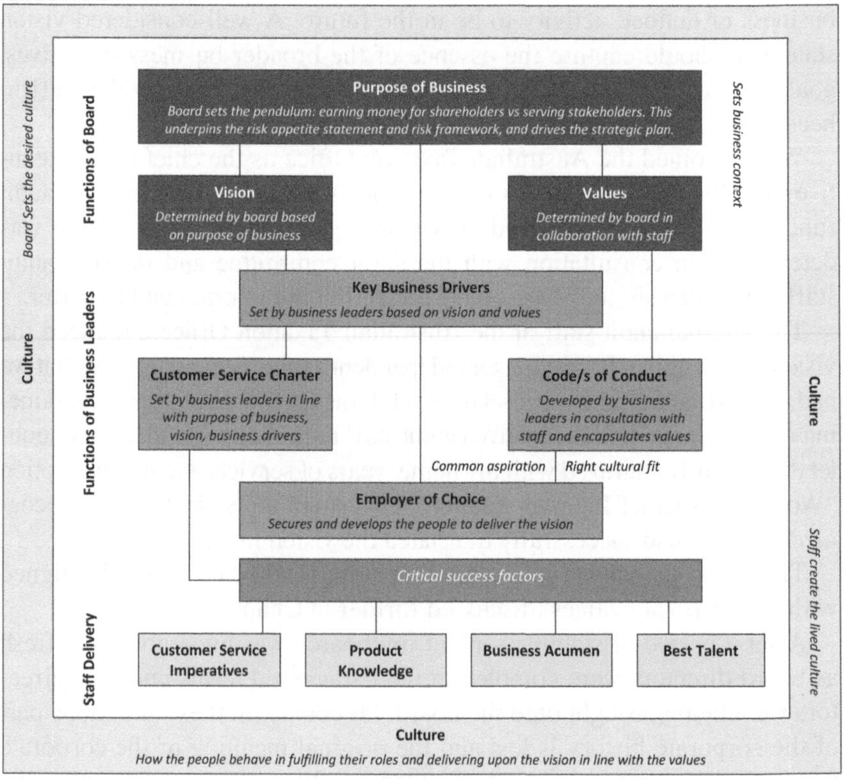

EXHIBIT 2.2 Foundations for delivering business success.

The board, audit committee, and business leaders have differing roles in shaping the culture of the organization and gaining assurance that the lived culture is consistent with the desired culture determined by the board. These roles are illustrated in **Exhibit 2.3**.

Vision statements don't just happen, they need to be considered carefully, and key stakeholders, including the staff, need to be engaged in the process. The starting point is to articulate what the business or activity does now, and then imagine what it would look like if it became the optimal version of itself.

Stakeholders will be inspired by a vision statement where it builds a picture in people, and captures the mind, heart, and soul of the business. It needs to be clear and succinct; passionate, powerful, and memorable; realistic in describing the ideal state; and avoid jargon, numeric measures, and typical "business speak."

While the vision captures *where* the business wants to go, the values reflect *how* it wants its people to behave in getting there. The success of most organizations is underpinned by a clear set of values,

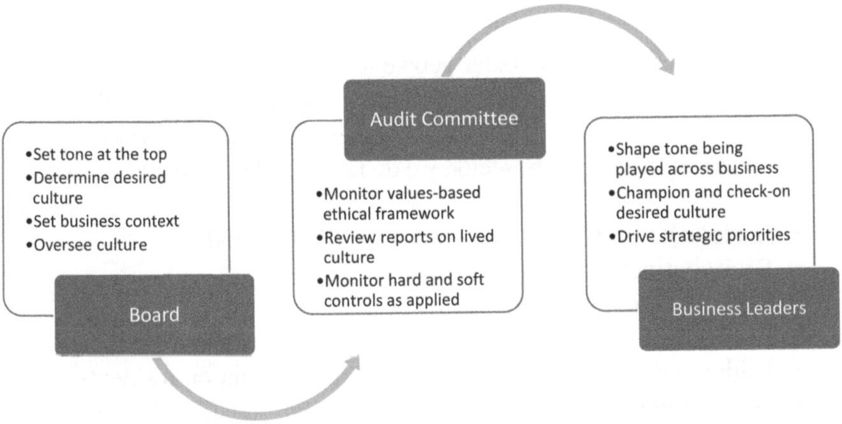

EXHIBIT 2.3 Board, audit committee, and business leaders monitoring the culture.

that are agreed, understood, and championed by business leaders and employees.

Corporate values typically reflect a combination of the principles the business stands for; the beliefs and attitudes of the workplace; and acceptable standards of behavior. The values should align with the kind of service customers expect when dealing with the business. Chapter 12 delves further into corporate values.

Understand the Culture

Setting the Scene

When I shifted into the rail services industry, I had to understand a totally different culture (discussed in Chapter 8). I learned early on that there was less focus on maintaining confidentiality within the rail industry than I was used to; the culture at the central bank was that confidentiality was at the heart of its credibility and, as such, nothing leaked. The incidence of fraud, corruption, and other wrongdoing was also significantly higher within a rail organization. So, when I conducted fraud and corruption awareness workshops with train drivers, guards, revenue compliance officers (i.e., ticket inspectors), and the like, I established the tagline that "just because others do it doesn't make it right."

It is important to tailor the messaging for the audience, and reshaping the culture of a large and long-established organization is challenging.

It is even more difficult to tackle a poor industry-wide culture, and the following examples in the aged care and financial services sector illustrate the importance of people on the ground embracing a tagline that *just because others do it doesn't make it right.*

Aged Care

As a community, we expect older people to be treated well, especially when they need some help at home or can no longer live independently and therefore receive aged care for their daily living through nursing home services. As key stakeholders of the aged care sector, we do not expect (nor should we accept):

- Inadequate prevention and management of wounds.
- Poor continence management.
- Dreadful food, nutrition and hydration.
- Insufficient attention to oral health.
- High incidence of assaults, and physical restraint on residents.
- Widespread overprescribing of drugs which sedate residents.
- Patchy and fragmented palliative care.

However, these are examples of major quality and safety shortcomings identified by an independent review across the whole aged care industry in one jurisdiction.

Financial Services

Within the financial services industry, media reports of scandals over the last decade caused significant reputational damage and impacted fundamental practices, products, advice, client dealings, regulatory compliance obligations, and other accountability, integrity, and fairness provisions. Having worked in the banking sector for an extended period, I was astonished at the range of scandals being reported by the media throughout the second decade of the twenty-first century, which included:

Impacts on Customers	Impacts on the Market as a Whole
• Bribery and theft.	• Breaches of compliance standards.
• Fictitious trading entities.	• Under-reporting of money laundering.
• Forging client signatures.	• Breaches of continuous disclosure.
• Mishandling client money.	• Insider trading.
• Misleading and deceptive conduct.	• Market manipulation.
• Misleading loan advertisements.	• Misconduct causing share price hike.
• Misleading product disclosures.	• Sub-prime mortgage class action.
• Other unethical practices.	• Unauthorized trading.

As a consequence of recurring scandals, the Australian Government established a Banking Executive Accountability Regime and commissioned a Royal Commission (i.e., wide-ranging inquiry) into the industry's conduct. The government's treasurer reflected on the importance to the economy of a strong banking system, but equally stressed that banks needed to be held to account and operate fairly.

The banking royal commission revealed further alarming and unconscionable conduct. It opined that no matter whether the motive was "greed," "avarice," or "pursuit of profit," the conduct ignored basic standards of honesty; the prevalence and persistence of the conduct that was uncovered would require changes to culture, regulation and structure. It also reflected that while there is no best practice for creating a desirable culture, there are six basic norms:

1. Obey the law.
2. Do not mislead or deceive.
3. Act fairly.
4. Provide services that are fit for purpose.
5. Deliver services with reasonable care and skill.
6. When acting for another, act in the best interest of that other.

I still find it difficult to reconcile how the banking culture had shifted so far adrift from the culture of "doing more for you personally." Sure, the culture needed to evolve to embrace more efficient, effective, and economic business practices, but it is evident that the fourth "e" – ethics – was lost somewhere in the translation.

What It Means for Business

Setting the right organizational culture is critical to the success of all organizations, as strategy and culture need to work together in order to achieve the objectives and goals of the organization. The strategy reflects the "what" and the culture represents the "how." The various influences on evolving the culture are illustrated in **Exhibit 2.3**.

Defining the values (see earlier) provides the basis for establishing the desired culture, and how this is played out is reflected through the tone at the top (behaviors and/or statements of senior management). It is also influenced by the organization's arrangements for governance, risk management, internal audit, remuneration and incentive, and whistleblower and customer feedback.

The culture reflects the way people behave, and their shared assumptions, values, and beliefs. Business failures often occur when there is an unacceptable gap between the desired culture and the lived culture (an example of this gap is contained in Chapter 12).

- The desired culture is set by the board, to reflect the values and operating principles that guide the organization's internal conduct from the boardroom to the frontline employees. It sets the basis of dealing with customers, suppliers, partners, regulators, shareholders, other stakeholders, and the wider society.

- The lived culture dictates what internal control practices and behaviors are applied by staff and are evident in practice. In essence, policies and procedures identify the internal controls employees are expected to follow, but the lived culture dictates what internal control practices are actually applied in practice.

Boards and business leaders are expected to set a tone at the top that helps to shape a values-based culture that drives ethical conduct, and where everyone in the organization is engaged and understands the type of conduct and behavior expected of them.

Grasp Key Business Drivers

Setting the Scene

One of the critical success factors for any business is to ensure all parts of the operation work together seamlessly. Yet, I still witness restaurants, hotels, and other service companies that have a clear divide between the frontline service staff and the cooks and other staff working behind the scenes. There seem to be invisible divides that are arbitrarily created by staff to form an "us and them" mentality. It happens in all types of situations; as a young banker, the branch was split into upstairs and downstairs; as a leader, there were situations between different interstate locations. It is unhelpful, and management needs to watch for it and inspire all parts of the business to work together in a consistent, cohesive, and seamless manner.

Effective business cohesion is well-evident in some high-performing restaurants. As an example, I enjoyed great interaction with all parts of the restaurant during a recent visit for a conference in the South-Pacific nation of Fiji. Having to eat gluten-free food can be challenging where restaurant staff don't understand the adverse consequence. Having brought this food allergy to the attention of the wait staff, the sous chef would come and see my wife and me at every meal and talk us through the safe options. The wait staff were obsessive at protecting our interests through every phase of their service. And on our last day, all of the restaurant staff came to our table and sang us a traditional Fijian farewell song. It was a most memorable experience.

There are occasions when I still shake my head about the unnecessary administrative requirements imposed from businesses and governments on individuals and commercial entities. In one week in 2020, I was asked to complete documentation in respect to my roles on two different audit committees. In one case, I was asked to complete, sign, and return five different forms containing personal information and common information that was repeated on every single form. In the other case, I was asked to complete and return multiple forms and return them by noon the next day even though it would take an hour or two to prepare; and of concern, I was expected to pass this information back through an unsecured email at a time when identity fraud was rife. In both cases, I wondered why no one ever bothered to design a single form that contained everything needed, and even better, one that was automated and could be transmitted securely through the use of technology. The words of one of my former bosses resonated, "We need to make it easy for customers to do business with us."

What It Means for Business

The vision, values, strategies, goals, and objectives of any business are highly dependent on its identified business drivers and their order of importance.

Of course, there are myriad business drivers that cannot be directly controlled, including international trade relations, the price of raw materials, geopolitical unrest, and economic conditions. So, business leaders need to manage the risks of these drivers, and focus on the drivers they can directly control.

- Internal drivers within the business support its work and typically have a common goal. This could be related to excellent customer satisfaction levels, or a financial growth measure like the percentage of market share (i.e., sales relative to the size of the industry as a whole). These measures are influenced by the seamlessness of the design, development, production, marketing, service delivery, and product sales areas.
- The external drivers usually involve elements like customers, economic conditions, competitors, disruptive innovation, and regulatory agencies. Drivers that influence the businesses sales performance include the number of calls people make, the effectiveness of the follow-up or referral service, and the number of active visitors on the business website. Key drivers are different across industries; in technical or professional areas, like an accounting or a law firm, thoroughness is more important than speed of delivery; however, for fast food outlets and food delivery providers speed is paramount.

Business leaders should identify and understand their business drivers, and optimize those that are under their control. An understanding of the key business drivers should influence the work of the governance, risk management, compliance and assurance functions.

Develop Business Acumen

Setting the Scene

Emerging and successful business leaders display a savviness or sense of the business, including the risks and opportunities that underpin success.

These traits are what distinguishes them from others, in that they think like an executive or business owner, understand how all the parts of the business work together, and satisfy the needs and expectations of the CEO and board. This, in effect, is business acumen.

Because I had excelled in completing the bank's training programs and had mastered each area of the business both technically and practically, I was often coming up with better ways of doing things during my first decade in the workforce. I never accepted the usual response that, "It's always been done this way." I was encouraged to pursue my ideas as long as I still met the spirit of the bank's detailed instructions and legislative compliance obligations. I learnt early in my career to "challenge the status quo," and this set me apart from my peers. In the modern business world this way of thinking like a business owner demonstrates business acumen and innovation, which are now increasingly encouraged to give businesses a competitive advantage.

What It Means for Business

I well remember during my second decade when one of my audit colleagues was completing an assessment of the bank's credit card arrangements (then called Bankcards, but ultimately the Visacard and Mastercard brands). The boss suggested the option of introducing an annual credit card fee be explored as part of the assessment given that some customers were unprofitable because they paid off the credit card bill before interest started accumulating. He was clearly thinking differently and I was impressed with how business savvy he was. Detailed scenario analysis confirmed the suggestion was valid. The bank's senior management baulked at the suggestion, and rejected what were well-founded recommendations. A few years later, the bank did introduce an annual credit card fee after other commercial banks had done so. It was all in the timing. The bank was a follower rather than a leader.

Conversely, I was astonished some years later when an auditor demonstrated a total lack of judgement, objectivity, and business acumen during an assessment of the organization's fleet of vehicles. He had shifted away from the approved audit objectives and scope, and pursued a biased personal agenda by recommending the organization's fleet of senior executive vehicles be disbanded. There was an absence of meaningful analysis and fact-checking. Somehow the draft audit report made it onto my desk as I was required to clear every report as the chief audit executive. Naturally, I changed the report and allowed it to pass with significant edits, a softening of language, and more realistic recommendations aligned to the approved objectives. The auditor had missed a significant fact: the motor vehicles in the "senior executive fleet" were actually paid for by the senior executives through a salary-sacrificing arrangement (i.e., the vehicle was within policy and the cost was part of the executives' approved total remuneration package). I was relieved that we had dodged a bullet, as a report lacking credibility (as did the draft) had the potential to damage the reputation of the whole internal audit department. The auditor still missed the point, and doubled-down on his lack of judgement; he raised an allegation of wrongdoing against me for changing audit reports (discussed further in Chapter 8). This and other allegations he made were frivolous, vexatious, and could not be substantiated; he ultimately withdrew the allegations. He found another job.

*The **chief audit executive** is the head of internal audit, a person in a senior position responsible for effectively managing the internal audit activity in accordance with the internal audit charter and the mandatory elements of the International Professional Practices Framework (including professional auditing standards and the code of ethics and core principles for internal auditors).*

Evolve Product Knowledge and Customer Service Imperatives

Setting the Scene

At age 17, I was developed to be a bank teller (cashier), initially on standby to be used during lunchtimes and when the banking chamber became busy. The bank's rules were "bent" a little as you had to be at least 18 to be a teller given the amounts of cash handled and controlled, and the high risk of robbery (bank security was considerably less developed in the 1970s, though I did have a pistol in the teller's box). Customers warmed to me.

I enjoyed the customer interactions involved in being a teller, and excelled at the job which I held for a few years. In addition to people management skills and product knowledge, once again numeracy skills were essential as you had to manually record all of your transactions and then tally the cash in and out throughout the day to determine how much cash you should have at the close of business. At this time, each teller was solely responsible and accountable for the cash under their control and had to make up cash shortages from their own money; "shared telling" arrangements came much later.

By the age of 19, I had been elevated to the "number one" teller position which required a high level of expertise and involved broader responsibility (but no supervisory authority over others). In addition to customer service duties, the tellers were required to undertake clerical duties before and after opening hours. We also had the round-the-clock safe (night safe) deposits to process for business owners. There were typically four tellers operating in the branch at any one time. One of the corner teller's boxes was obscured by a pillar, and the teller used that to great effect to minimize the energy she exerted at work.

The bank manager impressed upon everybody the importance of putting the needs of the customer first. He would often prowl the banking chamber to ensure that optimal customer service delivery was practiced by all front-line banking staff (even occasionally re-energizing the teller hiding in the corner). He had a good rapport with the customers, and handled any feedback promptly and professionally. He was a hard taskmaster for the staff, but the customers were always a priority – that was an enduring lesson.

What It Means for Business

A customer service charter (also called a charter of customer rights or a customer charter) articulates the organization's primary customer-centric objectives, based on the organization's overarching business strategies, objectives, and goals. It is usually developed by the business leaders in consultation with customer representatives and/or consumer groups where they are established. Once the customer service charter has been established, it is rolled out through the organization with appropriate staff training and awareness, coupled with periodic refreshers. It is also made publicly available to customers, and included on the organization's website.

The customer service charter has three key audiences as illustrated in **Exhibit 2.4**:

- First, customers by articulating their rights in terms of standards of quality, issues, complaints, feedback, privacy, and conflict resolution.

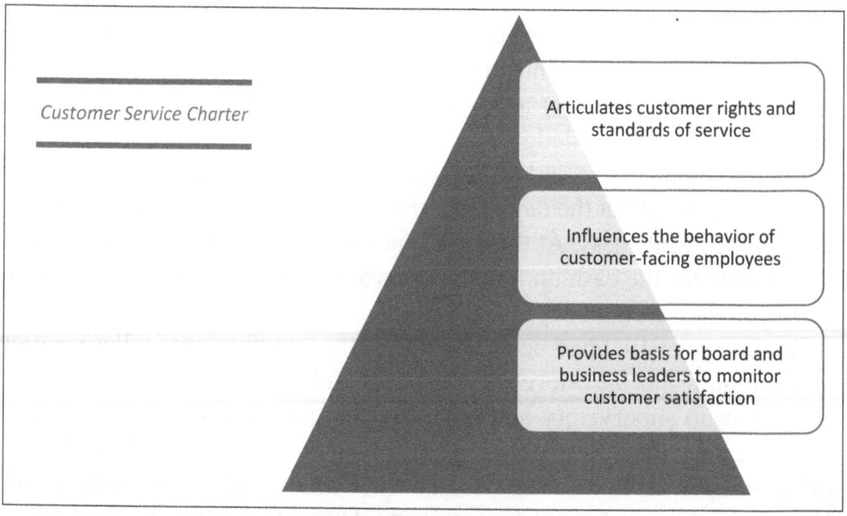

EXHIBIT 2.4 Key audiences for the customer service charter.

- Second, employees by letting them know the kind of behavior that is expected from them when dealing with customers, it should be part of the employee training for new employees, and periodically discussed in staff meetings.
- Finally, the board and senior leaders as a basis of monitoring the level of customer satisfaction, and to determine how best to rectify service issues, make changes to existing offerings, and to identify new products and services sought by customers.

Customer service charters are relevant to all industries, and their adoption is continuing to expand. The product and service commitments and standards contained in the charter should be translated into key performance indicators (KPIs) which are measured, monitored and reported periodically to the board and within public reporting (e.g., periodically on the organization's website; in the published annual report).

Boards and audit committees should seek information on the organization's customer service vision and how this is communicated to its customers, including the availability of a customer service charter. Where one is in place, its reasonableness should be considered in terms of current business strategies, objectives and values; competitor offerings; availability and ease of access across face-to-face and digital mediums; workforce socialization and periodic reinforcement; and integrity and timeliness of reporting of non-financial customer service standards and assurance arrangements.

Understand the Purpose of Business

Setting the Scene

Senior leaders need to gain assurance that the organization's actions are consistent with its vision, values, and stated purpose. Whether the purpose of business is oriented towards customers and other stakeholders or toward profitability for shareholders, there are myriad contemporary issues, for instance:

- Customer-centric – such as delivering against the customer charter; managing complaints; and maintaining the privacy of personal information.
- Central to both – combatting cybercrime.
- Business-centric – preventing wages theft; avoiding modern slavery exploitation; and reducing, eliminating or better managing red tape.

One of the first things I look at when completing my "due diligence" on an organization that I am looking at joining is its customer service charter and the meaningful reporting of associated performance indicators. Most organizations will publish a customer service charter, policy, or mission statement on their website and this provides an insight into what the business values are and what they expect of their staff. Armed with this knowledge, I can then direct my questions to the prospective employer on how they put life into their charter, how they know whether their staff embrace the commitments, and how they monitor the level of customer satisfaction against their rights and the organization's obligations. Remember that this is the time when you can ask well-meaning questions as the business wants you to join their team. It is essential that the corporate values and your personal values are in alignment.

When I was in frontline positions within the commercial banking environment, I always believed that the organization's success would come naturally if customer service excellence was consistently delivered. I thought that the focus on "marketing" ultimately became excessive and obsessive. I always factored in my personal experiences as a customer, and knew I especially enjoyed exceptional service though I distanced myself from customer service representatives who pushed hard with the salesmanship. I didn't need people to tell me every single time I transacted with them that they had a better product for me.

I still recall researching my first ever non-staff bank account when I left the banking sector after nearly three decades. There were two reputable banks at the local shopping center and I carefully analyzed their products against my needs. I finally opened my selected account. Just three months later, I received a letter from the bank advising that they were closing the branch … on the pretext that fewer branches would provide me with better service. Welcome to the real world! They did of course commit to maintaining the ATM (Automatic Teller Machine); and they did for some time before removing it too, to provide me with other options a few miles away.

It was clear that financial institutions had shifted their focus from putting their customer first, into putting profit optimization before all else (as had other industries). This is illustrated in **Exhibit 2.5**.

What It Means for Business

A Statement on the Purpose of a Corporation signed by 181 CEOs of the largest companies in the United States in 2019 reflects, "Businesses play a vital role in the economy by creating jobs, fostering innovation, and providing essential goods and services. The co-signing CEOs commit to delivering value to customers, investing in employees, dealing fairly and ethically with suppliers, supporting their communities, and generating long-term value for shareholders."[1]

[1] "Update: The Purpose of Business," *Internal Auditor* (October 2019): 10–11.

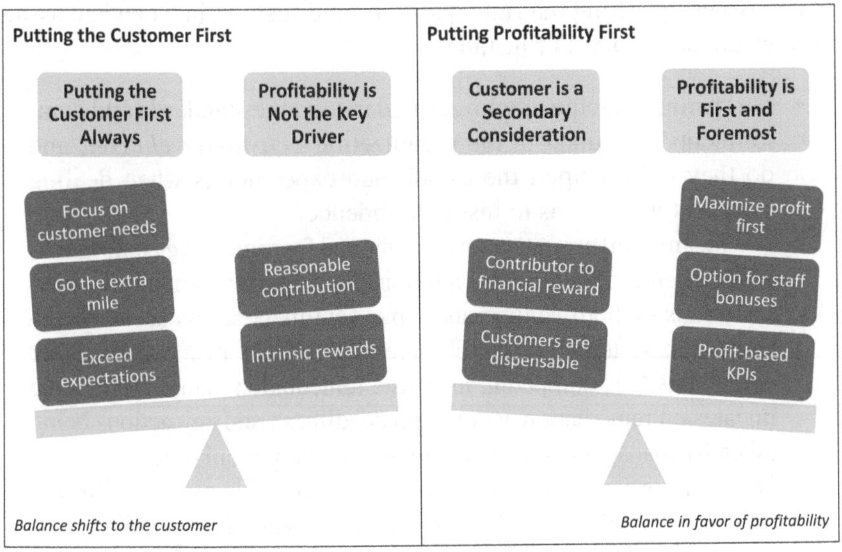

EXHIBIT 2.5 Balancing the scales between profitability and putting the customer first.

As businesses grapple with key business drivers and how these drivers shape the culture of the organization, this refreshed statement is likely to influence the thinking in boardrooms across the world. As an example, there has been a heightened interest in reevaluating the purpose of corporation in the United Kingdom and France.

An article on "The Dutch Stakeholder Experience" reflected that the Dutch stakeholder model had "evolved over time into a truly workable model in a successful market-based economy." The article drew out "some important lessons for those seeking to adopt a more stakeholder-oriented governance model (including) three key requirements to make such a model work. These are: (i) embed a clear stakeholder mission in the fiduciary duties of the board, (ii) give teeth to that stakeholder mission, while creating appropriate checks and balances, and (iii) foster a stakeholder-oriented mindset and environment."[2] Boards and audit committees should draw on the Dutch experience in considering how the three key requirements would help to make such a model work for their organization.

The Statement on the Purpose of a Corporation has the potential to shift the boardroom mindset from one of earning money for shareholders to serving stakeholders. Boards and audit committees need to remain abreast

[2] Christiaan de Brauw, "The Dutch Stakeholder Experience," 2 August 2020. https://corpgov.law.harvard.edu/2020/08/02/the-dutch-stakeholder-experience/ (sourced 20 August 2020).

of key issues by asking the right questions and seeking independent assurance where necessary. For instance:

- Do customer-facing employees understand the standards and commitments contained in the organization's ***customer charter***, and do they deliver upon the established expectations when dealing with customers so as to instill confidence?
- Are meaningful arrangements maintained for ***managing complaints***, including metrics and trend analysis on customer complaints covering trends by both volume and topic; sentiment across social media platforms; systemic issues observed; individual material customer complaints (i.e., complaint, its cause, remediation plan, and periodic updates on remediation actions and deadlines); and key actions being taken by management and how these are being monitored.
- Does the organization have robust controls for maintaining the ***privacy of personal information*** of individuals (including customers, employees, and other stakeholders) and adhere to strict regulatory obligations?
- Are the organization's technological controls sufficient to combat ***cybercrime***, including crimes where the computing device is the target (e.g., network access); crimes in which the computer is used as a weapon (e.g., launch a denial-of-service attack); and crimes where the computer is used as an accessory to a crime (e.g., to store illegally obtained data)?
- Do the payroll controls of the organization prevent and detect any incidence of ***wages theft*** (i.e., inadvertent and/or deliberate underpayment or non-payment of wages, allowances, entitlements, or retirement benefits, including superannuation)?
- Do the checks and balances for the organization's supply chain recognize and avoid products and services from suppliers that use ***modern slavery*** to exploit people by subjecting them to abuse, inhumane and degrading treatment, or force, deceive, or coerce them by threats or violence to work for little or no pay?
- Are business leaders actively working to reduce, eliminate, or better manage ***red tape*** to streamline internally or regulatory imposed requirements that are seen to be overly bureaucratic, cumbersome, and/or redundant?

Nurture a Reputation as an Employer of Choice

Setting the Scene

An organization where employees are happy and fulfilled at work, understand the vision, live the corporate values, and help to deliver against the business objectives will often be an employer of choice.

Senior leaders benefit from their organizations being recognized as an employer of choice because they become a magnet, attracting and retaining the best talent and having a lower attrition rate. Other benefits include:

- Having the best talent in the organization, to provide a competitive advantage.
- Leveraging the capability of higher quality of employees (i.e., the best talent) to boost customer satisfaction through the quality of the services or the product they deliver.
- Working with highly motivated and highly productive employees, as they consciously chose to work in the organization, which makes management and supervision of them less challenging.
- Boosting profitability as a consequence of the higher employee productivity and reduced recruitment costs because of a low attrition rate, as both directly affect the bottom line.

I transitioned well into various organizations that maintained a strong focus on the wellbeing of its employees and customers, and shaped an excellent work culture and workplace environment. These are the types of organizations that attract and retain superior employees.

I recognized early that my employer of choice may very well be different to someone else's, as there are also situational factors at play. Not everyone in these organizations was happy, and often this was because they could not, or were not willing to, live up to the expectations of delivering against a well-formed vision shaped by the corporate values. These people were usually in the minority, and it was their failure more so than the organization's (though in some cases senior leaders had not done enough to address the poor performers – see Chapter 4).

What It Means for Business

Leading-edge technology companies often have a buzz about them, and that attracts people of a certain personality. While these companies will be an employer of choice for employees who are compatible and thrive in the environment, others will not enjoy the expectation they participate in socializing and activities with coworkers that neither interest them nor appeal to their personality.

As I progressed into more senior roles, I focused on the reputation of the areas I was leading to ensure that they were gravitating towards being recognized as an employer of choice. As part of this, I invested time and energy in professional outreach, knowing that, internally, our reputation was increasingly positive. And when we were recruiting, I took a keen interest in recruiting the best talent. The common threads of an employer of choice and securing the best talent are illustrated in **Exhibit 2.6**.

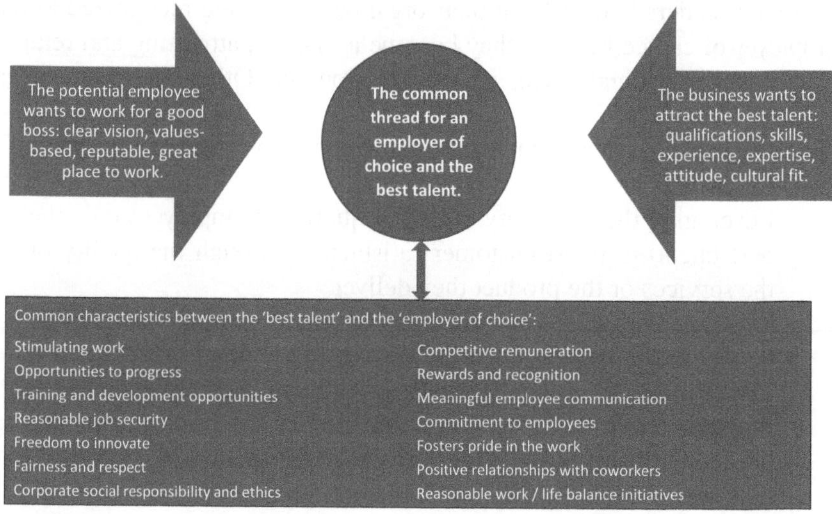

EXHIBIT 2.6 Common threads of an employer of choice and securing the best talent.

During my five years at the Australian Taxation Office, for example, I spoke personally with every recommended candidate, even when I was not directly part of the selection panel. Where candidates were being put forward to me to approve, I wanted to speak with them directly and informally, regardless of the level, to ensure they understood my vision and that I had high performance expectations of my people; I was not bringing people into a "cushy role," rather into a professional practice with tight and closely monitored key performance indicators that were sharply focused on outcomes that benefited the stakeholders. For the most part, we got the recruitment and retention right (I reflect on some challenges in Chapter 8).

CHAPTER 2 – TEN CLOSING REFLECTIONS

- A crucial role for boards is to establish a vision that captures *where* the business wants to go, and the organizational values that reflect *how* it wants its people to behave in getting there; business leaders then need to agree, understand, and champion the vision and values.
- Employees need to have a vision that clearly and succinctly articulates a mental image of what the business leaders want their business to be in the future, and it needs to reflect the broader business objectives, goals, and aspirations to provide a clear values-based focus that inspires people at all levels in the organization.

- Boards and audit committees need to maintain a keen eye on the organizational culture as it is critical to organizational success, with the strategy (the "what") and culture (the "how") needing to work seamlessly together to achieve the objectives and goals of the organization.
- Boards and business leaders are expected to set a tone at the top that helps to shape a values-based culture that drives ethical conduct, and where everyone in the organization is engaged and understands the type of conduct and behavior expected of them.
- Business leaders need to take steps to ensure business cohesion, with confidence that all parts of the operation are working together seamlessly and that governance, risk management, compliance, and assurance functions are in tune.
- Business leaders should identify and understand their business drivers, and optimize the internal drivers those that are under their control such as excellent customer satisfaction levels or a financial growth measure which are influenced by the seamlessness of the design, development, production, marketing, service delivery, and product sales areas. Conversely, they must monitor and manage the risks of external drivers such as international trade relations, the price of raw materials, geopolitical unrest, and economic conditions.
- Governance, risk management, compliance, and assurance specialists – together with emerging and successful business leaders – should operate in a business-savvy manner, thinking like a business leader or business owner, understanding how all the parts of the business work together, and satisfying the needs and expectations of the board and CEO.
- Boards and audit committees should seek information from business leaders on the organization's customer service vision and how this is communicated to its customers, including the availability of a customer service charter.
- Boards and audit committees should monitor developments arising from the revised Statement on the Purpose of a Corporation and how this will reshape business drivers and the culture of organizations throughout the world during the 2020s and beyond (including theirs and competitors).
- Business leaders should recognize the importance of attracting the best available talent by positioning their organization as an employer of choice, where employees are happy and fulfilled at work, understand the vision, live the corporate values, and help to deliver against the business objectives.

3 Oh No – Another Surprise Audit; the Business Is a-Changing

Internal auditing has evolved through varying styles over the last 40 years, with each new style building on the one before to satisfy the changing business needs and the emerging expectations of key stakeholders. The capabilities of internal auditors have continued to expand to satisfy these demands, and this introduced a new wave of trail-blazers. There is now recognition by business leaders that there are many areas of organizations that provide assurance (in addition to internal audit), and that collaboration between these areas is crucial to containing assurance costs. This chapter provides a reminder of the continuing merits of obsolescent practices (like surprise audits) in some circumstances ... and it also reflects on the personal triumph of getting back up after a brutal and unprovoked life-changing experience. It puts career planning into perspective through the advice of Gail Kelly (South African-born Australian businessperson) who said, "Whatever you are doing, give it all of your attention. Prioritize what you're going to do carefully, and then be in the moment."

Entity Profile and Role

Sector:	Financial services sector – retail banking.
Entity:	Rural Bank of New South Wales.
Entity description:	See Chapters 1 and 2.
Entity metrics:	For entity metrics see Chapter 4.
Primary role:	Internal auditor.
Main responsibilities:	Undertake internal audits of retail bank branches (two years), then audits for the first time of head office corporate activities (two years).
Timeframe:	Cusp of the First and Second Decades.

PERSONAL STORY

The bank usually transferred its staff around to different locations after several years. As an employee you were *directed* by the bank's management to a new location, and were not generally asked.

I had been very lucky to have spent just over five years at the Rural Bank's Penrith branch. It was close to my home (a few 100 yards to the east) and close to the local tertiary college (a further few 100 yards to the north). I had completed the first two years of a four-year commerce (accounting/banking) course at the local college so the timing of a transfer was not ideal.

I was appointed to the bank's internal audit team in February 1977 and spent a four-year rotation in the role. From a personal perspective, it was the most challenging time as I was working fulltime; travelling to my Sydney Central Business District (CBD) base most days; studying commerce part-time (four to five nights a week after work) during 1977 and 1978; I was engaged in mid-1977 to be married a year later; during 1977 my fiancée and I bought land and built our first home through to mid-1978; and our first child Nicole was born in mid-1980. Oh, and I was mugged and badly injured the day before Nicole was due (but more on that later).

I was exploring my new horizons in the Rural Bank headquarters in Oxford Street Sydney when I fortuitously bumped into David Harrison, one of my former branch accountants. "What are you doing in internal audit?", he enquired seemingly surprised. I was a bit taken aback at first, until he explained that I was not the typical style of person appointed to the area.

I found out later that I was part of a "new breed" of internal auditors, as the function was undergoing a transformation and needed knowledgeable, polished, and capable people with exemplary interpersonal skills. It was an all-male domain when I joined the ranks of internal auditing, but that gradually changed during my time in the State Bank.

Internal auditing in the 1970s was an "inspectorate" type role and, as such, was vastly different to now. It was very routine and involved a lot of rechecking of what the branch examiners and accountants had already checked. The auditing process was detailed, labor intensive, costly, and largely ineffective. Over time, that would change!

The bank had a talented staff member, David Walsh, who drew, captioned, and delivered humorous cartoons for the bank's monthly-staff newsletter and additional publications like the bank's calendar. In one cartoon, several serious-looking auditors simultaneously jumped unexpectedly through the door, window, and manhole surprising the regular cartoon characters "The Loan Arranger" and "Wampon" ... their reaction is captured with the caption, "Oh no, not another surprise audit" (see cartoon later).[1] This is a reaction that mirrors the perception that others across the bank had of internal audit at the time.

Old-style auditors had a culture of drinking after work, especially during field trips away. For any new auditors coming on board, there was considerable peer pressure to partake in the consumption of alcohol. As a teetotaler I was happy to accompany my colleagues to the hotel for a

[1] The Loan Arranger "Oh no, not another surprise audit" cartoon by David Walsh was used with permission.

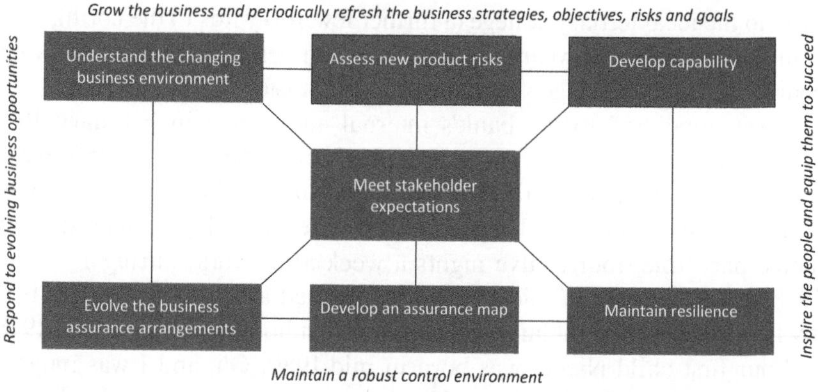

EXHIBIT 3.1 Sustaining a nimble and well-controlled business environment.

drink after work, but always made my personal preferences known without judging others. I had one colleague boast that it would only take him a couple of weeks to change that; he underestimated my resilience, and never succeeded. On the odd occasion my drinks were spiked, but my sense of smell and taste detected that quickly. Fortunately, that boozy culture was ultimately diluted by an influx of professional auditors.

The key insights from this phase of my story are:

- Understand the changing business environment.
- Assess new product risks.
- Meet stakeholder expectations.
- Develop capability.
- Evolve the business assurance arrangements.
- Develop an assurance map.
- Maintain resilience.

CONTEXT

Stakeholder expectations typically sit at the heart of business-growth strategies and the board's response to new business opportunities, and are underpinned by a well-equipped staff and robust control environment. These elements are discussed in this chapter and illustrated in **Exhibit 3.1**.

KEY TAKEAWAYS AND DEEP DIVES

Understand the Changing Business Environment

Setting the Scene

The primary focus of audits at banks had traditionally been on the retail-banking arm of the business, which was represented by a network of branches across the state. Teams of auditors would undertake audits at metropolitan and country (regional) locations. The movements of auditors were kept very secretive so that the surprise element would not be lost. This was always more difficult out in the country, as the locals could usually "sniff out" any out-of-towners very quickly.

> ***Surprise audits*** *are typically performed without notice to the business area, with the intention of examining the internal controls that are intended to prevent and detect fraud. The primary objective is to identify weaknesses in the control of assets and to establish whether the weaknesses have been exploited to misappropriate assets. The Association of Certified Fraud Examiners (ACFE) has reported that surprise audits are one of the most effective but least used forms of anti-fraud controls. Unscheduled cash counts and stock-takes performed by auditors are examples of approaches used in surprise audits.*

I learned early that auditors need to maintain professional skepticism in undertaking their work. This involves objectively gathering the facts, appraising them, and drawing conclusions solely from the facts.

A common audit objective in relation to the value of assets recorded in the balance sheet is to determine the existence, ownership, and valuation of those assets.

An Australian not-for-profit search and rescue organization, the National Safety Council Victorian Division, collapsed in the late-1980s with a shortfall in funds of about $300 million. Some 27 international banks had lent substantial amounts to the company.

While the company's external auditors had qualified the audit reports for several years, the board was not aware. The qualifications had apparently been removed by the CEO before distribution of the financial reports to the board. Alerted to the anomaly, the board looked below the surface to discover fraudulent financial records, particularly in respect of major trade debtors and a category of non-current asset known as "containerized safety equipment"; these were sealed shipping containers allegedly packed with expensive rescue equipment. The supposed tangible security (i.e. physical assets) the banks had been relying on for loans, totaling many millions of dollars were simply empty crates!

Subsequent enquiries revealed:

- The lack of caution by the banks and ineffective security monitoring was induced by the organization's social objectives and its reputation for being sophisticated.

- The CEO had a reputation as a respected leader. He was charismatic, affable, driven, and motivated, with a mesmerizing personality and a talent for cutting through bureaucracy. This created a "halo effect."
- The situation was exacerbated by inadequate regulation, inattentive bank lending, and poor oversight of "auditcd" financial statements.

The CEO committed suicide in the early-1990s before his trial. It is alleged that he had made false claims regarding his qualifications to obtain an initial appointment as a safety engineer at the company, before securing promotions ultimately to CEO.

Because of changes in the business environment, the pendulum had shifted through the late-1970s and 1980s, and the previous cautious nature of banks had been replaced with a more aggressive and less conservative lending regime, and their moral principles had become somewhat clouded (Chapter 7 delves further into the need to inspire a culture of integrity). Similarly, some auditors had not maintained professional skepticism when undertaking their audits.

What It Means for Business

Many large and prestigious business brands no longer exist, and, for some, this is because they failed to respond to the changing business environment.

It is possible for two longstanding retail brands in the same market to move in different directions, with one bounding to success while the other fails and is ultimately wound up. What can differentiate these businesses is the stability of leadership (e.g. one retained the same switched-on CEO for a decade, whereas the other had a succession of CEOs) coupled with a consistent strategy. The failing business realized it was stagnating, then pursued a cost-cutting strategy which resulted in a smaller range of products and dated stores with its fixtures getting older and its shops becoming dull and uninteresting. It was unprepared when another competitor moved into its traditional space and began heavily discounting its products.

Lego is a company that has operated since 1932, and has remained successful by responding astutely to the changing business environment. Conversely, Commodore Computers was founded in 1954 and became one of the world's largest PC manufacturers in the 1980s. But Commodore did not respond well enough to its competitors' product offerings, market positioning, and marketing efforts, and ceased to exist in 1994. Their respective tales are summarized in **Exhibit 3.2**.

The business environment is constantly evolving. This is often driven by a desire to improve business performance, implement better ways of working, or position the organization to succeed in a more competitive

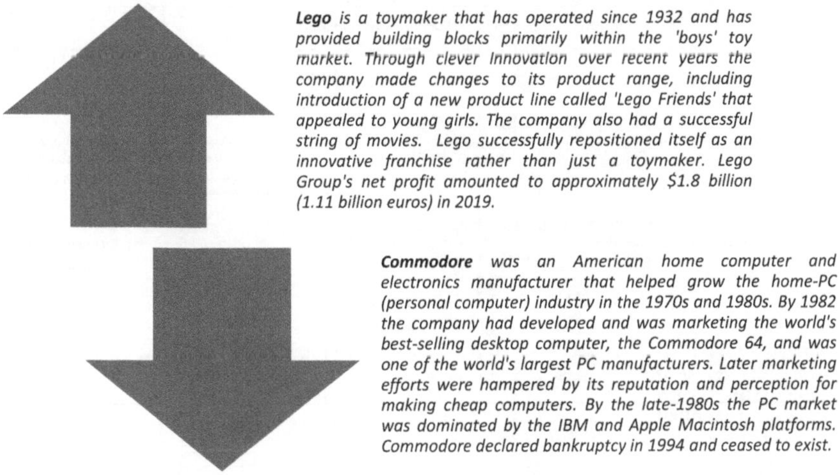

EXHIBIT 3.2 Examples of companies responding differently to the changing business environment.

industry. This can involve an upgrade to products and services, and implementation of improved technologies. The changes should be underpinned by a meaningful staff communication strategy and an investment in staff training to equip staff with skills to implement a new changed system.

There are many events that influence changes in the business environment. These include:

External Factors	*Internal Factors*
• Globalization.	• Decrease in performance.
• Geo-political events.	• Deterioration in profit.
• Disruptive innovation.	• Financial or cash flow restrictions.
• Recession or financial crises.	• Reductions in budget or funding.
• Increased market pressures.	• Changes in organizational structures.
• Advances in technology.	• Improved efficiency.
• Increased competition.	• Changes in industrial obligations.
• New or changed government legislation.	• Improved operations of the organization.
• Changes to regulatory requirements.	• Refreshed customer-centric initiatives.
• Increased expectations of customers.	• Changes in the supply chain.

When business leaders undertake an environmental scan and identify significant changes to the business environment relevant to the organization, the information needs be delivered to the board who will, in turn, consider a refresh of the organization's vision. Where changes are agreed, the CEO will then collaborate with the board and other stakeholders with a view to revising the business strategy; this will be informed by a gap analysis completed by the business leaders. The process is illustrated in **Exhibit 3.3**.

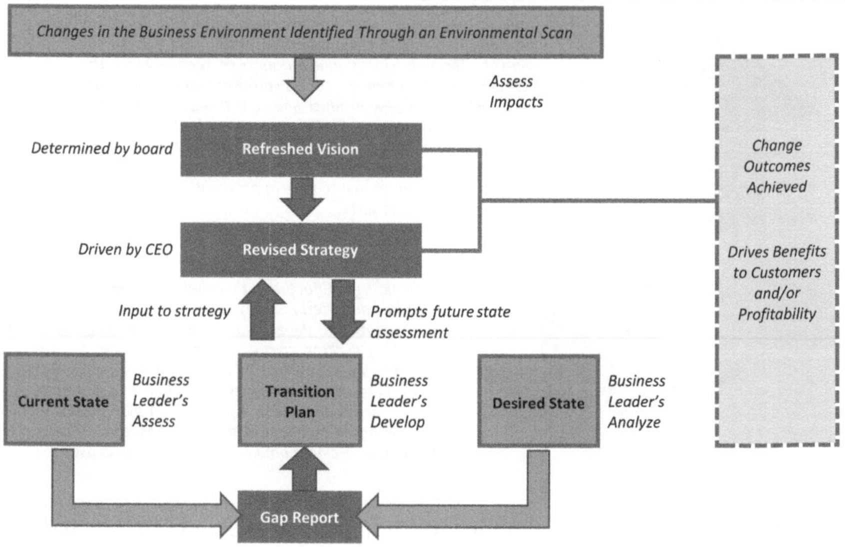

EXHIBIT 3.3 Process for responding to changes in the business environment.

Assess New Product Risks

Setting the Scene

The opening up of the global financial markets in the 1980's, enabled Australia's major banks to begin offering loans denominated in foreign currencies to personal (non-corporate) borrowers. The primary objective for banks to introduce these loans was enhanced profitmaking from higher margins, with secondary objectives focused on mitigating the perceived threat of new institutional lenders and anticipated potential regulatory lending restrictions.

The foreign currencies used included the majors – Japanese yen (JPY), Swiss francs (CHF), and the US dollar (USD). At the time, Australia's domestic interest rates were rising to unprecedented levels (e.g. rates on commercial bill facilities reached over 20 percent) while the interest rates on some foreign currencies (especially the Swiss francs) were considerably lower (around 7 percent).

The foreign currency loans provided exceptional value if the major currencies remained stable. However, when the Australian dollar was unexpectedly devalued, the benefit of achieving a lower interest rate on the foreign currency loans diminished and the adverse currency movements were soon seriously detrimental to the borrowers. A common example for a foreign-currency loan denominated in Swiss francs was that the principal owed was soon twice the amount that had been borrowed.

Borrowers initially, then bankers, started to panic at the swift change in fortunes. The banks had seriously misread the new product risks and were accused of misleading borrowers. They had fallen down on their promise to minimize the exposure of borrowers to exchange rate risks. In a classic risk-management move, the banks took steps to minimize their own losses and shift the responsibility of risk-taking to the borrowers. Litigation between the borrowers and the banks ensued through the courts from the late 1980s into the early 1990s.

SMASHED BY CURRENCY MOVEMENTS IN FOREIGN CURRENCY LOANS

As an example, a small-scale property developer had a commercial bill facility for a small development with climbing interest rates. He became an early foreign-currency loan borrower. He needed $250,000 to replace his existing commercial bill facility but ended up with a $500,000 foreign currency loan over two years in 1982 denominated in Japanese yen ($500,000 was the minimum borrowing for this type of loan). He lodged half the borrowings on term deposit. By early 1984, the principal debt had risen to $620,000, at which time the borrower was permitted by the bank to switch currencies. The loan was subsequently extended for a further three years. By 1987 the original foreign currency loan of $500,000 had blown out to a debt of nearly $1.8 million which the borrower was required to repay.

At the time that the foreign-currency loan debacle was taking shape, my career was at a crossroads. I had been identified as having the capability to shift into the high-stakes corporate lending world and this was to be my next step. However, as fate would have it, an opportunity opened up in the internal audit area of the bank and I achieved a promotion into an audit-manager role. I am glad that I was never a lender who was involved in leaving the bank's customers in a lesser state because of poor advice (fortunately, the State Bank was not one of the banks whose image was tarnished by the foreign currency loans crisis).

What It Means for Business

The assessment of product risks is an important part of product development, especially when introducing a new product or service in the market. Despite positive indications from research and consumer surveys, a new product offering might fail to make a connection with the customers. A robust product risk assessment will equip business leaders with the information needed to understand the merits, or otherwise, of launching the product, and whether it is a good investment for the business.

EXHIBIT 3.4 Product risk-assessment elements.

The risk assessment should consider the performance of similar products, the behavior of the market, potential for innovative disruption, soundness of the marketing plan, and potential profit contribution considering the costs of production, marketing, distribution, and sales. Examples of other lenses to be considered in the product risk assessment are illustrated in **Exhibit 3.4**.

New product offerings will be influenced by digital transformation. This includes both future innovations and developments we already know about (e.g. artificial intelligence, big-data analytics, biometrics, blockchain, conversational commerce, dark web, Internet of Things, augmented and virtual reality, and robotic-process automation).

In a broader sense, disruptive innovation should also be considered, with business leaders needing to recognize it as often rapid fire, reshapes new markets, drives economic volatility, creates new regulations, and, in some cases, is the result of a catastrophic event. Disruptive competitors like ride-share operations can usurp part of the established taxi industry's market share, but these operations need to manage longer-term risks and maintain acceptable corporate values for sustainable success.

> ***Disruptive innovation*** *refers to the process of developing and introducing new products or services into a well-established industry. It often drives transformation of the industry because it is more cost-effective and/or performs better. As a consequence, the previous "market leaders" are often displaced.*

Meet Stakeholder Expectations

Setting the Scene

I had received advice of my transfer from the Penrith branch of the Rural Bank onto the internal audit staff. The date was still to be finalized. It would require a daily commute of just over an hour from my home to the Sydney CBD if I was to catch the express train from the Blue Mountains into the city. I was older and wiser than my train trip five years earlier for my first day at the bank (discussed in Chapter 1). I worked out which train I would catch; it would be leaving about 7.30 am from Penrith.

The media had been reporting on frequent failures of the railway entity and I was about to experience that firsthand. It was clear that there was a disconnect between stakeholder expectations of a clean, safe, and reliable train service and what was being delivered.

On the morning of 18 January 1977, news was coming into the branch that there had been a serious train derailment at Granville about 25 miles (40 kilometers) to the east. By mid-morning some bank colleagues who survived the crash were making their way into the branch. We started piecing parts of the story together. Just after 8.00 am, an express commuter train from the Blue Mountains heading into Sydney had struck one of the steel-and-concrete pillars supporting the bridge carrying Bold Street over the railway cutting near Granville railway station.

It became clear that this was a major disaster, with the full extent to be revealed later. In all, 83 people died and another 213 were injured. Several Rural Bank colleagues and many locals including customers were killed or injured. It was an extremely sad day!

At the time, the state of the railway system was described as ramshackle, with subsequent investigations and inquiries revealing an alarming lack of investment in maintenance, coupled with ageing infrastructure. The government committed to modernizing the railway.

It takes great effort for sustained improvements to take shape, particularly integrating the government's modernization initiatives with the organization's culture for safety mindfulness. This was tragically evident when subsequent major train accidents happened:

- Near Glenbrook in December 1999 when 7 passengers were killed and a further 51 passengers were hospitalized when a Blue Mountains express train collided with the rear wagon of the transcontinental Indian Pacific long-haul train.
- Near Waterfall in January 2003 when a train derailed killing seven people aboard. The driver suffered a sudden heart attack and lost control of the train when it was travelling at 73 miles per hour (117 kilometers per hour) as it approached a curve.

Coincidentally, the train involved in the Granville tragedy was the one that I had selected to catch when I started my new job in internal audit a few weeks later. I had clearly dodged a catastrophe. And I did not know it at the time, but the Glenbrook accident would be a catalyst for me to leave the financial services sector to join the railways (discussed in Chapter 6) to transform the internal audit function, a job I held when the Waterfall tragedy occurred.

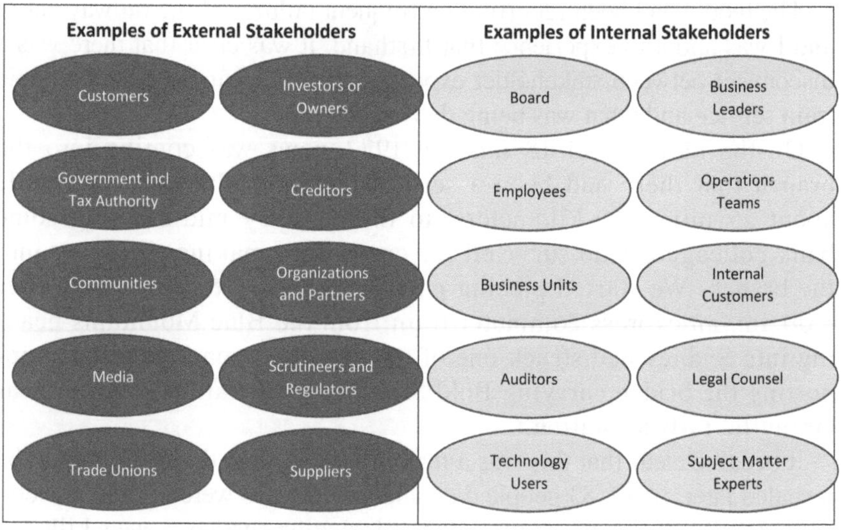

EXHIBIT 3.5 Examples of business stakeholders.

What It Means for Business

A critical success factor for any organization in determining its effective and sustainable future is how well it engages with its stakeholders impacted by organizational deliverables or outputs – all of the people and enterprises that work with it as partners in business development and decisions; those who provide goods and services; and those who receive the organization's goods and services. Examples of stakeholders are summarized in **Exhibit 3.5**.

This is underpinned by stakeholder engagement strategies that include proper stakeholder analysis and management. The support of all stakeholders makes achieving business objectives considerably easier, whereas disaffected stakeholders can damage positive work and threaten the achievement of business objectives. Stakeholder engagement is a key accountability of the CEO.

> ***Stakeholders*** *are individuals or groups that have an interest or investment (i.e. a stake) in the manner in which an organization designs, funds, governs, or operates it services.*

The first step is to establish a formal, systematic, and cohesive stakeholder engagement program that ensures that opportunities and risks posed by stakeholders are identified, evaluated, and managed. Development of such a program involves a rational assessment of the influence, impact, and priority of stakeholders. The program should be championed by the CEO and have engagement of key organizational staff.

> ***A stakeholder-engagement program*** *is a structured approach for identifying key stakeholders, documenting and implementing a plan for communicating with these stakeholders, and periodically reviewing the plan (more frequently when there is a significant restructure or change in the nature of the organization's business or its competition).*

The benefits of a stakeholder-engagement program include:

- Minimizes the risk of not meeting stakeholder expectations, or meeting them inconsistently.
- Maintains support (e.g. approval, resourcing) from business leaders and/or the board for proposed or ongoing programs.
- Optimizes successes and limits failings through effective consultation and decision-making.
- Helps to identify and monitor emerging risks, trends, and issues.
- Drives meaningful communications with stakeholders (discussed in Chapter 8).

A stakeholder-engagement program typically involves the following features:

- Respects the rights of key stakeholders (customer charter was discussed in Chapter 2).
- Documents a program to facilitate two-way interaction with key stakeholders.
- Requires a periodic review (e.g. annually or every two years), or when there is a significant change to the nature of the organization's business, its key processes, or its competitors.
- Ensures information about the organization's functions and governance structure is freely available (e.g. published on the web as well as in the published annual report).
- Provides an easily accessible and understood complaints handling policy and procedure.
- Delivers prompt responses and actions towards complaints and grievances (Chapter 2 mentioned the need for meaningful arrangements for managing complaints).

Once the stakeholder-engagement program has been developed, steps need to be taken to understand stakeholder expectations so that they can be met. A key driver for business leaders is the clarity of the purpose of business (discussed in Chapter 2), and whether the board has it oriented towards customers and other stakeholders.

A useful dialogue between the business leaders and identified stakeholders will be something like this:

- Do you agree that you are a stakeholder of the business?
- What is your interest or stake in the organization?
- What are your expectations of the organization in engaging and communicating with you as a stakeholder?
- How do you anticipate those expectations will be realized in practice?
- Are your expectations already in place or do they need to be implemented or altered?

Develop Capability

Setting the Scene

After working for about three years, I thought it was time to pursue part-time accounting studies, and the local college was offering a four-year commerce (accounting/banking) course. I signed up.

On the first night I was astonished that over 100 students were in the classroom. But the teacher assured us that people would gradually drop off and we would establish a new norm. He was right, and after a few months we had a normal class size. We had fewer students in the second year of the course because subjects were failed or students dropped out. It was the same pattern in the third and fourth years of the course. In fact, just five students completed the four-year course in the minimum four years (fortunately I was one of them). A handful of other students who had to repeat subjects finished a year or two later.

The workload was significant, with a fulltime job, studying part-time, and attending lectures four to five nights a week. My results were consistently strong throughout the four years of the course, and I managed straight A's in the first two years, achieving the prize for topping the course in those years.

The final two years of the course were tougher, as I was working in the Sydney CBD which required a daily commute. Additionally, my fiancée and I had bought land, and had a builder constructing our first home. We were married midway through the final year. So, plenty was happening 24/7.

The final exam in the fourth year was management accounting. I was comfortable with how I'd handled the papers for the three other subjects, and was quietly confident of a good result for each. The management accounting exam was in two parts with three hours allocated for each part. You were required to pass both parts.

I opened the paper for part one. The first question was worth 70 percent of the marks for that paper. The question cleverly combined two totally different concepts into the one question, one concept that we had learned through practical application and we had learned the theory for the other concept. I didn't know how to answer the question. I was stumped. I was shattered.

I had to think quickly. I needed to first answer the other questions worth 30 percent of the marks, and see what transpired. I was pretty confident with my answers for that part of the paper, and thought if I could secure 25 percent of the 30 percent on offer, it meant I needed to somehow get 25 percent from the remaining 70 percent … the impossible practical question to answer. I established my strategy; fess up and tell the markers I knew the concepts but couldn't combine them in a single answer. Then I set out to write down in narrative form all I knew about the theoretical side of both concepts.

I went home after the exam feeling quite despondent. To come so far and fail at the last hurdle would be too much to bear. At the time I just didn't have the heart to front up to complete another year if I failed. I completed the second part of the exam a couple of days later and it flowed nicely.

About six weeks later my results came in the mail. My mother rang me at work to let me know. She read carefully and slowly through all the results and I just waited and waited for the one that worried me – management accounting. It's a B pass she said … and I was elated (even a C would have been sufficient). It was a tough four years, but I had successfully completed the course.

The bank supported my studies with a few days' study leave each year, and time off (on pay) to complete the exams. I was always grateful that my chief audit executive, Jim McConville, arranged my travel itinerary in my final two years so that I travelled intrastate only during semester breaks, and worked in the Sydney CBD or in the metropolitan area when I was required to attend lectures. On successful completion of the course, I received a small incremental increase in my base salary.

I completed further studies throughout my career, but this first one when I was in my late teens was the pivotal one that helped build my confidence and showed me that I had the capacity, commitment, and academic cognition to succeed.

In addition to the learning from the content of the course, it meant I well-understood the challenges of combining fulltime work with part-time study, as well as the importance of business leaders supporting their staff through continuing education. I was thrilled when my own staff in later years invested in developing their own capabilities by completing a range of postgraduate courses, from professional certifications and master's degrees through to the doctorate level.

What It Means for Business

Staff capability is a central building plank for organizational performance. The efficient and effective achievement of business objectives depends on the organization's commitment to developing the capabilities of their people. This requires a systematic approach to workforce planning, including the planning, integration, delivery, and evaluation of staff learning and development.

An important success factor for individuals and business leaders is that staff don't just need the training ... they actually need to learn. Esteemed chief audit executive coach and author Jason Mefford has reflected on the differences between training and learning, "You can take training and not learn anything, and you can learn without going to training. To learn you need a combination of knowledge, skills, abilities, and experience. Training only helps you with the first two." He further reflects, "One of the best ways for people to improve their abilities is through community with others. Without this aspect of learning you really don't integrate and 'learn' the information fully."[2]

Developing staff capability requires business leaders to determine the principles and characteristics for building capability, then design a suitable framework to achieve the desired results; this will include a combination of the following elements:

- Reflect the broader business objectives.
- Define the organization's longer-term capability needs and how best to source them, for instance:
  - Investing in the continued learning and development of existing staff to build the necessary capability, and/or
  - Undertaking selective recruitment (including through an entry-level employment program) to fill capability gaps and achieve a well-balanced and capable team.
- Create a learning culture where continuous improvement becomes part of the DNA of the organization.
- Articulate how learning and development will be planned, promoted, and evaluated.
- Reflect how it will be aligned and integrated with workforce planning, performance management, and business outcomes.

Having the right people with the right skills at the right time does not just happen. It is the result of effective workforce planning, and this requires the same rigor and attention by business leaders as their other accountabilities. An appropriate investment in well-managed learning and development initiatives helps in delivering business objectives and outcomes into the future. This is illustrated in **Exhibit 3.6**.

Elements of developing capability are explored in other sections, including creating a learning environment (Chapter 1), developing business acumen (Chapter 2), identifying talent (Chapter 4), dealing with poor performance (Chapter 4), and building capacity and capability (Chapter 5).

[2] Used with permission.

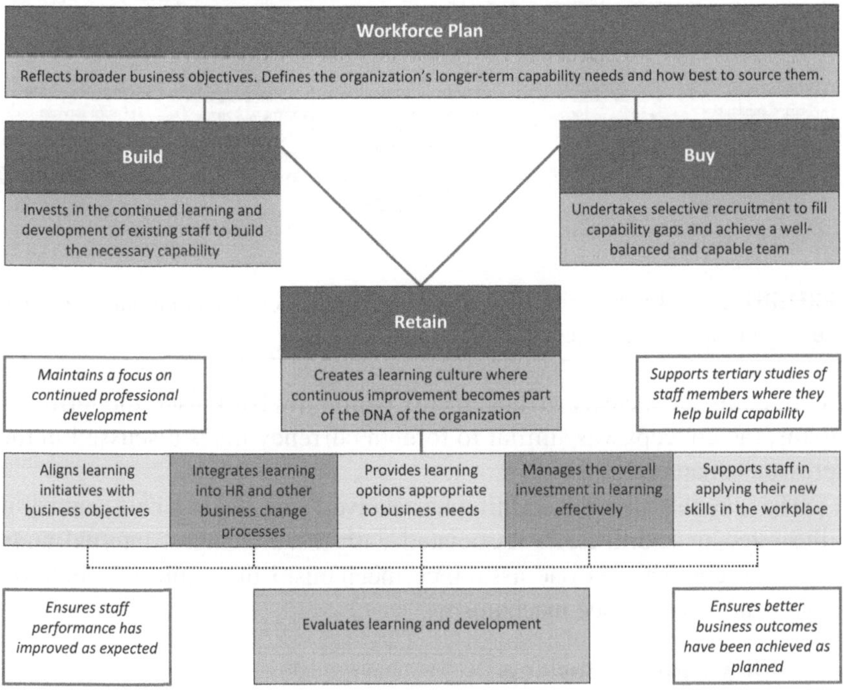

EXHIBIT 3.6 Process for establishing learning and development initiatives.

Evolve the Business Assurance Arrangements

Setting the Scene

To preserve the surprise element in regional audits, logistical arrangements were typically arranged so that the start of the audit was unexpected; for instance, the auditors could commence an audit at the close of business rather than the start of the day to throw the local branch staff off the scent.

The breadth of internal audit's focus has expanded as a consequence of the changing business environment and new product risks. But this did not always occur in a structured or systematic way.

The bank's internal audit team used a "standard" internal audit program when they visited the retail bank branches, and I was asked by the new chief audit executive to review the program for reasonableness. The retail-bank auditors were routinely reviewing loan paperwork and securities in branches where the average commercial/business loan was less than $100,000, and I quickly noticed that they didn't look at foreign exchange (FX) loans. The FX loans were introduced a couple of years earlier and were managed centrally, but they weren't part of the internal audit work program – anywhere! And the FX loans represented a far greater risk, averaging over $500,000 with inherent currency risks and

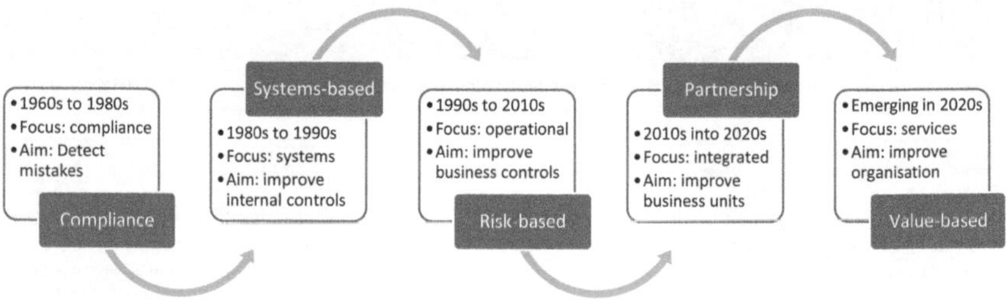

EXHIBIT 3.7 Evolving internal auditing techniques. Contemporary internal auditing practices are discussed in Chapter 6.

more complex security arrangements (while my bank used the term FX loans, the concept was similar to foreign currency loans discussed in the previous chapter).

The way that internal auditing has evolved over the last half-century is illustrated in **Exhibit 3.7**. Associated with these changes, internal audit is now recognized as one assurance mechanism in a suite of whole-of-organization assurance mechanisms.

What It Means for Business

Boards and audit committees expect business leaders to maintain effective internal control arrangements that reduce the residual risk of business activities to an acceptable level within the organization's risk appetite. They then rely on efficient and effective assurance arrangements to confirm internal controls are operating in practice as designed and to identify any weaknesses in controlling the risks.

Where boards and audit committees are relying on internal audit or other assurance functions that are weak or ineffective and they don't recognize it, they can be lulled into a false sense of assurance and could easily conclude that all is well because no red flags have been raised. This could result from an under-resourced, ethically compromised or ignored internal audit and other assurance functions, or ones with inadequate skills or a lack of independence.[3]

There are also potentially serious implications when business leaders fail to properly support internal audit. The board and audit committee are responsible for ensuring that that this does not happen and they should watch for potential "red flags" including when the chief audit executive:

- Avoids high-risk areas or accepts scope limitations.
- Ignores organizational culture.

[3] Richard Chambers, "No internal audit? it could be worse," 24 October 2016, https://iaonline.theiia.org/blogs/chambers/2016/Pages/No-Internal-Audit-It-Could-Be-Worse.aspx (Sourced 17 September 2020).

- Fails to perform follow-up to ensure recommendations are addressed adequately.
- "Waters down" reportable issues, that conceals or distorts the facts.
- Fails to provide adequate reporting about internal audit, including its performance, plans, budgets, staffing requirements, training needs, and quality.[4]

To combat these restrictions, boards and audit committees need to ensure they have a strong, credible, and credentialed chief audit executive. And the audit committee should meet with the chief audit executive "in camera" – without management present – periodically (at least annually) for frank and open discussions.

> ***Assurance*** *refers to the outcome of an independent assessment of governance, risk management, and control processes for an organization that is based on an objective examination of evidence.*

Because assurance is expensive, business leaders need to make conscious decisions on the right coverage and mix for their business environment. This involves establishing boundaries and assigning assurance responsibilities to each risk and control group so gaps and duplication of effort are avoided. Their aim should be to deliver strong, integrated, and cost-effective organization-wide assurance activities that do not consume more effort and money than necessary.

There are typically a wide range of specialist risk and control areas that undertake assurance activities. Boards and business leaders now utilize business assurance models within the organization that reflect the discrete areas relied upon within the organization to provide assurance, which may include three levels internally – management controls (first level); governance, risk, and compliance functions (second level), and ultimately internal audit (third level).

- The first level is concerned with management controls and generally has a real-time focus aimed at reviewing governance and compliance arrangements to demonstrate "checks and balances" are working effectively.

[4] Richard Chambers, "5 ways internal audit can fail to adequately serve its organization," 11 February 2019, https://iaonline.theiia.org/blogs/chambers/2019/Pages/Five-Ways-Internal-Audit-Can-Fail-to-Adequately-Serve-Its-Organization.aspx (Sourced 17 September 2020).

- The second level centers on risk oversight and involves some degree of real-time activity, with a mandate to review first level activities. It encompasses the work of specialist areas like risk management, technical and regulatory compliance, and safety, and aims to confirm the effectiveness of governance and compliance arrangements, and to identify and action improvements.
- The third level involves independent assurance that evaluates the adequacy and effectiveness of both the first and second levels of the organization's risk-management approaches. It is typically undertaken by internal auditors to independently confirm governance and compliance effectiveness, and to recommend improvements.
- Assurance is also provided to boards and audit committees by external scrutineers.

Scrutineers *refers to a person or entity from outside the organization that has the power to scrutinize any process or activity that requires rigorous oversight, with a focus on detecting noncompliance, corruption, and errors (e.g., external auditors, regulators, coroner, taxation authority, parliamentary committee, federal or state investigation).*

An assurance strategy helps to articulate how the organization leverages its overall investment in assurance, and aids the board and audit committee to grasp the effectiveness of these arrangements against the organization's risk and assurance requirements.

The establishment of an assurance strategy helps to:

- Formulate a cohesive, comprehensive and fit-for-purpose risk, and assurance process.
- Provide comfort to stakeholders about the reasonableness and adequacy of assurance.
- Ensure there is a comprehensive risk and assurance process.
- Define risk and assurance roles and accountabilities.
- Assess assurance coverage against the organization's key risks.
- Identify skills required to deliver necessary assurance as a guide to resourcing.
- Minimize assurance costs by getting optimal value from the organization's assurance investment, through minimizing duplication of effort and identifying assurance gaps.

Assurance maps (discussed in the next section) are generally the first step in this process and provide comfort that key organization risks are adequately covered by a coordinated combination of assurance activities.

Develop an Assurance Map

Setting the Scene

There are many players in organizations that have the responsibility to provide assurance. A good example is in respect to safety, where we often see people assessing elements of safety on a daily and periodic basis. The following safety-related assurance elements provide an illustrative example of ten common elements of safety assurance (not intended to be a complete picture):

First Level

- Work, health and safety coordinators undertake thorough checks of workplaces and operational sites to ensure that appropriate safety notices and emergency evacuation procedures are displayed, potential risks and hazards in the area are identified, risks are mitigated, and that safety practices are observed. They will also ensure that all hazards are properly assessed and recorded.
- Management has primary responsibility for managing workplace safety on a day-to-day basis.
- Corporate lawyers monitor legislative and regulatory changes and identify changes to safety regulations, and flow into organizational policies, procedures, and safe working instructions.
- Safe working inspectors are required in some industries (such as manufacturing, energy, and transport) to maintain safe working practices.

Second Level

- Work, health and safety committees have an oversight responsibility, and, in part, consider the consolidated insights of the work, health and safety coordinators.
- HR specialists monitor the safety culture of the organization and deliver safety training and refresher courses, some of which is mandatory.
- Compliance specialists monitor the safety-related licensing provisions at an individual, functional, and organizational level.
- Corporate investigators may be called upon to investigate safety breaches or near misses, to identify serious breaches of safety policies and to identify lessons learned.

Third Level

- Safety auditors provide an in-depth review of workplace safety programs with the objective of assessing the organization's compliance to applicable regulations or codes as well as the identification of unsafe conditions in the workplace. They typically report to management and the board safety committee.

- Internal auditors complete independent assessments of the organization's higher risk areas, which may include its safety management system. They usually report primarily to the board audit committee.

Notwithstanding the various assurance lenses being applied to safety, until recent years the various areas often worked in isolation with each other. There seemed to be a scattergun approach rather than a systematic and coordinated safety assurance effort. This resulted in duplication of effort and, in some cases, gaps in coverage. Boards, board safety committees, and board audit and risk committees rarely received a consolidated assurance view of the organization's safety arrangements.

An assurance strategy establishes a more disciplined approach that compels specialist safety-related areas and assurers to work together to provide a consolidated perspective on what safety regulations mean from a risk-management perspective, and how the three lines of defense are to be applied to educate employees, ensure full and active compliance, deliver independent periodical assurance, and keep their employees and the community safe.

The concepts around consolidation of safety assurance apply to other areas of the business where assurance is sought by the board, audit committee, and business leaders (e.g. *internally* – financial stewardship, performance, compliance, system security; *externally* – shared services, outsourced services). The breadth of the organization's assurance needs is broad, and assurance mapping provides a systematic approach for illustrating the different elements.

What It Means for Business

The audit committee's role and responsibilities have expanded significantly over the past two decades, with audit, finance, risk, and compliance specialists providing assurance through their separate reporting channels. The breadth of assurance reporting to the audit committee is illustrated in **Exhibit 3.8**.

Assurance mapping reflects the organization's assurance strategy (previous section) and underpins a collaborative reporting approach (Chapter 11). An assurance map is a high-level document that helps to establish a sound understanding of the holistic risk coverage and various assurance activities and how effective they are.[5] It is increasingly common for assurance maps to be constructed across three levels of assurance to rate the overall

[5] Andrew Cox and Bruce Turner, *Internal Audit in Australia Second Edition* (Sydney, Australia: The Institute of Internal Auditors Australia, 2020), 30.

EXHIBIT 3.8 Breadth of internal reporting to audit committees.

effectiveness of assurance activities, helping to bring to light overlaps, gaps, and other inefficiencies. It is a useful basis for promoting and informing combined assurance.

While internal audit is only one in a suite of assurance mechanisms, an assurance map developed by internal audit or another governance area feeds into the development of the internal audit plan.

> *An **assurance map** is a high-level document that identifies the holistic risk coverage across the organization by a range of assurance providers. It helps to identify gaps and duplication of assurance coverage, and illustrates the level of assurance brought by the various assurance activities.*

The example of an assurance map contained in **Exhibit 3.9** illustrates how the audit committee can identify areas where assurance arrangements are weaker (e.g. management accounting) and those where efficiencies may be possible (e.g. payroll and workplace safety).

Maintain Resilience

Setting the Scene

I was working in the State Bank's Head Office located at Number 1 Oxford Street Sydney, undertaking the first ever audit of the bank's marketing and

Risk Categories	Management 1st Line of Defense			Functional Oversight 2nd Line of Defense				Independent 3rd Line of Defense	
	Accounting Team Leader	Human Resource Manager	Business Reporting Coordinator	Risk Management Coordinator	Financial Controller	Compliance Manager	Management Safety Committee	Internal Audit	External Safety Auditor
Financial									
Financial Reporting	●	-	◑	◑	●	-	-	◑	-
Accounts Payable	●	-	-	◑	●	-	-	◑	-
Payroll	●	●	●	◑	●	●	-	●	-
Accounts Receivable	●	-	-	◑	●	-	-	◑	-
Management Accounting	○	-	-	○	○	-	-	○	-
--- <Other> ---									
Human Resources									
Recruitment	-	●	-	◑	-	-	-	◑	-
Training	-	●	◑	◑	-	-	-	◑	-
Succession Management	-	●	-	○	-	-	-	◑	-
Workplace Safety	◑	●	●	◑	-	●	●	●	●
--- <Other> ---									

Legend:

● = Complete risk coverage	◑ = Partial risk coverage	○ = Limited to no risk coverage	- = Risk not covered by this area

EXHIBIT 3.9 Abridged example of an assurance map.[6]

publications area. I was enjoying the work immensely and discovering new things. The people in the area were very generous with their time and were wonderful to deal with. I spent most of my working day in the area to document and assess the control arrangements.

I had a bounce in my step and a whistle on my lips in mid-July 1980 as I made my way back to the office after a stroll in the majestic Hyde Park directly opposite the bank's headquarters. It was a bright and sunny day, and I was excited at the pending arrival of my first child, due the next day. I crossed the street and was on the footpath a few yards from the bank when I was suddenly and unexpectedly hit with what would be termed these days as an unprovoked "coward punch."

I lost consciousness briefly as I fell awkwardly to the ground. While I was down, I was kicked and badly injured. It happened so quickly. I was

[6] Aligns to "The IIA'S Three Lines Model – An update of the Three Lines of Defense" released in July 2020 by the Institute of Internal auditors, Lake Mary, Fla., USA. https://global.theiia.org/about/about-internal-auditing/Public%20Documents/Three-Lines-Model-Updated.pdf (Sourced 20 August 2020).

confused, and people rushed to my aid with the realization of what had happened … a brutal attack that was so quick and without warning. The assailant took off, running down the busy Oxford Street. He was chased by some lunchtime joggers, but they lost him in the crowd.

I was unaware of the true nature of my injuries. Immediately after the attack, my first concern was that I would be late back from lunch; it was nearly 1:00 p.m., so I was cutting it a bit fine. I was also alarmed that the jacket of my trendy light tan three-piece suit had been bloodied.

Some folk recognized me and helped me up to the bank's onsite registered nurse. My Internal Audit colleagues were notified. I was taken to the nearby Sydney Hospital and treated. I had severe lacerations on the scalp of my head which required many stitches; the anesthetic didn't take properly and I could feel every single stitch. I was concussed, my face was swelling badly, and I had several chipped and broken teeth. My nose was badly broken and was standing at an odd angle to my face. The doctors wanted to keep me in hospital for further observation but I insisted on going home to be with my wife, Bea, given she was heavily pregnant and 40 miles away.

My colleagues transported me home. Bea was certainly shocked when she saw me … and I, too, was really shocked when I saw myself in the mirror for the first time, still battered, bruised, and bloodied. It was straight to the bathroom for a cleanup, and my request for a photo was summarily dismissed.

Thankfully, our first child, a little girl who we named Nicole, waited for a few days. She was born just four days after my assault. I looked a mess in the birthing suite, and Bea reckons I was treated by the nurses better than she was, being fussed over with cups of coffee and other comforts. My nose required surgery, and I was booked into Auburn Hospital (30 miles to the east) to have it repaired, a few days after the birth. It was too much for a stoic Bea when told she could go home, when I was still in Auburn Hospital. Once the medical staff knew the circumstances, they kept her in a little longer until I had been released.

I was off work for six weeks recovering from the assault, having further medical treatment, and having my teeth repaired. The one positive note was that I was able to share some nice quality time with my two girls, Bea and Nicole, during the early days. The initial visible wounds healed a lot quicker than the mental wounds; I suffered frequent debilitating headaches and anxiety over the ensuing four decades which I have had to carefully manage.

Once I was cleared to return to work, I endured the trip to Sydney for another half year. I was then transferred back to a retail bank branch in Springwood in the Blue Mountains where I was to be a loans officer.

While the assault was an unpleasant moment in my life, I remember the kindness, efforts, and empathy of so many people who helped me and my family through a most difficult period. I did bounce back, though the experience tested my resilience.

What It Means for Business

Workplace resilience reflects an employee's capacity to "bounce back" by handling the effects of a crisis event, responding to pressure, dealing with stress, and managing the demands of daily life. Resilient employees are usually well-equipped to handle the ever-challenging workplace demands of the modern business-world, including frequently changing priorities and heavy workloads.

The COVID-19 event (see deep dive in Chapter 14) certainly tested the resilience of people across the world, and stretched crisis-management efforts beyond what many people ever anticipated throughout the last half-century. To navigate these situations effectively, business leaders rely on the behaviors and mindsets of their people, coupled with an ability to look ahead.

Workplace resilience is an increasingly important factor in the turbulent world in which we are operating, and is important for both individuals and organizations that are striving to thrive and survive. When business leaders act to establish a great place to work that manages workplace stress and addresses mental health issues, they help to establish a resilient workplace where employees perform at their peak.

Business leaders can pursue a range of strategies to shape a resilient workplace. These include:

- Creating a comfortable work environment (e.g. natural light, suitable décor, plants, quiet spaces, standing desk options, social meeting spaces).
- Embracing smart work design concepts (e.g. flexibility in working roles and hours).
- Inspiring an inclusive work culture, including making coaching, and mentoring programs available.
- Establishing and communicating the leadership's commitment to support those with mental health challenges, then following-through by:
    - Increasing awareness through mental-health education and training.
    - Providing early intervention options, such as an Employee Assistance Program or similar.
    - Establishing programs to support recovery (e.g. return-to-work programs, flexible sick or care leave provisions).

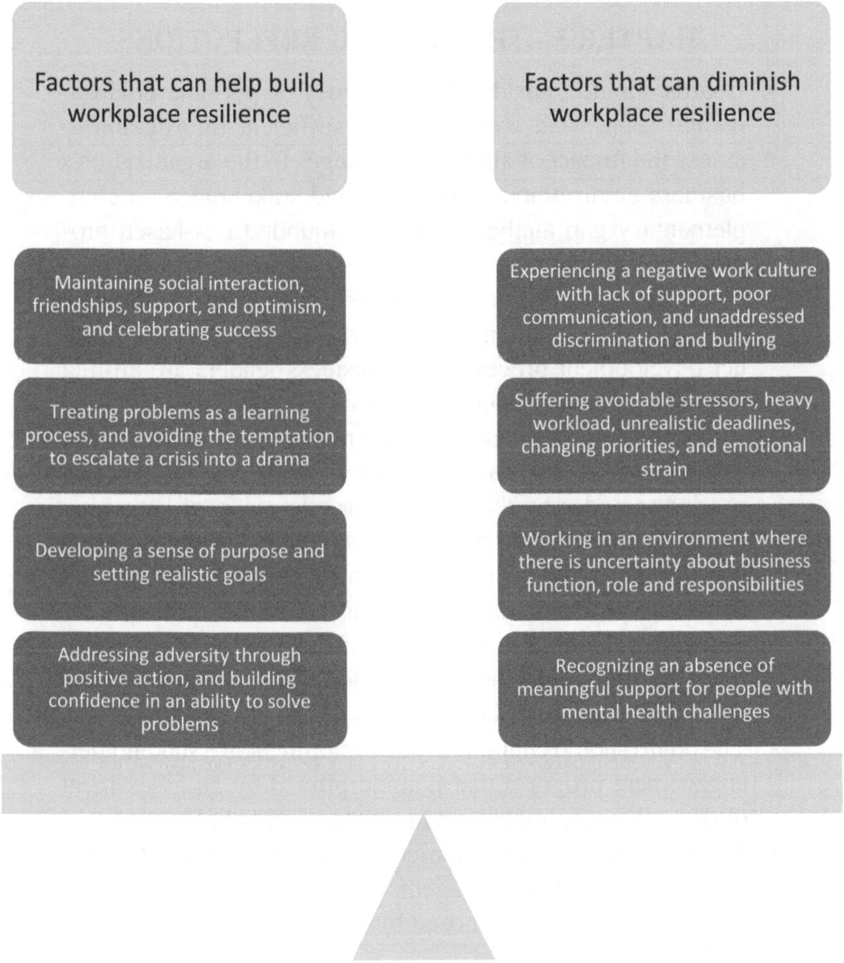

EXHIBIT 3.10 Examples of factors that help build or diminish workplace resilience.

At the core of these strategies should be a rebalancing of the pendulum so that factors that help build resilience far outweigh those that diminish workplace resilience. This is illustrated in **Exhibit 3.10**.

There are factors of resilience building interspersed throughout this book, including maintaining a fun business environment (Chapter 1), leveraging emotional intelligence (Chapter 1), maintaining communications with staff (Chapter 6), maintaining focus when under attack (Chapter 8), focusing on mental health (Chapter 10), understanding the lived culture (Chapter 12), and getting inspired (acknowledgements).

CHAPTER 3 – TEN CLOSING REFLECTIONS

- Boards should consider the outcomes of periodic environmental scans, and should receive sufficient information to assess the impact of significant changes to the organization's business environment, customers and stakeholders, a complementary gap analysis, and well-founded risk-based proposed changes to the organization's vision and strategy.
- Audit committees should seek assurance that meaningful product risk assessments are undertaken as part of the product development process when business leaders are aiming to introduce new products or services in the market.
- Audit committees need to understand how product risk assessments equip business leaders with the information needed to understand the merits, or otherwise, of launching any new products or services and whether it represents a good investment for the business, by considering the performance of similar products, the behavior of the market, potential for innovative disruption, soundness of the marketing plan, and potential profit contribution considering the costs of production, marketing, distribution, and sales.
- The board should champion the development of a stakeholder-engagement program that is underpinned by an assessment of the influence, impact, and priority of stakeholders.
- Business leaders should maintain a formal, systematic, and cohesive stakeholder-engagement program that ensures that opportunities and risks posed by stakeholders are identified, evaluated, and managed.
- Business leaders should establish a systematic approach to workforce planning, including the planning, integration, delivery and evaluation of staff learning, and development.
- Boards and audit committees should make business leaders accountable for maintaining effective internal control arrangements that reduce the residual risk of business activities to an acceptable level within the organization's risk appetite.
- Audit committees should require efficient and effective assurance arrangements that enable them to confirm internal controls are operating in practice as designed, and give them confidence that the control framework remains effective in identifying any material weaknesses in controlling the organization's risks.

- Audit committees should champion a systematic and coordinated assurance effort that avoids duplication of effort and potential gaps in coverage; they should insist on receiving an assurance strategy – informed by assurance mapping – that compels governance, risk, compliance, and assurance specialists to work together to provide a consolidated perspective and meaningful reporting.
- Business leaders should maintain an eye on workplace resilience – given the frequently changing priorities and heavy workloads in the modern work environment – to help manage workplace stress and address mental health issues so employees are equipped to perform at their peak; common strategies include creating a comfortable work environment, embracing smart work design concepts, inspiring an inclusive work culture, and communicating their commitment to supporting those with mental health challenges.

4 Rising Above the Norm

Governance, risk, compliance, and assurance are multi-faceted activities requiring a helicopter perspective … looking across the whole organization. Senior management strives to achieve internal alignment and external focus, and these professionals need to do likewise. This chapter explores the challenges of gaining assurance for highly complex activities, some of which are in overseas markets, and others are continuing to evolve … and it also showcases how internal audit saved an organization tens of millions of dollars through timely audit work prior to a significant market crash, and poses a common dilemma for high-achieving auditors – when business and/or audit leaders are on a different page to me, what should I do? It also highlights the negative impact from progressive staff development programs that are allowed to fizzle and fail because of lack of commitment by business leaders. It also puts staff capability into perspective, in the words of Jim Rohn (1930–2009), "If someone is going down the wrong road, he doesn't need motivation to speed him up. What he needs is education to turn him around."

Entity Profile and Role

Sector:	Financial services sector – merchant banking and retail banking
Entity:	State Bank of New South Wales (SBN) and European Asian of Australia (Euras)
Entity description:	By the early-1980s, the State Bank had expanded its local operations beyond its traditional state boundaries, establishing operations in Canberra and Melbourne. And it then established treasury and lending operations in the overseas global markets of London and New York. By 1984, it had entered into a joint venture with Deutsche Bank to establish a merchant banking operation based in Sydney called European Asian of Australia (Euras)
Entity metrics (1990):	• Total assets (on balance sheet) \$A18.4 billion • Total capital resources (including equity) \$1.5 billion • Annual operating profit before tax \$34.8 million • Net interest income \$561 million • Staff 7,300 (including 191 overseas and subsidiaries) • Number of branches 370 (Source: SBN 1989/90 annual report)

Sale of entity:	The State Bank was ultimately sold to Colonial in 1994 through a trade sale, with the New South Wales state government receiving net proceeds of $527 million (the purchaser secured guarantees and indemnities to protect itself from bad debts above a specified threshold). The Colonial State Bank carried on until 2000, when it was taken over by the Commonwealth Bank
Primary role:	Manager Wholesale Banking and Treasury Audits at State Bank, following a year-long secondment with Euras to establish their internal audit function
Main responsibilities:	Establish contemporary internal audit activity and undertake audits of assigned areas with the wholesale banking and treasury arms of the bank
Timeframe:	The Second Decade

PERSONAL STORY

My father had endured long periods without meaningful work during the high-inflationary and high-unemployment era of the late-1960s and 1970s; he was unemployed for over four consecutive years during the 1970s.

In the 1970s and early 1980s, banking was seen as a "career for life" for its male employees. As a young father with three young children in the 1980s – and the impact of my father's unemployment as a backdrop – I was glad for the job security as I was committed to maintaining a stable home life.

The situation was vastly different for female employees as illustrated by the following examples:

- If a female banker was getting married, she was required to resign from the bank and then reapply. This policy was only amended in the late-1960s just before I started at the Rural Bank.
- Women were also paid less than men. A policy of equal pay for doing the same job did not come into effect until the mid-1970s, though it would be quite some years before maternity leave was introduced to cater for women who were having children.
- Banks provided concessional interest rates to its staff for home loans. This also involved differential treatment, with the interest rate on staff loans for men being 4.5 percent in 1979 (about half the normal home lending rate), compared to 7.5 percent for the females.

The improved conditions for bank employees – especially the removal of inequities for women – were the result of the energy, effort, and conviction of trade union officials like the State Bank's Donna Churchland who championed the rights of women. The hard-fought successes are part of business-as-usual for subsequent generations, though there are other causes that have since come to the fore.

By the end of the 1980s, the banking landscape was beginning to change as a result of a stronger banking competition, changes to government policy, computerization of manual processes, streamlining banking processes, improved customer interface arrangements, and more aggressive marketing.

These changes were ultimately accelerated by the market crash of 1987. I was undertaking an audit of the bank's corporate lending portfolio (the large multi-million-dollar loans) when news of the market crash hit. I experienced the emotions of the bank's lending executives first-hand, which were understandably downcast given the significant exposure to many highly leveraged borrowers. It was an unbelievable and unforgettable sensation. A 100-million-dollar business in Australia was now worth a mere 60 million dollars; while banks had a security valuation buffer it was not enough, with some borrowers owing considerably more than the equity and market capitalization of their business.

*The **market crash of 1987** that occurred on Monday 19 October 1987 was a sudden, severe, unexpected, and generally unpredicted stock market crash that severely impacted the global financial market system. The Dow Jones Industrial Average in the US fell 22.6 percent (508 points) on that day and resulted in crashes in the futures and options markets. All of the 23 major world markets experienced similar market declines in October 1987; of these, three declined by more than 40 percent, three by between 30 and 39 percent, and eight by between 20 and 29 percent. The severity of the crash caused panic, with fears of extended global economic instability.*

Because of the changed business environment, many bankers had become unemployed by the end of the 1980s and had skills that were not readily transferable to other industries. So much for banking being a "secure" job for life! I had to cautiously navigate the impact of changes within the banking industry; fortunately, I had gained another set of skills through my auditing work, so I was not a "one trick pony" like many other bankers.

The key insights from this phase of my story are:

- Identify talent.
- Maintain professional development.
- Deal with poor performance.

- Balance internal alignment and external focus.
- Manage business restructuring.
- Drive excellence in leadership.
- Learn from the international scene.

CONTEXT

There are many ways that business leaders can inspire and support their people to rise above the norm. The commitment to developing capability (discussed in Chapter 3) provides a firm foundation. Excellent business leaders continue to grow the talent pool, and they optimize business outcomes by responding to or creating opportunities that result in changes to the organization's business strategies, objectives, risks, and goals. When hard decisions need to be taken, strong business leaders don't hesitate in making them. These elements are discussed in this chapter and illustrated in **Exhibit 4.1**.

KEY TAKEAWAYS AND DEEP DIVES

Drive Excellence in Leadership

Setting the Scene

Once in a career (if you're lucky), you might come across an exemplary leader who influences the course of your career. For me, that was Nihal Fernandopulle who was the consummate chief audit executive. I credit him with teaching me about professional internal auditing and how professional auditing standards underpin the work of internal auditors. He also challenged me to think beyond the norm.

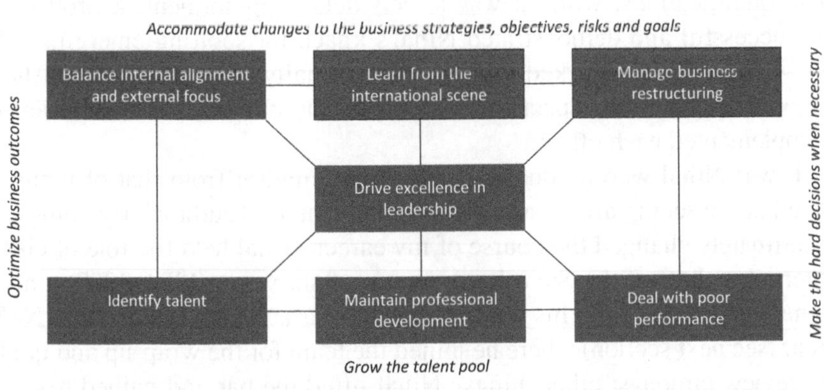

EXHIBIT 4.1 Shaping better business outcomes.

I met Nihal within a few months of me being promoted back into the State Bank internal audit team (from Euras); a few retirements had resulted in a new leadership regime. Nihal was appointed from outside the bank to the position of chief internal auditor. He was an experienced, highly polished, and charismatic leader who brought a fresh energy and passion for internal auditing to the team, though some of the "old timers" found it difficult to change to a new way of thinking and doing things.

Nihal was tasked with modernizing the bank's internal audit function to keep abreast of banking regulation changes introduced by the Australian government. He also provided business improvement advice to top management and assurance to the board on the bank's foreign exchange management activities including the overseas offices in New York and London.

Nihal understood modern internal auditing and was committed to maintaining professional internal auditing standards. He introduced the team to Sawyer's Internal Auditing written by the "Father of Modern Internal Auditing" Lawrence B. Sawyer (the book was first published in 1973, and remains relevant today, with the seventh edition published in 2019). He also promoted the professional body, the Institute of Internal Auditors (IIA), and arranged for his audit staff to attend relevant training courses delivered by the IIA. It was a very structured, and thoughtful approach to the training and development of his staff.

It was an inspired appointment by the State Bank executive. And Nihal set about transforming the bank's internal audit activity. I was a keen learner, and enjoyed Nihal's leadership style, the bounce in his step, his friendly demeanor, his willingness to share a laugh, and his intelligent approach to the work.

Nihal promoted Leonard Yong to the position of Senior Manager Head Office Audits, which was one of Nihal's direct reports, and was the position I reported to. At the time, Leonard was an information systems audit manager in the State Bank's internal audit team and he held post-graduate qualifications; while it was a "left field" appointment, it proved to be successful and demonstrated Nihal's knack for spotting emerging talent. Leonard and I worked together exceptionally well, as we established a good rapport and respect for each other, and our skills and experience complemented each other.

It was Nihal who gradually changed my mindset from that of being a "banker" to seeing myself as a professional "internal auditor." By doing so, it ultimately changed the course of my career. Nihal held the role of chief internal auditor at the State Bank for about six years (1984–1989), and I benefited directly from his wisdom on overseas audits to London and New Year (see next section) where he joined the team for the wrap-up and quality review (amongst other things). Nihal lifted the bar and gained respect across the bank.

The successful transformation of the State Bank internal audit function was confirmed in mid-1989 through an independent evaluation that reported (amongst others) that it functioned as an independent unit with a high level of professionalism; the overall control and direction was well-executed; audits are performed in a competent manner with due professional care; and, the function is willing to use outside technical expertise where required. It was professionally and personally rewarding to work within a creditable area.

It was a surprise when Nihal announced he was leaving the State Bank to move to the Reserve Bank of Australia as Head of Audit (chief audit executive). He mentioned that he would be filling several senior roles in a few months' time and encouraged me to apply. I mentioned that I had been at the State Bank for 18 years, was happy there, valued the job security, had a young family, and was not looking for a change.

The branch audit team had found it more difficult to transition to the modern style of auditing, more so than the technology and head office (or corporate) groups. Even the senior manager of the branch audit team (one of the "old timers") was reflective about Nihal's departure, notwithstanding their differences over the years, and commented at his farewell that "… maybe it's better the devil you know!"

A new chief internal auditor was appointed by the State Bank executive a couple of months later. It was another external appointment. It was obvious quite early that the new person was like "chalk and cheese" compared to his predecessor. He was from an information technology background, and made it clear he was going to reform the internal audit function by leveraging technology through computer assisted audit techniques (CAATs) for pretty much everything. He had no interest in listening to the wise souls who pointed out that a large part of the audit universe (especially the higher risk areas) had not been computerized. And you can't apply CAATs to manual processes! He then made uninformed declarations … everyone in the team has to be degree qualified; audit reports would no longer be issued; professional auditing standards had no relevance; if you don't like the direction, then leave. He was not friendly at all, and would not speak to anyone as he moved through the office. Quite a contrast to "the devil we knew"!

I was trying to come to grips with the style of auditing being introduced by the new chief internal auditor and it was clear to me that we were on a totally different page to each other; I thought the mooted changes were illogical, ill-considered, and retrograde steps. As I was seriously pondering what I should do, Nihal contacted me out of the blue, and reminded me that he would soon be recruiting several senior managers to the internal audit team at the Reserve Bank and encouraged me to apply. He stressed that there were no guarantees as it was a merit-based recruitment process.

He got me thinking, and I realized what I needed to do … but more on that in Chapter 5.

What It Means for Business

Business leaders should be motivated to drive excellence across all leadership and management levels to underpin the organization's success in achieving business objectives, strategies, growth, and investing in the development of their people. Excellent leaders boost customer outcomes, increase staff productivity, inspire and maintain a capable workforce, and ultimately produce financial benefits.

The challenge for business leaders in cultivating excellence in the next generation of leaders is to identify people who display certain qualities and then help them to refine those qualities by creating the right situation where they can develop and succeed. The effects of excellent leaders compared to uninspiring ones is illustrated in **Exhibit 4.2**.

It is beneficial for boards and audit committees to engage with leaders below the CEO, so they understand the benchstrength and strategic nous across the team. It also helps them to understand the succession options (at least in the short to medium term) in the event that the CEO is suddenly and unexpectedly unavailable (e.g., illness). Ten attributes of excellent

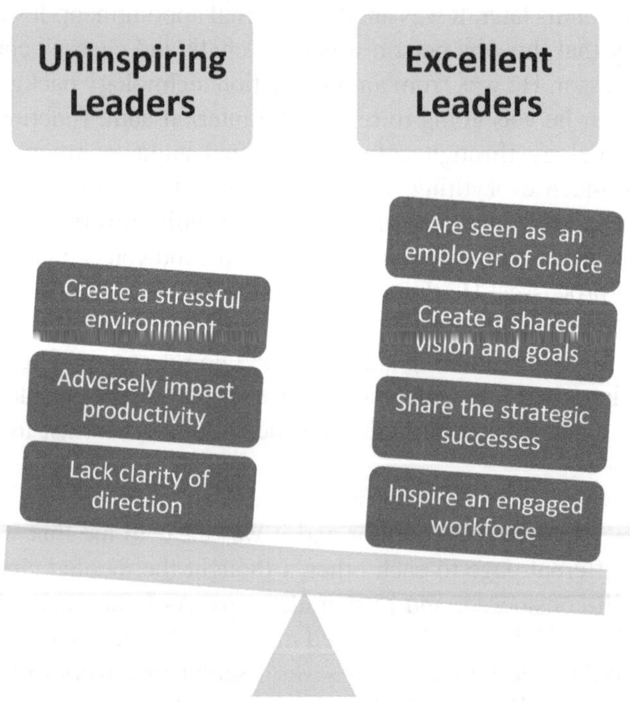

EXHIBIT 4.2 Effects of excellent leaders compared to uninspiring leaders.

EXHIBIT 4.3
Ten attributes of excellent leadership

Attributes	What is expected of the leader
A**L**ignment	Ensures seamless business practices and operations across the organization.
Strat**E**gic	Translates strategies into clear actions and goals to deliver business objectives.
Inspir**A**tion	Motivates the workforce so the people are engaged, innovative and productive.
Kin**D**ness	Promotes empathy and compassion through all levels of management.
Int**E**grity	Acts with honesty, shaping organizational values and the tone at the top.
Cou**R**age	Prepared to make the hard decisions and keep people informed.
Focu**S**	Maintains meaningful communications with all stakeholders.
Humility	Willingness to accept that someone else's way might be better.
Vis**I**on	Establishes and drives a clear, consistent and unambiguous business direction.
Coo**P**eration	Promotes collaboration across the workforce to achieve seamless outcomes.

leadership that boards and audit committees will be able to consider are summarized in **Exhibit 4.3**.

For people aspiring to pursue leadership opportunities, further tips are included in **Exhibit 14.3** – *PANTHERS planks for achieving career success.*

In researching this chapter, ***Coaching for Leaders*** *was regarded by many one of the best initiatives they had come across regarding leadership, and they offered it up as a great place to start an individual's web-based leadership development efforts. The site features "Insightful Conversations with Dave Stachowiak" and is reported to have attracted 15 million downloads of conversations with bestselling authors, expert researchers, and everyday leaders. It is available at* https://coachingforleaders.com/

Identify Talent

Setting the Scene

The Rural Bank and State Bank required all staff to have a performance assessment completed at least annually. The best performers across the whole of the bank were eligible to receive a special incremental increase in their salary (colloquially called a "special") as a reward, recognition, and encouragement. It was a rare achievement. Around March each year, local staff would await the advice from head office as to whom within their workplace had been granted a special.

My performance was consistently rated "exceeds expectations" (or similar) and I was awarded a special each year for over a decade from my second year in the bank until 1983 when I was appointed to a management-level position.

The State Bank's executive committee reviewed the special increments scheme in 1982, and announced that the existing scheme would continue and that it would be supplemented with the introduction of a management development scheme. The special increments were increased to $100, $150, and $200 (equivalent to $265, $398, and $530 in 2020) with those people in the higher group eligible for inclusion in the management development scheme and a special increment of $300 in the first year increasing to $500 in the third year.

The purpose of the management development scheme was *to identify those officers with above-average potential and to ensure that their progress was in keeping with their ability.* In selecting officers for the scheme, consideration was to be given to present and previous staff performance reports, training and development course reports, the results of external courses of study, and the officer's ability to apply the knowledge gained from the study to work performance.

I actually believe the State Bank's management development scheme was leading practice at the time; however, it was allowed to fizzle and fail because of lack of commitment by business leaders and those who had had carriage of administering it. The State Bank then lost the opportunity for identifying the talent within the organization and ensuring business leaders optimized that potential. I could tell from my first meeting with the Careers and Recruitment Manager soon after being appointed to the scheme that this was something that was imposed upon him by the Executive Committee and that he didn't have any great interest in the scheme. When I resigned from the State Bank a few years later after 18 years at the bank (all highly successful), not one person from the management ranks made contact with me. So much for identifying and nurturing talent!

What It Means for Business

Business leaders in the twenty-first century have to grapple with a shortage of high-caliber talent, so it makes sense to identify and nurture the untapped potential sitting inside the business. Uncovering and identifying talented individuals should be driven by business leaders as a normal part of the business process, and boards should oversight these accountabilities.

Research suggests that the value of high potential talent is about 90 percent greater for a business than employees at the other end of the spectrum (i.e., those not identified as having high potential), and these rare gems can help to lift the effectiveness of other team members by between 5 and 15 percent; alarmingly, as many as 95 percent of organizations fail to follow-through on high potential development plans.[1]

Building talent requires an investment in the continued learning and development of existing staff to leverage their capability and longer-term potential (the concepts of building, buying, and developing talent were discussed in Chapter 3, see in particular **Exhibit 3.6**).

Performance appraisals and supervisor nominations are not in themselves reliable methods for identifying talent within an organization. Another important consideration is the personality of the person (emotional quotient was discussed in Chapter 1) especially when their future roles are likely to involve the management and/or leadership of people.

Business leaders will often start to identify individuals they consider to have high potential based on the person's resilience, passion, enthusiasm, level of collaboration, drive for success, the extent to which they are objective-oriented, their commitment to learn and grow, and the organizational fit. Business leaders are keen to find the people who clearly stand out from their peers.

High performance does not always translate into high potential. There are three lenses beyond performance that help to identify the organization's high potential talent – capability, social skills, and energy.

Capability: These people demonstrate their potential for performing at an executive level through their strategic thinking and transformational leadership abilities. They demonstrate vision, imagination, and an entrepreneurial mindset, engage well with stakeholders, and communicate clearly about strategy and objectives.

Social skills: These are genuine and well-respected people who have the skills to manage themselves while connecting with others. They live the corporate values, connect with the vision, handle workplace pressure, deal with adversity, maintain dignity, act with integrity, show respect to their colleagues, communicate across the organization, manage stakeholder relationships, and collaborate effectively.

Energy: These people have innate levels of ambition, commitment, conscientiousness, drive, and the motivation to achieve and succeed. They often put in the extra discretionary effort, work hard and diligently, jump at opportunities for personal growth and professional development, and are willing to take on extra duties and greater responsibility.

Employees with high potential will know they are out-performing their peers, and will often wonder if any of the business leaders have noticed

[1] These percentages were sourced from training materials and media articles. They are intended to be indicative and illustrative. They have not been separately verified.

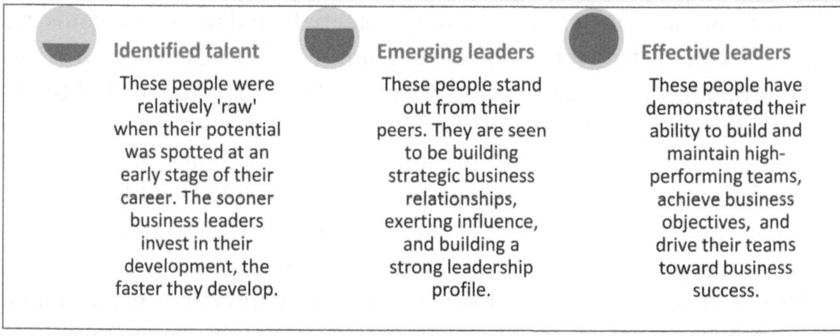

EXHIBIT 4.4 Converting potential into leadership effectiveness.

their potential. Managers should engage with them and discuss what their future at the organization might look like. It is worthwhile to inform them they are on the organization's radar for a management development program, and/or for career fast-tracking and a future leadership position; otherwise, there is the risk they will look elsewhere for opportunities.

Once talent has been identified, business leaders should establish appropriate career path planning, and monitor progress. Career path planning will help to convert the identified talent into effective leadership as illustrated in **Exhibit 4.4**. While the planning will guide the development, there needs to flexibility to accommodate personal and professional changes that occur.

Maintain Professional Development

Setting the Scene

The Rural Bank had an impressive induction and training program that catered well for my style of learning and helped me to adapt quickly and successfully to a banking career (mentioned in Chapter 1).

My strong performance assessments that led to me being selected for the management development scheme (discussed in the previous section) were complemented with me excelling at the bank's intensive and extensive training courses and successfully completing my accounting studies in 1978 (discussed in Chapter 3). From 1976 to 1983, I attended three training courses, examiner, loans officer, and proficiency assessment. I came top in each of the three courses.

At age 28, I was one of the youngest ever staff selected to attend the proficiency assessment course (the average age of the participants of my course was 32); a strong performance at the course was a necessity for bankers to be appointed to the relatively senior position of branch accountant (the second most senior person in most branches, below the branch manager).

I had moved up from the loans officer role into the equivalent of an assistant branch accountant role (called a signing officer) at the Penrith branch close to home when I was appointed to the management development scheme. It was an exciting moment!

That excitement dulled relatively quickly when I was asked to move to the Sydney CBD (about 40 miles away) on a secondment to establish the internal audit function at the European Asian of Australia (Euras) merchant bank which had been established as a joint venture with the State Bank. I declined, as I had a good chance to taking on the lead role of one of the branch's agency (or satellite) offices close to home. I was then *directed* by the State Bank's HR management to take on the role. I did so. My children were 5, 3, and 1. Alas, I then commuted into Sydney and travelled extensively for the next 25 years!

When I finished at Euras, the State Bank was restructuring its internal audit function and I secured a management-level position in its Head Office audit group, which meant I skipped through several levels in the hierarchy. This ultimately morphed into me being the Manager of Wholesale Banking and Treasury Audits. In an odd twist, when I was in my early-30s, I was then senior to some of my prior managers who were considerably older; the old rule of "rank has its privileges" (mentioned in Chapter 1) seemed to have been forgotten or dispensed with as none of these gentlemen called me Mr Turner in line with the traditional concept of the pecking order (which humored me). In fact, I don't recall ever being called "Mr" during my career except on the odd first meeting with someone or when I was conducting employment interviews. Quite a dramatic change in practice and protocol between one generation and the next!

In the mid-1980s, I was inspired to complete further banking studies when one of my close colleagues decided he was going to do so (he dropped out but I persevered). Upon successful completion, I achieved professional status with the Australian Institute of Bankers. As I had topped the state (New South Wales), I was awarded the prestigious Henry Young Memorial Award for 1987. Successes like this helped to evolve a personal brand (discussed in Chapter 10 – see **Exhibit 10.2**).

My progress through the bank to the management level was achieved through effective professional development that included meaningful induction and orientation, on-the-job training, attendance at structured training courses, secondment to another entity, and successful completion of tertiary studies.

What It Means for Business

Professional development is the process that leads to a person's professional growth. Business leaders invest in the professional growth of their staff to gain improved business outcomes and to better leverage the talents and skills within its workforce.

The planning of professional development is equally important for the individuals working within the business who are keen to learn and grow. Professional development is ultimately a shared responsibility between the business and its staff. Examples of professional growth are contained in **Exhibit 13.5**.

Professional development doesn't just happen, it needs to be meaningfully considered, well-planned, and reflect the broader requirements of the organization's workforce plan. Business leaders should never take a passive or haphazard approach to professional development, rather they need to take an active role in the development of the workforce to deliver longer-term benefits for the organization and the individuals concerned.

Professional development planning is a strategic driver that supports the organization's investment in developing its overall workforce capability. A well-considered structured and documented longer-term professional development plan provides the impetus for the continued investment in developing organizational capability even when the organization is tightening its spending.

The five-step process for delivering a structured, systematic, and well-founded professional development plan is illustrated in **Exhibit 4.5**.

The capability assessment will help to identify skill gaps at both an individual and business function level for inclusion in the professional development plan. For instance:

- An individual working in a frontline position and shifting into a supervisory role might benefit from attending a training course on *managing staff* or receiving business support to complete an *MBA*

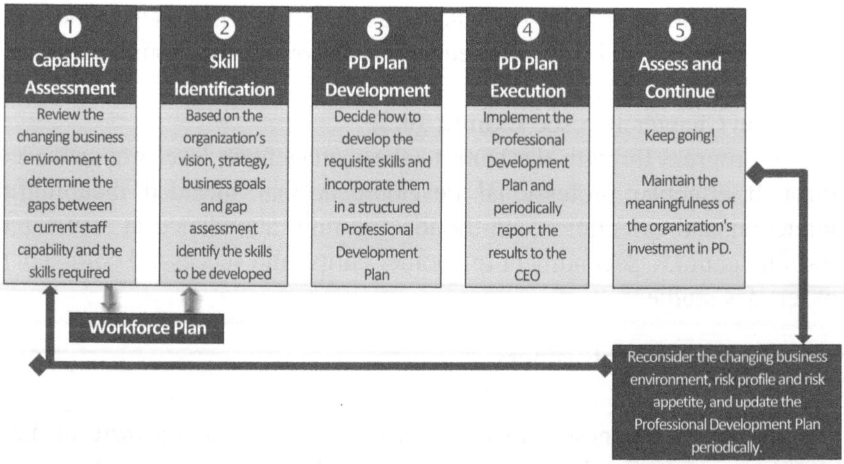

EXHIBIT 4.5 Overview of professional development planning.

(master of business administration). Whereas, another staff member with back-office responsibility for managing complaints might benefit from attending a national conference on building customer confidence that includes sessions on analyzing and actioning complaints.

- Areas within the business dealing with customer communications might have identified a need to better communicate in "plain English" which requires all staff in those functions to undertake a tailored *better writing workshop.*
- The business function might have identified the need to provide function-wide training for all frontline staff when it was rolling out a new *customer relationship management system* (CRMS) to better manage its interaction with current and potential customers.
- The business might have refreshed its vision, risk appetite, strategies, and customer charter and needs to embed these in the mindset of its staff as a whole. That might involve an *executive roadshow* to inform the staff and boost their understanding and commitment.

A professional development plan should also focus on the longer term, and ensure that the professional development of staff is aligned to the needs identified in the workforce plan and the business plan. As an example, the government's health bureaucrats might recognize the need for a significant increase in its investment in mental health over the next decade, and would work with the education sector to boost the number of nurses and allied health professionals trained in mental health specialization.

Deal with Poor Performance

Setting the Scene

Throughout my career, I have found that most people perform well, though there are often a handful of poor performers. I felt it was my duty as a supervisor to help the poor performers to improve, or to apply the organization's policy on poor performers. It was often a time-consuming and thankless task.

There is considerable time and energy required in having tough conversations with underperforming staff, following through on the improvement plan, and documenting each step. But too many managers continue to skirt their responsibilities and leave it up to others. That's why some notorious and longstanding poor performers survive for many years.

At times I have been seriously let down by my own senior staff, particularly when I was younger and less experienced. In one instance, one of my managers accompanied me on a road trip as part of a site visit and we discussed how a relatively new employee (a lawyer) was progressing after a few months. The assessment was quite negative, and I couldn't understand why this was the first time I was hearing about it. I suggested that we take firm action in respect to the employee's under-performance as he was still on his 6-month probationary period (meaning the legal processes to exit employees were simpler and less onerous). The manager agreed and we planned to meet with the staff member together the next morning. Unfortunately, the manager and the staff member had terse words the next morning before I had arrived, and the staff member walked out. For some weeks afterwards we tried unsuccessfully to contact him, but to no avail. Calls were not answered, messages were not responded, mail was returned, and registered mail was not collected. We were snookered by the law and how cunningly the lawyer played it … the 6-month probation period elapsed, and under the law, the employee had to be confirmed in the job. He ultimately returned on the basis that he would no longer work with that manager. After a short period, he secured another job and left our employ. He lasted just a month or two in the new job before he was sacked!

In another organization, I was dealing with a manager who was clearly not delivering to the standard expected … in fact, he was not delivering anything at all. He was based interstate, but I contacted him regularly. He promised outputs, then failed to deliver time and time again. I sent him a formal warning letter. He did not improve and did not respond, so I sent a second warning letter and ultimately a third. I had followed the organization's industrial processes to the letter; the under-performance issues were exceptionally well-documented, so I engaged with the HR manager on the next steps. We decided to dismiss the manager, and arranged a flight the next day with all of the requisite documentation … termination advice, formal letter, and various forms. When he realized he was being sacked, the manager became aggressive. The security guards were on standby, and escorted him off the premises. The dismissal was upheld some weeks later through the organization's formal independent appeals process.

As I progressed through the ranks, I realized that I was spending too much time on dealing with the poor performers compared to the time I was investing in the growth and development of the better performers. So, I pivoted the triangle illustrated in **Exhibit 4.6** to boost the time available for the better performers and arranged strategies to spend less time and effort on the poorer performers while still remaining committed to helping the poor performers to develop their skills or find somewhere better suited to their talents.

I still dealt with the poor performers in a structured and systematic manner. But I had learnt a few tricks along the way through experience, and I engaged with the HR and industrial relations specialists early to

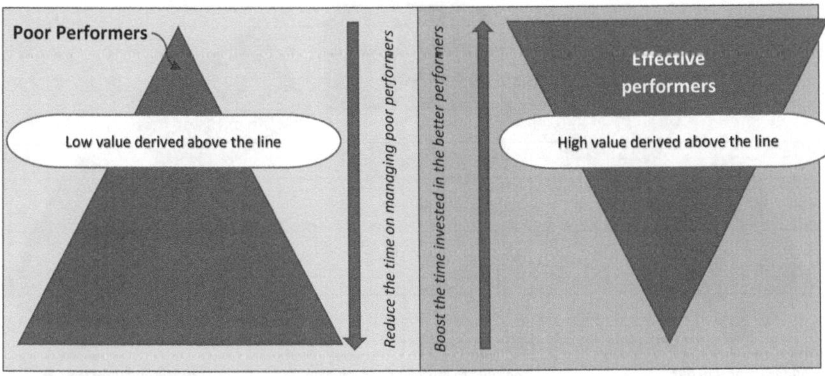

EXHIBIT 4.6 Pivoting the triangle to invest in effective performers.

leverage their skills, experience and knowledge of the law. I consciously rebalanced my time so that the effective performers received more of my time and attention.

What It Means for Business

Successful business leaders hire the right people, then they proactively manage their performance against expectations (explored further in Chapter 8). They take steps to manage staff performance through the establishment of clear performance goals, meaningful feedback, effective development, and helpful day-to-day coaching. Despite these efforts, not all staff are equal in their performance; **Exhibit 4.7** illustrates how staff could be assessed across five different categories, typically creating a bell curve.

Bell curves *are commonly used in statistics to depict the normal distribution in a graph which has a symmetrical shape like a bell. The top point of the curve represents the most probable event in a series of data (i.e., mean, mode, and median), while all other possible occurrences are symmetrically distributed around the mean, creating a downward-sloping curve on each side of the top of the bell.*

There will be occasions when business leaders need to manage staff who are performing below the level expected of them. When the under-performance is not addressed and managed promptly, these people can create unhealthy and unproductive outcomes that affect the entire workplace.

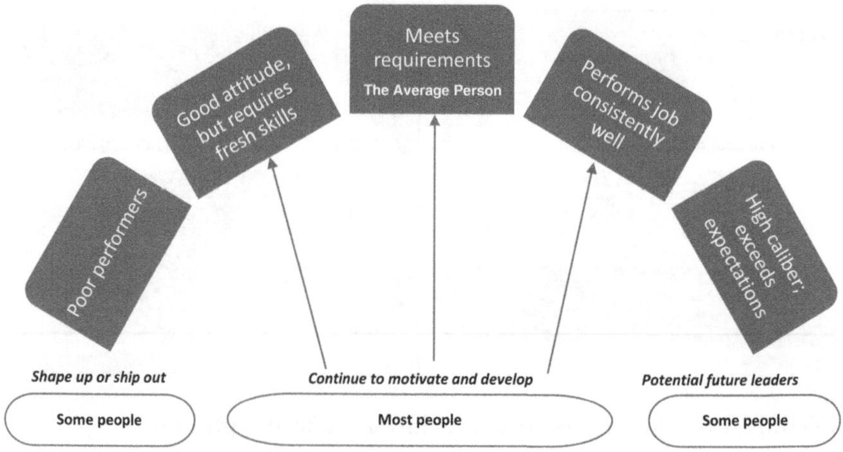

EXHIBIT 4.7 Typical employee performance levels.

Underperformance or poor performance can be revealed in the following ways[2]:

- Unsatisfactory work performance, that is, a failure to perform the duties of the position or to perform them to the standard required.
- Noncompliance with workplace policies, rules, or procedures.
- Unacceptable behavior in the workplace.
- Disruptive or negative behavior that impacts on co-workers.

When handling poor performers, business leaders need to do so appropriately and sensitively, and they need to stay strong, focused, just, fair, and reasonable. They should confer with the HR experts to determine the best way to respond in line with the organization's human resource policies.

Business leaders need to be direct in dealing with underperformance, otherwise staff members who are not aware they are performing below the level expected are not likely to change their performance. If underperformance is not addressed, the issues have the potential to become more serious over time which can affect the productivity and performance of the entire workplace.

The common approach for managing underperformance is illustrated in **Exhibit 4.8**. Where the first five steps do not achieve a sustained improvement in performance to the level expected, then the business leader should devise an exit strategy. This could involve a demotion to a level

[2] *Best Practice Guide Managing Underperformance,* Fair Work Ombudsman, https://www.fairwork.gov.au/how-we-will-help/templates-and-guides/best-practice-guides/managing-underperformance (sourced 30 May 2020).

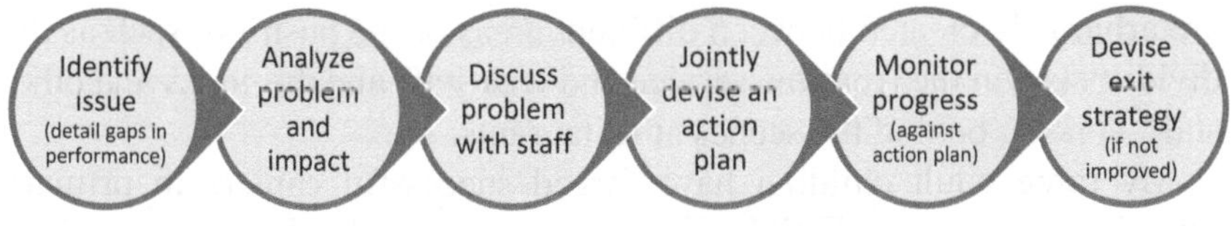

EXHIBIT 4.8 Common approach for managing poor performers.

commensurate with the staff member's ability, a move to another area of the business where the staff member has skills to succeed, a suggestion the staff member finds another role outside the organization, or dismissal.

In some cases, the business leader may have to deal the underperformance of a staff member who has a mental health or substance use disorder (e.g., depression, anxiety, bipolar, eating disorders, schizophrenia, intellectual developmental disability, alcohol and drug use disorders). These situations need to be handled sensitively; there is a legal obligation to provide a safe place for staff and for staff to perform their duties effectively, but there is a fine line between being supportive to a staff member with a mental health disorder and invading their privacy.

The changing behavior of some staff might point to signs of mental illness, especially where they unexpectedly become disruptive and counterproductive. In these cases, the business leader should confer with the HR experts to determine an appropriate management plan primarily aimed at ensuring the staff member gets connected to the right resources (e.g., counsellor, Employee Assistance Program, or other resources). The management plan should support the staff member and minimize disruption to the workplace. Not all people with a mental illness fall into the underperforming category; in fact, many staff with a mental health disorder will not disclose their diagnosis and they continue to perform well, demonstrating positive behaviors and high productivity levels.

Governance, risk, compliance, and assurance professionals should satisfy themselves that the organization has an effective and well-applied performance management framework that is linked to organizational objectives and outcomes. The audit committee should ensure the chief audit executive periodically includes an independent review of the performance management framework in the internal audit plan.

Balance Internal Alignment and External Focus

Setting the Scene

One of the critical success factors for any business is to ensure all parts of the operation work together seamlessly (discussed in Chapter 2 under key business drivers). This requires the removal of invisible divides that are arbitrarily created between different areas of the business, such as the divide between the frontline service and wait staff and the cooks and other staff working behind the scenes at restaurants.

My three adult children have forged successful careers in primary school teaching with STEM expertise (science, technology, engineering, and mathematics), as a law, justice, and white-collar crime specialist, and high school sports teaching. Each expanded the learnings of their base degrees by completing post-graduate studies. At one stage, however, while they were at university, they each held part-time jobs at a local steak restaurant, the Black Stump. Mother's Day was a peak time for the restaurant, so in 2001 when they all had to work at the restaurant my wife and I enjoyed lunch at the Black Stump, with one of the children in the kitchen, one behind the bar, and one as our wait-staff server.

Through their practical restaurant working experience, each learnt the importance of the linkage between the internal alignment within the business and the external focus on the customers as illustrated in **Exhibit 4.9**. This has held them in good stead throughout their professional careers.

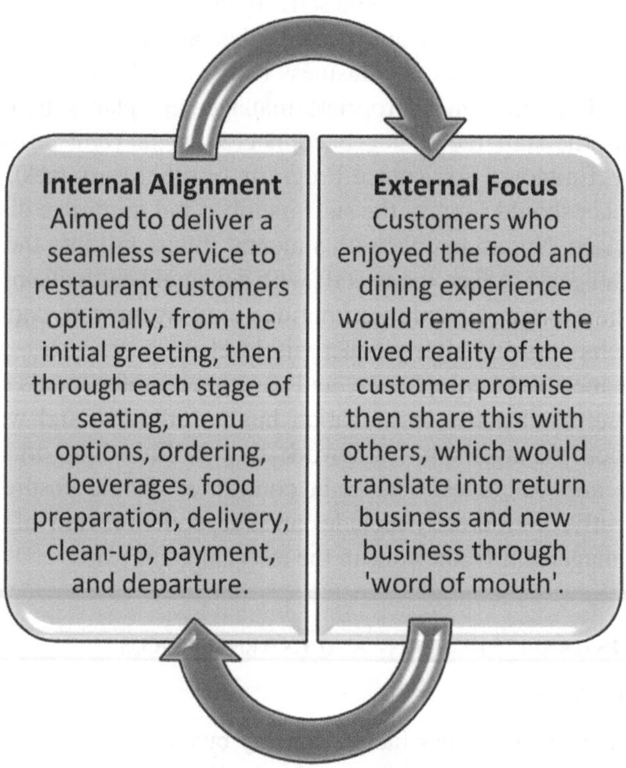

EXHIBIT 4.9 Example of internal alignment and external focus in a restaurant.

What It Means for Business

I have seen businesses flounder and fail to achieve optimal results because they have been too inward-looking. They may have done business "with themselves" extremely well, but they often failed to grasp the external factors that are required for sustained success. Accordingly, I realized that one of the essential planks for achieving career success is external focus/internal alignment (see **Exhibit 4.9**).

> ***Internal alignment and external focus*** *achieve a balance when the needs and expectations of customers and other stakeholders external to the organization are delivered through seamless, focused and aligned internal service providers who are guided by the overarching customer service charter commitments (see Chapter 2) and the brand promise. This is illustrated in* ***Exhibit 4.10****.*

One way of assessing whether your organization is externally focused is to consider whether the business leaders invest time in understanding the issues and challenges facing the customers (great!) or whether they are substantially focused on understanding how the organization's products and services are working for the business (not so great!).

I well remember the change pursued by some commercial banks when they transformed their tellers and other frontline staff into sales people and spent time training them on how to sell the bank's product offerings. An externally focused organization would have also educated them on the business issues and challenges faced by their customers.

EXHIBIT 4.10 Achieving sustained success through internal alignment and external focus.

Internal and external factors will influence the success or failure of a business.

- Business leaders can significantly influence internal factors within the business, and how they handle them will have a substantial impact on business growth, success, and sustainability. Internal factors include the mission, strategies, vision, values, risk appetite, business leadership, and staff engagement.
- Business leaders have little to no control over external factors, but they must anticipate and/or respond to external factors for the business to achieve sustained success and growth. External factors include the economy, regulatory requirements, advances in technology, disruptive innovation, competitors, and the changing needs, expectations, and behaviors of customers.

When business leaders promote an external focus, and embed this mindset throughout the organization, then internal alignment is often realized through a greater level of collaboration, silos and turf battles being diminished, continuous improvement becoming the norm, and productivity being boosted.

Externally focused business leaders will also recognize how the outside world is changing, and this leads to creative thinking and innovation of new business opportunities; it also minimizes the risk of disruptive innovation and other surprise attacks by competitors. The primary benefit is for customers who gain clear accountability for their real needs. And, ultimately, the business grows.

In undertaking their work, governance, risk, compliance, and assurance professionals should consider how well-balanced the organization has established internal alignment and external focus in line with its vision, values, objectives, strategies, performance management framework, and business model.

Manage Business Restructuring

Setting the Scene

Australian banking has changed quite dramatically since I took my first tentative steps into the industry in the early 1970s. I joined the state-based Rural Bank, just as Australian banks were consolidating, which resulted in the rationalization of major national commercial banks through mergers and acquisitions.

I also experienced first-hand the effects of a change of government policy that allowed foreign banks to operate in Australia (foreign banks were excluded from operating as banks in Australia between 1942 and 1984). That decision was taken at a time when Australia was emerging from an insular and protectionist regime, and coincided with the lifting of exchange controls, floating the exchange rate, and removing restrictions on interest rates for both loans and deposits. These decisions opened up opportunities for Australia and its banks to compete on the world stage, with the Australian banking system establishing a reputation globally as being reliable, transparent, sophisticated, and competitive, backed by a strong regulatory system.

Banks in Australia offered traditional services, and gradually expanded their services into business banking, financial markets trading, stockbroking, and funds management. This meant that the banks were often reinventing themselves. Consequently, for much of the three decades I spent in the banking industry, there were frequent announcements of business restructures and job losses. These announcements are still occurring.

The "Big 4" banks in Australia had 176,870 full-time-equivalent employees in 1991 (around the time that I left the State Bank), and over the next decade gradually reduced employee numbers by 28 percent to 127,705 by 2002. As the "Big 4" banks bought out smaller banks and moved into a range of other products (e.g., superannuation, insurance, investment advice), employee numbers increased again to 178,817 by 2012 (though the roles were vastly different to "traditional" banking roles), before further rationalization and downsizing saw the numbers reduced again by 15 percent to 151,883 by 2019.[3]

In my early career, many of the restructures were the result of computerization, centralization of processing, and increased competition. The more recent job losses have resulted from bank amalgamations, branch closures, automation, and digitization, and have been partly offset by an increased investment in people with technology capabilities (e.g., software engineering, data, architecture and security).

It was an awkward and stressful experience for bank employees to have the risk of losing one's job almost constantly hanging over one's head, especially during periods of high-unemployment and recession. This feeling was compounded for those bankers who were the sole breadwinner and with a young family to support.

In 2018, one of my former colleagues, Brian Woodham, organized a reunion of former members of the State Bank internal audit team from the late-1970s. It was the first time that many had seen each other for about 40 years. Some had been terribly hurt, unprepared, and psychologically affected when they were laid-off from senior and mid-level roles at the

---

[3] Employee numbers for the "Big 4" Australian banks were kindly provided by the Australian Bankers Association (ABA) and are intended to be indicative. The data was sourced from the annual reports of the banks, and include just the four majors as the ABA does not have data going back as far as the 1990s for any of the other banks. Data received 9 June 2020 directly by the author from the ABA's Director, Research and Data Management.

bank which they thought they would have as an employer-for-life. Many were thrust into a broader business world they didn't know, and were ultimately left to swim against the tide. I reflected after the reunion:

> I had some wonderful conversations; loved how the folks (re)connected so easily with each other after forty years or so; enjoyed the casualness of the night; reminisced about old times through conversations, attendee profiles, and artifacts; was stoked that whilst we were all older, the voices, larrikinism, mannerisms, and idiosyncrasies of old were exactly the same. But the real highlight was 'the healing' the gathering provided to some of our former workmates who left the bank in less than ideal circumstances (and for some this involved some quite hurtful exits). Nice to see them reconnecting with our professional roots … and remembering what was nice about our former bank.

We established at the reunion that just one of our former auditing colleagues had seen out his career as a banker, one stayed in the internal audit profession, and another dozen moved into other business sectors and roles, including professional services, retail, education, and rail transport. The diversity of their roles after leaving the banking sector (often due to restructuring and redundancy) is illustrated in **Exhibit 4.11**.

Business leaders have used many descriptors to reflect on their strategies to reduce the number of employees in their organization. Some of the more common descriptors are illustrated in **Exhibit 4.12**.

Bank restructuring continues across the world. In 2020, HSBC – with its history spanning 155 years – had steps in train to cut about 35,000 roles over the ensuing three years as part of a significant structural overhaul worth $6 billion and involving mergers between its retail banking, private banking, and wealth management divisions into a single operation. (HSBC

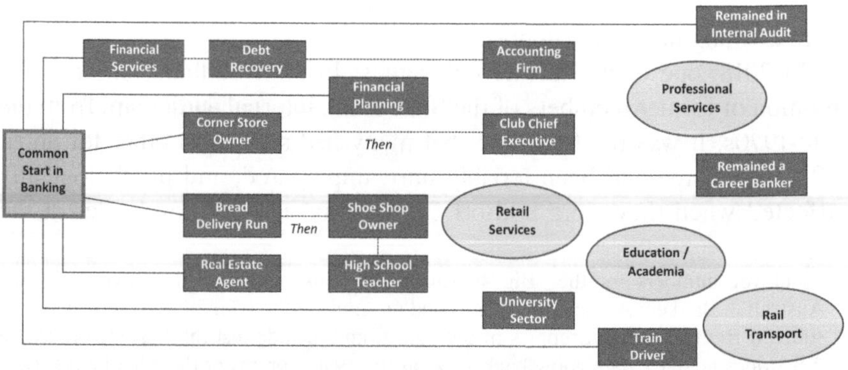

EXHIBIT 4.11 Diversity of roles of a selection of former banking colleagues.

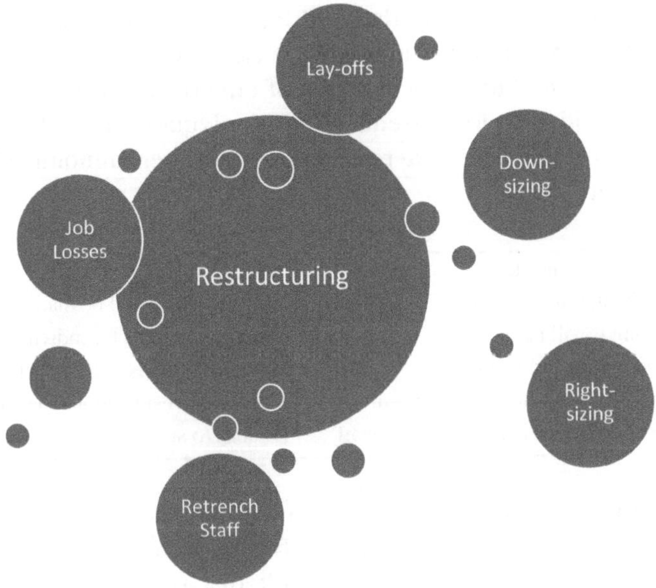

EXHIBIT 4.12 Descriptors used by business leaders when restructuring.

was reportedly the largest bank in Europe in 2018, and the seventh largest bank in the world.)

What It Means for Business

The current pace of change that businesses are experiencing is not expected to drop any time soon, with increased competition, shifting consumer trends, and changing market conditions all impacting the traditional business models. Business restructuring is inevitable that can lead to uncertainty and resistance. Business leaders need to consider the impact of restructuring on their employees, and be proactive in maintaining meaningful, honest, and transparent communications.

> ***Business restructuring*** *in the context of this chapter refers to changing the structure of an organization, such as reducing hierarchical levels, downsizing the number of employees, job redesign, and altering the structural reporting relationships. This is often driven by a cost-cutting objective. It can also result from changes to the organization's ownership structure (e.g., merger or takeover), adverse economic conditions, disruptive innovation, and technological advances (e.g., artificial intelligence, big data analytics, biometrics, blockchain, conversational commerce, dark web, Internet of Things, augmented and virtual reality, and robotic process automation).*

Restructuring can spook the workforce, and can be stressful at all levels within the organization. Any sense that layoffs are likely will be the catalyst for rumors and a host of employee questions. Business leaders should develop "frequently asked questions" (FAQs) with responses for staff once a restructure has been announced. FAQs should cover:

• Why change is needed.	• Whether layoffs are likely.
• What changes are coming.	• How decisions will be made.
• How long it will take.	• Specific concerns for individuals.
• Any points of clarification.	• How the changes will impact customers.
• Roles, activities, and tasks affected.	• Financial considerations to be offered.
• Changes to teams, departments, or staff.	• Persons to speak to for personal issues.

Meaningful communications need to be maintained even after the restructuring, because many of the staff who were not made redundant and remain may suffer feelings of guilt that they survived and their workmates didn't.

Boards need to monitor the restructuring arrangements, and how they align with any revised strategies, and the risk appetite determined by the board. In particular, they should understand the overarching restructuring plan including the implementation and communications strategies. While the business leaders are likely to understand the vision for the restructured organization, it is the people within the organization who are the ultimate change agents, and the senior and line managers who are the critical restructuring partners as they deal with the staff on the ground on a daily basis. Successful restructuring applies a considered approach, similar to the steps illustrated in **Exhibit 4.13**.

Audit committees need to monitor changes to the control environment, as a result of restructuring, and should assign the chief audit executive specific responsibilities for assessing and reporting upon significant operational and internal control changes. Even if the board and/or audit

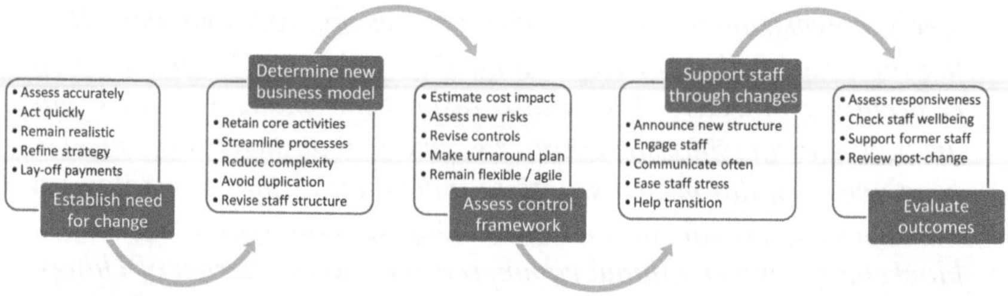

EXHIBIT 4.13 Business restructuring steps.

committee have approved changes to the internal audit staffing levels and budget as a subset of the broader business changes, these changes should not be effected until after all other business restructuring has been finalized. This reflects the need for internal audit resourcing to be optimized while restructuring is underway because the likelihood and impact of errors and fraud is heightened during these periods.

Once the restructure has been completed, business leaders should undertake a post implementation review to determine the extent to which the anticipated benefits have been realized. The outcome of that review should be reported to the board and/or audit committee. Where business leaders do not complete a post implementation review of a significant restructure, the audit committee should ask the chief audit executive to include such a review in the internal audit plan.

Learn from the International Scene

Setting the Scene

I conducted audits at the State Bank's offshore offices in London and New York each year between the mid-to-late-1980s (five visits to each city), together with my senior audit manager Leonard Yong. The audits were well-planned to ensure that we optimized the time we spent on-site. The extensive preparation allowed us to hit the ground running, even though the distance and time difference meant we were jet-lagged for the first few days; the travel time from Sydney to London (or New York, depending on the audit sequence) was between 26 and 30 hours door-to-door without stop-overs.

Each audit was scheduled for three weeks, and we travelled across the Atlantic on the weekend, ready to resume in the next city on the Monday. It was hard work, and the days were especially long. The aim was to complete at least half the fieldwork in the first week, as tying up the loose ends and wrapping up the audit were time-consuming steps in the process. If you didn't break the back of the work in week one, then you would more likely to fail to navigate the unexpected events that lay ahead in the final two weeks. The third week largely involved report-writing, coordination with the external auditors, the quality review by the chief audit executive (Nihal Fernandopulle), and discussion and clearance of the draft audit report with the executive team.

Banks had become very creative with a range of synthetic products, so you never knew what to expect. On an audit of the London treasury book, I found that the office had established a "swaption" as a new synthetic product. At that time, I had come across both options and swaps previously. But this was something of a different product, so I had to review the risks and assess the adequacy of the internal controls relatively quickly, and establish how the product fitted with the bank's centrally established policies and counterparty limits. Despite the best laid plans and preparation, you never knew what might eventuate when you were travelling overseas, and often with no precedent to draw on. You had to be focused, and agile.

***Synthetic products** in the finance sector are structured to suit the cash flow needs of the investor, and are inherently derivatives. They allow financial market traders to take a position without laying out the capital to actually buy or sell the asset. The term "synthetic" refers to financial instruments that are artificially created in the form of a contract by simulating other instruments with different cash flow patterns, maturities, and risk profiles.*

On my first visit to New York in 1986, I discovered that many bankers moved between organizations. The concept was quite different to Australia, where bankers had traditionally stayed with the one bank. It opened my eyes, and the realization of other opportunities probably led me to ultimately leave the State Bank a few years later, to join the central bank.

I couldn't get over the busyness of New York, where everything was fast-paced; even ordering a sandwich at lunchtime was a bit intimidating initially as I found the café staff to be quite impatient while I was deciding my order. At the time, New York still had a poor reputation for its law and order; when I went to the office in the financial district on a Sunday, I never knew whether I should feel comfortable or more alert when there were police cars at every second intersection! I experienced snow in New York on my second visit and the temperatures were extremely cold; in the same month, the very next year we experienced a heat wave with temperatures over 100 degrees Fahrenheit. You just never knew what to expect, and had to be agile enough to respond to the circumstances.

The pace of London was distinctly different, and I had to get used to the later start with many folks commencing work at 9:30 a.m., then working later into the evening. I had the chance to experience England's long history, and a highlight was walking from my hotel to the office in Fenchurch Street along the north bank of the River Thames in central London past the Tower of London (built in the eleventh century). The character of the bank's office was quite different also; I still have memories of my first trip to London, when the growth of the office had outstripped the leased space, and my colleague and I had to share a small space on the corner of a desk in the dealing room. It was a hive of activity, and was constantly loud and boisterous, and every dealer seemed to be smoking several cigarettes simultaneously so the visibility in the smoke-filled dealing room was poor (and no doubt unhealthy).

The international experience also helped in sharpening the auditing skills and finetuning risk awareness as illustrated in the case study below.

SHOWCASING HOW INTERNAL AUDIT SAVED A BANK TENS OF MILLIONS OF DOLLARS[4]

A preliminary assessment of the quality of a financial institution's high-value loan, coupled with the assessed inherent risk because of complexity of structural and security arrangements, led the internal auditors to schedule a review of securities at the interstate offices of a regional financial institution. The financial institution had used a type of securitization approach to borrow $700 million from the bank, and in effect, was secured by a "book" of hundreds of home loans and commercial loans (typically "bricks and mortar") pledged by the regional financial institution.

A right-to-audit clause in the loan documentation allowed a visit by the bank's internal auditors to the regional financial institution's head office in an adjoining state to review firsthand the myriad pledged securities and the overall quality of the underlying security.

A high proportion of poor-quality securities were identified within the book by the internal auditors, and senior management subsequently had the regional financial institution swap these out for higher-quality securities. Senior management also saw the value in the audit assessment approach and subsequently changed their lending and monitoring arrangements to apply similar concepts.

In a postscript, the regional financial institution collapsed a year or so after the audit visit with debts in excess of $2 billion and significant unrecoverable losses; it was placed in liquidation. The reasons for the collapse were similar to the US sub-prime debacle – essentially bad loans with a lack of quality security and ultimately securitization (selling off) of the loans. The collapse was fueled by rapid expansion of the business, commercial property lending for speculative projects, and a small net interest margin on the loans.

The bank avoided significant losses of tens of millions of dollars, as a consequence of the insights delivered by the internal audit team.

The environment in Papua New Guinea was very different to the global financial centers of London and New York. I had been sent to PNG to provide technical assistance to the internal audit team and the cash handling operation. We were collected at the airport and warned to be vigilant throughout

[4] Bruce R. Turner, *Team Leaders Guide to Internal Audit Leadership* (Lake Mary, FL: Internal Audit Foundation, 2020), 70. Modified and abridged by author.

the month-long trip because the capital Port Moresby had a serious law and order problem. Our hotel was surrounded by razor wire and was patrolled by guards with machine guns. We were always escorted, from the hotel to the high-security bank premises and back to the hotel. It was a surreal experience. The people were lovely, and were interested in learning.

Having thc opportunity to work in London, New York, Port Moresby (and others) provided a window to another world. You learn a great deal from experiences on the international scene, and these learnings differ greatly between first world and developing nations. While physically and mentally draining, they are experiences I look back on fondly.

What It Means for Business

The world is getting smaller with the continued increase in global connectivity and as companies grow and spread across the globe; this creates professional development and career opportunities internationally. The number of workers taking on global assignments is expected to increase by up to 50 percent over the decade to 2030. Even companies that don't have an international presence will more than likely have customers, suppliers, and/or colleagues from other countries.

International work experience will arm individuals who undertake overseas assignments with fresh skills and insights so that they are better equipped to deal with cultural differences when they run into them in the workplace. It will also equip them with enhanced communication skills so that they are able to communicate with all types of people more effectively than coworkers who have never left the country. Employers, co-workers, customers, and other stakeholders come from different walks of life, and working abroad enables expatriates to appreciate the differences and similarities that exist. This richness of experience is reflected in each new day that delivers something different and fresh through an enduring (and often fun) way of learning and developing.

In countries where English is the primary (or native) language, international experience helps people to better understand the unique cultural nuances and barriers that must be overcome; for example, English is the primary language of the United States, the United Kingdom, Australia, and New Zealand (among others), but there are cultural differences between people of these nationalities that need to considered to effectively communicate with them. There are even cultural differences that need to be understood for people within the same nations. When dealing with people whose first language is not English, people also learn how to effectively communicate with different levels of English in the workplace.

International work experience will also help expatriates to sharpen some of their personality traits and skills that future employers in their home country may be looking for; these include being adaptable, adventurous,

EXHIBIT 4.14 Personal outcomes of international experience.

courageous, driven, independent, open-minded, patient, resilient, self-sufficient, and tolerant, among others. Working abroad enhances the expatriate's life experience because they have tried new things, experienced more of the world, shaped a new way of thinking through the different everyday occurrences, and have met new people from different cultural backgrounds. This experience and the international network that they have developed will help them make better more well-rounded decisions in the future.

People who stay in a sheltered "bubble" with their parents, family, and childhood friends limit their chances of discovering their real selves. Some of the main personal outcomes of gaining international experience are illustrated in **Exhibit 4.14**, and these translate at the individual level into the development of transferable skills that ultimately boost the individual's employability. For people who do not have an opportunity for international travel, some of these characteristics can be developed by gaining broader experience across different areas of business, such as financial, medical, law enforcement, military, agriculture, retail, wholesale, industrial, and others (a tapestry of experience in illustrated in **Exhibit 9.2**).

Business leaders have the opportunity to provide high potential staff-members with the international experience that will help them to convert the potential into leadership effectiveness and make them a more valuable asset (see **Exhibit 4.4**). This experience will stretch the staff member so that the business leaders can monitor how well they handle the broader responsibilities, challenges, and expected social behaviors. Living abroad will throw all sorts of new and unexpected challenges at the staff member, well beyond their normal day-to-day work experiences; for instance, altered living arrangements, changed cuisine, different modes of transport, varied business and stakeholder practices, different organizational culture, foreign government bureaucracy, employment restrictions, cultural nuances, and, in some cases, a different language. The staff member's confidence in solving problems will grow as each new challenge is dealt with and conquered.

CHAPTER 4 – TEN CLOSING REFLECTIONS

- Business leaders should establish workable strategies – as a normal part of the business process – to uncover and identify talented individuals.

- Boards should oversight the accountabilities of business leaders in building talent through an adequate investment in the continued learning and development of existing staff to leverage their capability and longer-term potential.
- Business leaders should develop a longer-term professional development plan for the organization as a whole (or discrete areas of the business) to ensure the professional development of staff is aligned to the needs identified in the organization's workforce plan, and the respective operational and business plans.
- Business leaders should take an active stance in managing staff who are performing below the level expected of them, otherwise continued underperformance can create unhealthy and unproductive outcomes that affect the entire workplace.
- Audit committees should ensure the chief audit executive periodically includes an independent review of the performance management framework in the internal audit plan, and should seek comfort from governance, risk, compliance, and assurance professionals that the organization has an effective and well-applied performance management framework that is linked to organizational objectives and outcomes.
- Business leaders should invest time in understanding the issues and challenges facing the customers (external focus) rather than focus on how the organization's products and services are working for the business (internal focus).
- Business leaders need to consider the impact of restructuring on their employees, and be proactive in maintaining meaningful, honest, and transparent communications.
- Boards need to monitor organizational restructuring arrangements, and how they align with any revised strategies, and the risk appetite determined by the board, and they should pay close attention to the overarching restructuring plan including the implementation and communication strategies.
- Boards and audit committees should engage with business leaders below the CEO, so they understand the bench-strength and strategic ability across the team, and are well-placed to consider succession options if the CEO is suddenly and unexpectedly unavailable (e.g., illness).
- Individuals who avail themselves of opportunities for international work experience will gain fresh skills and insights, and become better equipped to deal with cultural differences and to communicate with all types of people.

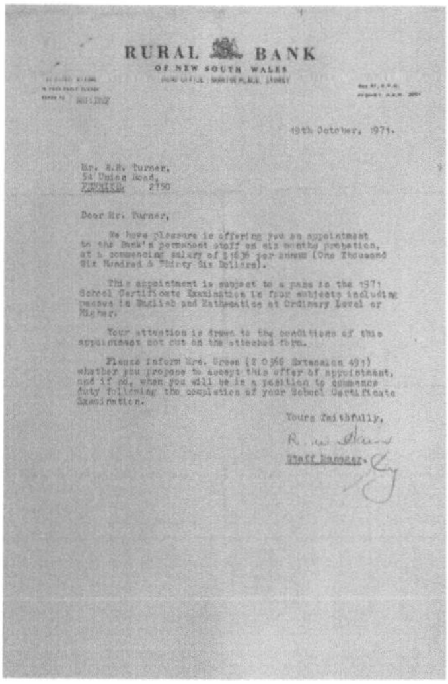

RURAL BANK
OF NEW SOUTH WALES

19th October, 1971.

Mr. B.R. Turner,
54 Union Road,
PENRITH. 2750

Dear Mr. Turner,

We have pleasure in offering you an appointment to the Bank's permanent staff on six months probation, at a commencing salary of $1636 per annum (One Thousand Six Hundred & Thirty Six Dollars).

This appointment is subject to a pass in the 1971 School Certificate Examination in four subjects including passes in English and Mathematics at Ordinary Level or Higher.

Your attention is drawn to the conditions of this appointment set out on the attached form.

Please inform Mrs. Green (2 0366 Extension 491) whether you propose to accept this offer of appointment, and if so, when you will be in a position to commence duty following the completion of your School Certificate Examination.

Yours faithfully,

Staff Manager.

Business leaders need to onboard younger employees thoughtfully. Above, Bruce secured his first fulltime job at at age 16. (Source: Personal archives.)

Professional development is a shared responsibility between business leaders and individuals and should be aligned to the needs of the organization. Above, Bruce is awarded professional membership of the Banker's Institute after successfully completing tertiary studies in accounting and banking. (Photo: Personal collection.)

When you apply yourself during your organization's staff training and development courses you never know where it might take you. Bruce front row second from left at the intensive State Bank Proficiency Assessment course in 1983, after his first stint in internal auditing. He topped the course and was later appointed to the State Bank's Management Development Scheme which proved to be a stepping stone back into internal auditing and onto a secondment with the European Asian of Australia Merchant Bank. (Photo: Personal collection (from a *"State Banker"* staff magazine article).)

A favorite cartoon from the State Bank Calendar from June 1985. The "stars" were the Loan Arranger and Wampum but the caption reflected the times, albeit a little overstated. (Photo: Personal collection (from State Bank calendar). Cartoonist: David Walsh © used with permission.)

Opportunities for working in different parts of the world are helpful in providing fresh ideas, new experiences, and different perspectives. Above left, Bruce visiting the Tower of London in 1985 on his first international auditing engagement (on the way to the office on a Saturday, dressed in his State Bank tracksuit). Above right, Bruce with his senior manager (and acclaimed author) Leonard P Yong at their first audit in New York in 1986. (Photos: Personal collection.)

Gaining professional qualification helps to build credibility. Bruce (4th from left) standing next to the State Bank Managing Director John O'Neill (3rd from left) at a certificate presentation ceremony at the Banker's Institute in 1987 where the MD encouraged all bankers to "get stuck into the books." (Photo: personal collection (from *"State Banker"* staff magazine).)

Auditor Bruce top in state

Senior HO auditor Bruce Turner was presented with the 1987 Henry Young Memorial Prize on 15 September.

The annual award, established in 1971, is the major award sponsored by the Australian Institute of Bankers for students undertaking TAFE banking and finance courses. The award is presented to the student in each state who gains the top mark in Banking Practice.

To be eligible, candidates must gain at least 85%. Results attained in other subjects are also taken into consideration.

At the presentation ceremony at Sydney Technical College, Bruce received a framed certificate and $120.

Bruce, his wife, Bea, and their children, Nicole, 7, Jacqueline, 5, and Glen, 3, live at Emu Plains, quite a distance from Sydney Tech. He did the course by correspondence.

Bruce completed the commerce accounting Procedures course in 1978 and is a member of the Institute of Affiliate Accountants.

He started with the Bank at Penrith 16 years ago, and five years later joined the Audit staff. Four years after he was back in the branch system and worked at Springwood for 10 months before returning to Penrith for two years. Bruce was then seconded to EURAS merchant bank, in which the Bank had a 50% stake. For the past four years he has been with head office audits and now works mainly in the corporate and treasury areas.

Bruce Turner

Sharing professional profiling and staff member successes with audit committees and other key stakeholders is important to boosting their confidence in audit outcomes. Bruce was the recipient of the "Henry Young Memorial Award" in 1987 for topping the state in academic studies. (Source: Personal collection (from *"State Banker"* staff magazine).)

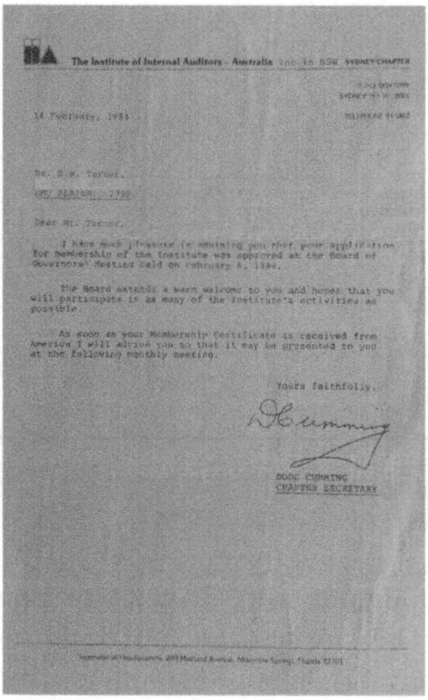

The Institute of Internal Auditors – Australia Inc. in NSW SYDNEY CHAPTER

14 February, 1984

Mr. D.R. Turner,

Dear Mr. Turner,

I have much pleasure in advising you that your application for Membership of the Institute was approved at the Board of Governors' Meeting held on February 6, 1984.

The Board extends a warm welcome to you and hopes that you will participate in as many of the Institute's activities as possible.

As soon as your Membership Certificate is received from America I will advise you so that it may be presented to you at the following monthly meeting.

Yours faithfully,

DOUG CUMMING
CHAPTER SECRETARY

A strong and mutually productive association with the Institute of Internal Auditors for nearly four decades. (Source: Personal archives.)

Building an excellent leadership team is vital to the success of any internal audit department. Chief Internal Auditor Nihal Fernandopulle (far right) scouted for the best emerging talent to establish a fresh senior management team for the Reserve Bank of Australia internal audit department in 1990. This was the first time the central bank had recruited so widely for senior roles from outside the organization. He is flanked by his senior managers Claire Warner, Clarita Imperial and Bruce. (Photo: Personal collection (originally supplied by the RBA).)

Working with developing nations is highly beneficial in boosting internal audit capability and professionalism across the world, as was this technical assistance mission with the central bank of Papua New Guinea in Port Moresby in 1995. Bruce pictured with Mark Ward at a Kokoda Track memorial in PNG. (Photo: Personal collection.)

Part 2

Embracing Executive Challenges

Key message: Help others succeed by investing in their growth, taking an interest in their opportunities, and caring about their success.

"Bruce, please accept my sincere thanks for your outstanding guidance and support over the last three years. I could not have wished for a better mentor.

During your time as chair of the audit committee we have benefitted from your extensive experience and wise counsel and most importantly we have been able to work through a reform program to mature the internal audit, risk management and compliance functions. You have brought a very effective balance of knowledge, expertise and high expectations, generous mentoring of staff, and active management of the committee and its members. This has enabled these reforms to progress in a considered and measured way.

On a personal note, thank you for the leadership and clear advice you have provided to me through some very challenging circumstances. It has been critical for me to be able to seek independent advice and test my views with someone who I hold in the highest regard."

Terry Bailey
Chief Executive
Office of Environment and Heritage
September 2016

---

5 Don't Worry ... They're All Honest Here

Stepping up into a senior executive role in auditing involves much more than replicating what was a recipe for success in prior roles. Whilst internal auditing transcends all industries, there are unique risks elevated in new business models and product types. This chapter explores the decision to centralize a national audit team, introduce modern audit practices, establish an integrated auditing regime, rebuild capacity and capability, and embrace the competitive neutrality challenges of the business ... and it also tackles the challenges of a complacent auditing culture, poor performance, and communication shortcomings, coupled with the expanding expectations of business leaders. The storytelling emphasizes the sage advice of Jack Welch (1935–2020) who said, "Before you become a leader, success is all about growing yourself. After you become a leader, success is about growing others."

Entity Profile and Role

Sector:	Financial services and manufacturing sectors – central bank with note printing manufacturing arm
Entity:	Reserve Bank of Australia (RBA) with Note Printing Australia (NPA) subsidiary
Entity metrics (2001):	• Total assets $A58.1 billion • Net assets $9.4 billion • Annual net profit $3.1 billion • Total annual revenues $4.2 billion • Total annual expenses $1.1 billion • Annual production at NPA of polymer banknotes 276 million • Staff 800 (excluding NPA). (Source: RBA 2000/01 annual report)
Primary role:	Senior manager internal audit (reporting directly to chief audit executive)
Main responsibilities:	National responsibility for operational and IT applications audits across Australia of the RBA's commercial activities, including banking, registry, gold bullion, gold lending, note issue, and currency. Responsibility for audits of the manufacturing arm at Note Printing Australia
Timeframe:	The Third Decade

PERSONAL STORY

After 18 years in commercial banking (with a short stint in merchant banking), I realized the time was right for me to explore other opportunities. By this time, I had changed my mindset from being a banker to being a professional internal auditor. In the previous chapter, I reflected on the importance of driving excellence in leadership, and had formed the view that the style of auditing being introduced by the State Bank's new chief internal auditor was illogical, ill-considered, and retrograde; we were on a totally different page to each other.

That led to my decision to leave the State Bank and take on fresh challenges at the Reserve Bank of Australia (the nation's central bank). I was appointed Senior Manager Branch Audit Group and was soon followed by Claire Warner Senior Manager Head Office Audit and Clarita Imperial as Senior Manager IT Audit. Nihal Fernandopulle established a strong senior management team to support him in transforming the internal audit activity at the Reserve Bank. It was unusual for the Reserve Bank to appoint four senior executives from outside the bank to lead a function, but in 1989 the government had set a precedent by appointing Bernie Fraser (the former Treasury Secretary) as the Reserve Bank Governor (i.e., CEO and chairman of the board), the Reserve Bank's first external appointee to that position.

Nihal Fernandopulle had been head-hunted to the Reserve Bank as Head of Internal Audit and held the role for about 7 years (1989–1996). He was tasked with introducing a major change management program relating to the bank's risk management, internal control, and audit processes, including introducing professional auditing standards and risk-based financial, compliance, and performance auditing. He was in charge of the central bank's internal auditing function in Australia and overseas.

My role included primary responsibility for auditing banking, registry, and cash operations maintained at branches in each of Australia's eight capital cities (Adelaide, Brisbane, Canberra, Darwin, Hobart, Melbourne, Perth, and Sydney). I was also tasked with audits of the information systems supporting those business operations. While I was not initially responsible for audits at the currency manufacturing arm – Note Printing Australia – I was allocated this responsibility after a few years.

Half of the Reserve Bank's internal audit team reported to me (initially I had 38 auditors) before we commenced restructuring and centralizing the function to Sydney with a satellite site in Melbourne. The remainder of the internal auditors were split between Clarita Imperial (information technology general controls, superannuation, and the health fund) and Claire Warner (head office operations including international and domestic markets).

I had been hesitant at leaving the commercial bank that I knew because of the perceived job security it provided in a business that I understood and excelled in. But I was enjoying the new challenges, the broader remit of the role, and a chief audit executive I understood and supported.

Then after just 6 months or so, my world was turned upside down. The Reserve Bank announced a major restructure affecting every area of the bank. Every senior executive position would be reopened and you had to reapply for your position and, if unsuccessful, you could potentially be laid-off. The process was merit-based, involved a global search for some positions, and decisions were to be made by independent selection panels. In a major shock, some of the most senior, respected, and longstanding executives were replaced by others. It was a worrying time because I was still establishing myself at the bank and I had a young family with children aged 10, 8, and 6. Fortunately, I survived and was reappointed to my position.

It took me a while to comprehend the information systems auditing part of my role, because it was unfamiliar and didn't come to me naturally. I also had information systems auditors who were set in their ways and created a sense of mystery as to the work they were completing. We had identified a need to implement integrated auditing, where information systems auditors and financial/operational auditors work together. I felt exposed by my lack of technical information systems ability. I was encouraged by the chief audit executive to undertake the Certified Information Systems Auditor (CISA) certification, which I did. I absorbed myself in the CISA studies and attended nightly lectures in North Sydney for several winter months. It was worthwhile, and I passed the exam and achieved CISA certification. It all made sense to me then!

When Nihal left the Reserve Bank, Clarita Imperial was promoted internally to replace him. She was a good appointment. She was a smart and engaging professional, and we had worked well together as peers. The transition was smooth, and Clarita and I forged an even stronger working relationship. My role expanded further, taking on some of Clarita's former areas of information technology general controls, as the decision was made in a smaller bank to reduce the number of senior managers from three to two.

My decade at the Reserve Bank was a period of profound change, which I explore within this chapter in sections covering once-in-a-lifetime events and competition pressures. We attained great success at the Reserve Bank in achieving credibility for the internal audit activity. We had consistency of vision, values, direction, and approach under Nihal and then Clarita. This was aided by having constancy at the helm of the bank by the Governor Bernie Fraser initially, then Ian Macfarlane AC. The Reserve Bank was a fantastic employer, and I enjoyed my time there immensely.

My role had required extensive travel, and I visited each of the five major interstate branches at least twice a year, then the others at least annually. By the early 2000s, the business functions for which I was responsible for auditing had shrunk in size and complexity. They were less challenging, had lost their luster and the joy, and business activity at the sites had lessened considerably. I still enjoyed the people I worked with, but the job was less fulfilling and it was clear that I was "typecast" as an auditor so internal moves were unlikely.

After a decade at the Reserve Bank, I was at thc crossroads. Do I stay until I retire in another decade, and enjoy the corner office with all the mod-cons and classy mahogany walls or do I start another adventure?

The key insights from this phase of my story are:

- Lead the change agenda.
- Build capacity and capability.
- Address professional blind spots.
- Shape business transformation.
- Inspire others.
- Respond to once-in-a-lifetime events.
- Consider competition pressures.

CONTEXT

The business of banks was reshaped enormously through the 1990s, partly as a consequence of external changes. This drove a need to boost the strength of the team to support the business transformation. There are many factors that underpin business transformation, with some of these elements discussed in this chapter and illustrated in **Exhibit 5.1**.

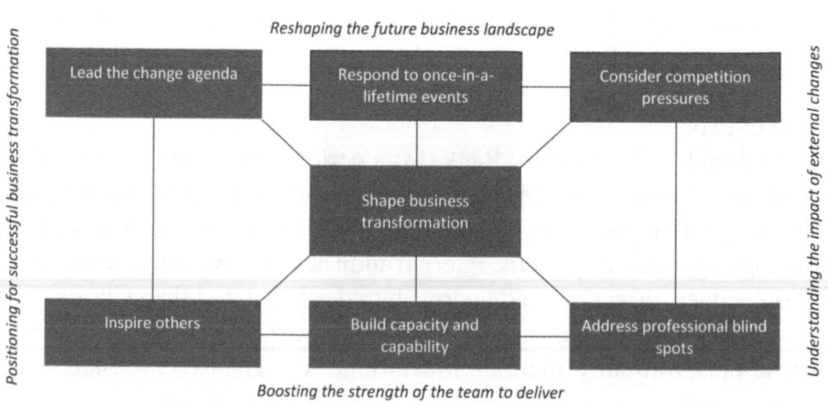

EXHIBIT 5.1 Transforming the business by responding to changes, challenges and opportunities.

KEY TAKEAWAYS AND DEEP DIVES

Lead the Change Agenda

Setting the Scene

Reshaping the future business landscape does not just happen by chance, it needs someone to determine and lead the change agenda. The starting point when assuming my role at the Reserve Bank was the need to transform the internal audit team from an outdated inspectorate role into a modern, credible, and more professional internal audit activity. The proposed changes would boost performance and require centralizing the audit team.

Internal and external stakeholders had expressed the need for a more effective internal auditing approach. We identified the initial changes which were focused on building team capability, establishing a risk-based auditing methodology, developing a cost-effective program of audits, boosting the use of technology, and establishing robust stakeholder relationships.

We crafted the change agenda in consultation with the chief audit executive (who conveyed advice from the audit committee), audit team members, and stakeholders. We recognized that there was much to be done, and the change agenda would take at least 2 years to be fully implemented, though significant foundations would be in place within the first year. Our motto captured the essence of the endgame, which was audits that were recognized as being "High value. Right quality. Low cost."

Prior to the new internal audit leadership regime, the bank's external auditors had placed only limited reliance on the work of internal audit. By mid-1991 (just a year into the transformation), the external auditors reported on the considerable improvement that had occurred under the new regime in the quality of the work performed by internal audit and their increasing reliance on this work.

In early 1992, an external review of the internal audit function by a big-four accounting firm reported very favorably that the bank now had a solid, efficient internal audit group in place. They reflected that they placed our internal audit team amongst the best they had seen, commenting favorably on the standard of work, quality of auditors, methodology, content of reports, commitment of staff to achieve top quality auditing, and the integrated auditing approach. There was much to celebrate at the time, though there was still much to be done. That early success ultimately inspired further success!

We continued to focus on continuous improvement, further lifting the caliber of internal audit staff, maintaining professional standards, proactive stakeholder engagement, and delivering reporting and insights of a high standard. Those efforts were recognized through the positive outcomes of subsequent independent reviews by big-four firms, and through the external auditors commenting very favorably on the high standard of assistance and cooperation provided by internal audit.

At one stage at the Reserve Bank, I had three audit managers reporting to me, whose names were Peter Richards, Paul Phibbs, and Mary Hoare. This was a rather apt quirk, given the success of a highly successful American folk group from the 1960s and 1970s named Peter, Paul, and Mary who had as one of their hits the song "The Times They Are a-Changin," written by Bob Dylan.

What It Means for Business

The business environment is constantly evolving and organizations need to change to stay relevant to survive. Throughout history, some companies survived and thrived by responding well to the changing business environment, whereas others failed because they did not identify the need for change or did not respond quickly or appropriately enough. **Exhibit 3.2** provides an example of two companies (Lego and Commodore Computers) that responded differently to the changing business environment.

Even major companies that were highly successful and apparently invincible in the late-twentieth century no longer operate as they did, including the Polaroid Corporation (synonymous with instant photographs) which filed for Chapter 11 bankruptcy protection in 2001, and Swissair (Switzerland's then flag carrier airline) which faced bankruptcy in 2002. The business landscape is littered with similar stories.

An organization's change efforts need to be focused in the right areas, for the right reasons, and at the right times. Organizations that don't innovate and change in response to an evolving market will often fail. The change agenda needs to consider the needs, expectations, and changing behaviors of current and potential customers, and the impacts on the corporate culture.

The change program should be driven by a clear strategic objective, and the people affected need to understand the reasons for the change and how it will impact them. Business leaders need to establish the competitive advantage the organization will realize if the change agenda is successfully implemented, need to be pragmatic through all stages of the process, and they need to closely monitor progress through a disciplined project management approach. Employees need to be kept well-informed as the project progresses, and they need to be trained in any new arrangements that affect them and their workplace.

Business leaders charged with leading a change agenda should not be daunted as it is not as complex as it first seems. The key steps are illustrated in **Exhibit 5.2**.

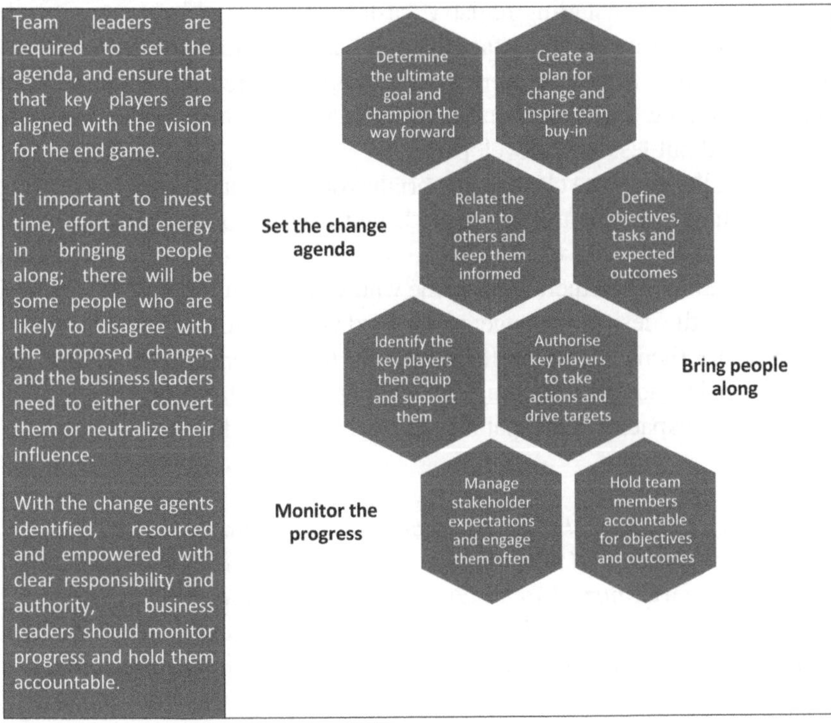

EXHIBIT 5.2 Key steps for leading the change agenda.

The board needs to approve any significant change agenda. It should be kept informed of risk mitigation, communication strategies, budget and cost control, impacts on employees, affects for stakeholders, overall progress, and outcomes. The board could delegate some of this oversight to the audit committee.

Build Capacity and Capability

Setting the Scene

I inherited internal audit staff spread right across Australia, and an early decision was made to centralize the audit team to Sydney with a satellite office in Australia's second largest capital city, Melbourne. We were shifting from an inspectorate-type auditing approach, to risk-based auditing. This was a significant change requiring different skillsets, and resulted in us offering redundancies to most of the interstate auditors. We were also boosting the focus on applying professional internal auditing standards.

I had come into the job with a proven track record at the State Bank, and had well-developed internal auditing and traditional banking skills. But my role at the Reserve Bank was much broader, and several business areas were new to me, including registry, cash handling, and information technology (and ultimately manufacturing). I had much to learn in an environment of change where we were laying off people, recruiting fresh talent, and introducing a new auditing approach. My executive leadership skills were sound but less well-developed.

The challenges were clear. Some bright young talented people were being brought into the team, and they were keen to learn. Some of the older auditors were also attuned to the change agenda, and would help to lead the transformation. Then there were some who were disruptive and did not have the skills or the desire to change; we worked with HR to find suitable alternative roles for them. My initial three areas of focus needed to be: Addressing professional blind spots, shaping and leading the transformation agenda, and building the capacity and capability of the internal audit team.

In May 2015, one of my early recruits into the Reserve Bank internal audit team, Valaria (known as Val or Valerie) Dennis passed away. She was just 51 and was survived by her husband Garry and two teenage daughters Lauren and Emily. It was a shock to all. Val had been an important member of the branch audit team throughout its transformation. As testament to her professional contribution and likeability, and the team comradery we established, former team members from the 1990s attended her funeral from all points of the compass, including interstate from Melbourne and Perth (about 2,500 miles or 4,000 km). I have recognized Val as one of the "Twenty-four Legends Who Inspired Me" within the acknowledgments towards the end of the book.

What It Means for Business

Once you understand the change agenda, the next step is building the capacity and capability of the team you require to deliver upon the vision and promise. In bringing people into the team, an important element is their cultural fit; when you get this right, you build team comradery that underpins longer-term success.

Leaders need to consider the associated elements of build, buy, and retain in determining their strategies for establishing the capacity and capability of the team. This involves investing in the development of existing staff to build the necessary capability (i.e., build), coupled with selective recruitment to fill capability gaps and achieve a well-balanced and capable team (i.e., buy), and then nurturing a learning culture (i.e., retain). These elements are illustrated as part of the process for establishing learning and development initiatives in **Exhibit 3.6**.

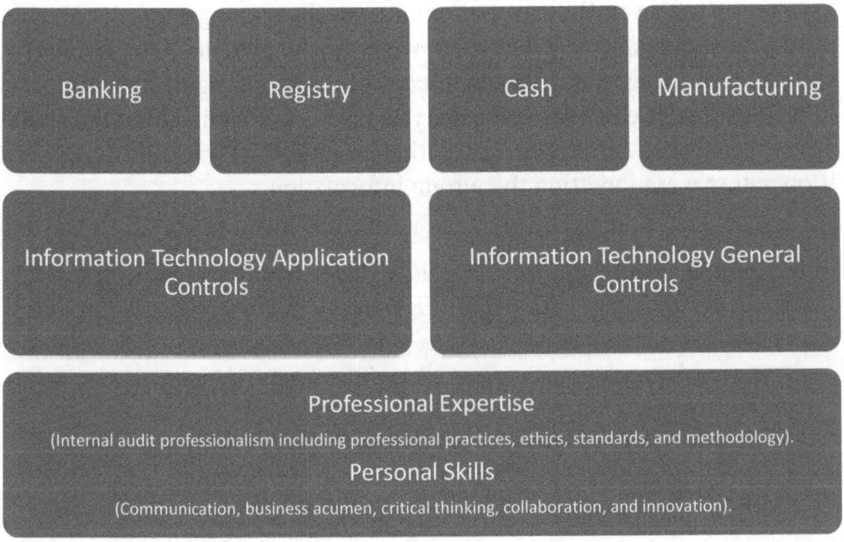

EXHIBIT 5.3 Example of applying the build, buy, retain strategies in practice.

In establishing a robust branch audit team, we realized that we needed to apply a structured and systematic approach as depicted in **Exhibit 5.3**:

- We brought business experts into the team (as represented by the first row), with the intention of building them into internal auditors. They understood one or more of the business areas with a high level of expertise, and would incrementally gain exposure and skills in the other business areas.
- We brought information systems specialists into the team (represented by the second row), including some that we recruited (or bought) from outside the organization.
- We gained a good blend of professional expertise and personal skills that would provide a firm foundation for service delivery and help in cross-fertilization across the team (represented by the third row). This was complemented with intensive training in areas like the professional practices framework, the new auditing methodology, and communications skills (covering all elements including active listening, presenting, managing meetings, body language, and report-writing).

We established an integrated auditing approach (which was progressive at the time), which meant the top two rows worked in sync with each other, rather than separately as in the past. Operational/financial auditors needed to work side-by-side with information systems auditors to arrive at an opinion on the overall control environment. This recognized the need of clients to understand whether there were any end-to-end gaps in internal control. Reporting that operational controls were strong meant little if an IT audit found weak logical security; conversely, confirming that inbuilt system controls over interest calculations were robust was of little comfort if operators were inputting the wrong information.

***Integrated auditing** draws together team members with different knowledge and expertise to deliver a more effective outcome through the holistic approach of a single audit. An integrated audit differs from a traditional (non-integrated) audit in terms of scope and overall complexity and the depth and breadth of coverage. The audit report should be written in "one voice" so that jargon is removed, technical elements are properly explained in plain English, the flow of the report is fluent, and recommendations are consolidated and meaningful.*

Business acumen was recognized as an important skill, because it helps to ensure service areas understand the client and its business areas, its culture, the way it works, the sector it operates in, competitor pressures, and the local and global factors. It ultimately helps organizations accomplish their objectives.

***Business acumen** reflects a "big picture" sense of how a business works to make money or deliver services. It requires people to maintain a strategic perspective and possess a wide-ranging knowledge and capability. These people understand and cope with typical business situations through their grasp of business strategy, a marketplace perspective, a big-picture focus on organizational interdependencies, and aligned business objectives.*

In building capability, we established a professional development planning approach along the lines illustrated in **Exhibit 4.5**. Our capacity planning underpinned the development of the annual internal audit plan that considered the source and application of resources, and was monitored through a series of key performance indicators that optimized the time that auditors spent on auditing rather than non-audit administrative tasks. We also leveraged Computer-Assisted Audit Techniques (CAATs) to maximize the audit coverage.

Audit committees should seek periodic (at least annual) updates on the capacity and capability of the areas that report to them; they rely on these specialists as their eyes and ears within the business. These include governance, risk, compliance, assurance, financial, and internal audit areas.

Address Professional Blind Spots

Setting the Scene

I recall one of the early conversations I had with one of my direct reports at the Reserve Bank, an older gentleman (perhaps mid-50s, so about 20 years older than me at the time) who had been in the bank's internal audit area for a long time. I excused myself. He ignored me. He was clearly pretending to be busy. I excused myself again. He responded begrudgingly. I asked him a technical question about fraud controls, and he glared at me commenting, "You don't need to worry about that, they're all honest here." I was shocked by the assessment, and it was clear to me that complacency had been allowed to breed and fester. I held my fire at the time, though I would tackle the issue and the attitude a little later once I had completed further research.

How wrong he was! Sometime later, the newspaper headlines rang out, "Bank Employee Stole $100,000" and "Worker Robbed Reserve."

While the bank had robust physical and logical controls over its cash processing area, a worker had stolen $100,000 in cash and the bank's existing controls failed to prevent or detect the theft (**Exhibit 5.4** reflects how robust internal controls can be circumvented).

The employee ultimately confessed, was charged, and went before the courts. The media reported that the employee was angry at being overlooked for a promotion and had been transformed from a shy, quiet gentleman, who was diligent and dutiful at work, to a moody and withdrawn individual with the onset of a mental illness. He reportedly gave $80,000 of the proceeds to a prostitute as a gift and spent the rest on the woman and himself.

The internal control framework for the cash handling operation were strong, reflecting the inherent risk of holding cash which is, of course, highly liquid and easily transferrable. **Exhibit 5.4** outlines 14 of the most critical internal controls, then reflects on how the controls can be circumvented.

I have discussed the above internal control framework at internal audit conferences globally, and asked the audience how would they would rate the residual risk or likelihood of theft in the cash processing area (polling question options were – rare, unlikely, possible, likely, almost certain). The response was overwhelmingly rare or unlikely.

This story is not about the theft per se, rather about the professional blind spot of an experienced internal auditor whose objectivity had been diluted.

EXHIBIT 5.4

Example of robust internal controls being circumvented

Internal Control	How the Control was Circumvented
Rigorous employee vetting	Long-term employee considered to be honest and a good performer
Code of conduct reminders	Ignored by employee; motivated by being overlooked for promotion
CCTV covers all banknote movements	Dropped physical banknotes in areas not covered by CCTV
Impregnable physical security	Retrieved banknotes later and snuck them out in loose clothing
Strict segregation of duties	Lapsed when passwords of colleagues were discreetly "stolen"
Movements under triple control	Cash on hand transported as required; but some was already stolen
Custodianship under triple control	Lapse in triple control when employee re-entered work area alone
Senior staff hold keys and combinations	Cash on hand agreed to computer and paper records
Auto destruction of damaged banknotes	Changed destruction transactions to agree with computer system
Passwords for cash entries involve triple control	Stole passwords of two workmates; discreetly watched their keystrokes
Transactions computerized	Entered false destruction transaction of $100,000
Daily reconciliation of all transactions	Falsified paperwork so it "looked right"
Daily scrutiny of records	Changed paper records to accord with transaction; unnoticed
Regular surprise cash counts	Concealed by changes to records

***Objectivity** requires that internal auditors do not subordinate their judgment on audit matters to others. It is an unbiased mental attitude that allows internal auditors to perform engagements in such a manner that they believe in their work product and that no quality compromises are made. (According to the International Professional Practices Framework of the Institute of Internal Auditors.)*

What It Means for Business

Internal auditors and other governance, risk, and compliance specialists must avoid professional blind spots. It is imperative that they consider inherent risks in a manner where they always remain alert, suspicious and objective, apply challenging "what if" scenarios, and never become complacent.

A tip from a global luminary of the internal audit profession, Norman Marks, (retired chief audit executive and author) is, "Master the fundamentals—the business, risk management (the way it should be, not the way it generally is), and internal control. Seek to understand why people do the things they do, the way they do them, and always think about what would be best for the organization as a whole."[1]

Internal audit team leaders have a crucial quality assurance role that helps to ensure that auditors have maintained objectivity throughout audit engagements. This requires a commitment to the ongoing monitoring of internal audit quality at every stage of an audit – planning, fieldwork, reporting, and the follow-up of recommendations. The ongoing monitoring considers whether:

- Audit objectives and scope were achieved to a high standard.
- Audit evidence and analysis is clear, complete, and supports the conclusions.
- Output is reasonable with overall audit opinions that are defensible and have a firm basis.
- Audit recommendations are reasonable, meaningful, practical, actionable, and useful.
- The audit report provides a clear and unambiguous written conclusion or opinion on each audit objective.
- The audit could withstand independent scrutiny at a corruption, coronial, or parliamentary inquiry, a federal or state prosecution investigation, a royal commission, or an external quality assessment.
- Business leaders consider that the audit added value to the business, and the recommendations were useful.

The quality review by internal audit team leaders should always extend beyond a desk review of the workpapers, and should ideally involve other techniques, such as observations during a site visit and/or walkthrough; environmental scan; one-on-one discussion; team meeting; and/or a challenge session.

In my experience, auditors tend to maintain a sharper focus and objectivity when they know that their team leader – and perhaps the chief audit executive – are going to challenge what they have done and found. It is often useful for team leaders to sit down with the auditors involved in

---

[1] Bruce R. Turner, *New Auditor's Guide to Internal Auditing* (Lake Mary, FL: Internal Audit Foundation, 2019), 203.

high profile or higher-risk audits to test their individual thinking by talking through the way the audit was undertaken and the audit observations identified. A "devil's advocate" approach helps in exploring matters beyond the individual issues, including culture, soft controls, risk appetite, and alignment with the organization's strategies, objectives, and risks.

There are times when an auditor does not grasp the seriousness of a particular observation when they view it in isolation, or they might overstate the importance of a matter. It is helpful to ponder the real meaning of audit observations in terms of business strategies, objectives, and risk appetite; whether there is a broader message; how the audit observations relate to other areas of the business; and whether there are potential operational risks or crisis events that have not been thought about and for which management is unprepared to respond.

As an audit leader, I found that on-site visits provided a wonderful opportunity to walk around the site with the auditor to see firsthand what they looked at and how they formed their conclusions. I would ask lots of questions … where does this come from; where does this go; what's the purpose of this; etc. After the site visit and tour, I would have a good sense of the auditor's capability, and would equally understand the process from "cradle to grave" when I fronted the audit committee and senior management.

The quality review approach used by internal audit team leaders is equally helpful for other governance, risk, and compliance professionals.

Audit committees should seek an annual assertion from the chief audit executive on compliance with professional auditing standards and the international professional practices framework. This should complement the chief audit executive's reporting to the audit committee on its internal quality assurance and improvement program.

Shape Business Transformation

Setting the Scene

My time at the Reserve Bank coincided with many significant business changes in response to market changes and the evolving needs of customers, including (within my areas of audit responsibility) new business systems, release of counterfeit-proof banknotes (the first in the world printed on polymer substrate rather than paper), introduction of a new funds transfer systems between banks (i.e., Real-Time Gross Settlement System or RTGS), establishment of a joint venture, and corporatization of the manufacturing arm (i.e., Note Printing Australia or NPA). The timeline in **Exhibit 5.5** illustrates these changes, with each change requiring system under development or other internal audit coverage.

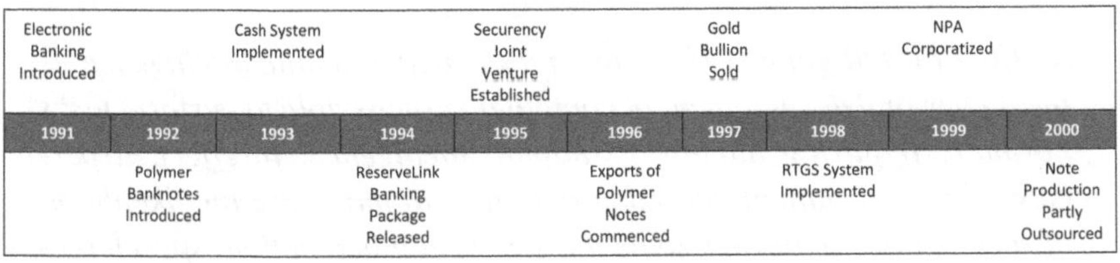

EXHIBIT 5.5 Timeline of business changes in the 1990s.

These business transformation initiatives were in addition to externally influenced or imposed changes, such as the Y2K remediation, and the substantial sale of gold bullion (next section) and changes associated with the national competition policy (following section).

Further changes were implemented in the 2000s, including a shift in 2001 (around the time I left the bank) to a National Note Processing Centre rather than state-based cash operations.

In addition to completing "business as usual" audits, we needed to embrace an early form of agile auditing to effectively assess a business environment that was constantly evolving. As a result of our approach to building capacity and capability (discussed in an earlier section of this chapter), we were well-positioned and well-equipped to do so. For much of this time, the implementation of new systems required explicit internal audit sign-off. This required us to work closely with the business areas as trusted advisors to determine whether sign-off prerequisites had been sufficiently satisfied and evidenced before the changes were allowed to proceed.

***Agility** is expected to deliver a nimble response and approach for the changing dynamics in the organization's risk landscape.*

What It Means for Business

Disruptive innovation and the rapidly evolving digital landscape are likely to profoundly shape business transformation over the next decade. As discussed in Chapter 3, disruptive innovation can occur rapidly to create new markets, economic volatility, and ultimately new regulations.

Digital transformation is already occurring through artificial intelligence, big data analytics, biometrics, blockchain, conversational commerce, dark web, internet of things, and robotic process automation (among others). Artificial intelligence, in particular, is already having an enormous impact on people's lifestyles and their decision-making. Even if people don't realize it.

Artificial intelligence *(AI), sometimes called machine intelligence, is the theory and development of computer systems able to perform tasks normally requiring human or animal intelligence. In effect, it perceives its environment and takes actions that maximize the likelihood of successfully achieving goals through visual perception, speech recognition, decision-making, and translation between languages.*

As examples of how AI is now accepted as part of people's normal lifestyle, smartphones have built-in assistants; motor vehicles are becoming more autonomous with safety features and parking help; drone delivery programs are already a reality in some parts of the world; social media decisions are being influenced by AI; travel is aided by digital maps for navigating, connecting with ride-share providers, and booking flights; banks are sending automated emails to customers whenever they detect unusual transactions, perhaps warning of a potential fraud; smart thermostats adjust the temperature in people's homes based on their preferences; and email users are helped by AI when they want to exclude spam messages and categorize important messages.

Chief audit executives will need to be smart in leveraging technology to drive internal audit efficiencies. In many organizations, CAATs have been used to great effect to reduce the human workload and expand audit coverage. This will need to continue, but should be supplemented with other digital solutions like artificial intelligence and robotic process automation.

If an internal audit function has the right level of funding, the only thing that can inhibit their use of technology in the audit process is the level of creativity within the internal audit team. This needs to be nurtured, and innovation encouraged. You don't want auditors always running down rabbit holes in experimenting with technology, so there needs to be an overarching and longer-term audit technology strategy that guides the investment in technologies, how they are used, and how the auditors are trained in their use. Networking with other technically savvy auditors in other organizations helps to generate fresh and creative technology solutions.

Chief audit executives will need to further expand the multi-disciplinary skillset of their team by recruiting people with a high level of digital expertise. These digital specialists will need to understand the potential risks for the business and establish themselves as trusted advisors to management, but will also need to determine how digitization can help internal auditors adopt new technologies such as artificial intelligence in the conduct of their audits. They should also be tasked with cross-fertilizing their digital skills with other auditors in the team to boost internal audit's overall digital expertise.

There is an opportunity to use new technologies in assessing the integrity and completeness of non-financial information, especially regular reporting provided on an organization's website or used for decision-support. As an example:

- Within the broader public sector, this could involve reporting to government ministers, boards (where they are in place), and to the community.
- Within the transport sector, this could cover on-time running statistics.
- Within the health sector, it could be used to identify and assess breaches of privacy, such as inappropriate or unauthorized access to patient records across a 24/7 work environment.
- Within commercial organizations, the focus could be on decision-support information provided to boards and the CEO.

Without people intelligently conceptualizing enhanced technology options in audits, it becomes an underutilized and potentially wasted resource. Optimal use of auditing technology is underpinned by ideas, innovation, and design that identify the best ways of doing things. The sharing of ideas and practical examples by internal auditors leads to greater success as a profession, and ultimately, recognition as trusted advisors.

Audit committees and chief audit executives need internal auditors to challenge the status quo and pursue new technologies and contemporary auditing strategies. Technology is one element of that, but the biggest factor of an internal auditor's success is a combination of their smarts and how they engage with stakeholders; that is, a nice blend of IQ and EQ.

Inspire Others

Setting the Scene

At the State Bank, I had a small loyal and polished team, and was equally well-respected within the business and across the internal audit team. My reputation alone was a catalyst for me being able to inspire others.

The situation was very different when I joined the Reserve Bank as a relative unknown, with new people to manage, a change agenda, a broader national role, a vastly different culture, key stakeholders in senior positions, and a much larger internal audit team that included interstate auditors. The bank was also undertaking a major restructure.

Having established the change agenda in consultation with the chief audit executive and the team (see earlier section in this chapter), I had managed to set a clear path that we intended to roll-out incrementally across the interstate branches, initially in South Australia.

Fortunately, I had leaders within the team on whom I could rely to help rally the rest of the team members. Some were direct reports to me, while others were individuals within the team (i.e., the informal leaders) who were respected and therefore were able to influence the behavior and support of others. I took the time to get to know the informal leaders within the team, and to engage them in implementing the change agenda. In turn, they helped me to understand the business and its culture.

Together with these formal and informal leaders, we ultimately inspired the team to establish and implement a totally revised auditing strategy and methodology. We also established strong stakeholder relationships with the business leaders across the nation, and they, in turn, recognized that the revised audit approach delivered better value for them. This was an important milestone, given the impending implementation of the national competition policy (see competition section later in this chapter), and the need for internal audit costs to be lowered, while delivering more effective and higher-quality audit services.

A philosophy of continuous improvement had paid dividends in the standing of internal audit within the bank and with key external stakeholders, and this continued to inspire the members of the team.

Sometimes being challenged to take on a different role can prove to be inspirational. In 1998/99, I was asked to undertake the annual audit of the Reserve Bank market operations in London and New York. While it was not part of my formal remit, it was a chance to do something different for a couple of months and for a fresh set of eyes to consider the bank's overseas risk and control environment. Some of the new ways of working I employed during these audits were adopted as standard practice for future overseas audits. The experience proved to be challenging, re-energizing, and refreshing. It also proved to be a clever act by the chief audit executive to enhance her succession planning options should they be required.

The New York office was situated at One Liberty Plaza, within the Wall Street precinct, and right next to the World Trade Center. Just a couple of years later in 2001, the World Trade Center collapsed and many people died following the September 11 terrorist attacks. One Liberty Plaza sustained significant facade damage, windows were blown out, and at one stage there was a rumor that the building was in danger of collapse. We watched in Australia as the news alerts were coming through, and it was a terrible feeling. As depicted in the movie Forrest Gump, it is sometimes a strange and curious manifestation when history collides with the paths of individuals.

What It Means for Business

John Quincy Adams, the sixth president of the United States from 1825 to 1829, is quoted as saying, "If your actions inspire others to dream more, learn more, do more, and become more, you are a leader."

The term ***inspire*** *reflects on one person's ability to create an environment that makes another person feel that they want to do something and that they are able to do it. Leaders who inspire others typically influence them to reach an optimal level of performance and success for themselves and for their teams.*

I heard a story once about an ambitious worker having separate dinners with two different business leaders. After the first dinner, the worker left feeling *the business leader* was one of the most witty, charming, and brilliant people in the country. After the second dinner, the worker left feeling that *he* was one of the most witty, charming, and brilliant people in the country. In this scenario, the second leader inspired the worker by making him feel special; he therefore established his credibility and drew loyalty.

Successful business leaders have identified the ability to inspire others as the single most important leadership skill. Where the business leader demonstrates integrity, credibility, and a sense of caring, inspiration generates in their employees' clarity, commitment, connection, energy, and passion for the organization's vision, values, and direction.

The starting point for inspiring others is for a business leader to clearly articulate what they believe in, why they exist, and where they are heading. That is initially established by having and sharing a clear vision, objectives, and values that help employees visualize the possibilities. Employees need to feel safe, to feel like they belong, and to feel like they matter, so business leaders need to maintain meaningful communication and provide opportunities for employees to contribute their ideas and insights. The follow-through becomes important, so that employees see the business leader as being credible, trustworthy, and committed to the course they have set.

While people often use the terms inspire and motivate interchangeably, they are actually quite different in nature as illustrated in **Exhibit 5.6**.

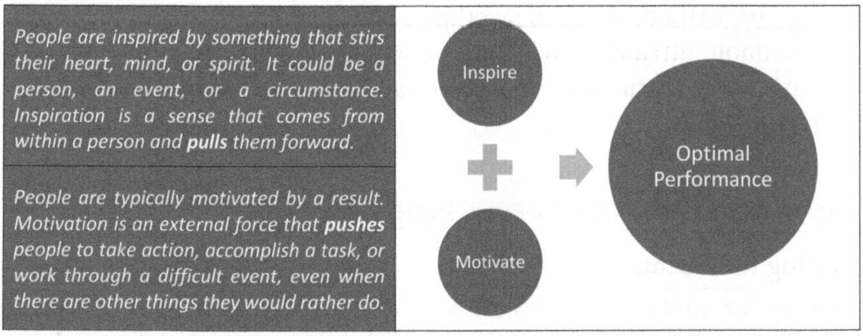

EXHIBIT 5.6 Comparing inspire and motivate.

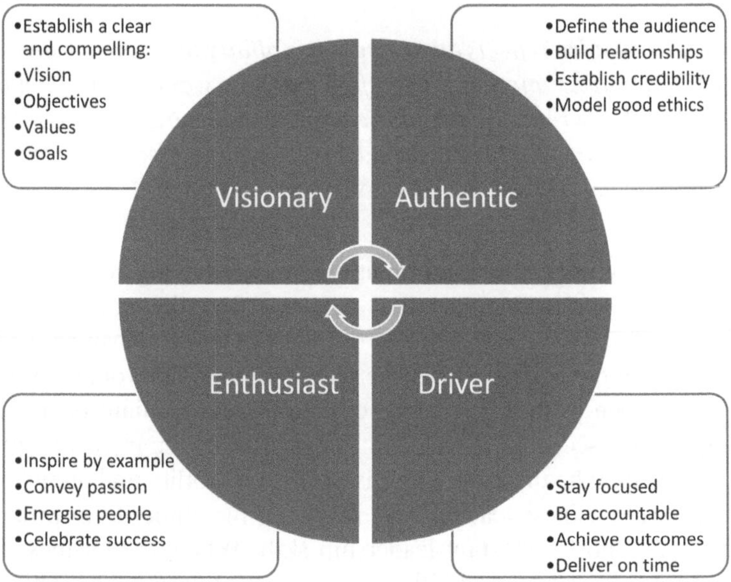

EXHIBIT 5.7 Common attributes of leaders who inspire.

Leaders need to both inspire and motivate their staff if they are to deliver optimal performance. The approach for getting the best out of one employee is different for another as everyone has a different driver that drives their performance. For some employees, they are influenced by a leader who inspires them, while others work best when they are motivated. We discuss the importance of remaining motivated later in the book in the post-face.

The ability to inspire others does not come from how much a leader knows, rather it comes from people seeing how much they care and sensing their passion. That will often ignite the spark within their employees who deliver optimal performance and typically apply discretionary energy (or extra drive) in the workplace.

Common attributes of leaders whose actions inspire others to dream more, learn more, do more, and become more are illustrated in **Exhibit 5.7**.

Respond to Once-in-a-Lifetime Events

Setting the Scene

During the mid-to-late-1990s, I was directly involved in two separate "once-in-a-lifetime" events. Both required significant audit effort and were without precedent. They required a fresh way of thinking and working.

***Once-in-a-lifetime** refers to an event or opportunity that literally will not be repeated within a person's lifetime, or is an exaggeration of an event or opportunity that happens infrequently.*

The first event related to the Reserve Bank selling gold bullion from its international reserves, which required discretion and confidentiality so as to not disrupt the market and influence the global price of gold. The bank sold 167 tons of gold bullion in 1997, with the value of gold holdings in its balance sheet falling by $1.8 billion, and the value of foreign exchange rising by $2.3 billion (i.e., proceeds of the gold sales with other factors such as valuation changes).[2] In announcing the sale, the bank commented:

> Over the past five years, a number of central banks have sold gold from their reserves, the most prominent being the central banks of Austria, Belgium, Canada, the Netherlands, Portugal and South Africa. The Australian sales program followed a review by the Bank of the costs and benefits of holding a significant part of international reserves in the form of gold. Following the review, the Bank's Board concluded that, while there was a case to hold some gold as a contingency against unforeseen events, the previous holdings (which amounted to about 20 per cent of international reserves) were no longer justified. The principal reason for this conclusion was that a country in Australia's position, with large gold reserves in the ground, and high annual production, derives negligible diversification benefits from holding a significant proportion of its international reserves in the form of gold.[3]

The second event was colloquially called the Y2K bug, Year 2000 bug, or Millennium Bug. An unanticipated risk surfaced in the late-1990s with regard to a problem in the coding of computerized systems that was projected to create havoc in computers and computer networks around the world at the beginning of the year 2000. The problem related to the coding of computer applications that typically used six digits for the date as dd/mm/yy (or mm/dd/yy in some parts of the world). This coding did not account for years that started with a prefix of "20" rather than "19."

---

[2] Reserve Bank of Australia Media Release, *Official Sales of Gold*, number 1997-13, 3 July 1997. https://rba.gov.au/media-releases/1997/mr-97-13.html (Sourced 17 June 2020).

[3] Ibid

The bank's Y2K project was controlled by a high-level steering committee reporting to the Governor and to the bank's board.

- The bank had to address its own business operations and systems, with its technical preparations for the Year 2000 commencing in 1996.
- The bank had to consider the broader system-wide issues in Australia, with a comprehensive program of work covering the preparedness of the Australian payments system, the availability of cash, and the maintenance of public confidence in the financial system.

Internal audit reviewed the Y2K project, participated in the high-level steering committee and on working groups, and worked with management to identify risks and provide an independent check on reported progress. We also implemented a rolling program of surprise cash counts to verify the existence and security over Reserve Bank cash spread throughout Australia and held in trust by the commercial banks and armored car companies (the cash was held in local communities in case of a run on banks if computer systems failed in January 2000).

Australian banks and other financial institutions spent more than $1 billion working to ensure that Y2K did not disrupt their normal operations. This involved them:

- Devoting a large number of staff to checking and updating their computer systems, and fixing problems where they were found.
- Replacing outmoded ATMs and EFTPOS machines; rewriting computer programs; and, where necessary, installing new software.
- Testing and retesting their computer systems, both individually, and on an industry-wide basis, and participating in successful worldwide testing conducted by major international banks.[4]

What It Means for Business

The concept of agile auditing has evolved over recent years in response to the speed of change within organizations. The aim is for internal auditors to be more agile in responding to significant business changes so they work directly with operatives and share insights on an ongoing basis, and ultimately provide more timely assurance to the audit committee and CEO on the management of risks and the implementation of revised controls.

---

[4] Reserve Bank of Australia Annual Report 1999. *The Reserve Bank's Role in Preparations for the Year 2000.* https://www.rba.gov.au/publications/annual-reports/rba/1999/prep-y2k.html (sourced 17 June 2020).

***Agile auditing** is a contemporary approach, that delivers a nimble internal audit response, and approach for a changing business environment and aims to provide timely assurance and insights to senior management.*

Agile auditing is not of itself a new technique, as illustrated by internal audit's involvement in the sale of gold bullion and the Y2K bug. Auditors have needed to be increasingly agile in conducting their audits for much of the twenty-first century, especially during the global financial crisis and more recently the global pandemic. What has changed is the increasing proportion of work that is agile.

Where agile auditing is embraced by the chief audit executive, there remains a need to focus on delivering firm assurance to the audit committee and CEO for higher-risk business practices through more traditional auditing techniques, including clear recommendations for improvement.

Internal auditors should not be rooted in their office looking at their computer screens when they will see much more of the organizational culture and operational practices when they visit sites and spend time there. Auditors need a balanced approach, with audit technology used wisely and strategically, complemented with physical interactions with clients.

Research suggests that 44 percent of internal stakeholders believe that internal audit is adding significant value, and this rises to 88 percent where the internal audit function is perceived to be operating in an agile fashion.[5]

Boards should seek plans from the CEO when significant business changes or dealings are proposed, and the accompanying business case should discuss the pros and cons, the governance arrangements, and how the arrangements align to the business strategies and the risk appetite. Audit committees should seek advice from the chief audit executive on significant changes in the organization's business, risks, operations, programs, systems, and controls (especially those that involve once-in-a-lifetime events).

Audits of these events should be factored into the internal audit plan in line with professional internal auditing standards (standard 2010 planning). Where these events are unanticipated when the audit plan is initially established, the chief audit executive should confer with the audit committee chair with a view to effecting appropriate changes to the audit plan to accommodate the independent audit assessment.

[5] "Can Internal Auditing Become Agile? Seven Keys to Thinking the Unthinkable," *Steve Denning* blog, https://www.forbes.com/sites/stevedenning/2017/03/21/can-internal-auditing-become-agile-seven-keys-to-thinking-the-unthinkable/#75c9f1512e08 (sourced 19 June 2020). March 21, 2017

There are different approaches that the chief audit executive can potentially embrace when significant business changes occur. These include internal audit's involvement in steering committees or working groups, systems-under-development reviews, agile auditing, or consulting and advisory engagements.

Governance, risk, and compliance specialists should similarly consider the impacts on their distinct areas of operation with the aim of providing advisory support, and consequently updating the related policies, frameworks, and reporting.

Consider Competition Pressures

Setting the Scene

Government moves were afoot in the early-1990s to pursue changes to trade practices legislation in Australia with a view to adopting competition policy principles. A review committee was commissioned by the-then Prime Minister against a backdrop of major microeconomic reforms, and recognizing that slow progress was being achieved on areas of the economy sheltered from competition. Professor Fred Hilmer, who chaired the review, presented a report on the outcomes of the committee's deliberations, commonly referred to as the "Hilmer Report," in 1993. The federal and state governments acted on the recommendations. It took several years for the national competition policy to be fully adopted (it proceeded in three tranches from 1997/98 through to 2005/06).

Within the Reserve Bank, the contestable businesses within my portfolio of responsibilities (such as transactional banking services and registry services) were most affected by the policies around competitive neutrality. Separate financial data was recorded for these businesses, which fully met all competitive neutrality and devolved banking requirements, including allowance for all relevant taxes. The bank took early steps to embrace competition principles within the banking and registry businesses with these services re-engineered from as early as 1994.

The bank took steps to reduce its processing costs once competitive neutrality requirements took hold, and this included the outsourcing of cheque processing (a high-volume activity) in 1997 followed by the outsourcing of other support services the following year. The federal government devolved its banking arrangements in 1999.

*The term **National Competition Policy** refers to a set of policies introduced in Australia in the 1990s with the aim of promoting microeconomic reform, and which proved to be pivotal in removing unwarranted barriers to competition. Australia's state and* *federal governments endorsed the principles of the new competition policy that included introducing competitive neutrality so government businesses did not enjoy unfair advantages, restructuring public monopoly businesses to increase competition, extending prices surveillance, and reviewing all laws that restricted competition (amongst others).*

Competitive neutrality *requires that government business activities should not enjoy any net competitive advantages simply by virtue of public sector ownership. This allows market competition to drive the efficient production of goods and services by the lowest cost business. As an example, resource allocation distortions for government business activities do not occur (i.e., are neutralized) because prices charged are required to fully reflect resource costs; cross-subsidization is not permitted.*

While government policy and laws will impact businesses, competitors are always looking for ways to optimize their market share and return on investment. This can occur as a result of unanticipated market shifts through disruptive innovation.

Disruptive innovation has affected the world as we know it already with readily-available resources like online encyclopedias, smartphones that disrupted the laptop market, and cell-phone cameras that disrupted the photography market. And there are other potential impacts in the future when other innovations mature, including drones to deliver shopping and online education that is expected to disrupt traditional forms of higher education.

Netflix forged a niche in the market and disrupted the traditional video store (or DVD store) when it pursued customers who it perceived were being under-serviced. Netflix established a new business model based on affordability, accessibility, and availability of a huge movie and series content and quickly evolved into a powerhouse video streaming service.

Disruptive innovation *is the process of developing and introducing new products or services into a well-established industry. It often drives transformation of the industry because it is more cost-effective and/or performs better. As a consequence, the previous market leaders are often displaced. Disruptive innovation is distinguished from disruptive technology in that it concentrates on the use of the technology rather than introducing new technology in and of itself.*

There will be other competitors that don't fit neatly into the definition of disruptive innovation, but have nevertheless transformed a market by reshaping an existing service offering, as an example, the impact that ride-share providers like Uber have had on the taxi industry

What It Means for Business

Competition inevitably exists in every successful market, and this requires business leaders to focus on well-considered competition strategies to sustain and grow the business. These strategies typically feature pricing, quality and service, and marketing as illustrated in **Exhibit 5.8**.

Staying one step ahead of competitors requires business leaders to understand their customers while recognizing the strengths and weaknesses of their competitors and the changing business environment. The business will prosper where management understands what their customers need and want, and are well-positioned to react quicker than the competitors; this provides a competitive advantage. Business leaders must always ensure that the business complies with relevant competition laws, and chief audit executives and compliance specialists need to provide periodic assurance that this occurs.

There will be times that business leaders need to react to disruptive innovation. In these situations, they should avoid over-overreacting by unnecessarily unsettling or unwinding businesses that are still profitable. Rather, they should focus on bolstering relationships with key customers and other stakeholders, and identify and implement sustainable innovations. There may be opportunities for business leaders to pursue growth opportunities themselves through disruptive innovations of their own making, and these are best managed separately to the core business so as to not distract from business-as-usual activities.

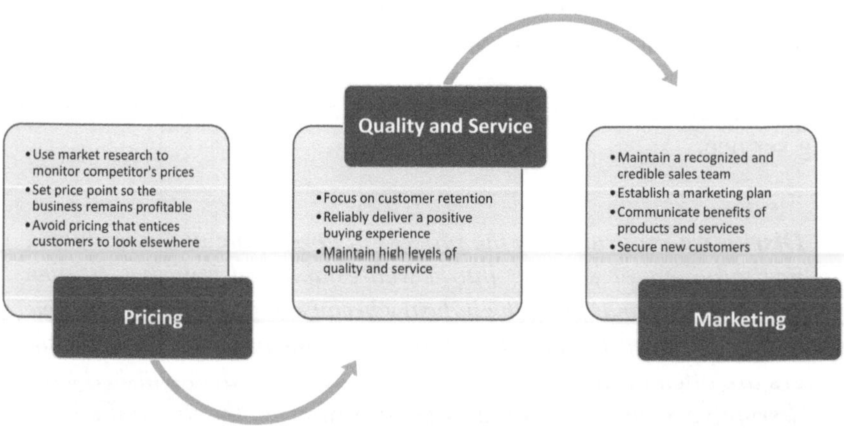

EXHIBIT 5.8 Common features of a marketing strategy.

There are, of course, downsides to disruptive innovation. It typically focuses on new markets that are either high-end or low-end, so solid profits and increased revenues can take time to achieve; it rarely generates profits very quickly. Disruptive innovation also requires business leaders to determine the futuristic market based on what they predict customers will need or want.

There will be occasions when competitors initiate steps to engage in a price war. Business leaders need to weigh up the potential downside risks in taking on the challenge of a price war because it almost always results in a reduced profit margin and lower prices across the market. A better strategy might be to reinforce the organization's unique selling proposition for its goods and services to avoid the challenge.

CHAPTER 5 – TEN CLOSING REFLECTIONS

- Boards should approve any significant change agenda, and then be kept informed of risk mitigation, communication strategies, budget and cost control, impacts on employees, affects for stakeholders, overall progress, and outcomes; the audit committee could be tasked with monitoring progress.
- Business leaders should drive any change program through a clear strategic objective that ensures the people affected understand the reasons for the change and how it will impact them, and are well-informed as the project progresses and trained in any new arrangements that affect them; business leaders must remain pragmatic through all stages of the process, and monitor progress through a disciplined project management approach.
- Audit committees should seek periodic (at least annual) updates on the capacity and capability of the areas that report to them (i.e., governance, risk, compliance, assurance, financial, and internal audit) as they rely on these specialists as their eyes and ears within the business.
- Internal auditors and other governance, risk, and compliance specialists must avoid professional blind spots, and can do so by considering inherent risks in a manner where they always remain alert, suspicious and objective, apply challenging "what if" scenarios, and never become complacent.
- Audit committees should seek an annual assertion from the chief audit executive on compliance with professional auditing standards and the international professional practices framework, and this assertion should complement the chief

audit executive's reporting on the internal quality assurance and improvement program.

- Audit committees and chief audit executives should encourage internal auditors to challenge the status quo and pursue new technologies and contemporary auditing strategies.
- Business leaders should recognize their ability to inspire their employees to gain clarity, commitment, connection, energy, and passion for the organization's vision, values, and direction, and can do so by demonstrating integrity, credibility, and a sense of caring.
- Business leaders should focus on well-considered competition strategies (including pricing, quality and service, and marketing) to sustain and grow the business.
- Chief audit executives should respond to significant business changes by involving internal audit in steering committees or working groups, systems-under-development reviews, agile auditing, or consulting and advisory engagements.
- Governance, risk, and compliance specialists should similarly consider the impacts of business changes on their distinct areas of operation with the aim of providing advisory support, and consequently updating the related policies, frameworks, and reporting.

Further reading: *The books I wrote on* ***New Auditor's Guide to Internal Auditing*** *and* ***Team Leader's Guide to Internal Audit Leadership*** *(Internal Audit Foundation, 2019 and 2020 respectively) provide practical insights for people moving into the internal audit profession and those taking on leadership roles. These books complement the strategic-level content of* ***Sawyer's Internal Auditing: Enhancing and Protecting Organizational Value, 7th Edition*** *(Internal Audit Foundation, 2019).*

The Internal Audit Ambition Model *produced by The Institute of Internal Auditors Netherlands in 2018 may also be of interest for chief audit executives, boards, and professional bodies. The aim of the model is to substantively enhance the practice of the internal auditing profession and to challenge colleagues around the world to continue on their way to further professionalization. See* www.iia.nl

6 I've Been Working on the Railroad

Taking on a chief audit executive role for the first time can be unnerving, especially when it involves rebuilding a large internal audit activity and reversing a prior audit committee decision for outsourcing. The challenge is amplified when the responsibilities include major investigations into poor behavior and corruption prevention in an industry rife with fraud. This chapter illustrates how a "back to basics" approach helped to strengthen a lax control environment and, ultimately, delivered global recognition for internal audit quality … and it also considers the responsibility to protect whistleblowers even after leaving an organization, and the impact of poor probationary management practices. In the immortal words of Nelson Mandela (1918–2013), "It always seems impossible until it's done."

Entity Profile and Role

Sector:	Transport sector – passenger rail services
Entity:	State Rail Authority of New South Wales (StateRail)
Entity metrics (2004):	• Net Assets \$A4.2 billion • Annual revenues \$A2.1 billion • Annual net profit \$A81 million • Staff 9,700
Primary role:	Director Audit and Investigations (chief audit executive)
Main responsibilities:	Lead three main branches – internal audit, corruption prevention, and major investigations. Responsible for driving performance improvements across a diverse and complex rail operation, and for ongoing assessments of compliance obligations. Leader of multi-disciplinary audit team of 25. Primary adviser to board audit and risk committee on governance, risk management, internal control, and fraud and corruption control arrangements
Other executive roles:	Chair of ethics committee. Member of internal disciplinary review panel (dealing with staff wrongdoing). Chair of internal investigations coordination group. Protected disclosure coordinator for whole entity (dealing with whistleblowers)
Timeframe:	The Fourth Decade

PERSONAL STORY

After over a decade at the Reserve Bank, I felt it was time to move on. During my lunch breaks, I had several discussions with an agent for the role of chief audit executive at the State Rail Authority of NSW (StateRail) and had been shortlisted for the role. I was invited for a formal interview by StateRail senior executives and took the day off work so that I could attend the interview and give it my best shot.

My wife accompanied me into Sydney so we could enjoy lunch and do some sightseeing after the interview. The interview went well, and I came out with a bounce in my step. My wife and I met for lunch, and partway through lunch I received a phone call from one of the StateRail executives wanting names and contact details for my referees, as they wanted to proceed to the next stage of the recruitment.

I was surprised by the speed in which things had progressed. So, I promised to revert by the end of the day as I wanted to speak personally to my referees so as to not blindside them. I called my boss, Clarita Imperial, and asked if I could drop into the office for a quick chat. She was happy to oblige. When we met in her office, I mentioned that I was in the mix to fill the position of chief audit executive at StateRail, and wanted her as a referee. I was emotional during the discussion, as we had worked together for over a decade and had an excellent working relationship. Clarita then dropped the bombshell that she too was entertaining an offer to move to the World Bank. That presented a potential opportunity for me at the Reserve Bank, so I revisited my reasons to want to move on and realized I was best served elsewhere.

I was offered the role of chief audit executive at StateRail, which I accepted, commencing in mid-2001. My core responsibilities included internal auditing which represented about two-thirds of my resourcing, and extended into new areas for me in major investigations and corruption prevention which collectively represented about one-third of my resourcing but ended up consuming about 75 percent of my time. The internal audit staff were quite circumspect when I started, wondering how long I would last; I gained some perspective of their thinking when they mentioned they'd had six chief audit executives over the previous five years.

Before taking on the role, I was aware that StateRail had been restructured several times in the previous five years. What I had not expected was the impact of those restructures on the workforce and the underlying behavioral issues in some of its business areas. In the previous decade, the independent corruption watchdog had undertaken numerous investigations into allegations of wrongdoing at StateRail, often with damning results. The internal audit function had been outsourced to a big-four firm as part of those changes, and part of my brief was to bring it inhouse again.

This involved boosting staff numbers (or upsizing), just the opposite to my downsizing brief when I had joined the Reserve Bank.

I heard that part of the reason for my appointment from a banking background was that the new executive team wanted to strengthen the control of cash at railway stations. It was rumored that there had been a substantial theft of cash at one of its locations and nobody could be held accountable because the controls were so weak, notwithstanding a police investigation.

I experienced a very different culture to my banking days. In the Reserve Bank, everything was quite civilized, and nothing leaked; within the railways, the opposite seemed to be the case. In one of my early meetings with one of the most senior StateRail executives, I was brought into his office by his executive assistant and was seated ... then he just ignored me for about ten minutes in an obvious powerplay. He had heard it all before! I eventually won him over, and we established a fruitful working relationship.

I had always been a member of a trade union because I believed it important for genuine and ethical trade unions to protect and enhance the rights of workers. My longstanding bankers union did not service the railways, so I wrote to the two main railway unions, asking them to provide a few reasons why I should join their union, rather than the other one. Neither trade union responded, so I let my union membership lapse after 28 years.

StateRail's leadership and board seemed to be in a constant state of change, and that was quite a different experience to the consistency of leadership that I had enjoyed at the Reserve Bank. In three years at StateRail, I ended up having five different CEOs with whom I had to forge effective working relationships. And many changes right across the senior executives ranks.

Despite the odds, I led StateRail's Internal Audit team to achieve the prestigious IIA-Global Commitment to Quality Improvement Award for audit leadership in 2004; one of only two ever Australian recipients.

The constant changes at the CEO and executive level proved to be too much in the end. Less than a month after being presented with the Commitment to Quality Improvement Award by the then-International Chairman of the Institute of Internal Auditors, Bob McDonald, I was stunned when I was made redundant. A few months earlier, the government had established a new entity called Rail Corporation New South Wales (RailCorp) that brought StateRail and the Rail Infrastructure Corporation back together. The deck chairs above me had shifted again, and I wasn't required to lead RailCorp's internal audit function. I learnt the harsh lesson that contractual and charter protections for chief audit executives (to preserve their independence) have little meaning when a new entity is created through a merger.

I had learned a great deal in my three years as StateRail's chief audit executive, and had refined my leadership experience in the rough and tumble environment of the railways. I often quipped that my three years at StateRail felt more like ten years, as so much had happened, so often, and at such a fast pace.

Fortunately, I was well-placed to move in a new direction after StateRail, and I was asked to assume responsibility for corporate governance at an energy company (discussed in Chapter 7). My wife and I had a chance to reflect and re-energize during an interstate road-trip prior to me taking on my new role.

The key insights from this phase of my story are:

- Step-up the internal audit vision.
- Monitor outcomes from shared services and outsourcing.
- Establish key performance indicators.
- Manage whistleblowers meaningfully.
- Maintain effective communication with staff.
- Maintain behavioral standards.
- Manage mergers and acquisitions.

CONTEXT

Business leaders need to promote corporate values in all that they do and how they do it. When they are changing the operating model, they need to keep a keen eye on maintaining proper behavioral standards. There are many factors that help to shape behavioral standards leading to the anticipated business outcomes, with some of these elements discussed in this chapter and illustrated in **Exhibit 6.1**.

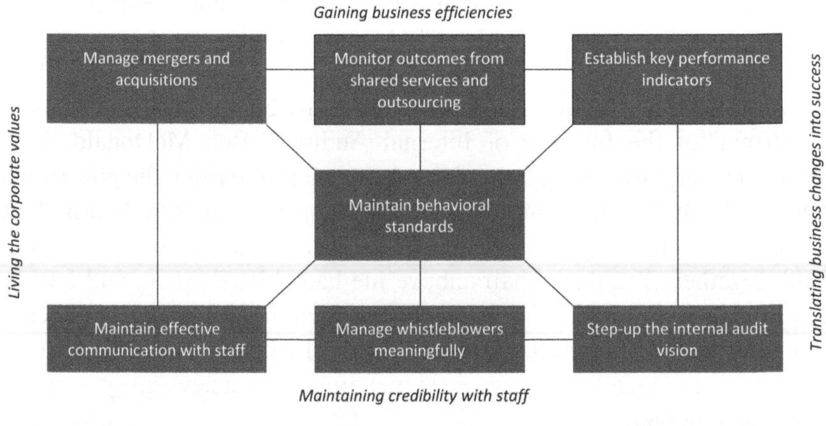

EXHIBIT 6.1 Translating corporate values and business changes into sustained success.

KEY TAKEAWAYS AND DEEP DIVES

STEP-UP THE INTERNAL AUDIT VISION

Setting the Scene

I was fortunate to have the strong support of the audit committee chairman, Arthur Butler; the Deputy Chief Executive, Fran McPherson; and the Chief Financial Officer, Peter Scarlett, throughout most of my three years at StateRail. While the CEO position changed often, I at least had a degree of stability in setting the direction for internal audit, and pursuing that direction through these three critical StateRail leaders.

This was important because the State Rail Authority (under its state government ownership) had been restructured several times in the five years prior to me starting there.

When I joined StateRail in 2001, we established in collaboration with the audit committee, the CEO, and my staff for the vision of internal audit: *To be recognized by the end of 2004 as a world class internal audit unit that has the resources, skills and acumen to make a positive difference to the business.*

The turn-around in the perception of StateRail's internal audit function can be illustrated, in part, with two key measures (other typical measures used in balanced scorecard are illustrated in **Exhibit 6.6**):

- First, of 1,644 internal audit recommendations raised, 98 percent were accepted and implemented, reflecting a positive client satisfaction outcome in terms of the usefulness of recommendations.
- Second, 91 percent of internal audits were assessed as "adding value" to the business based on client surveys in 2003/04 (the highest two ratings on the five-point scale), reflecting a positive client satisfaction outcome in terms of the value add.

The government established a new entity – Rail Corporation New South Wales (RailCorp) – in January 2004 that brought back together the remaining railway entities. RailCorp was to run passenger train operations (i.e., CityRail metropolitan passenger rail services and CountryLink long-distance services) and maintain the greater metropolitan network.

By that time the StateRail internal audit function (including the corruption prevention and major investigation arms) had realized its vision … being recognized as a world class internal audit unit that had the resources, skills, and acumen to make a positive difference to the business. The function was credible, was operating at a high level, and was adding value to the business leaders.

The next phase of the journey involved the amalgamation of the StateRail and Rail Infrastructure Corporation internal audit teams into a single RailCorp structure under new leadership as I had left the organization.[1]

What It Means for Business

An important role for the audit committee is to establish a vision for internal audit in consultation with the board, CEO, and chief audit executive. The vision should encapsulate the future state of the internal audit function in three to five years' time. It provides the chief audit executive with the basis for determining their strategic priorities for maintaining the momentum, building capability, embracing leading edge practices, and enhancing the organization's governance arrangements.

Exhibit 6.2 illustrates different levels of internal audit maturity that could align with the audit committee's aspirations, and illustrates abridged examples of common features. The cost for achieving a "world class" internal audit activity is likely to be greater than settling on a vision for an "implemented" level of internal audit maturity.

Once the vision has been agreed and included in the internal audit charter, the chief audit executive should develop a strategic roadmap aligned to the vision to articulate its strategic priorities and guide its evolution to further align with the organization's strategies, objectives, and risks and its assurance needs. The strategic roadmap should be reviewed and approved by the audit committee, and implementation should then be monitored by the audit committee through quarterly or half-yearly progress reporting.

> *The* ***internal audit competency framework*** *developed by the Institute of Internal Auditors (and promoted in 2020) reflects the outcomes of a multi-year research effort. It provides useful intelligence for chief audit executives aiming to invest in the development of the internal audit cohort. Sourced from* https://global.theiia.org/standards-guidance/Pages/Internal-Audit-Competency-Framework

Internal audit's strategic roadmap should capture strategic and tactical improvement ideas to present a visible illustration of the internal audit "end state." The strategic roadmap should reflect the chief audit executive's leadership

[1] From 2013 RailCorp's operation and maintenance functions were transferred to Sydney Trains and NSW Trains, leaving RailCorp as an asset owner.

EXHIBIT 6.2

Different levels of internal audit department maturity[2]

Internal Audit Maturity Levels		
Internal audit demonstrates business acumen, and learns from inside and outside the organization, with a constant focus on continuous improvement: • Innovates good practice. • Seen as a strategic business partner and trusted advisor. • Leader in the internal audit profession.	**World Class**	**High Aspiration**
Internal audit integrates information from across the organization to improve governance, risk management, control and compliance practices: • Emphasizes good practice. • Anticipates and responds to change. • Expands its role in response to business needs.	**Managed**	*Determine Audit Committee Vision*
Internal audit management and professional practices uniformly applied: • Generally conforming with the *International Professional Practices Framework* for internal auditing, including professional internal auditing standards.	**Implemented**	
Sustainable and repeatable practices: • Partially conforming with the *International Professional Practices Framework* for internal auditing, including professional internal auditing standards.	**Defined**	
Few sustainable and repeatable practices: • Not conforming with the *International Professional Practices Framework* for internal auditing, nor professional internal auditing standards.	**Initial**	**Lowest Level**

[2] Bruce Turner, *Resourcing Internal Audit* (Sydney, Australia: The Institute of Internal Auditors Australia, 2020), 3 Modified and updated.

assessment, risk profile, priority actions, prioritization, allocation, timeframes, monitoring arrangements, and funding where necessary. It may include:

- What its future audit work profile should be to best support the organization, and this is likely to include greater use of technology for auditing.
- What technology capability may be necessary to support the future work profile.
- What professional development may be necessary to assist transition to new ways of working, which may require advanced technology audit skills.
- How service provider specialist knowledge and skill can best be transferred to in-house auditors.
- Succession planning.

Chief audit executives need to have sufficient budget/funding commensurate with the vision that has been established. Audit committee charters typically include a requirement for the audit committee to periodically advise the board (or CEO) on the adequacy of internal audit resources to carry out its responsibilities. Audit committees should have a reasonable, defensible basis for informing the board as to whether or not the internal audit activity is sufficiently resourced with competent and objective professionals able to carry out the forward audit plan with the aim of enhancing and protecting organizational value (**Exhibit 6.3** illustrates elements that influence internal audit budgets).

While there is no simple formula for determining an internal audit budget and the appropriate level of resourcing, a combination of techniques can be considered to arrive at a reasonable, objective, and scientific basis.

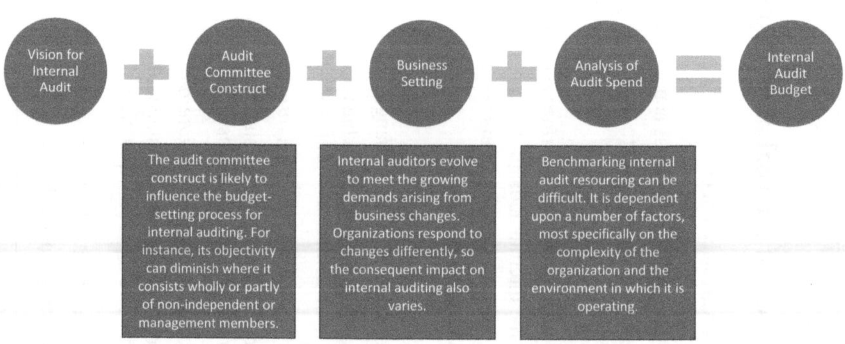

EXHIBIT 6.3 Elements that influence internal audit budget-setting.[3]

[3] Ibid, 3–4.

EXHIBIT 6.4
Environmental assessment[4]

The Environment in Which Internal Audit is Operating			Determining Internal Audit's Spend
Define Audit Universe	**Assess Risk Profile**	**Develop Audit Plan**	
Geographical coverage International operations Number of locations Extent of centralization Business maturity Assurance arrangements Regulatory requirements	Risk appetite of board Risk management maturity Business specific risks Disruptive innovation effects Control effectiveness Maturity of lines of defense Collaborative reporting	Vision for internal audit Extent of audit plan Resourcing model Size of activity Capability of audit team Efficiency and productivity Technological tools	Employee costs (total) Co-sourcing expenses Consulting costs Investment in training Technology license costs Travel expenses Administrative costs
Greater complexity of an organization typically needs more funding	A stable, mature, well-controlled organization might neutralize funding	Expectations for broader coverage will require more funding or more efficiency	Development of auditing capability and/or technology solutions needs to be funded

A comprehensive environment assessment will consider a range of elements that will impact on internal audit achieving its vision, creating its audit plan, determining its funding/budget, and establishing its resourcing and capability. Common environmental factors are illustrated in **Exhibit 6.4**.

Audit committees and boards that are assessing the adequacy of the internal budget can ask the chief audit executive to provide a report on the ten considerations outlined in **Exhibit 6.5**.

Monitor Outcomes from Shared Services and Outsourcing

Setting the Scene

While at StateRail we recruited wisely, and we secured a gem with experienced audit professional, Siri Thongsiri (recognized as one of the

[4] Ibid, 4. Modified and enhanced.

1. Assess whether the internal audit activity has the right amount of competent and professional resources to provide the right blend of internal audit services to the organization in line with the vision, approved internal audit service catalogue, and audit plan.
2. Identify and document the features of the audit universe that cannot be reasonably covered in the internal audit plan, particularly the top five risks that internal audit may not be able to cover with its current resources.
3. Identify any unique features of the audit universe that influence operational risks and internal audit coverage, such as the geographical coverage, international operations, number of locations, extent of centralization, business maturity, assurance arrangements, and regulatory requirements.
4. Assess the reasonableness of internal audit's coordination with other internal and external assurance providers and whether there is a reasonable spread of assurance costs.
5. Determine the chief audit executive's insights on whether they consider their resources to be sufficient.
6. Assess past internal audit budgets within the organization, including the performance against the budget (e.g. reasonableness of variances) and the organization's adjustment factors (e.g. efficiency dividends in the public sector).
7. Obtain comparisons of the organization's internal audit spend for similar organizations, and analyze this data using global and local benchmarks.
8. Undertake an environmental assessment of the typical factors that influence the internal audit resourcing and budget-setting.
9. Establish how internal audit has considered the velocity of risks, or the speed at which risks are likely to develop, in its environmental assessment.
10. Consider how well the internal audit activity is performing in the context of its Key Performance Indicators (e.g. as reported in the Balanced Scorecard Report or equivalent if this structured style of KPI reporting is used).

EXHIBIT 6.5 Ten considerations for assessing internal audit's budget.[5]

legends who inspired me at the back of the book). Siri leveraged his unique ability to "think outside the box" and regularly applied fresh and creative auditing techniques to his work. In one of his audits, Siri's analytical techniques accurately predicted a major shortfall of services from a third-party security supplier, where outsourced services were systematically charged but not provided (the technique is also referred to as "ghosting rorts"). Using a right-to-audit clause, the service schedule (attached to the invoice) was compared with the supplier's employee and payroll records to prove that the supplier never had the resource levels to deliver the services charged for in the service schedule. Management strengthened the system of internal controls, and recovered a large sum of money from the supplier.

A few years ago my auditors were assessing a sample of higher-risk contracts. As part of this audit, they reviewed an important security-destruction contract. Their initial work established that there was a strong security culture within the organization. The auditors then assessed the associated outsourced security destruction arrangements to gain a complete picture.

A third-party provider had been contracted to destroy computer hardware in a highly secure environment; the hardware contained sensitive corporate and personal information. The auditor activated the right-to-audit clause and arranged to assess the destruction process at the service provider's premises. This was the first time the service provider was audited under a right-to-audit clause.

Notwithstanding the credible reputation of the contractor, the auditor identified, and raised serious breaches of critical contractual conditions,

[5] Ibid, 5.

including lax custodianship, absence of security clearances for contractor's staff, poor timeliness of destruction, and deficiencies of separation of hardware from other non-secure items.

He was especially alarmed that security bins used to store the organization's computer hardware were left open, which allowed people to just take any hardware without challenge. The risk was exacerbated by the contractor employing many itinerant casual staff who had no security clearances despite it being a requirement of the contract (i.e., the clause was intended to ensure the good standing of the people handling the hardware). The business leader responsible for security recognized the escalated reputational and compliance risks should the organization's highly sensitive information make its way into the public domain. Further, the organization was paying for a premium service, but the third-party supplier was delivering a second-class service.

It is also important to focus on other external arrangements beyond shared services and outsourcing, such as joint ventures, subsidiaries, and associated or controlled entities.

A joint venture company, Securency Pty Ltd, was formed in 1996 as a manufacturer of polypropylene films used in banknote production. It marketed its products widely. There was a practice in some countries to which the company marketed its products to seek "facilitation payments." Several senior managers were accused of paying lucrative commissions to middlemen in order to secure government contracts. The media has reported on court proceedings, in which the company and several of its executives pleaded guilty in 2012 to bribing, or conspiring to bribe, foreign officials in several South East Asian countries in order to secure banknote contracts. The reputational damage to the manufacturing company and its parent has been significant, and it is clear that the corporate values of Securency and its parent were at odds with each other.

***Facilitation payments** are payments made to public or government officials to incentivize them to complete an action or process that is beneficial to the party making the payment. They are illegal in most countries and are tantamount to bribes.*

What It Means for Business

Many organizations now have shared services or outsourcing arrangements with third-party providers for all or part of their routine processing tasks, and activities requiring specialist expertise. While these processes are typically non-core and may be low value/high-volume, they can involve many job types, including manufacturing, information, communications and technology, finance, software-as-a-service arrangements, computer programming, customer service (e.g., call centers), record-keeping, and some human resources functions (e.g., employee benefits management and payroll).

Both ***outsourcing*** *and* ***shared services*** *arrangements are usually established to reduce costs, improve efficiency, boost quality, or improve customer service.*

Outsourcing *is an arrangement that shifts tasks, operations, jobs, or processes to an external workforce (either offsite or onsite), through a contract established with a third party. These arrangements can also be called "contracting out," and where they involve outsourcing to a third party in a country other than the one where the outsourcing company is based, they may be referred to as "offshoring."*

Shared services *arrangements typically consolidate related administrative services (such as payroll and accounts payable) into a single area; these service tasks would have been previously completed in multiple areas of the organization or group (e.g., defined business units and locations, or across several government entities). The arrangements result in the funding and resourcing of the service to be shared, with the providing department effectively becoming an internal service provider.*

Boards and business leaders that are considering entering into outsourcing or shared services arrangements need to initially challenge the business case, the underlying assumptions, and projected savings. It is imperative for a risk-based business case to be constructed objectively, and that it includes a clear baseline of costs together with robust estimates of the initial expenditure required and the timeframe for achieving the savings. The assessment should also encompass cultural elements to establish whether the proposed service provider is a good fit that shares similar corporate values.

Once these arrangements are implemented, qualitative and quantitative benchmarks and key performance indicators (KPIs) should be established and monitored by the business leaders and the board as a basis for measuring the success or otherwise of the outsourcing and shared service initiatives; these measures will typically include cost, timeliness, quality, and customer satisfaction.

Shared services and outsourcing continue to represent operational risks for the business requiring effective controls. It is incumbent upon business leaders through their legal counsel to incorporate appropriate clauses in the contracts or service level agreements with service providers that address internal controls. This is typically done through two key clauses:

- First, the service provider should be tasked with delivering to the business receiving the service a periodic (at least annual) certification or attestation that agreed internal controls have been effectively maintained.
- Second, a "right-to-audit" clause should be included in all third-party contracts.[6]

When parts of an operational process that is being audited and is within the internal audit scope have been outsourced to a third-party supplier or delivered through a shared services arrangement, the chief audit executive should ensure the auditors invoke the right-to-audit clause in the contract, and then independently and objectively assess controls maintained by the third-party supplier.

*A **right-to-audit clause** is often included in significant tenders and critical contracts, based on the overall contracting risks (e.g., value, duration, and industry-specific). The clause provides internal and external auditors access to information, books, records, and assets held by contractors (and subcontractors) for purposes of auditing, including a right to make copies. The right to audit relates to the specific contract and typically covers operational practices and procedures; security arrangements; accuracy of invoices and reports; compliance with confidentiality, privacy, and security obligations; books, records, and accounts; and any other matters determined as being relevant to the contract.*

There are usually provisions requiring the records and information to be in a data format and storage medium accessible by the customer who, in turn, must provide reasonable notice of the audit. A suitable onsite space for the auditor to work is also a common feature in these clauses. A right-to-audit clause does not establish any obligation to undertake an audit – it merely reserves the right

[6] The Association of Certified Fraud Examiners website has a Sample Right-to-Audit Clause as an example - https://www.acfe.com/uploadedFiles/ACFE_Website/Content/documents/sample-documents/sample-right-to-audit-clause.pdf (sourced 24 June 2020). Organizations should seek their own independent legal advice.

for auditors to conduct an audit where they determine a need. It will usually have survival provisions to enable it to be used for 7–10 years after the termination of the contract.[7]

Chief audit executives also need to alert their auditors to remain vigilant for any transactions that point to potential facilitation payments when reviewing the revenue and expenditure cycles for organizations active in foreign markets.

Audit committees should ensure that the audit universe (that is, the list of potential audits) includes entities that are subsidiary, controlled, or associated with the organization, with a view to the internal audit function periodically assessing the reasonableness of the overarching governance and risk management arrangements, and financial stewardship. The internal audit and audit committee charters should clearly articulate boundaries (if any) to the audit coverage and audit committee oversight (that is, areas "out of scope"). The results of the internal audit/s of subsidiary, controlled, and associated entities should be reported to the audit committee

Establish Key Performance Indicators

Setting the Scene

On several occasions I have taken on the role of chief audit executive in organizations where the audit committee and senior management have lost confidence in the internal audit function and do not see that they are getting value from their investment.

These internal audit functions did have a few narrowly framed inward-facing performance measures, but they did not have measures that addressed the full range of expectations of key stakeholders.

The most visible part of an internal audit activity is characteristically the final audit report. My predecessors had overlooked the fact that internal audit functions are typically measured on more than the outcomes of individual audit assignments, with key stakeholders interested in having a well-considered set of KPIs that help them evaluate the overall success of the internal audit activity.

One of my first acts upon taking on the role of chief audit executive was to develop, in consultation with the audit committee, a set of KPIs that aligned with the vision for internal audit. The audit committee supported

[7] Bruce R. Turner, *New Auditor's Guide to Internal Auditing* (Lake Mary, FL: Internal Audit Foundation, 2019), 119–120.

the establishment of a balanced scorecard for internal audit with the KPIs split into four elements:

1. How well the internal audit function partners with the audit committee.
2. How well the internal audit function supports management in achieving their business objectives.
3. How well the internal audit processes are managed.
4. The innovation and capabilities of the internal audit team.

In some organizations, I incorporated a fifth element – the professional outreach of the internal audit team.

I understood the importance of organizations establishing a performance culture, as discussed in *rising above the norm* in Chapter 4, which is underpinned by identifying talent, maintaining professional development, and dealing with poor performance.

Internal auditors are more likely to help an organization accomplish its objectives where their personal performance goals and objectives align to the mission and objectives of the internal audit activity, which, in turn, should align with the strategic direction of the organization. So, once the KPIs and the balanced scorecard reporting concept were established, they were communicated to all members of the internal audit team. The KPIs were cascaded through the audit managers to all of the auditors so the auditors had clear visibility between their personal goals and those of the internal audit activity.

While there were some initial teething problems, these were ironed out so the individual performance measures on which an auditor's performance were to be assessed corresponded to their agreed performance goals, and involved qualitative and quantitative factors.

We also established KPIs for other arms of our function. In terms of corruption prevention, the Corruption Prevention Officer and I participated in the intensive induction program of new staff, including train drivers, guards, revenue protection officers, and other frontline staff. In reshaping the organization's lived culture, it was important for us to impress upon the people being onboarded that "just because everyone does it doesn't make it right." It was also important to put a face to the people who handled protected disclosures. We participated in dozens of training workshops each year and recognized the impact we were having through participant surveys; our impact was reflected in the *overall presentation, knowledge, and delivery* ratings which were rated as either excellent or very good by 100 percent of participants on a five-point rating scale, the two highest rating levels (excellent = 87 percent; very good = 13 percent).

What It Means for Business

Audit committees and business leaders are increasingly expecting chief audit executives to report on both the value of the insights the internal audit function delivers, as well as the performance metrics that facilitate effective oversight of the internal audit function. This requires chief audit executives to establish a structured and practical approach for providing "balanced" reporting on the performance of the internal audit activity.

Balanced scorecards are designed to translate internal audit strategy into action, with the aim of helping to manage and measure the performance of the internal audit function, and, consequently, achieving alignment with organizational strategies. They are becoming an increasingly well-established means for reporting quantitative and qualitative KPIs to the audit committee in a balanced way; the KPIs should be a blend of inward-facing and outward-facing measures.

*A **balanced scorecard report** is part of a performance management system that is widely used by organizations and has become a leading management framework for strategy execution throughout the world. Within the context of internal auditing, balanced scorecards help to translate strategy into action, and to manage and measure internal audit performance (through KPIs used to evaluate the success of the internal audit activity); they help to connect the internal audit function's strategy with that of the organization.*

The performance culture of the internal audit function is driven by absolute clarity of the organization's strategies and business objectives, coupled with the steps that the chief audit executive establishes to ensure the auditors perform in alignment with the direction of the organization and the vision for internal audit. A firm foundation is established through effective goalsetting and clear KPIs that are consistently applied at the both the internal audit function and auditor levels (see examples in **Exhibit 6.6**).

The essential features to the successful implementation of a balanced scorecard report include:

- Making the internal audit strategy explicit in establishing the basis of the scorecard.
- Choosing the measures that are aligned to the strategy, and have clearly understood relationships between the measures.
- Defining and refining the performance measures so that the scorecard is well-understood and remains front-of-mind for all internal audit staff.

EXHIBIT 6.6

Examples of KPIs included in balanced scorecard reports for internal audit[8]

Balanced Scorecard Element	Examples of Internal Audit Function Key Performance Indicators (KPIs)	Measure Type	Inward or Outward Facing Measure
Partnering with the audit committee	Board (or audit committee) expectations met	Qualitative	Outward (delivers value for critical stakeholders)
	Percentage of audit plan complete	Quantitative	Inward
Supporting senior management	Client satisfaction goals – value added	Qualitative	Outward (delivers value for critical stakeholders)
	Client satisfaction goals – usefulness of recommendations	Qualitative	Outward (delivers value through useful recommendations for critical stakeholders)
	Cycle times (duration period of audits)	Quantitative	Outward (drives timely reporting for stakeholders)
Managing internal audit processes	Performance against the internal audit financial budget	Quantitative	Inward
	Availability of current and relevant internal audit charter, intranet, audit manual	Qualitative	Outward (provides useful resources for stakeholders)
	Budget to actual audit times	Quantitative	Inward
	Conformance with quality assurance and improvement standards (based on internal and external quality assessments)	Qualitative	Outward (adds to credibility of work for stakeholders)
Managing Innovation and capabilities	Internal auditor workforce satisfaction	Qualitative	Inward
	Completion of initiatives in professional development plan	Quantitative	Inward
	Optimizing innovative practices and utilization of internal audit resources (to conduct audits while minimizing 'administration')	Quantitative	Inward

[8] Bruce Turner, *Balanced Scorecard Reporting* (Sydney, Australia: The Institute of Internal Auditors Australia, 2019), 4.

- Managing the mindset of people involved in internal audit activities so that the performance measures are embedded in their psyche.

Where the internal audit activity seeks client feedback, after each audit in the form of a client satisfaction survey, the "scores" for the value added from the audit and the usefulness of audit recommendations are qualitative measures that are directly influenced by how well the auditors have completed their work.

As an example, within the balanced scorecard, the internal audit function had a target of 3.5 out of 5 for the client satisfaction goal KPIs "value added" and "usefulness of audit recommendations," and for "cycle times (duration period of audits)" a KPI of 14 weeks or less. The following example (**Exhibit 6.7**) shows how KPIs could be met at a function level, even though one of the audit team leaders was falling behind the targets in the audits for which he was responsible. In this example, the chief audit executive would use the outcomes while discussing the half-yearly or annual performance assessment with the team leaders. They would have the chance to explain the outcomes, especially when KPIs were not met; there could well be valid reasons for the outcomes for team leader B, such as an audit with a high level of difficulty that resulted in the identification of many issues, while dealing with a poor business leader who was attempting to deflect his or her unsatisfactory audit result.

Audit committees should direct the chief audit executive to establish KPIs and report them periodically to the audit committee in a balanced

EXHIBIT 6.7

Example for using KPIs to inform performance assessment discussions

	Target	Team Leader A	Team Leader B	Internal Audit Function as a Whole
Client satisfaction goals – value added	≥ 3.5 out of 5	4.2	3.2	3.7
Client satisfaction goals – usefulness of audit recommendations	≥ 3.5 out of 5	4.6	2.6	3.6
Cycle times (duration period of audits)	14 weeks or less	11 weeks	15 weeks	13 weeks
Outcome		KPIs met	KPIs not met	KPIs met

scorecard report. The committee should also ensure that the KPIs are embedded within the internal audit function and applied in the performance assessment arrangement for all audit team leaders and auditors. The audit committee chair should use the balanced scorecard results as a significant input into the assessment of the chief audit executive's performance.

Manage Whistleblowers Meaningfully

Setting the Scene

StateRail had a contemporary whistleblower policy which was underpinned by protected disclosure legislation (which is now called public interest disclosures in government entities). Senior management had anointed protected disclosure officers across the organization, whose role was to receive complaints (or allegations) from whistleblowers, then maintain an ongoing dialogue with them. My role was twofold – I was an anointed protected disclosure officer as well the protected disclosure coordinator for the whole of the organization.

The whistleblower policy helped to promote transparency, compliance, and the fair treatment of people who came forward with allegations of wrongdoing. The challenge in dealing with whistleblowers was to ensure that the disclosures were being made in good faith and without malice, based on the person's honest perceptions.

In my role as protected disclosure coordinator, I was responsible for coordinating all disclosures provided to nominated protected disclosure officers and ensuring they were referred to the appropriate area for preliminary assessment, and, if warranted, further investigation. I also informed the state's corruption watchdog of any corruption-related allegations. There were reporting and feedback provisions that needed to be closely monitored.

My office was set up well for dealings with whistleblowers, with a doorway directly into a secure confidential meeting room from the lift area, and a connecting back-door into my office. It allowed me to speak with whistleblowers in an environment that they found to be quiet, safe, private, comfortable, and unobservable. I was usually accompanied by one of my trusted senior staff so that we could take the information confidentially, without me exposing myself personally to accusations of wrongdoing; there were situations where whistleblowers came forward with allegations that were frivolous or vexatious as a way to "damage" their managers or work colleagues. It was a constant balancing act to determine which allegations had merit to pursue further.

I was acutely aware of the importance of caring for whistleblowers. This awareness was heightened further when the story of a massive $3.8 billion accounting fraud at WorldCom broke in 2002. The chief audit executive at

WorldCom (and ultimate whistleblower), Cynthia Cooper, and her team of auditors worked together in secret to investigate and unearth the substantial fraud after initially discovering some suspicious entries in the company's financial records. Her book about her life and the WorldCom fraud, *Extraordinary Circumstances: The Journey of a Corporate Whistleblower*, was published in 2008. It was a fascinating and inspiring story.

The responsibility in caring with whistleblowers does not cease if you move away from the organization, where the whistleblower originally came forward. There was one whistleblower who I handled confidentially and discreetly until the matter was finally resolved about 6 months after I had left StateRail. The whistleblower was fearful of any reprisals, and I continued to protect the identity; I never provided the name to anyone, despite the interest of managers to know the name.

What It Means for Business

Whistleblowing is of vital importance to business leaders in directly protecting their organization from wrongdoing. If they don't recognize, address, and close-down violations, they risk the consequences of legal prosecution, major fines, reputational damage, public scrutiny, and loss of capital (e.g., fraud losses). Business leaders should familiarize themselves with whistleblower rights and responsibilities so that they are well-equipped to promote a whistleblowing culture across the organization.

Boards and audit committees need to ensure that their organization has a whistleblower (or similar) policy in place that is consistent with their legislative obligations and aligned to the corporate values. The policy should include common provisions, including:

- A requirement for secure information management systems for the receipt, storage, assessment, notification, and reporting of disclosures.
- Details of the internal reporting structure, identifying the roles and responsibilities of those in the reporting structure.
- A secure process and environment for receiving disclosures.
- A means of identifying a person (or persons) who can receive disclosures from whistleblowers.
- Responsibility for management to investigate suspected wrongdoing and take appropriate action.
- A secure means of notifying external law enforcement agencies or corruption watchdogs of reportable disclosures under the relevant legislation.
- Training and education for selected staff in the receipt, handling, assessment and notification of disclosures.

- Training and education for selected staff in the welfare management of whistleblowers.
- A process to collect and collate statistics, themes and trends on all allegations of wrongdoing with confidential reporting to the board and audit committee.

Once a whistleblowing policy has been established and disseminated appropriately, business leaders should focus on raising awareness, and delivering meaningful training as the foundation for an open culture that helps to combat workplace wrongdoing.

***Whistleblowers** are individuals or groups of individuals who make disclosures about wrongdoing and improper conduct. This can include fraud and corruption, criminal offences, serious professional misconduct, dishonesty, misuse of information, perverting the course of justice, falsifying scientific research, someone covering up wrongdoing, and serious health, safety, or environmental risks.*

In government entities, whistleblowers could also raise issues regarding maladministration and serious and substantial waste. This could extend to situations where a public officer or entity performs their functions dishonestly, which results in the person, or an associate of the person, obtaining a benefit for which they otherwise would not have obtained, such as a license, permit, approval, authority, or other entitlement; an appointment to a statutory office or board; or a financial benefit (e.g., real or personal property, or a direct or indirect monetary or proprietary gain).

Legislation concerning whistleblowers is typically established for three primary purposes:

- Encourage and facilitate disclosures of improper conduct and detrimental action made in reprisal by senior management or the organizations.
- Provide protection for people who make disclosures or who may suffer detrimental action in reprisal for those disclosures.
- Provide confidentiality of the content of disclosures and the identity of people who make them.

Whistleblowers can make disclosures that relate to conduct or action that may have already taken place, may be occurring now, or may happen in the future. While legislation is different across jurisdictions, common protections for whistleblowers include:

- Immunity from civil and criminal liability and disciplinary action for making the disclosure.
- Immunity from liability for breaching confidentiality provisions.
- Protection from actions in defamation for making the disclosure.
- The right to sue for damages or to seek an injunction to stop actions in reprisal.
- Protection of their identity and any information that would lead to their identification.

Not all allegations of wrongdoing are substantiated; in fact, the majority (around 60 percent) are not. It is important for business leaders to establish a charter of rights for people who are the subject of allegations (discussed in Chapter 8).

Maintain Effective Communication with Staff

Setting the Scene

I thought I had settled well into my senior executive role and had maintained a strong commitment to keeping the team informed of developments and significant matters. Several surprises sharpened my attention to maintaining effective communications.

First, as part of my ongoing stakeholder relationship arrangements, I met periodically with partners from the major accounting firms. As I did with all meetings, regardless of the audience, I closed my office door. I was quite shocked when one of my staff mentioned that others in the team were unsettled because they had deduced that I was talking to the partners as part of a strategy to outsource the internal audit activity. It was a case of oversensitive staff feeling threatened and adding fuel to the rumor mill. I addressed the issue at a whole-of-staff meeting, guaranteeing that there were no outsourcing plans, and when I closed the door it was simply to stay focused on the conversations.

Second, my staff and others were required to complete a 360-degree feedback survey as part of an intensive executive-level training course I was undertaking. My direct reports were away at the time, either on vacation, or working interstate, so I asked the next level down to participate. When I received the results I was taken aback, because the staff had rated my communication down, though my peers and boss had rated me highly. I subsequently found out that key messages that I had conveyed to my audit managers had not been passed down the line. I realized then that I needed to continue meeting with my direct reports, but I also needed to connect regularly with staff at all levels to ensure there was clear and succinct common messaging about our strategies and direction.

Third, we had determined the need for change and had created strong messaging around moving from "good to great." I thought the staff were on board. Then, I found errors were creeping into reports; sloppy attention to detail had created avoidable problems with key stakeholders; and staff were forgetting basic tasks that impacted on the timing of reporting to the audit committee. Despite my close coordination with audit managers and coaching efforts to help raise the bar, things did not improve. At our all-staff meeting I reflected on the various incidents and how they were affecting our overall performance and the perceptions of stakeholders. I shook the tree a little when I said quite bluntly that I thought we might have moved from bad to worse … rather than good to great! This opened up the communication channels, and allowed us to better understand the root cause of our problems, which we addressed through collaborative solutions. The staff rallied, and we were soon delivering a consistently good performance. That ultimately elevated to a consistently great performance through sustained effort.

The bruising I had endured through these incidents put me on a firmer footing. I established a more well-rounded communication approach with my staff, that was both vertical and horizontal as illustrated in **Exhibit 6.8**.

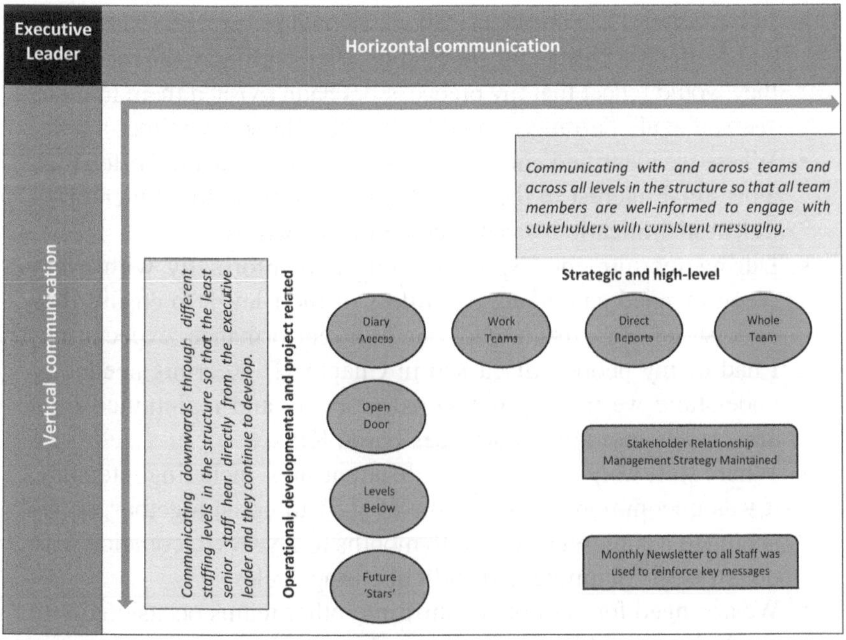

EXHIBIT 6.8 Examples of horizontal and vertical communication approaches.

My communications included some that were face-to-face or as team huddles, whereas others were through video-conferencing or teleconferencing. As my communication approach matured and I gained experience, I had all bases covered, including:

- Fortnightly meetings with my direct reports (or more often if required) with a fixed agenda focused on strategic initiatives, the progress of the audit plan, and any staff issues arising.
- Ad hoc discussions with individual direct reports on issues arising.
- Monthly whole-of-team meetings with an agenda and minutes, usually with a presentation.
- Monthly meetings with each of the audit managers and their working teams focused on the progress of their audits and significant observations arising, any issues with the methodology, and options for innovation.
- Six-weekly meetings with the staff two levels below me and, separately, with those three levels below me without the audit managers present. These were free-flowing conversation-style. (While the audit managers initially felt threatened by these sessions, they soon relaxed when they saw the value.)
- When we had graduates (see Chapter 1, including **Exhibit 1.2**), we would meet as a group each six to eight weeks to check on their progress and to discuss management-level techniques to enrich their learning.
- In some roles I had interstate staff who would be surprised when I visited them for a "meet and greet" soon after starting in the role; often they would reflect that my predecessors hadn't visited them in many years, if at all. I arranged to visit each site at least three times a year.
- Where we identified emerging "stars" within the team, I often took a personal interest in their development through direct mentoring (talent identification was discussed in Chapter 4).
- During recruitment I spoke directly and informally with every recommended candidate, regardless of their level, to ensure they understood my vision and the high-performance expectations I had of my people (discussed in Chapter 2). Recruits needed to understand we ran a professional practice, and maintained tight and closely-monitored outcomes-based KPIs.
- Where staff were spread across different sites, including interstate, it was uncommon for the whole of staff to come together, so we arranged a conference every 18 months to 2 years to coincide with our strategic planning and audit planning cycles.
- We arranged for auditors to shift into other teams occasionally to break down working team silos and to use their expertise on specific audit engagements or to cross-fertilize skills.

- I implemented and issued a monthly one-page (double-sided) newsletter to all staff reflecting on key messages, highlighting recent successes, and listing all of my key meetings and travels scheduled for the ensuing month.
- I opened up my electronic diary so that my direct reports had full access, and others in the team would have read access. I mentioned that there would occasionally be confidential meetings in my diary that would be marked "private;" these would be rare but as the chief audit executive there were sometimes highly sensitive matters to be handled, and the staff recognized that.

I maintained an open-door policy and the regular interactions with staff at all levels meant that people felt comfortable approaching me, especially if something meaningful needed to be handled. People did not abuse the openness, and my executive assistant would usually coach them on the best times to connect with me directly; staff could also view my electronic diary. I often had routine conversations with my direct reports while I was driving between sites (e.g., my regular trips between my home and Canberra (and vice versa) involved a three-hour drive, and the highway through the Southern Highlands and away from the city outskirts – the mid-hour of my journey – were quiet and relatively risk-free; my car was equipped with legally approved hands-free cell phone capability).

What It Means for Business

Maintaining effective communications with staff involves considerable effort and energy as illustrated in **Exhibit 6.8**. In some instances, it can appear to be over-reaching. But when it is done in an open, constructive, and systematic manner, it helps to shape a culture of professionalism and integrity. When you are working in organizations subject to significant (and sometimes continuous) change, it is imperative that staff are well-informed and engaged in the process, regardless of whether it is a business-as-usual or changing environment.

The benefits of effective two-way communication are gained through a common understanding of the organization's strategies, objectives, and goals; engaged employees; a more consistent approach; better sharing of ideas and knowledge; improved legislative and regulatory compliance; and a positive attitude towards change. Conversely, business leaders who fail to communicate effectively will likely see a negative shift in any or all of the above benefits, and this could be detrimental to the organization's operational efficiency, customer satisfaction, and ultimately profitability and market share.

Having well-informed staff does not just happen. It requires the right culture, underpinned by communicating openly, with clarity and conciseness, being approachable, encouraging feedback and acting on it, and updating staff regularly with meaningful information. These elements involve the following:

• Shaping the right culture	The importance and benefits of understanding the culture (Chapter 2) and maintaining a fun business environment (Chapter 1) underpin successful communication strategies. Business leaders should never see communication as something they tick off a task list, rather, it should be crafted to breathe life into the lived culture of the organization and help to keep staff morale high.
• Communicating openly	Open communication helps to build trust and make staff feel valued; it is demonstrated when staff at all levels contribute in meetings. Staff perform at their best when business leaders seek their input, and when they understand why a task needs to be done. Effective communicators make their messages clear, succinct and simple, and avoid technical jargon.
• Being approachable	Most workplace communication is nonverbal, so it means nothing when a business leader encourages staff to talk with them if their body language sends a different message. Business leaders need to remain conscious of their attitude and the level of openness they project to their staff; this is aided by a friendly, positive attitude at all times that encourages staff to talk openly with them.
• Encouraging feedback	Honest and meaningful communication provides a conduit for legitimate staff feedback and ideas. This feedback, in turn, is great for business as it helps to embed a customer-centric culture (Chapter 2) while showing staff that the business leader values their opinions. Business leaders should always be appreciative of well-meaning staff feedback and take it seriously.
• Updating staff regularly	Business leaders should never keep their staff in the dark about what's going on with the organization and the business area, including significant projects, and other business-critical activities. Staff will feel more connected to the organization and the direction it is taking when they are well-informed, and when they are thanked and congratulated for successful outcomes.

Well-informed and engaged staff provide an important conduit through to key stakeholders (discussed in Chapter 3) when they understand the strategies, objectives, and risks of the area. **Exhibit 6.9** illustrates staff at

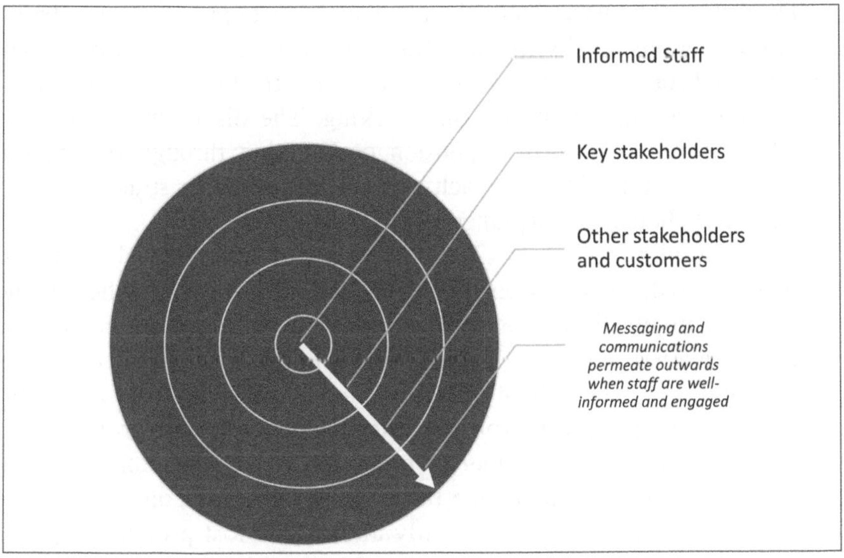

EXHIBIT 6.9 Targeted communications with staff permeating to stakeholders.

the center who are equipped to share a consistent message to stakeholders (including customers); the power of communication comes from many people sharing this task, rather than it being left solely with the executive leader.

Maintain Behavioral Standards

Setting the Scene

One of the downsides of frequent leadership changes was the difficulty in maintaining consistent behavioral standards across a large and disparate workforce. If a long-term worker behaved badly in one area of the organization, he might be given a slap on the wrist. Another worker committing a lesser transgression in another area of the business could be subjected to stern discipline, possibly dismissal. There was no consistency. And when the organization's leadership did take a strong stance against poor behavior, many staff operated on the basis that they would hold back for a while, and wait until the next "new regime" before reverting to their old unacceptable behaviors.

To combat this, StateRail established a Disciplinary Review Panel. Each week StateRail's Deputy Chief Executive, Corporate Counsel, and I would come together as the Disciplinary Review Panel to assess investigation reports covering behavioral matters. The organization had several discrete units undertaking investigations, including the major investigations unit (under me), fraud and corruption (under the chief investigator), and behavioral matters (under HR management).

The aim of the Disciplinary Review Panel was to provide values-based recommendations for disciplinary outcomes that were fair and consistent based on substantiated and well-evidenced investigation reports, irrespective of the area the employee was working. The disciplinary outcomes could range from dismissal, suspension, or demotion, through to a caution, warning or training. The approach was part of a broader strategy to nurture cultural change, underpinned by honesty and integrity.

The Disciplinary Review Panel took a dim view of substantiated allegations, with firm action recommended regardless of whether the allegations involved serious transgressions or less serious behavioral matters. An average of nine investigation reports were considered every month, and just over half of these resulted in dismissal. As an example, if someone stole $50 from a wallet handed into lost property – it resulted in dismissal. If someone breached strict no-alcohol or drug policies – dismissal. If someone threw a hot cup of tea on a co-worker – dismissal. If someone fraudulently altered the lost property register to steal a bunged-up bicycle – dismissal (breach of trust). The more serious issues of fraud, corruption, and theft also resulted in dismissal, as well as the matters being reported to the appropriate law enforcement authority (e.g., police or the Independent Commission Against Corruption [ICAC]).

All employees who were the subject of adverse disciplinary outcomes could appeal the decision to an independent external review board. Over the nearly three years of operation of the Disciplinary Review Panel during my time at the organization, the vast majority of decisions (in the vicinity of 95 percent) were upheld and the disciplinary outcomes were confirmed. This reflects the fair, just, and reasonable conclusions reached by the investigations staff, coupled with the objective assessment of the evidence supporting the investigation reports that was undertaken by the Disciplinary Review Panel. It also reflected the industrial relations environment of the time when trade unions were supportive of management's commitment to addressing behavioral shortcomings.

I also chaired a separate Investigations Coordination Group to ensure that the respective investigation efforts were coordinated, didn't interfere with each other, and systemic issues were determined and actioned. It also armed me with intelligence on emerging themes that informed the corruption prevention arm of my team, and the communications strategy that they maintained.

As part of my external coordination role, I maintained a reporting channel directly with the state's corruption watchdog – the ICAC. The Investigations Coordination Group helped to ensure the completeness and integrity of the regular reporting to the ICAC, and the appropriate handling of matters reported by the ICAC to the StateRail CEO.

What It Means for Business

Well-founded values underpin behavior and decision-making at all levels of an organization, and these values need to be reinforced (as discussed in Chapter 2). It is typically a condition of employment for staff to meet standards of professional behavior, and this, in turn, helps the organization to create a respectful working environment for everyone. It is incumbent upon business leaders to lead by example in applying the standards that govern their workplace, and to promote these standards to staff so their behavior is acceptable and they are positioned to succeed in their job.

*The **behavior** of a person or an organization is reflected in the way in which they act or conduct themselves towards others. **Standards of behavior** are a set of official guidelines based on corporate values that are usually promulgated in a code of ethics or code of conduct; they are intended to govern the actions, speech, and attitudes of staff.*

An organization's standards of professional behavior are usually encapsulated in a code of ethics and a code of conduct (illustrated in **Exhibit 12.5** for disseminating organizational values). These codes reflect, respectively, principles-based guidance and the manner of implementing the guidance. They serve as a commitment to how staff will treat and interact with each other, and will help to normalize staff behavior by clearly articulating the level of behavior expected on a daily basis. They help to set the tone of the organization and its lived culture, especially when the corporate values become a part of their day-to-day language so staff and business leaders don't realize they are using those words or practicing those behaviors.

Standards of professional behavior typically cover areas such as accountability, appearance, communication, respect, and service. As an example, staff may be required to commit to:

- Taking ownership of all that they do and responsibility for the outcomes of all their actions.
- Respecting their personal appearance, work environment, and all areas visible to customers.
- Maintaining clear, open, honest, and timely communication.
- Treating others as they would want to be treated.
- Providing customers, co-workers and other stakeholders with courteous, prompt, and safe service.

Business leaders and audit committees need to ensure that the corporate values and standards of professional behavior are:

- Embedded across the organization.
- Rolled-out, periodically reinforced, tied into training and development, and included as part of the onboarding and orientation process for new staff.
- Applied consistently across the organization, with allegations of breaches dealt with promptly and in a fair, just, and reasonable manner.

These are matters for the CEO to monitor in consultation with the head of HR. The audit committee should receive a report at least annually from the CEO or HR asserting that these arrangements are maintained effectively, and highlighting any trends or systemic issues.

Board directors play a vital role in governing an organization on behalf of its shareholders or members. While the legal duties of each director are contained in various legislations, there are hundreds of other laws and legal requirements for which directors may be personally liable. Beyond these legal requirements, directors should maintain proper behavioral standards which should be publicly acknowledged (the board code of conduct was discussed in Chapter 2). At a minimum, each director should recognize acceptable behavioral standards and agree to uphold them, with examples of common requirements summarized as follows:

- Assume personal responsibility for impartially contributing to board decisions.
- Actively develop reasonable and adequate knowledge about the business of the organization, and its strategies, objectives and risks.
- Actively contribute to the development of relevant organizational policies, values, and codes.
- Maintain focus and strong support for the organization's longer-term strategies.
- Prepare properly and fully for all board and board committee meetings and strategic decisions.
- Promote the need for sufficient and complete decision-support information.
- Undertake all tasks and assignments delegated by the board or a committee of the board.
- Actively manage conflicts of interest, and avoid personal gains for oneself, family, or associates.
- Identify differences between personal and board positions on controversial matters so the board can make informed and balanced decisions that are ultimately beneficial for the organization.

- Devote sufficient time, energy, focus, and skills to the duties of a director.
- Uphold and champion high ethical standards at the board level.
- Step down from the board if any of the above points are no longer possible.

Boards of multinational companies should also determine whether their morality and behavior in developing nations mirrors how they would be expected to behave in their domestic markets, regardless of the local laws, given the impact that global transparency can have. The increasing global media attention being given to the overseas activities of multinational companies is influencing consumer buying trends, with people no longer purchasing clothing made in sweatshops or other goods produced by child labor, and motorists boycotting service stations supplied by oil companies that disregard environmental impacts. The heightened risk of modern slavery was mentioned in Chapter 2 and is discussed in the postface.

Manage Mergers and Acquisitions

Setting the Scene

I have been involved in or experienced the effects of merged entities both as a senior executive and as an audit committee chair. Despite mergers promising improved performance, some have failed because of poor planning, ineffective risk management, and inadequate oversight.

My first employer was the Rural Bank; it was corporatized as the State Bank and ultimately merged with the Commonwealth Bank of Australia. I spent several years at Integral Energy Australia which was the result of a merger between Prospect Electricity and Illawarra Electricity; the retail arm of Integral Energy was subsequently sold off to Origin Energy while the electricity distribution division was rebranded to Endeavour Energy.

And I spent several years at the State Rail Authority; it ultimately merged with the Rail Infrastructure Corporation to form RailCorp after it had been restructured several times in the five years prior to me starting there in 2001. Notably:

- In 1996, the State Rail Authority was split into four distinct entities to separate infrastructure from operations as part of the process of moving to an open access regime (in response to the national competition policy mentioned in Chapter 5). The four entities were Freight Rail Corporation (providing freight services); Rail Access Corporation (managing track and providing access to public and private operators); Railway Services Authority (maintaining track and rolling stock); and the State Rail Authority (delivering passenger services through CityRail and CountryLink).

- In late-1996, the Freight Rail Corporation was corporatized and was relaunched as FreightCorp; it was ultimately sold to a private operator in early 2002.
- In 1998, what remained of the State Rail Authority was split into four operating divisions under the StateRail banner, being CityRail Stations; CountryLink; Operations; and Passenger Fleet Maintenance.
- In early-2001, the Rail Access Corporation and Railway Services Authority were merged into the Rail Infrastructure Corporation and that new entity took responsibility for ownership and maintenance of all railway infrastructure.

It became clear that the government's decision in 1996 to split the State Rail Authority into separate entities had not achieved the outcomes anticipated. The strategy was rethought amidst reported criticism of operational failings and public perceptions of blame shifting, particularly after the Waterfall train accident in 2003 (mentioned in Chapter 3).

In January 2004, the government established a new entity, Rail Corporation New South Wales (RailCorp), that brought back together the remaining railway entities that were split just seven years earlier. RailCorp assumed responsibility for passenger train operations from the residual StateRail (CityRail metropolitan passenger rail services and CountryLink long-distance services) together with responsibility for owning and maintaining the greater metropolitan network from the Rail Infrastructure Corporation.

Not all business changes "feel right." I stood down as audit committee chairman from one public sector entity following changes announced by a departmental secretary because the changes would have a profound effect on the organization's governance, risk, control, and compliance arrangements and its external accountability obligations (discussed in Chapter 11). Subsequent events validated my decision to stand down.

What It Means for Business

Boards may look to mergers and acquisitions when the growth of their company has stalled or when they are responding to disruptive innovation. The board might be looking for value creation or value enhancement by removing excess capacity, increasing market access, acquiring technology more quickly, developing new businesses, or improving the target company's performance.

A well-founded merger or acquisition can help to solidify the company's market position, eliminate competitors, fuel growth, and expand its operations. They can also help to quickly establish a brand in a growth market where the company being acquired is already in that market. The ultimate performance and finances of the merged entity will be shaped by elements overseen by the board, including the acquisition premium, bidding process, and due diligence.

The most successful mergers and acquisitions are delivered and stand the test of time when the board's strategy and the CEO's transition planning are strong and clear so that synergy benefits, economies of scale, and cultural compatibility are achieved. The smooth transition is typically underpinned by proper communication, clear strategies, and effective implementation.

Mergers and acquisitions *are transactions which transfer or consolidate the ownership of companies, other business organizations, or their operating units with other entities. The transactions are strategic in nature, aimed at changing the nature of the business or its competitive position through growth or downsizing. The assets and liabilities are usually consolidated into a single entity. An acquisition occurs when one entity takes ownership of the stock, equity interests or assets of another organization.*

Within the public sector, governments can use machinery of government changes to achieve a similar effect to mergers and acquisitions. For instance, they can create a new government agency; create a new portfolio or cluster; move agencies between portfolios; close an existing government agency; and/or move functions and responsibilities between agencies. Within this section, machinery of government changes will be treated as mergers and acquisitions.

Machinery of government *relates to the interconnected structures and processes of government, such as the functions and accountability of departments in the executive branch of government.* ***Machinery of government changes*** *refer to variations made by the government to established systems of public administration, including changes to the structure of government and the allocation of government functions between departments and ministers. It can involve the movement of functions, resources and people from one agency to another. Could also be called "administrative re-arrangements."*

While the board (or governing body) will usually establish an overarching strategy that knits together all of the pieces of the merger or acquisition into a cohesive model, the operational integration will usually be the responsibility of the CEO. Well-informed boards will utilize a structured framework to manage strategic elements of the merger or acquisition, covering elements such as market and purchasing power; market similarity and compatibilities (i.e., complementarities); and production operation similarity and compatibilitics.

The development of a new vision for the merged organization is imperative. The board needs to determine a broad, forward-thinking image for the organization before it sets out to reach its objectives and goals. In turn, the CEO will need to ensure that each business leader defines their role by determining how their business area fits into the new vision, and how it will work with other departments to fulfill this vision. Well-chosen business leaders, from line managers to executive management, will set in motion the structures, systems, technology, communications, and training to achieve the vision and shape the ideal culture.

The board will monitor progress strategically and should seek an independent post-merger review to help measure the success of the integration, commonly considering three lenses – absolute performance, relative performance, and the realization of synergies.

The CEO will need to develop a comprehensive transition plan with an eye for detail that covers all operational angles for the merged organization, including achieving a return on investment, understanding and embracing the regulatory environment, avoiding fragmentation, bringing employees along, retaining talent, aligning two cultures, coordinating employee benefits, determining product mix, integrating information communications and technology, merging the best processes, shaping innovation and collaboration, avoiding or closing service gaps, retrofitting physical spaces, and updating branding and signage.

Employee turnover can be a barrier to successful mergers and acquisitions, with some reports suggesting a significantly greater employee turnover in merged organizations in the ensuing decade compared to static or unmerged organizations. The CEO together with the head of HR need to address organizational behavior as a high priority, factoring in the relative size, cultural differences, and other variables of the respective organizations.

A communication strategy is imperative to clearly communicate to all invested parties how the integration will proceed, so as to alleviate fears, build trust, and motivate the new combined team. The communication strategy will serve to:

- Provide a relatable human face for the new merged entity for staff.
- Offer consistent messaging.
- Allow staff to engage in transition discussions through, say, town-hall-style meetings.

- Deliver regular updates on the transition process and information on upcoming changes.
- Encourage ideas from the frontline for innovation and integration.

The audit committee needs to carefully consider the impacts of mergers and acquisitions on the merged organization's overarching governance arrangements, risk management, control and compliance arrangements, and especially on the people. The committee should receive regular reports on progress.

CHAPTER 6 – TEN CLOSING REFLECTIONS

- Audit committees should establish a vision for internal audit in consultation with the board, CEO, and chief audit executive to encapsulate the future state of the internal audit function in 3–5 years' time; the chief audit executive should leverage the vision in determining the strategic priorities for maintaining the momentum, building capability, embracing leading edge practices, and enhancing the organization's governance arrangements.
- Audit committees should make reasonable enquiries to ensure the chief audit executive has sufficient budget/funding commensurate with the vision for internal audit; they should apply a reasonable, defensible basis to inform the board whether the internal audit activity is sufficiently resourced with competent professionals able to carry out the forward audit plan.
- Chief audit executives should invoke the right-to-audit clause in third-party supplier or shared services contracts when parts of an operational process that are being audited are within scope and are delivered through these arrangements; the third-party controls should be independently and objectively assessed.
- Audit committees should require the chief audit executive to establish KPIs, report them periodically to the audit committee in a balanced scorecard, embed the KPIs within the internal audit function, apply the KPIs in the performance assessment for all audit team leaders and auditors, and use the balanced scorecard results as a significant input into the assessment of the chief audit executive's performance.
- Boards and audit committees should ensure their organization has a whistleblower (or similar) policy in place that is

consistent with legislative obligations and aligned to corporate values.

- Business leaders should maintain effective communications with staff through open, constructive and systematic initiatives that shape a culture of professionalism and integrity, regardless of whether it is a business-as-usual or a changing business environment.
- Business leaders and audit committees should ensure that the corporate values and standards of professional behavior are embedded across the organization; rolled-out, periodically reinforced, tied into training and development, and included as part of the onboarding and orientation process for new staff; and applied consistently across the organization.
- Boards of multinational companies should determine whether the morality and behavior in operating divisions in developing nations mirrors how they would be expected to behave in their domestic markets, regardless of the local laws, given the impact of global transparency.
- Boards pursuing mergers or acquisitions (or similar) should establish an integration strategy; utilize a structured framework; develop a new vision and brand for the merged organization; consider structures, systems, technology, communications and training proposed by the CEO; monitor progress strategically including the CEOs transition plan; and commission an independent post-merger review to measure the success of the integration.
- Audit committees needs to carefully consider the impacts of mergers and acquisitions (or machinery of government changes in the public sector) on the merged organization's overarching governance arrangements, risk management, control and compliance arrangements, and especially on the people, with regular reports on progress.

7 Another Nudge in the Right Direction

Excellence in internal auditing can be a catalyst into other associated professional roles involving governance, risk, and compliance. These professions share a common language and are well-placed to engage with audit committees at a meaningful level on organizational performance and conformance. The chapter promotes the need for shared learning, meaningful workplace integration, and reporting collaboration … and it shines the line on egotistical investigation practices that can unconscionably disrupt the strategic direction of an organization and its leadership, and underlines the importance for audit committees to monitor investigation frameworks and activities. The words of the Greek philosopher Socrates (470–399 BC) remain valid to this day, "The secret of change is to focus your energy not on fighting the old but on building the new."

Entity Profile and Role

Sector:	Utilities sector energy distributor and retailer.
Entity:	Integral Energy Australia.
Entity metrics (2007):	• Net assets \$A1.1 billion. • Annual revenues \$A1.4 billion. • Annual net profit \$A191 million. • Staff 2,300.
Primary role:	Head of Audit and Risk (chief audit executive).
Main responsibilities:	Strategic responsibility and leadership for developing a strong internal audit and risk management function (including insurances), and for directing risk- based audits. Initial role covered entity-wide corporate governance, compliance, business continuity management, and fraud / corruption control.
Other executive roles:	Member of executive committees, including - Australian Financial Services Governance; Executive Audit; Business Compliance; Fraud Disclosure; and Contract Probity.
Timeframe:	The Fourth Decade.

PERSONAL STORY

Overall my time at StateRail was enjoyable and professionally rewarding. I especially valued the opportunity to work with many highly capable and committed people within my team, on the audit committee, at the executive level, and on the frontline. I had broadened my skillset through higher-level executive responsibilities, including direct oversight of major investigations, corruption prevention, and whistleblowers. We had assembled a well-regarded internal audit function that had embedded many innovative practices.

It was, however, a highly challenging three-year period as a result of the constant organizational and leadership changes, and the impact of the Waterfall tragedy in January 2003 (mentioned in Chapter 3). The executive's focus had shifted largely to the Special Commission of Inquiry into the Waterfall Rail Accident which ran for nearly two years, until the final report was released in January 2005 (the report was known as the McInerney Report, named after the judge who chaired the inquiry). The executive's focus on the inquiry was understandable; under workplace safety laws, executives could be held personally liable for negligence and faced hefty fines and potentially jail time.

As a result of the changes, the inquiry, the lived culture across the organization, constant daily travel, further restructuring, and the transformational agenda for my areas of responsibility, I was physically and emotionally drained when I left StateRail. Given my state of mind, I knew I needed a break from internal auditing after over two decades in the profession. It was a dignified exit, and I didn't realize it at the time but that would work in my favor a few years later when I was looking for an audit committee role (discussed in Chapter 11).

The corporate governance role at Integral Energy was just what I needed. I could leverage my experience while taking on broader responsibilities for corporate governance, risk, insurance, compliance, business continuity management, and fraud and corruption control. And, importantly, it gave me a break from internal auditing. I took a relatively significant pay-cut (of around 20 percent), which I felt was appropriate if I was to have the space I needed to reenergize and refresh my mental strength. A short vacation between StateRail and Integral Energy helped, and I was ready for the new challenge. Fortunately, I was well-equipped to make an immediate impact in my new corporate governance role.

After having my own office for much of my career beyond junior roles, it took me a while to adapt (well, *try* to adapt) to the open plan concept at Integral Energy where only a handful of the most senior executives had their own office. My designated work area was reasonably quiet as it was situated close to the CEO's office.

One of the things that open office planners tend to overlook is that the needs of introverts, like me, are different to others. Introverts need personal space, and this includes being in an office alone with the door closed to think and figure things out uninterrupted, and regain energy; being around others is tiring so introverts do need time alone.

There were some rumblings within the organization about the value of the internal audit function. There was also a sense that the incumbent chief audit executive felt threatened by my presence given my internal auditing pedigree. I made it clear that I was there to focus on corporate governance, and I had no interest in moving back into the world of audit.

Almost a year into my time at Integral Energy, I was asked to take over the internal audit area. I baulked, as I wasn't keen to do so. The CEO and the CFO spoke with me encouraging me to take on the challenge. I relented after a while on the condition that it would not be a clean swap; I would give up some of my functions, such as compliance management, but would retain the others. I was not trying to build an empire, rather I was keen to finish reshaping these areas and to broaden my skills and experience. The change was announced. It did not accord with what I had agreed, and I was to lose key areas of my portfolio like risk management. So, I made the difficult decision to resign, partly reflecting my personal values (i.e., deals should be honored) and partly because I was still mentally fragile. This caused quite a kerfuffle. The board had been informed of the change.

Hasty discussions were arranged to convince me to stay. And I agreed to do so when the originally proposed arrangement was to be honored. I committed to being the Head of Audit and Risk, and I reported administratively to the newly appointed Company Secretary, Irina White, who I had worked with briefly at StateRail in the lead-up to the 2004 merger (I reported functionally directly to the board audit committee). Irina was an excellent leader; I enjoyed reconnecting and driving the change agenda. With the support of a strong well-balanced audit and risk team, we managed to reshape the function and enhance its reputation.

After several years at Integral Energy, I was ready to move back into a more significant chief audit executive role. I accepted the Chief Internal Auditor role at the Australian Taxation Office, one of the largest public sector organizations in the Southern Hemisphere. In a further twist, my former role at Integral Energy was filled through the appointment of Clarita Imperial, my past colleague and boss from the Reserve Bank of Australia.

The key insights from this phase of my story are:

- Work within the business.
- Shape good investigations governance.
- Inspire a culture of integrity.
- Apply risk management across the business.
- Maintain effective compliance.
- Ensure business continuity.
- Monitor insurance arrangements.

EXHIBIT 7.1 Working within the business.

CONTEXT

A critical success factor for governance, risk, compliance, and assurance specialists is their ability to work within the business to deliver what boards and business leaders truly need. Some of these elements are discussed in this chapter and illustrated in **Exhibit 7.1**.

KEY TAKEAWAYS AND DEEP DIVES

Work within the Business

Setting the Scene

When I joined the railways, I knew very little about its people or its operations. Soon after I joined, the executive team established an "At the Front" program that required every senior executive to spend at least half a day each month in the field working with or shadowing people in critical frontline positions.

It was a fantastic program that allowed me to develop an understanding of the business, particularly its three key customer commitment themes for a clean, safe, and reliable railway. It was a program I committed to, and I had my executive assistant build time into my diary every month. In the end, I visited 27 different work locations across almost three years, and on these visits, I completed cleaning tasks (on trains and on stations), provided customer service (ticket-selling, barrier ticketing control, lost property), assisted with revenue protection, maintained crowd control at major events (including a rugby union world cup), observed closed circuit television (CCTV) operations, completed customer surveys, and helped at a health and wellness fair. I also observed train maintenance, rail management, and train drivers at the wheel on several different types of train.

The two most challenging visits were:

- Carriage cleaning at night at a site where the ground temperature was 95 degrees Fahrenheit (35 degrees Celsius). It was physically exhausting work, compounded by the heat (the air-conditioning is turned off at night) and the risk of needle sticks (unfortunately drug users occasionally leave their equipment on the trains).
- Customer service on the XPT (express train service) from Sydney to the regional city of Dubbo, a round trip of 500 miles (800 km) which took 12 hours. I thought I'd rest on the return trip and do some work-related reading, but the staff were so excited to have a senior executive on the journey they planned activities for me for the whole trip. Naturally I obliged.

After the visits, I received positive notes from the staff with whom I interacted. As an example, one station assistant commented, "I am grateful that firstly you are taking part on this 'At the Front' program as someone like yourself can learn about the work we do and how we operate at a station level. This is a great initiative. Although I was nervous at first, I was pleased to have met you. Secondly, you have made a wonderful impression. And last, our team were pleased that you were pleased with your visit."

The visits provided lasting memories, and my jottings reflected upon the following: The hustle and bustle at ticket barriers; the wrath of customers when trains were delayed; most customers were understanding in a crisis as long as they were well-informed; the physical work; the need for caution in using tongs to pick up needles, and, the enthusiasm of staff for the program at every location.

After each visit, I provided feedback to the operations executives, and this was wide-ranging, including suggestions to improve the train driver's development program; personal safety concerns of revenue protection staff (ticket inspectors); problems of serving alcohol on long-distance country trains; duplication of work effort on manual and computer systems; verification of third-party bookings; bad practices for which the local staff didn't know who to inform; and, in one instance, the station assistant was using a broken old mop because they didn't have enough money for a new mop.

What It Means for Business

To be truly effective, governance, risk, compliance, and assurance specialists should never sit at the side of the business as an afterthought, rather they need to operate within the business. And this requires them to gain the respect of business leaders and operational staff by *knowing* the business. It is imperative they develop wide-ranging knowledge and capabilities with an extensive business perspective to do their jobs well. They should also be able to consider business operations through both the performance and conformance lenses (discussed further in Chapter 12).

Research suggests working within the business requires governance, risk, compliance, and assurance specialists to present several distinct features.[1] Notably:

- Demonstrating a strategic flair with a "big picture" understanding of how the business works to make money or otherwise deliver services.
- Understanding what underpins the success of the organization – its industry, external environment, chosen strategies and business, and risks related to those strategies and business.
- Spending time with those in their organization who can help them think more like a business leader.
- Understanding the pulse of the organization, its objectives, its products and services, its customers, changes in competition, related industry developments, processes, operations and technologies, and its regulatory environment.
- Addressing issues from the stakeholder's point of view, communicating with them using language that they understand.

CEOs and business leaders should consider the merits of introducing an "At the Front" program that is tailored for their organization. While it is especially beneficial for governance, risk, compliance, and assurance specialists, it can be equally applied to other business leaders. Having gained so much from working within the business through an "At the Front" program, it is an approach that I adopted in all my roles over the final decade of my career. And I encouraged my staff to do likewise.

An "At the Front" program is beneficial on a number of fronts for the executives involved, the staff, and the organization. It helps the staff gain insights on the strategic direction, reinforces the benefits of customer service commitment, sharpens the focus on safety or other imperatives, enhances the communication loop, and builds workplace relationships.

[1] Bruce R. Turner, *Team Leaders Guide to Internal Audit Leadership* (Lake Mary, FL: Internal Audit Foundation, 2020), 29–30.

Executives gain firsthand exposure to operational risk management, gain insights into daily routines of frontline staff, identify improvement opportunities, demonstrate leadership, and help make things happen (even something as simple as a new mop for the station assistant). In turn, it helps the organization to drive its vision, mission, values, objectives, and strategies.

Shape Good Investigations Governance

Setting the Scene

Internal auditors have a broad mandate to operate in an independent and objective manner, and in some organizations, they are tasked with undertaking investigations of wrongdoing. However, internal auditors and others conducting investigations are still obliged to adhere to organizational policies and avoid activities that are not authorized under the internal audit charter and the approved forward audit plan. When left unchecked, corporate investigators could develop egotistical investigation practices that unconscionably disrupt the strategic direction of an organization and its leadership.

In one organization, we received allegations that a chief audit executive had been monitoring the emails of senior people, including the governing body, and audit committee, for no proper or authorized purpose (discussed in Chapter 11), in breach of organizational policies and the trust of the position.

There have been instances where I have been unintentionally misled by investigation reports that have (or could have) compromised my objective analysis. Examples include:

- On considering a "final investigation report," it became apparent that there remained "loose ends" that were never clearly identified in the report.
- There were errors of fact in the report, and incomplete and unvalidated data. For example, total amounts quoted in the report were not backed up by schedules of individual amounts contained in the investigator's work-papers; it then took eight weeks to substantiate the total amounts (which ultimately highlighted flaws in the investigator's analysis).
- Interpretations of legislative requirements were not supported by expert advice (and this was not disclosed).
- The outcome (or conclusion) was inconsistent with the facts reported.
- Procedural fairness was not demonstrated, and a reasonable due process was not followed. For instance, interviews were conducted without proper notice, interviews were recorded without actual confirmed consent and positive agreement, and a relatively junior staff member interviewed senior executives.

These examples (and others I have experienced) underline the importance for audit committees to monitor investigation frameworks and activities. Corporate investigators play an important role in an organization's governance and need to apply contemporary governance practices to provide credibility when reporting on the outcomes of investigations. Notably, these practices include:

- Applying investigation standards, independence, and principles; demonstrating the capability of investigative resources; maintaining overarching quality assurance practices; and according protections to employees under investigation (see discussion on charters of rights in Chapter 8).
- Enabling audit committees to minimize internal investigative process failures through effective governance oversight of the corporate investigation activity, while ensuring that the confidentiality and secrecy of individual investigations is maintained.

What It Means for Business

Different areas within an organization might be tasked with undertaking investigations of employee wrongdoing, including fraud, corruption, bullying, harassment, discrimination, and other poor behavior. Because investigations need to be undertaken confidentially, investigators typically complete their work with much less direct oversight and scrutiny than other governance, risk, compliance, and assurance roles.

Inevitably, every investigation conducted internally by corporate investigators has inherent downside risks irrespective of whether or not allegations are substantiated. Where allegations are substantiated, management will consider disciplinary action commensurate with the seriousness of the matters, and will assess the broader impacts on other workers, operations, internal controls, and culture in the same business unit. Even where employees who are the subject of investigations are cleared of the allegations (or the allegations are not proven), there is likely to be an adverse impact on their productivity through their disengagement, loss of morale, and de-motivation because of the stresses involved in any investigation that calls into question their integrity.

Audit committees and management typically maintain an "arms-length" approach that enables investigators to perform their role in an independent, objective, impartial, and confidential manner. This is appropriate. However, internal investigative process failures can and do occur. There are practical steps that audit committees can take to maintain effective oversight of the fraud and corruption investigations activity without affecting the confidentiality and secrecy of individual investigations.

Corporate investigators are usually very solid at undertaking their investigations and delivering a report specific to the allegations investigated.

They are less well-developed in applying their investigative mindset on strategic, leadership, human resource, and damage control considerations that the senior executives need to know when they receive investigation reports. Root cause analysis is an approach that corporate investigators could use to better inform management of actions they need to take to address the underlying conditions beyond the specific allegations that have been investigated. These insights can enhance the reporting on specific allegations, and on the control framework as a whole.

The chief audit executive (or the executive responsible for investigations if it is someone else) should take steps in consultation with the audit committee chair to:

- Establish and maintain a consolidated investigations manual that clearly documents investigation standards, protocols, methodology, techniques, quality assurance arrangements, and a charter of rights.
- Establish and maintain effective quality assurance arrangements, and periodically report the results to the audit committee (at least annually).
- Periodically deliver to the audit committee a profile of the capability, qualifications, and experience of investigators (at least annually, or when significant changes occur).
- Introduce (or enhance) high-level reporting to the audit committee on the outcomes of investigations.

The features of good investigations governance are summarized in **Exhibit 7.2**.

Inspire a Culture of Integrity

Setting the Scene

Former US President, Dwight D. Eisenhower, once commented, "The supreme quality for leadership is unquestionably integrity. Without it, no real success is possible, no matter whether it is on a section gang, a football field, in an army, or in an office."

> *The principles of* ***integrity*** *refer to the commitment to consider people equally without prejudice or favor; act professionally with honesty, consistency, and impartiality; and take responsibility for situations, showing leadership and courage. Within the public sector, it also encompasses a commitment to place the public interest over personal interest.*

EXHIBIT 7.2
Features of good investigations governance[2]

Element	Comments
Investigations manual	Audit Committees need to understand all elements of investigation activities, which should be documented in an approved and up-to-date investigation manual. The investigation manual will usually include appropriate information on: • Mandate of investigators and their rights to undertake investigations. • Legislative requirements and compliance obligations. • The standards, principles, protocols, methodology, and techniques applied. • Rules of evidence and documentation requirements, including secure storage and preservation of evidence. • The process for determining action for allegations. • Management of conflicts of interest and impartiality. • Planning, approval and escalation points. • Conduct (including proper protocols for recording interviews and timeframe KPIs). • Referrals to law enforcement and other outside agencies including police and the corruption watchdog. • Reaching conclusions and recommendations. • Delivering internal reporting. • The process for taking action against substantiated allegations. While Audit Committees will not need to have a detailed knowledge of the investigation manual, they should seek assurance that it is (and remains) "fit for purpose."

Quality assurance	Corporate investigators should be required to adopt a quality assurance and improvement approach that is consistent with the approach applied by internal auditors (in line with standard 1300 of the International Professional Practices Framework); that is, internal quality reviews; periodic external quality assessments; and, continuing professional development. Effective quality control processes will ensure (amongst others) that: • Investigations are not reported until the work is completed and reviewed by someone independent for reasonableness. • Any qualifications on the scope, objectives, and approach for an investigation are clear and unambiguous. • Recommendations are clear, understandable, and practical. • Emotion and personal bias are eliminated. • Boards and audit committees do not receive reports that are incomplete or unclear.
Profile of investigators	While the board, audit committee, and CEO rely on the expertise of investigators in the completion of investigations and in preserving an appropriate "tone at the top," these leaders rarely have a good understanding of the individual and collective backgrounds of investigation staff (e.g., business experience, qualifications, certifications, years of investigative experience (including level of complexity), and continuing professional development). A leading practice for audit committees is to receive a report each year on the profile of specialist governance, risk and audit professionals. That approach should be explicitly extended to investigation staff with a profile of investigators reported to the audit committee as least annually.

(*Continued*)

EXHIBIT 7.2 (*Continued*)

Features of good investigations governance

Element	Comments
High-level reporting	***Open Investigations*** Audit committees require consolidated quarterly reporting on open investigations, including: • Running tally (number of investigations brought forward from last period, new investigations, closed investigations, matters referred elsewhere (e.g., law enforcement agency), new total carried forward to next quarter). • Number of investigations (or allegations) currently open per category (e.g., *corruption* – conflicts of interest, bribery, illegal gratuities, economic extortion; *asset misappropriation* – cash, inventory, other assets; *financial statement fraud* – net worth / net income overstatements, net worth / net income understatements). • Source of investigations (which can be through internal channels including "whistleblowers," or external channels including corruption/ law enforcement agencies). • An ageing of investigations to indicate whether investigations are completed in a timely manner. • Information on the number of employees who have been stood down (on pay or without pay) or reassigned while investigations are being completed, with assurance that the status of these employees is being actively managed and the CEO is being kept informed. ***Completed Investigations*** Audit committees require consolidated quarterly reporting on completed investigations, including: • Number of completed investigations (or allegations) per category and whether they were substantiated, not substantiated, or other result. • The sanctions applied (where allegations have been substantiated) so the audit committee has visibility, to assess the consistency of decision-making. • Root cause/s for each substantiated allegation. • Any themes, systemic issues, or early indicators of emerging risks and how they will be handled, including strategic, leadership, human resource, and damage control considerations. • Lessons learned that can be incorporated into corruption prevention (or similar), risk management, and compliance activities, including training, ongoing reinforcement / education, and internal communications.

[2] Bruce Turner, *Audit Committee Oversight of the Fraud and Corruption Investigations Activity* (Sydney, Australia: The Institute of Internal Auditors Australia, 2020), 3–6

Integrity is reflected through people doing the right thing at all times and in all circumstances, irrespective of whether someone is watching or not. It can take many years for an organization or an individual to establish a reputation of integrity, and it is a value that lasts forever unless it is tarnished. As an example:

- WorldCom – MCI, Inc. (previously Worldcom and MCI WorldCom) was a telecommunications company. For a time, it was the second largest long-distance telephone company in the United States, after AT&T. The company grew largely by acquiring other telecommunications companies and filed for bankruptcy in 2002 after an accounting scandal, in which several executives, including CEO Bernard Ebbers, were convicted of a scheme to inflate the company's assets. Mr. Ebbers was convicted on nine counts of securities fraud and sentenced to 25 years in prison in 2005 (he was granted early release from prison in 2019 for health reasons after serving 14 years of his sentence). The former CFO, Scott Sullivan, received a five-year jail sentence.
- Barings Bank – Barings Bank was a British merchant bank based in London, and the world's second oldest merchant bank after Berenberg Bank. It was founded in 1762 by Francis Baring, a British-born member of the German-British Baring family of merchants and bankers. The bank collapsed in 1995 after suffering losses of £827 million (equivalent to £1.6 billion in 2019) resulting from fraudulent investments, primarily in futures contracts, conducted by its employee Nick Leeson, working at its office in Singapore.

Breaches of integrity can also adversely affect the bottom line. The Report to the Nations 2018 Global Study of Occupational Fraud and Abuse published by the Association of Certified Fraud Examiners (ACFE) estimates that organizations lose 5 percent of their annual revenues to fraud.[3] The ACFE "Fraud Tree" splits occupational fraud and abuse into a three-pillar classification system of corruption, asset misappropriation, and financial statement fraud.

Integrity shortcomings can also pervade wider industry. The final report into the Royal Commission into Misconduct in the Banking, Superannuation and Financial Services Industry (royal commission) in Australia was tabled in parliament in February 2019 (discussed further in Chapter 2). In his introduction to the final report, the commissioner reflected:

> The conduct identified and described in the Commission's (reports) includes conduct by many entities that has taken place over many

[3] Report to the Nations: 2018 Global Study of Occupational Fraud and Abuse, Association of Certified Fraud Examiners, 2018, p 8.

> years causing substantial loss to many customers but yielding substantial profit to the entities concerned. Very often, the conduct has broken the law. And if it has not broken the law, the conduct has fallen short of the kind of behaviour the community not only expects of financial services entities but is also entitled to expect of them.

The royal commission unleashed evidence of appalling behavior, reflecting examples of poor organizational and personal integrity, including bribery, forged documents, lying to regulators, charging financial planning fees to clients who had died, repeated failure to verify customers' living expenses before lending them money, and mis-selling insurance to people who cannot afford it.

The royal commission outcomes resulted in disastrous reputational damage for some financial institutions. For one, the media reported that because of revelations at the royal commission, $2.2 billion was wiped off the company's market value, its full-year profit plummeted 97 percent, revenue from ordinary operations slumped 55 percent, and its final dividend fell from 14½ cents to 4 cents per share.

What It Means for Business

The community's "pendulum of expectation" has shifted back towards a need for undoubted organizational and personal integrity because of recent scandals reported by public inquiries, corporate and employee misbehavior, and increased media focus.

Strong stakeholder awareness of organizational values helps to bolster the practical application of integrity and, consequently, minimizes the risk of fraud (including corruption). Building and sustaining good governance and employee integrity requires ongoing attention and effort. Effective leadership and positive organizational cultures enable the implementation of good governance systems and foster employee integrity. CEOs, managers, and employees each have a role to play in promoting integrity.

> ***Promoting integrity*** *means developing and maintaining an organizational culture and/or environment that supports ethical conduct. It involves making expectations about individual conduct clear and ensuring the entity has robust systems, policies, and processes in place to support ethical behavior. Importantly, entities need to focus on both the ethical conduct of individual employees and good organizational governance (i.e., performance and accountability).*

Complacency remains a significant challenge for most organizations in curbing fraud, especially where an attitude pervades of "It couldn't happen here!." A contemporary solution involves the ABCs of good practice, for example:

- **A**cknowledging fraud risks through monitoring fraud and integrity trends and events, understanding risk indicators, undertaking fraud risk assessments, and considering fraud risks in decision-making.
- **B**olstering preventive and detective controls through an awareness of fraud indicators, maintaining meaningful whistleblower programs and a conflicts of interest framework, conducting effective investigations, and maintaining a holistic compliance framework.
- **C**hampioning cultural awareness through strong leadership, clear organizational values and standards, a meaningful policy framework underpinned by an honest and ethical culture, and audit committee oversight.

In some organizations, the chief audit executive has a direct responsibility for fraud prevention, in which case the following action steps provide a basis for periodic review. In other situations, the organization's fraud prevention activities may be subject to periodic risk-based internal audits, in which case the action steps will aid in these independent evaluations. These action steps are equally relevant for other governance, risk management, compliance, and fraud prevention professionals; they are illustrated in **Exhibit 7.3**, followed by a description of steps to consider.

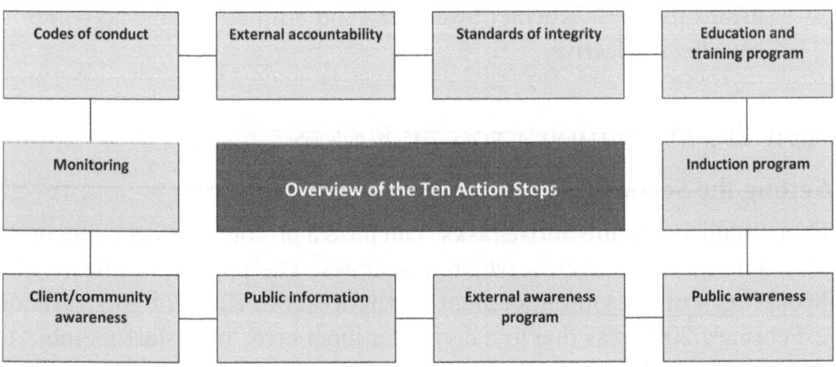

EXHIBIT 7.3 Ten action steps for shining the light on an organization's values of integrity.[4]

[4] Bruce Turner, *Fraud Prevention: 10 action steps* (Sydney: Institute of Internal Auditors Australia, 2019), 5.

The audit committee should receive periodic assurance on the ten action steps, covering the following (which are expanded upon – see appendices):[5]

1. Assess the currency, availability, and awareness of the organization's **Codes of Conduct** (that is, the code of conduct for employees, the Board Code of Conduct (if it is separate), and the Statement of Business Ethics for suppliers/contractors – see Chapter 12).
2. Assess the reasonableness and meaningfulness of the organization's reporting on its **external accountability** requirements.
3. Assess whether the organization has established and communicated clear and unambiguous **standards of integrity** under which it operates.
4. Determine whether the organization has a structured **education and training program** to assist employees recognize, detect, and prevent fraud.
5. Assess the adequacy of the organization's **induction program** including organizational values.
6. Assess the extent to which the organization has sufficiently raised **public awareness** by arranging for the general public to have easy access to key conduct and fraud-related documents.
7. Assess the adequacy of the organization's **external awareness program**.
8. Determine whether the organization has a robust **public information** and community relations role.
9. Assess the reasonableness of the organization's **client and community awareness** program.
10. Determine whether the organization maintains structured **monitoring** of its awareness program through surveys and other means to assess whether awareness and attitude change activities have been effective.

Apply Risk Management across the Business

Setting the Scene

Even "routine administrative tasks" can have a profound effect on an organization and the market in which it operates. The premature release of a Monetary Policy Announcement by the Reserve Bank of Australia on 2 February 2000 was due to a computer-input error by a staff member in the bank's Information Office.

The error resulted in the Monetary Policy Announcement being inadvertently released to 62 recipients of an email at 9:24 a.m., six minutes before the intended time of release at 9:30 a.m. The premature release had

[5] Ibid, 5–7.

a clear impact on trading on the Sydney Futures Exchange and in the foreign exchange market, though it did not seem to have had much impact in physical securities markets.

Some large trades took place in those six minutes which resulted in opportunistic profits for a small number of market participants estimated to be in the order of $A2 million on the foreign exchange market and a further $A2.15 million on the futures exchange (i.e., aggregate from trading, including March bill futures contracts $A800,000; June bill futures contracts $A150,000; three-year bond contracts $A1.2 million).[6]

A review of the bank's arrangements for the release of market-sensitive information established that the premature release was not motivated by malice or the desire for gain, and reflected:

> The immediate contributing factors (to the error) were the absence on leave of the officer who usually carries out this function, insufficient care by the relieving officer in carrying out her duties, and inadequate supervision. The more fundamental cause, however, is that, in order to try to provide the greatest possible level of service to "clients" in terms of timely receipt of releases, staff of the Information Office have adopted procedures which carry risks.[7]

At the time the error occurred, the Information Office was processing an average of 20 media releases a week (about 1,000 annually), with releases varying from highly market-sensitive information to more routine matters. There are five primary operational risks for the bank in releasing market-sensitive information, including:

- Premature release of the information through one of the various distribution channels.
- Errors in media releases.
- Leaking of information (deliberately or inadvertently).
- Transmission of an unauthorized media release.
- Delays in the release of information.

What It Means for Business

Business leaders who effectively manage risks are more likely to succeed in growing their business. They achieve this by integrating good risk management practices into their day-to-day operations and apply them to the

[6] Media Release: Statement by the Governor, Mr. Ian Macfarlane, *Review of the Reserve Bank's Arrangements for Releasing Market-Sensitive Information*, Number 2000-06, 18 February 2000. https://www.rba.gov.au/media-releases/2000/mr-00-06.html (sourced 17 June 2020).

[7] Ibid.

wider aspects of their organizational arrangements. This typically results in improving operational efficiency, enhancing governance and stakeholder confidence, establishing a strong foundation for decision-making, boosting health and safety performance, maintaining effective compliance with relevant legislation, encouraging proactive management, and minimizing losses.

The international standard for risk management (ISO31000) provides guidelines, principles, a framework, and a process for managing business risks to facilitate risk analysis and risk assessments. The standard is designed for all organizations, regardless of size, activity or sector. It was last updated in 2018 to:

- Review the principles of risk management, which are the key criteria for its success.
- Focus on leadership by top management who should ensure that risk management is integrated into all organizational activities, starting with the governance of the organization.
- Provide greater emphasis on the iterative nature of risk management, drawing on new experiences, knowledge, and analysis for the revision of process elements, actions and controls at each stage of the process.
- Streamline the content with greater focus on sustaining an open systems model that regularly exchanges feedback with its external environment to fit multiple needs and contexts.

*The **risk appetite** is the level of risk that the board (or governing body) is prepared to accept. **Risk management** is a process to identify, assess, manage, and control potential events or situations to provide reasonable assurance regarding the achievement of the organization's objectives. **Business risks** are all risks to the organization including operational, financial, compliance, and strategic risks. In turn, **internal controls** are any actions taken by management, the board, and other parties to manage risk and increase the likelihood that established objectives and goals will be achieved.*

The chief risk officer should establish enterprise risk management arrangements in line with the policies established by the board and in accordance with the international risk management standard (ISO31000). These arrangements will typically include:[8]

- Championing the establishment of enterprise risk management.
- Setting the risk appetite in collaboration with the board.

[8] *Position Paper: The Role of Internal Auditing in Enterprise-wide Risk Management* (Altamonte Springs, FL; The Institute of Internal Auditors, 2009). Elements recast and modified.

- Developing a risk management strategy for board approval.
- Imposing risk management processes based on board-approved policies.
- Developing and maintaining the risk management framework.
- Facilitating the identification and evaluation of risks.
- Coaching management in responding to risks.
- Coordinating risk management arrangements.
- Managing risk assurance arrangements.
- Determining the reasonableness of risk responses.
- Implementing specific risk responses when delegated by the CEO.
- Assuming accountability for risk management coordination.
- Consolidating the reporting on risks.

The audit committee should receive periodic assurance from the chief audit executive that core enterprise risk management elements are in place and operating as intended. These include:[9]

- Reflecting how well the risk appetite (introduced in chapter 1) is applied across the organization.
- Giving assurance on the risk management processes.
- Giving assurance that risks are correctly evaluated.
- Evaluating risk management processes.
- Evaluating the reporting of key risks.
- Reviewing the management of key risks.

RISK AWARENESS DOES NOT ALWAYS RESULT IN GOOD DECISION-MAKING

There are reportedly an estimated 5 million alligators spread out across southeastern US, and people in states with alligator populations recognize they are dangerous, frightening animals. Their jaws can exert up to 2,000 pounds of pressure when closed. It is well-recognized the reptiles present a high inherent risk of death or injury to humans.

A 58-year-old nail technician in South Carolina spotted an alligator in her back yard when completing a home manicure on her porch, while enjoying a glass of wine. Despite the risk, she decided to go down into the yard to take some photographs. She was undeterred, even after her friends mentioned that they'd seen an alligator kill a deer recently. The woman remarked, "I don't look like a deer" as she attempted to touch the alligator. The reptile attacked her, and

[9] Ibid.

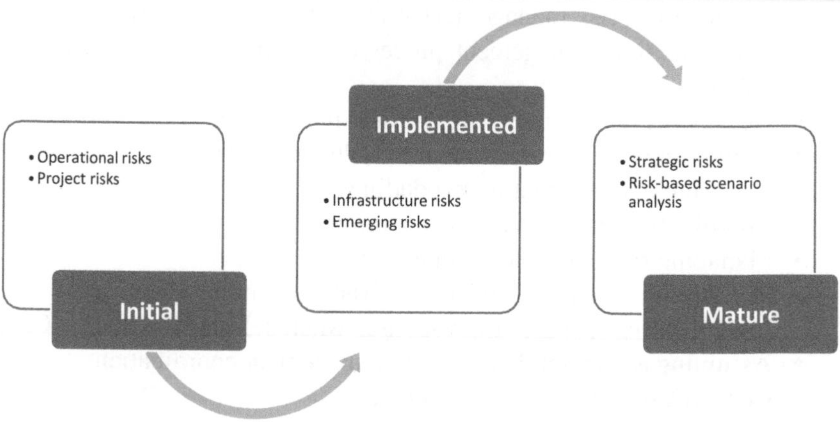

EXHIBIT 7.4 Risk reporting maturity.

dragged her into the pond. She was thrown a rope by her friends, and when she surfaced remarked quite coolly, "I guess I won't do this again." Alas! the alligator wasn't finished, and she was again taken by the alligator and was, sadly, killed.

Note: Developed by the author from media reports.

The board (or its audit or risk committee) should receive regular risk reporting covering strategic risks, operational risks, project risks, infrastructure risks, risk-based scenario analysis, and emerging risks.

The extent of risk reporting will usually reflect the maturity of the organization's enterprise risk management as illustrated in **Exhibit 7.4**.

Better risk reporting to the board and audit committee will improve the richness and strategic nature of the discussions. **Exhibit 7.5** contains examples of the different risk reporting types in a hospital setting to illustrate how this information will spark different conversations that result in strategic action.

Boards should expect an active and informed audit committee to provide independent and objective oversight of the organization's lived corporate culture and the overall control environment, including insights on emerging trends and risks. Audit committees tend to view their responsibilities through different lenses that have both a primary and secondary focus as illustrated in the example in **Exhibit 7.6** (these will change over time in line with environment factors).

Risks and hazards are managed through established internal controls with well-formed arrangements typically relying on three control layers – systems and processes; capability; and culture. The premise is that with these separate control layers, lapses, and weaknesses in one defense do

EXHIBIT 7.5
Examples of risk reporting types

Type of Risk Reporting	Example[10]
Operational risks	Hospital performance is below benchmarks and contracted levels due to a lack of capacity to meet demand for emergency treatment. Lost capacity for lifesaving surgeries due to closure of operating rooms because of dangerous levels of fungal contamination that is not responding to typical cleansing, and treatment protocols.
Project risks	An urgent decision is required on funding for digitizing new hospital wards in a property under construction as it will affect the design. Technology implementation would involve a long lead-time, potentially impacting the overall project timeline. A highly complex $100 million hospital development is underway on asbestos-related contaminated land with remediation of the land required within the project's funding envelope. There are significant variables and a tight government-imposed time-frame.
Infrastructure risks	Failure of medical imaging equipment is resulting in high-risk patients being turned away to other hospitals, requiring a two-hour commute.
Emerging risks	Global insights point to increasing cyber risks, which could severely impact critical patient care systems, and ultimately patient wellbeing if the hospital's technological security was compromised.
Strategic risks	An increase in patient demand due to unprecedented growth in local population is outstripping the capacity of the workforce to treat and care for patients. Deteriorating assets coupled with a significant asset maintenance backlog could compromise the hospital's capability to maintain its quality accreditation, agreed service levels, and its license to operate.
Risk-based scenario analysis	The CEO became aware of a small hospital that lost power and its backup generators failed due to extreme heatwave conditions (temperatures hit 110°F, whereas the generators were designed for heat under 90°F). Disruptions were minimized as the event occurred on a low-demand weekend. Under risk-based scenario analysis, the board would be informed of the event, and the current risk mitigation strategies at its organization. The board will then understand how this type of incident would be managed if it happened at one of their large hospitals at peak demand time.

[10] Bruce R. Turner, *Team Leaders Guide to Internal Audit Leadership* (Lake Mary, FL: Internal Audit Foundation, 2020), 142. Modified.

EXHIBIT 7.6
Examples of audit committee areas of focus

Primary Focus	Secondary Focus
• Tone at the top of the organization • How well the values are embedded in the organization • Whether the desired culture and lived culture are in sync • Effectiveness of management in achieving objectives • Effectiveness of governance and compliance processes • The completeness and effectiveness of assurance • How well board committees collaborate	• Cyber vulnerabilities • Financial reporting • Reputation risk • Security and safety • Operations and service delivery • Internal auditor "value add" • External auditor credibility

not allow a risk to materialize, since other defenses also exist, to prevent a single point of failure. The concept was originally presented by James Reason in 1990 as the "Swiss cheese model" (sometimes called the "cumulative act effect").

Maintain Effective Compliance

Setting the Scene

Compliance failures inevitably impact the reputation of an organization and its ability to operate, and can result in fines, prosecution, loss of contracts, complaints, and litigation for the organization and its senior officers, and potentially imprisonment for senior officers. By way of example:

- Media reports suggested that mining companies across the world in the early-2020s view the risk of losing their license to operate as the biggest risk to their businesses.
- A ride share company failed in its quest to be granted a new license to operate in London because it was found to be not "fit and proper" after repeated safety failures. London was one of the company's top five global markets with approximately 45,000 drivers; some drivers were found to have been unlicensed and uninsured.
- An iconic bank (one of the top 50 banks in the world) reached agreement in 2018 with a national regulator for a $A700 million penalty relating to serious breaches of anti-money laundering and counter-terrorism financing laws; quite simply, the bank failed to notify the regulator of thousands of cash transactions above the

legislated value. At the time, this represented the largest ever civil penalty in Australian corporate history.[11]

- Media reports in 2020 suggest that the national regulator is likely to fine another bank $A1.3 billion for breaching anti-money-laundering and counter-terrorism financing laws, and hindering tax enforcement action. "If the Federal Court determines the proposed penalty is appropriate, the penalty order made will represent the largest ever civil penalty in Australian history."[12]
- A Michigan facility for teenagers with behavioral problems lost its contract with the state to care for youth in the state's foster care and juvenile justice systems and its license to operate following the death of a teenager who was wrongly restrained by staff. The regulator identified ten licensing violations in 2020, including a failure to follow rules related to restraint and discipline.
- Companies using computer software outside of the license terms (i.e., piracy) could face prosecution or hefty fines; one UK company was fined a reported £250,000 for using unlicensed software.
- At an individual level, motor vehicle drivers in France can lose their driving loss license for up to six months if caught using mobile phones whilst driving (this includes talking (even while using headphones), texting, holding the phone or looking at it in a way that takes attention away from driving, touching the buttons or screen, or engaging with the device in any way).

Energy companies have to comply with strict legislative and regulatory requirements to maintain their license to operate given the inherent safety risks associated with handling electricity, gas, and other energy products. These requirements come on top of the usual legislative obligations associated with work health and safety, registration of business name, human resources, industrial relations, environment, security, information privacy, national competition, privacy, freedom-of-information, transparency, taxation, anti-corruption, external accountability (including financial reporting), and others.

There are also personal licensing obligations that energy companies need to monitor for some roles, including electricians, security guards, helicopter pilots, and motor vehicle, truck and fork lifts drivers. Motor vehicles in the organization's fleet will have compliance plates, while software licenses underpin technology solutions. Boards also need to comply

[11] Australian Transaction Reports and Analysis Centre (AUSTRAC) Media Release, 5 June 2018, "AUSTRAC and CBA agree $700 m penalty": 1–2.

[12] AUSTRAC Media Release, 24 September 2020, "AUSTRAC and Westpac agree to proposed $1.3 bn penalty."

with the organization's establishing legislation or constitution, and need assurance of compliance with significant contractual conditions.

All of these legislative, regulatory, and constitutional requirements are typically translated into company policies, procedures, and workplace instructions. After a few months at Integral Energy, the CEO decided that constant internal audit reports identifying outdated policies and procedures needed to be addressed holistically, rather than through a piecemeal approach. I was asked to head up a task force of executives from each division, to review and update every policy and procedure; there were thousands, given the dangerous elements of the organization (energy distribution and supply).

The task force successfully fulfilled its objectives, with impressive results. The exercise helped me to establish a reputation for getting things done, and, importantly, shaped strong stakeholder engagement across all business areas within a relatively short period of time.

To monitor compliance, the company had:

- Four board committees, all of which covered different elements of compliance – audit and risk; retail trading risk; remuneration and human resources; and high-value transaction approval.
- Five executive committees, each with a substantial compliance focus – major contract review; environmental; network capital governance; occupational health and safety; and financial services license.

As head of audit and risk, I maintained a multi-level compliance approach that included:

- Me attending key executive committee meetings as an observer and participant (the charters contained suitable wording to preserve internal audit independence).
- Training and developing internal audit staff to fulfil the full ambit of their compliance-related responsibilities under the internal audit charter and in the risk-based internal audit plan.
- Complementing internal resources with specialist technical compliance resources from a service provider firm (e.g., work health and safety specialists) where needed.
- Scheduling a periodic high-level internal audit to assess the compliance baseline, the register of compliance risks, and the overarching compliance framework to determine how well the core elements were operating in practice.
- Scheduling individual compliance-related audits in the approved internal audit plan to determine whether established controls over

compliance risks were operating in practice in line with established policies and procedures.
- Providing assurance to the audit committee on the organization's arrangements for undertaking compliance risk assessments, identifying compliance strategies, creating awareness, promoting compliance, fostering continuous improvement, establishing monitoring mechanisms, maintaining the compliance register, and producing meaningful compliance reporting.
- Overseeing regulatory reviews as the organization's central coordination point for the regulator's review team to ensure a smooth and seamless process.
- Monitoring the implementation of significant regulatory recommendations as part of the routine internal audit process for monitoring and reporting on the implementation of audit and other recommendations.

What It Means for Business

Effective compliance programs are a critical element of good governance as they ensure that organizations are adhering to laws, regulations, standards, licenses, policies, plans, procedures, contracts, guidelines, specifications, or other requirements relevant to their business. Some compliance obligations are mandatory (e.g., legislation, licenses, permits), whereas others are voluntary (e.g., internal codes of conduct, industry codes).

Compliance continues to be a primary concern for the boards and senior management of most organizations, with reputation risk pushed to new levels as a consequence of the complexity and pace of legislative and regulatory change, coupled with an increase in regulatory scrutiny and enforcement. Entities across all sectors – private, public, and not-for-profit – need to comply with obligations associated with their establishing legislation or constitution, as well as broader legislative and regulatory obligations on how they operate, account, and report.

An organization's compliance framework is designed to ensure that the organization achieves compliance with both externally and internally imposed requirements, and includes governance structures, programs, processes, systems, controls, and procedures.

A compliance framework is an important element in the governance of entities for:

- Preventing, identifying, and responding to breaches of laws, regulations, codes, or standards.
- Demonstrating a solid compliance regime to regulators.
- Promoting a culture of compliance.
- Helping the organization to be a good corporate citizen.

Regulators have the right to independently validate that an organization in their jurisdiction is compliant with legislation and regulations by conducting documentary and/or onsite reviews of the organization's policies, procedures, operations, activities, systems, premises, and related information. The outcomes of the regulatory review will often be reported publicly and to parliament.

Business leaders with the support of governance, risk, compliance, and assurance specialists need to ensure that the organization has a well-formed compliance framework. This will minimize the risk of compliance failures and associated reputational risks, as well as the consequent potential impacts of fines, prosecution, complaints, and litigation for the organization and its senior officers, and potentially imprisonment for senior officers. An effective compliance framework:

- Identifies, facilitates, creates awareness, and promotes compliance.
- Is underpinned by compliance risk assessments, a compliance register, and identified strategies.
- Establishes monitoring and assurance mechanisms.
- Fosters continuous improvement.
- Handles compliance breaches (including escalation and/or breach reporting).
- Provides internal and external compliance reporting.

Business leaders have a legal responsibility to report to the board, regulators, other scrutineers, counterparts, and stakeholders any breaches, potential breaches, and near misses of laws, regulations, standards, licenses, policies, plans, procedures, contracts, guidelines, specifications, or other similar compliance obligations.

Audit committees should expect clear and complete compliance reporting together with periodic analytical assessments. Governance, risk, compliance, and assurance specialists should undertake analysis of both the number and outcomes of wrongdoing allegations and the organization's breach reports to pinpoint trends, identify systemic issues, and gain pointers on the strengths and weaknesses of the organization's lived culture, both in terms of what is being dealt with and how it is being handled.

The maturity of compliance reporting is illustrated in **Exhibit 7.7**. As an organization's compliance reporting matures, the audit committee initially receives isolated reporting at the initial stage, which then adds on insights from the implemented stage, then finally the mature stage delivers insights covering all three stages.

As the organization's compliance arrangements evolve and mature, audit committees have an opportunity to promote shared learning between governance, risk, compliance, and audit specialists with a view to achieving meaningful workplace integration, and driving reporting collaboration.

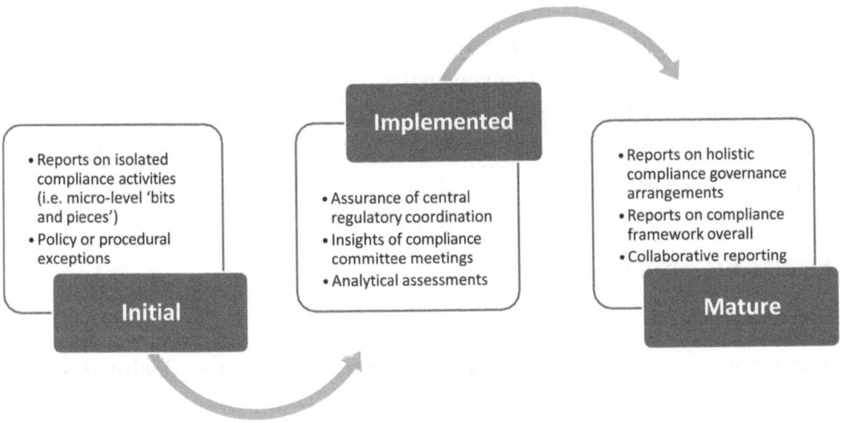

EXHIBIT 7.7 Maturity of compliance reporting to the audit committee.

Audit committees usually receive a great amount of reporting, but in the absence of collaboration amongst specialist areas reporting to it, the committee is left to its own devices to interpret the shadows that fall across the various separate reports; these specialist areas include governance, risk, compliance, assurance, quality, financial control, fraud investigation, and corruption prevention. These specialists are increasingly expected to work together to interpret and report on the patterns emerging in their collective work; through a well-coordinated approach, they will produce insightful information for the audit committee that helps the committee to fulfill its increasing obligations.

Collaborative reporting provides an overall conclusion or opinion on the outcomes of all of the work of the specialist areas, rather than merely summarizing their respective reports. The overall conclusion or opinion interprets the insights from the specialist areas and applies professional judgement to the trends, patterns, themes, and systemic issues. This ultimately provides the audit committee with an overall conclusion on the state of the organization's internal controls.

Audit committees should receive information from business leaders periodically (at least annually) on the status of all policies and procedures, so they can be assured that the policies and procedures are being reviewed and updated in line with the scheduled review dates. Where reviews are overdue, the audit committee should be informed of the action in train and target date/s to complete the respective reviews.

The **Open Compliance and Ethics Group (OCEG)** is a non-profit thinktank that (according to its vision) is dedicated to achieving a world where every organization and every person strives to achieve objectives, address uncertainty, and act with integrity. It created principles and other innovations aimed at "breaking down silos between governance, strategy, performance management, risk management, compliance management, internal audit and other departments." https://www.oceg.org/

Ensure Business Continuity

Setting the Scene

The frequency of strikes and other industrial action has declined significantly since the 1970s and 1980s in many industrialized countries. Industrial disputes were relatively common in the 1970s and 1980s, with the number of strikes in Australia peaking in the 1970s with over 2,000 work stoppages every year that decade; the conclusions of a recent study found, "The frequency of strikes and other industrial action has become extremely rare. Adjusted for population, the frequency of work stoppages has declined by 97% since the 1970s.[13] In Australia, there has been a significant decline in: [14]

- The average number of disputes per year from 2,368 (1970s) to 198 (2010s).
- The average number of work days lost per year from 3,146,000 (1970s) to 145,000 (2010s).
- The number of days lost per 1,000 workers per year from 542 (1970s) to 14 (2010s).

As a banker in the 1970s and 1980s, we often had to combat strike action to keep the business operating and to maintain our own livelihoods. On some occasions, railway services were closed down as a result of strike action, and when a snap strike was called during the middle of the day, many commuters were left stranded in the Sydney CBD. Overnight accommodation had to be hastily arranged. There was also a lengthy strike by elevator engineers where they refused to repair or maintain the elevators in high-rise buildings. The strike went on for several weeks, and people modified their behavior when they went to the office as they had to use the stairs; quite a task when you were situated on the 24th floor as businesses continued to operate, even though it would be decades before the interconnected world of the twenty-first century would allow people to work from home.

---

[13] Jim Stanford, "Historical Data on the Decline in Australian Industrial Disputes," The Australian Institute, https://www.tai.org.au/sites/default/files/Industrial_Disputes_Briefing_Note_FINAL.pdf (sourced 3 July 2020).

[14] Ibid.

During the peak of the industrial action, railway operatives were striking for increasingly longer periods. Commuters had to adapt. During a two-week strike, I took the decision to hire a bus to transport bankers into the Sydney CBD from a number of outer-Sydney cities and suburbs from about 40 miles to the west. The bank agreed to underwrite the cost if I made all the arrangements. We quickly filled one bus, then two, then three, then four for the duration of the strike. On seeing the success of the western initiative, bankers to the north and south soon followed suit. These were informal arrangements that kept the business operating, and were ultimately incorporated into the bank's formal business continuity safeguards.

Like the need to work around industrial action, the following stories illustrate that there are many angles that need to be covered to ensure business continuity.

- When I completed a technical assistance mission to Port Moresby (Papua New Guinea) in the mid-1990s, my workmate, Mark Ward, and I invested considerable time in our planning and preparation. For most of the time during our three-week mission, we were able to continue to operate. We were interrupted on one occasion when we were working in our respective hotel rooms at night, but had left our doors open so we could more readily collaborate across the hallway … the security guards armed with machine guns suggested the doors be kept locked, and we quickly obliged. And we were nearly caught out when we were setting up to deliver a PowerPoint presentation at the end of the trip to the central bank Governor (CEO) and his executive team, discovering that the electricity power points in the boardroom were different to elsewhere in the building and we did not have the right adaptor (we had wrongly assumed powerpoint standardization).
- A few years ago, my wife and I took a cruise along the Danube and Rhine Rivers in Central Europe. Over two weeks, we traveled from Budapest to Amsterdam stopping along the way and sightseeing at a dozen cities spanning Hungary, Slovakia, Austria, Germany, and The Netherlands. It was a relaxing and enjoyable voyage. Around the mid-point of the cruise, the captain announced that the water level in the river was too low for the boat to continue. But he had a work-around. The next morning, we would all pack our things and leave the vessel, where a coach would transport us around the low water point to link up with another vessel waiting for us. The cruise director would continue with us, but we would be saying farewell to the captain and the crew. For my wife and I and our fellow vacationers, it was a seamless transition, though I expect it was a stressful time for the captain, the cruise director, and the cruise company as they invoked their business continuity arrangements.

What It Means for Business

A survey of board members leading into 2020 found that just one in five (21 percent) believed their organization was prepared to respond to an adverse risk event from a planning, communications, recovery, and resilience standpoint.[15] The situation is likely to have changed quickly as a result of unanticipated impacts of a global pandemic (which are discussed in the postface, with key insights on changes in global business environment illustrated in **Exhibit 14.1**).

***Business continuity management** (BCM) is a holistic framework with its objective to provide the organization with the ability to effectively respond to threats such as natural disasters or data breaches and protect the business interests of the organization. BCM extends beyond information and communications technology (ICT) to encompass all business operations, and it includes disaster recovery, business recovery, crisis management, incident management, emergency management, contingency planning, and pandemic planning.*

Business leaders need to factor a range of features into their business continuity management arrangements as illustrated in **Exhibit 7.8**.

Business leaders must develop and articulate the organization's processes for continuing essential activities during and after an unforeseen event or disaster situation. As depicted in **Exhibit 7.9** and then discussed, they need clarity of overarching arrangements to be enacted when a business disruption, disaster situation, or crisis has a major impact on business

EXHIBIT 7.8 Features that influence business continuity planning.[16]

[15] "Continuity not Complacency," *Company Director* (July 2020, Volume 36, Issue 06): 51.
[16] Ibid. Modified and structured.

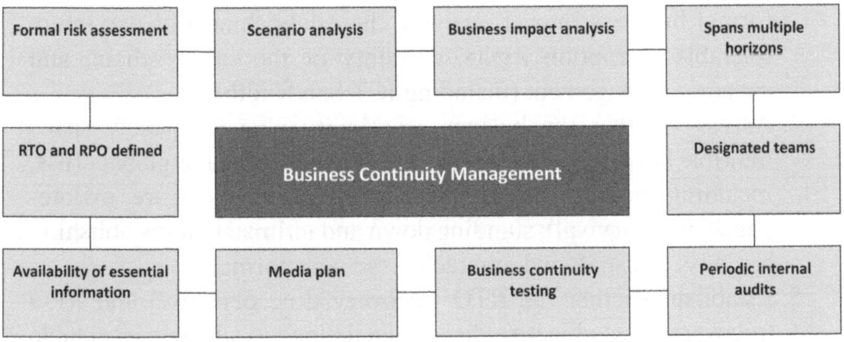

EXHIBIT 7.9 Ten Action Steps for Overarching Business Continuity Management Arrangements

operations that flows to service delivery. Effective business continuity planning will help to prevent interruption to critical services and re-establish operations as quickly and smoothly as possible. Once business continuity management arrangements (including plans) have been developed, the arrangements should be communicated appropriately across the organization and reinforced through the training of key people.

The audit committee needs to know how the organization's business continuity activities fit together, how effective they are, whether they are likely to be successful if a need arises to stand them up, and whether the customer experience sits at the heart of decision-making. This can be satisfied where business leaders provide the audit committee with periodic assurance on the ten action steps, covering the following:

1. Assess whether the organization has formally assessed the risk of potential business disruptions, disaster situations, or crises, and covers all major risk areas, including people (safety and wellbeing, availability, capability, and remote support), customer experience, supply chain, operations, financial stewardship (including cashflow and solvency), communications, continuity of critical control arrangements, and cyber risk management.
2. Determine whether business continuity management arrangements are sufficiently dynamic, and include scenario analysis at three levels – optimistic, expected, and pessimistic – with variables factored into the scenario analysis, such as time elapsed before normal operations can resume; economic markers covering the severity of the event; workforce health, wellbeing, readiness, and connect-ability; and commercial arrangements.
3. Determine whether the business impact been assessed should a business disruption, disaster, or crisis situation occur, including

formal business impact analysis, the establishment of maximum tolerable disruption limits, certainty of the supply chain, and capacity management (including ICT bandwidth).

4. Assess whether the business continuity plan adequately spans multiple horizons in the event of a serious national or global crisis, including initial emergency management response (care, maintenance, and survival); standing down and ultimately re-establishing business as usual; and embracing the new normal.
5. Establish whether the RTO (recovery time objective) and RPO (recovery point objective) have been defined to avoid unacceptable consequences after ICT disruption.
6. Determine whether designated teams have been identified and established with a designated crisis center, with clear definition of people responsible for business continuity, crisis management, and ultimately recovery.
7. Assess the availability of essential information, including accessible crisis kits of important information and resources, defined trigger points, an escalation process, and an up-to-date contact list of key management, employees, suppliers, and stakeholders, including contractual requirements of suppliers for call-out response times and effort.
8. Assess the adequacy and reach of the media plan to deal with the media following an unforeseen event, crisis or disaster situation.
9. Establish the availability and adequacy of a formal schedule of business continuity testing across a range of activities (e.g., desktop, configuration, platform, multi-platform, services, and realistic crisis scenario), and confirm periodic testing is carried out, recorded, and remediated, with post- test reports and improvement actions reported to the audit committee in a timely way and actively followed-up.
10. Ensure regular internal audits of business continuity management and ICT disaster recovery are performed and reported to senior management and the audit committee.

Monitor Insurance Arrangements

Setting the Scene

I assumed responsibility for monitoring Integral Energy's insurances, recognizing that insurance was only an effective risk mitigation strategy when policies were held with a reputable insurer, the coverage was right, the policies were appropriate, and the conditions were understood and managed.

There is little point in having insurance if there is a risk that legitimate claims are not paid when loss events occur. Not all insurers are the same, so it is important to understand their reputation in the market and creditworthiness as illustrated by the following examples:

- HIH Insurance was Australia's second largest insurance company before it was placed into provisional liquidation in March 2001.[17] The demise of HIH was the largest corporate collapse in Australia's history, with liquidators estimating that HIH's losses totaled up to $A5.3 billion.

  While some policyholders with particular types of insurance had their policies taken over and honored by other insurers, many policyholders did not have their insurance claims paid. The demise of HIH changed the insurance landscape in the region forever, particularly for public liability coverage.
- The need to understand and monitor the conditions of insurance is illustrated in a high-profile case involving missing gold bullion. In April 1995 about $A5.8 million of gold bullion was stolen from a private safe inside the Sydney office of Australia's then wealthiest man, Kerry Packer.[18] The gold was covered under the company's global property policy with per occurrence limits of $A5 million for bullion, with a deductible of $A1 million, some of which had been exhausted by other claims.

  A dispute over the deductible arose with the eight insurers after they paid $A4.02 million. Mr Packer's company sued for an additional $A742,049 which Mr Packer claimed he was entitled to because the policy was worded in such a way that the deductible should have been subtracted from the value of the gold, not the actual sum insured.

  An appeals court ruled in favor of Mr Packer, overturning a Supreme Court decision in favor of the insurers. In handing down the ruling, the judge said the policyholder was correct in that the deductible should be subtracted from the value of the gold and then the monetary cap should be applied. The judge reflected that the policy showed that the claim "is not the maximum amount which the insurer is obliged to pay under the policy, but the true value of the loss suffered."

What It Means for Business[19]

Treating risks (i.e., risk response planning) typically involves establishing a plan to treat or modify the highest ranked risks to achieve acceptable risk levels. This is influenced by the organization's risk tolerance and appetite levels and, broadly, advocates responses that will reduce, accept, avoid or transfer risks.

---

17 Prepared from media reports. Intended to be an educational and illustrative example.

18 Ibid.

19 Bruce Turner, *Insurable Risk Reporting* (Sydney: Institute of Internal Auditors Australia, 2020), 2–7.

Risk transfer involves redirecting the negative impact of a risk or type of risk to a third party through approaches including insurance (financial impact), outsourcing (supplier responsible for non-core work activities), hedging (exchange rate risk), and other financial instruments (such as leasing).

Insurance is arranged by organizations as a common risk treatment approach, though some organizations could opt to "self-insure" (in whole or part) in line with the organization's risk appetite statement, or government policy in the public sector. The primary aim of insurance is to reduce the financial impact of a business interruption, loss, or damage to a facility or equipment.

While insurance coverage for assets and obligations such as property, motor vehicles, and worker's compensation has been a traditional risk treatment approach for many years, the nature of insurances and the coverage arranged continues to expand in keeping with business changes. These include public and products legal liability exposures, professional indemnity, director's and officer's liability, cyber risks, specific construction projects and programs of work, and miscellaneous losses such as employee dishonesty, personal accident, overseas business travel, and event cancellation. Insurance policy exclusions eliminate coverage for some types of risk, and narrow the scope of insurance coverage by removing coverage for risks that insurers are unwilling to take.

Audit committees rely on management to establish and maintain mature and consistent practices for insurable risk reporting and the foundations that support it. Insurable risk reporting should align with the organization's corporate policy framework for risk management and provide assurance that the organization has the right level of insurance coverage, is managing particular conditions of insurance policies like exclusions and deductibles, insurers have the capacity to pay, and claims management is efficient, effective and represents value-for-money.

An ***insurable risk report*** *will inform the audit committee of the organization's corporate policy on insurances, including whether there is a corporate policy in place, whether it is current and applied, and the minimum requirements for insurance arrangements. The insurable risk report will contain four primary sections, (1)* ***right level of cover*** *(describing assets at risk, classes of policies, breadth and depth of coverage of individual policies, and amounts insured); (2)* ***creditworthiness of insurers*** *(providing assurance on insurers' capacity and intent to pay all reasonable claims); (3)* ***special conditions*** *(providing assurance of effective compliance monitoring of exclusions, special conditions, and deductibles); and,* ***claims management*** *(describing the nature and value of claims for the period, and providing assurance on effectiveness of claims management).*

Audit committees should expect mature, well-considered, and consistent insurance practices, and management can validate this through an annual insurable risk report that contains insights on:

1. The availability of an appropriate corporate policy framework for the organization's insurance arrangements.
2. Whether the organization has the right level of insurance coverage in terms of insurable risks (breadth) and the values for which they are insured.
3. Whether insurance cover is held with insurance companies that have the capacity to pay (i.e., credit-worthiness), integrity and market credibility in the event of a claim.
4. Whether there are any particular conditions, exclusions, or deductibles of the insurance policies that need to be managed and how this is handled.
5. Whether the management of the more frequent claims (such as workers' compensation, property damage, and motor vehicle) is efficient, effective, and represents value-for-money (regardless of whether claims management is inhouse, outsourced or a blended approach); it is also useful to have a summary of the history of insurance claims and the lessons learned (to avoid reoccurrences of incidents that led to the claims); together with details of when the claims management arrangement was last "market tested" for longstanding relationships.

CHAPTER 7 – TEN CLOSING REFLECTIONS

- Governance, risk, compliance, and assurance specialists should operate "within the business" to gain the respect of business leaders and operational staff by knowing the business through wide-ranging knowledge, capabilities, and a business perspective so they can do their jobs well.
- The chief audit executive (or an alternate) should establish and maintain a consolidated investigations manual, maintain effective quality assurance, and periodically report to the audit committee on quality assurance, investigator profile, and outcomes of investigations.
- Boards should expect an active and informed audit committee to provide independent and objective oversight of the organization's lived corporate culture and the overall control environment, including insights on emerging trends and risks.

- The chief risk officer should establish enterprise risk management arrangements in line with the policies established by the board, and the chief audit executive should provide periodic assurance to the audit committee that core enterprise risk management elements are in place and operating as intended.
- Business leaders should integrate risk management practices into their day-to-day operations and apply them to the wider aspects of their organizational arrangements, as a basis for improving operational efficiency, enhancing governance and stakeholder confidence, establishing a strong foundation for decision-making, boosting health and safety performance, maintaining effective compliance with relevant legislation, encouraging proactive management, and minimizing losses.
- The board (or its audit or risk committee) should receive regular risk reporting covering strategic risks, operational risks, project risks, infrastructure risks, risk-based scenario analysis, and emerging risks.
- Business leaders should ensure that the organization has a well-formed compliance framework that informs the work of governance, risk, compliance, and assurance specialists, with audit committees given periodic assurance that all policies and procedures are being reviewed and updated in line with the scheduled review dates.
- Business leaders should develop and articulate the organization's processes for continuing essential activities during and after an unforeseen event or disaster situation to provide clarity of overarching arrangements to be enacted when business operations and service delivery are adversely impacted by such events.
- Audit committees should obtain periodic assurance from business leaders on how the organization's business continuity activities fit together, how effective they are, whether they are likely to be successful if a need arises to stand them up, and whether the customer experience sits at the heart of decision-making.
- Audit committees should expect mature, well-considered, and consistent insurance practices, and management can validate this through an annual insurable risk report.

8 Composing the Melody in the C-Suite

Gaining a seat in the C-suite often reflects the level of professional breadth, maturity, and credibility of the chief audit executive. Direct and frequent access to decision-makers provides an opportunity to directly influence the organization's performance and conformance agenda, and the tone at the top, whilst safeguarding independence. This chapter focuses on a transformational agenda to deliver a high-performing internal audit "professional practice" with contemporary world-class features … and it also highlights the inherent vulnerability to "white-anting" when highly-accomplished professionals are appointed to transform a function that has individuals who are resistant to change. Everyone has a purpose in life and Mark Twain (1835–1910) captured this sentiment perfectly when he said, "The two most important days in your life are the day you are born and the day you find out why."

Entity Profile and Role

Sector:	Government sector – taxation and superannuation administration.
Entity:	Australian Taxation Office (ATO).
Entity metrics (2012):	• Total Assets $A1.0 billion. • Annual expenses: $A3.2 billion. • Annual revenue collection for government: $A280 billion. • Staff 25,000.
Primary role:	Chief Internal Auditor (chief audit executive).
Main responsibilities:	Responsible for providing strategic leadership to the internal audit function, with an executive advisory role to the Audit Committee and Commissioner's Plenary Governance Forum. Directed a comprehensive risk-based audit work program for up to 40 staff.
Other executive roles:	Senior executive "site sponsor" for the Penrith site (staffing of up to 1,400 staff). Was tasked with developing and driving social and business cohesion strategies to achieve stronger local results. Chair of Penrith's senior executive site leadership forum. Member of the executive team that led the corporate services and law division; one of the ATO's four operating divisions. This was a primary entity-wide corporate governance role that shaped ATO-wide governance, risk management, and control frameworks.
Timeframe:	The cusp of the Fourth and Fifth Decades.

*The **C-suite** refers to the most senior executive-level managers within an organization, such as the CEO, chief financial officer (CFO), chief operating officer (COO), and chief information officer (CIO).*

PERSONAL STORY

After several years at Integral Energy, I was approached to consider taking on the role of chief audit executive at the ATO. The timing was good, and I was willing to explore the opportunity. Following several after-hours interviews with the agent, I was flown to Canberra to meet with the senior ATO executive who was conducting the recruitment. I took a day off work. I checked with the agent and was assured I didn't need to bring anything along and I was just meeting with one executive.

When I arrived in the ATO's head office in Canberra, I was escorted to a meeting room. It was soon evident that some wires must have been crossed because this was not a casual one-on-one conversation, rather a full-on interview with about eight people in the room, including representatives from the audit committee, the external auditor, internal clients, and members of the executive. Fortunately, I handled the situation well and had brought some materials with me which I could inject into the interview as part of "show and tell." The interview went well and I was offered the role soon afterwards.

In negotiating the terms, conditions, and remuneration for the appointment, the senior ATO executive mentioned, seemingly as an afterthought, that there might be some travel involved. Looking back now, I should have explored the travel requirement a little more as I ended up traveling to Canberra on average at least three weeks out of four for the five years I spent at the ATO; it was actually a positive, as I was well-supported and it provided frequent and direct interactions with critical stakeholders.

After I was signed up, and about six weeks before I was to commence, I contacted the audit director of the Parramatta (western Sydney) team and arranged to join them for an informal meet-and-greet and a cup of coffee. I didn't know them and they didn't know me, so I thought it would ease the stress for them of waiting for the unknown. I was impressed with the energy and enthusiasm of the team. They had many ideas for improvement that I was keen to explore. I received a message later that day from the senior ATO executive in Canberra who recruited me, saying that the team was impressed with our earlier interactions that day. It was clear that the ATO "grapevine" was strong and traversed state borders.

The division that I would be situated in from an administrative reporting perspective was holding a strategic planning conference a couple of weeks before I was due to commence and I was invited to attend for two days. I took up the offer and built it in to an interstate road-trip that my wife and I had arranged to take between finishing at Integral Energy and commencing at the ATO. It provided a wonderful opportunity to meet key executives and to learn about the organization and some of its challenges.

On my first day, I travelled to Canberra and met the Commissioner (CEO), audit committee chair, and other senior executives during the morning. In the afternoon I travelled to Belconnen (a Canberra suburb) to meet the internal audit teams based there (the performance and IT teams). I came prepared, with the first cut of my "First 100 Days Roadmap" and a presentation that I made to staff, followed by an informal conversation. I surprised everyone with my preparedness and professionalism.

I spent the second day attending an audit committee meeting in Canberra as an observer, then flew interstate to Melbourne to meet the Victorian audit team on day three. Day four I was back in Sydney meeting with the New South Wales audit team.

While I was well-received by all of my staff during our initial interactions, there was a degree of skepticism as to whether we could deliver what I had said we would do. In the end we did, as a result of strong support from the Commissioner, audit committee, executives, and the internal audit team.

On my retirement after five years at the ATO, I was presented with a beautifully presented photo book containing memories of the time together, and heartfelt messages from the internal audit staff. It was clear that my decision to take on the chief audit executive role was the right one, and I finished my fulltime working career on a high. I have included below the comments of one of my loyal lieutenants, as it captures well the essence of the audit team's messages.

> It feels like only yesterday I was looking at your first 100 days document, thinking that I had heard it all before. I was questioning not only my choice in career, but my choice in employer. Our first meeting was over coffee. Our first of many coffee catch-ups. You sat, listened, and immediately gained my trust and respect. Maybe because you were a latte drinker, but probably because you had a passion for the profession that I had never seen before. It was contagious. I believed that you would make a difference, and you definitely have.
>
> For five years you were there to support me, and provide me with every opportunity to prove myself. Professionally nobody had ever showed that much faith in me and for that I am forever grateful. You have taught me more than any text book, university degree, or training course. Sometimes you gave me projects and sometimes (how pretentious am I) you made me feel that if I were not here, things

would not work. Which is not true. I am just a member of a team, but still you know how to get the best out of people. What a skill!

The team has been led by you in a way I have never experienced before. By a person with industry experience, but more importantly by a person with strength of character and with a heart of gold. You have indeed taken us from good to great, and hopefully you have taught us the skills to move onto even bigger and better things.

The key insights from this phase of my story are:

- Lead a transformation agenda.
- Establish meaningful stakeholder communications.
- Inspire innovation and improvement.
- Recognize good performance outcomes.
- Manage customer complaints well.
- Maintain focus when under attack.
- Prepare for "life's third act."

CONTEXT

Leading a transformation agenda successfully requires a clear focus on the needs and expectations of stakeholders coupled with a committed, engaged, agile, and innovative high-performing team. There will inevitably be challenges and changes that need to be navigated. There are many factors that underpin a transformational leadership, with some of these elements discussed in this chapter and illustrated in **Exhibit 8.1**.

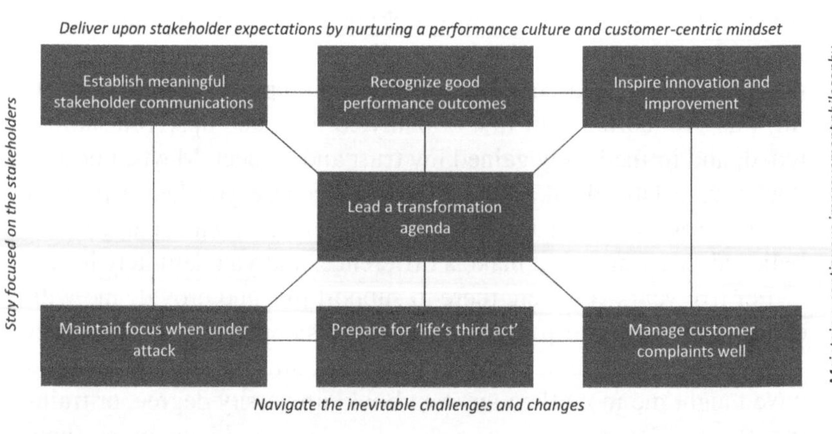

EXHIBIT 8.1 Leading a transformational agenda.

KEY TAKEAWAYS AND DEEP DIVES

Lead a Transformation Agenda

Setting the Scene

The sage advice I received from the Commissioner of Taxation when I started at the ATO still resonates, "You've got a good team, they just need leadership and direction." I always kept that in the back of my mind. The Commissioner's advice was well-founded as he had previously chaired the audit committee prior to taking on the top job a couple of years earlier.

The approach I had planned to take aligned nicely with the Commissioner's expectations. I had established a structured and analytical approach that I had intended to follow, and incorporated the high-level elements in "My First 100 Days Roadmap" (see **Exhibit 8.2**) that would provide the foundation for developing robust planning for the future.

We conferred with the audit committee, and agreed upon a revised timetable for the forward audit plan with the aim of clearing a backlog of audits to give us a fresh start. Through collaboration with key stakeholders, we developed a strategic audit plan that was focused on key initiatives for transforming the internal audit function in line with the vision.

With a clear plan in place, we implemented six critical steps in the first six months (our quick wins). These included:

- Moving two of the interstate teams closer to the business, so the auditors could get to know and become respected by the business (both management and staff).
- Quickening the pace of audits (they were taking too long to complete) and enhancing the quality of reports.
- Identifying common issues and root causes arising from audits (rather than considering each report in isolation), so as to provide a broader picture to the audit committee and senior management.
- Implementing a range of key performance indicators (KPIs) and introducing a balanced scorecard for measuring progress.

Wide Consultation and Representation - Meet:	Documentary Review - Assess:	Determine Strategies - Set Direction:
• Commissioner	• Charters	• Benchmarking / analysis
• Executive and managers	• Forward audit plan	• Strategic audit plan
• Internal audit staff	• Progress reports	• Three-year audit plan
• External auditors	• Methodology	• Annual audit plan
• Service providers	• Policies and procedures	• Staff development plan
• Peers	• Schedule of technologies	• Updated artifacts

EXHIBIT 8.2 My first 100 days roadmap for the ATO (excerpts).

- Upgrading the staffing and implementing a professional development plan.
- Establishing a stakeholder relationship program and building a relationship with the Institute of Internal Auditors in Australia.[1]

We were soon on our way transforming the function into a high-performing internal audit team, recognized for quality and value by its stakeholders. We recognized the importance of internal audit living and breathing the business, rather than living and breathing auditing. We achieved the turnaround by driving a range of pivotal changes to the way the function operated, notably:

- Developed a risk-based and strategically focused forward work program that ensured the internal auditors got into the right areas at the right times.
- Established an environment where the internal auditors were expected to be in tune with what was really going on in the business, and what was coming over the horizon.
- Ensured the audit conclusions took into account the internal operating environment and the impact of global events on traditional business drivers.
- Tailored the reports to the needs of the audit committee, keeping them short, sharp and succinct, and incorporating creative visual aids.
- Reported at a more strategic level, covering themes, trends and systemic issues, insights into the culture of the entity, and the efficiency, effectiveness and ethics of operations.

We ultimately achieved our vision of being recognized as a world class internal audit function. The balanced scorecard reports tracked our trajectory throughout the transformation. The satisfaction levels of all stakeholder groups improved markedly, including the audit committee, senior management, and internal audit staff.

What It Means for Business[2]

Boards, audit committees, and business leaders should expect the internal audit function to add value to the business. Where the function becomes

---

[1] Reflections articulated by Norman Marks, "Fine Article on the ABC of a Professional Internal Audit Practice," 26 March 2012 https://iaonline.theiia.org/blogs/marks/2012/Pages/Fine-Article-on-the-ABC-of-a-Professional-Internal-Audit-Practice.aspx (sourced 25 September 2020).

[2] This section draws on the content of an article: Bruce Turner, "The ABC of a professional audit practice," (Sydney: The Institute of Internal Auditors Australia), *IIA-Australia Journal* (Issue 1, March 2012): 15–22. Used with permission; the Institute of Internal Auditors Australia retains copyright and intellectual property rights.

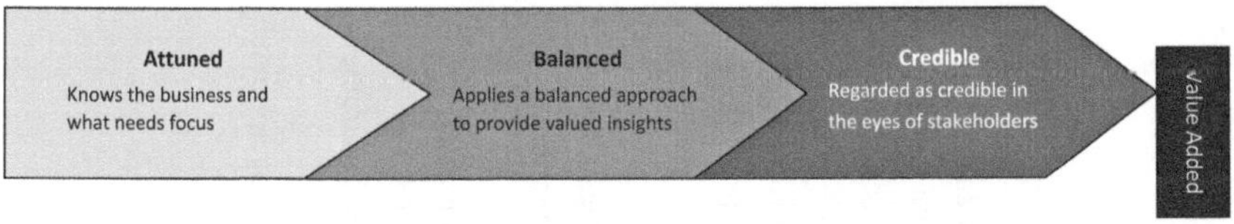

EXHIBIT 8.3 Delivering value by being attuned, balanced, and credible.

tired, lacks direction, and is not functioning at an optimal level, there is a risk that key stakeholders will miss out on critical insights. In these cases, the audit committee might need to appoint a chief audit executive as a change agent to transform the function.

The ABCs of professional practice illustrated in **Exhibit 8.3** are equally relevant to governance, risk, compliance, and assurance specialists.

Each element of being attuned, balanced, and credible is discussed over the next few pages, then the top ten practice tips for each ABC element are summarized in **Exhibit 8.4**.

Attuned

It is essential that governance, risk, compliance, and assurance specialists are attuned to what their audit committee and other stakeholders need, and consistently meet their expectations.

The responsibilities of audit committees have grown over recent years and their expectations of governance, risk, compliance, and assurance specialists in supporting them have similarly increased. The success of each is mutually dependent. Another important ingredient is the support of senior management, and their genuine commitment to introducing and maintaining effective governance arrangements.

The information available both within an entity and externally provides a rich harvest for governance, risk, compliance, and assurance specialists to "tune in" and shape their own work plans and activities. Notably:

- Entities usually document their vision, values, business objectives, and priorities in a carefully constructed strategic planning suite.
- The board and senior management have developed increasingly sophisticated information channels, including the enterprise risks (both current and emerging) and legislative obligations. An array of information channels and published information is available on the entity and its governance arrangements, reflecting the increasingly connectivity of entities to the outside world.

Governance, risk, compliance, and assurance specialists are expected to be in tune with what's really going on in the business, and what's coming

EXHIBIT 8.4
Top ten practice tips for each ABC element

Attuned

- Understand the environment in which the entity is operating, including external factors, and competition.
- Know the entity's strategic direction – what's happening now, what's likely to happen, and what are the emerging risks.
- Establish a constructive partnering arrangement with the audit committee, and build a high level of mutual trust.
- Keep abreast of audit committee expectations through regular discussions (mainly chief audit executive and committee chair). While formal reporting and presentations at audit committee meetings are vital, the informal discussions with members are often even more valuable.
- Establish a comprehensive and structured stakeholder relationship program to know what is coming "across the horizon."

Balanced

- Achieve a balanced coverage in the forward work program, blending traditional areas of financial audit coverage with efficiency, effectiveness, and ethics elements; incorporate deep dives and spot checks.
- Position internal audit so that it is looked upon as a source of advice and provider of quality value-add services.
- Expand involvement in activities that may be beyond traditional coverage, working with business leaders on areas like business continuity, risk management, and compliance until they reach a reasonable level of maturity.
- Access industry and economic information independently to reduce reliance on management's perspective of organizational and sector risks.

Credible

- Review the internal audit charter each year so it remains relevant, consistent with better practice models, and complements the audit committee charter.
- Maintain effective structural reporting lines, with functional reporting to the highest level, such as the audit committee and/or chief executive.
- Showcase the role, standing, independence, and contribution of internal audit in the entity's published annual report.
- Pursue positive trends in management's perception of internal audit, through key measures such as the value add and usefulness of audit recommendations.
- Tailor a balanced scorecard reporting approach that suits the nature of the entity.

• Develop a risk-based and strategically focused forward work program that ensures that the internal auditors get into the right areas at the right time. • Establish high-level themes within the forward work program to facilitate future reporting on trends and systemic issues, rather than just focusing on the results of individual audits. • Assist the entity to value independent scrutiny and embed early in major system developments, construction and similar projects, and business re-engineering projects. • Strive to always deliver auditor excellence in what, when and how they do their work. • Get into the business to see what really goes on.	• Tap into organizational health, and share impressions, and insights on emerging issues with audit committee members. • Showcase the contribution to the business of internal audit activities in a comprehensive annual report to the audit committee and key executives. • Deliver crisp reports that really matter, and pitch them in a manner that aligns to the critical business drivers. Reports must be short, sharp and succinct. • Enhance high-level reporting to the audit committee by summarizing and reporting the outcomes of all audits under agreed themes. • Write "without fear or favor," and "tell it as it is" but write in a balanced style "for the world to see" recognizing the concepts of freedom of information. • Undertake effective monitoring and reporting of the status of audit recommendations.	• Comply with professional auditing standards, and deliver an overarching quality assurance assertion to the audit committee each year. • Provide to the audit committee a periodic benchmarking report outlining the overall auditing capability (experience, average auditing years, qualifications, and professional certifications). • Establish recruitment and retention strategies that deliver a well-balanced auditing team with a professional culture. Complement the strategies with a professional development plan for internal audit. • Maintain internal auditor communication strategies to ensure consistency in dealings with stakeholders. • Maintain honesty and fairness in all reporting and relationships, at all times and at all levels; especially, handle sensitive matters in an impartial way.

over the horizon. There will be an increasing need to consider the entity's culture to determine whether it is in sync at all levels.

The role of governance, risk, compliance, and assurance specialists will continue to expand. Internal auditors, for instance, should already be involved in activities beyond the traditional compliance and accounting areas of internal audit coverage. As a source of advice, they will be positioning themselves to contribute to the enhancement of business processes and business outcomes. An assessment of "soft controls" can provide insights on how the business is really running.

Balanced

Increasingly, governance, risk, compliance, and assurance specialists are expected to discover things that the audit committee and senior management didn't know. They are well-placed to do so as they see right across the entity, but they need the right skills and focus to be able to provide a balanced perspective. In addition to business acumen, they need to be able to think strategically, and package their reports creatively. The establishment of a capability framework helps to shape the profile of these specialists for the future.

In turn, the internal audit forward work program needs to adequately address the main risk areas within the entity. Setting the right forward work program is vital, and it is essential to achieve a reasonable balance across the whole entity and the high-risk areas. While most audit activities have always had a plan, these days there is a need to sharpen the strategic focus. A blended approach is worthwhile, so that there is coverage of performance and strategic areas, coupled with sufficient coverage of the traditional "bread and butter" compliance and accounting areas of internal auditing.

Audit committees need governance, risk, compliance, and assurance specialists to help them in many different ways. For instance, these specialists are well-positioned to:

- Identify emerging issues and risks.
- Make the connections, so the audit committee can understand the trends, systemic issues, and reporting themes arising from their various streams of work.
- Provide insights on the culture of the entity, together with an opinion of the efficiency, effectiveness, and ethics of its operations.
- Deliver creative reports, where the "picture is painted" (where possible) through photographs, pictures, illustrations, graphs, video, or a site tour rather than many pages of written commentary.
- Provide assurance that management is embracing recommendations for improvement and achieving sustained improvements to the associated governance, risk and control arrangements.

Credible

The credibility of governance, risk, compliance, and assurance functions is underpinned by the three key pillars of professional excellence, quality of service, and professional outreach.

Professional excellence reflects that governance, risk, compliance, and assurance specialists:

- Maintain risk-based policies and methodologies that are efficient, effective, and contemporary, and lead to the timely discovery of issues and opportunities, while preserving value.
- Deliver value to the business and help management to achieve business objectives through governance, risk, and control insights.
- Establish a mandatory requirement for governance, risk, compliance and assurance specialists to maintain continued professional development to stay relevant.
- Establish well-balanced multi-disciplinary teams from a variety of backgrounds and with relevant industry experience.

Further, the chief audit executive is expected to:

- Have a contemporary auditing mandate coupled with an independence of mind.
- Understand and consistently apply professional auditing standards.
- Maintain a credible and capable auditing team that delivers the requirements of the internal audit charter and the forward work program.
- Provide strong encouragement for auditors to pursue auditing-specific certifications.
- Have sufficient standing within the entity so that the entity's annual report (published in the public domain) contains explicit commentary on internal audit, including its reporting lines, independence, role, level of maturity, and contribution.

Professional outreach strategies will help governance, risk, compliance, and assurance specialists to connect with professional leaders and practitioners from outside their entity to avoid becoming too inward-looking. The insights gained will help them to remain innovative, and to keep abreast of emerging risks, hot topics, and better practices. The sharing of their entity's "leading edge" practices with others is energizing, and helps to lift their credibility within both the profession and the eyes of internal stakeholders. **Exhibit 8.4** was developed for the internal audit function but can be modified for use by governance, risk, compliance, and assurance specialists.

Establish Meaningful Stakeholder Communications

Setting the Scene

As a young auditor in my mid-20s, I was assigned to undertake the first comprehensive audit of the bank's treasury dealing operation; the bank was expanding its treasury activities in the foreign exchange and domestic investment markets. It was a time when internal auditors used a systems-based auditing approach. This required auditors to identify every critical process, then flowchart the process, establish key controls, undertake a walk-through to validate the assessment of controls, develop an audit program, then complete the fieldwork.

When we commenced the review, we initially met with the chief manager of the treasury area. He was obviously an experienced operator recruited from Europe, though he seemed quite aloof, and had little time for auditors. After we had spent about a week in the area, the chief manager wandered past and asked what we were doing. We reminded him of the audit and that we were undertaking a walkthrough; he was quite dismissive, and bluntly commented that it seemed to him like a "crawl-through." I thought at the time, "welcome to the world of the elite, entitled and arrogant!"

It was a difficult audit given the embryonic stage of the operation, its complexities, and the attitude of its leadership. Having completed the preliminary assessment and walkthrough, we benchmarked the control framework with other more established dealing functions. The chief manager laughed off our suggestion to install recording equipment so that an audio record was maintained for all money market and foreign exchange dealing transactions. In his view, the cost could not be justified. My boss reflected that good audit recommendations never die, and internal auditors sometimes need to be patient and play the long game. Within 18 months the bank did install voice recording equipment in all its dealing rooms. The catalyst was a large foreign currency transaction (one of four near-simultaneous similar transactions) subsequently disputed by the counterparty financial institution. My bank lost millions of dollars when the exchange rate plummeted unexpectedly before the transaction could be reversed out of its books.

The dealing room experience sharpened my awareness of the impact of stakeholders and how to handle them. No two stakeholders are the same, and they need to be managed accordingly.

> ***Stakeholders*** *are individuals or groups that have an investment or interest (i.e., a stake) in the manner in which an organization designs, funds, governs, and/or operates it services.*

***Stakeholder engagement** is the process of managing the expectation of any person or entity that has an interest in a function or the performance level of the organization. Stakeholders are impacted by organizational deliverables or outputs. Proper stakeholder analysis and management are critical to an organization or project as the commitment and support of all stakeholders makes achieving objectives considerably easier, whereas disaffected stakeholders can damage much other positive work and threaten the achievement of objectives.*

As I gained more experience and rose through the ranks, I established formal stakeholder relationship management arrangements within each of the areas for which I was responsible. With a responsibility for transformational change in most of my later roles, effective stakeholder relationships were fundamental to achieving the successful outcomes expected by the boards, audit committees, and chief executives.

Even as I rose to the level of a board member, I continued to champion stakeholder management planning as a critical element of good governance. On his retirement in 2019, the CEO of the Western Sydney Local Health District, Danny O'Connor, wrote to me commenting, "I want to remind you of my reluctance to develop a stakeholder management plan! We discussed this several times and I did indeed develop such a plan. This has proven to be very beneficial in providing an organized framework to derive value from a very extensive range of stakeholders and partners associated with our broad base change program." He then reflected on the value of stakeholder engagement for the entity's multi-billion-dollar redevelopments, and ambitious plans to improve the experience of healthcare through integrated health services, digital technology, and development of a new concept for health services at a new hospital (then at the planning stage).

What It Means for Business

Successful relationships between organizations and their stakeholders are founded on working together towards common goals. Investors have a financial stake, and expect a financial return; customers who avail themselves of products and services that improve the quality of their lives will spread the word about the offerings of the business; employees depend on the business for their livelihoods and – treated well – they typically go above and beyond their job requirements to further the best interests of the organization.

A ***stakeholder engagement program*** *is a structured approach to identifying and evaluating an organization's key stakeholders, documenting and implementing a plan for communicating with these stakeholders, and periodically reviewing the program (more frequently when there is a significant restructure or change in the nature of the organization's business).*

Stakeholder engagement programs deliver improved business outcomes by promoting effective two-way communications. Notable outcomes include:

- Providing an opportunity for the organization to apply its risk appetite to optimize successes and limit failings through effective programs of consultation and decision-making.
- Identifying key stakeholders for the organization, garnering their input, and using the insights to support the organization and achieve its objectives.
- Ensuring stakeholders fully understand the benefits the organization offers by communicating with them frequently.
- Anticipating likely reactions of stakeholders to organizational communications and progress, which helps to refresh strategies to capitalize on positive reaction, while avoiding or addressing any negative reactions.
- Identifying conflicting objectives among stakeholders to facilitate the development of strategies to resolve any issues that may arise.

An effective stakeholder engagement program will help to mitigate the risks of not meeting stakeholder expectations, or meeting them inconsistently. It also boosts support from senior management or the board for proposed or ongoing programs (e.g., approval and resourcing), and boosts the ability of business leaders to identify and monitor emerging risks, trends, and issues.

Ten critical success factors of an effective stakeholder engagement program are:

- Founded on a formal, systemic, and cohesive process.
- Championed by an appropriate business leader with the engagement of key organizational staff.
- Requires a rational assessment of stakeholder influence, impact, and priority (see **Exhibit 8.5**).
- Drives clear and consistent engagement.
- Requires regular and relevant communication.
- Promotes transparent and honest conversations that build trust.

EXHIBIT 8.5
Example of stakeholder prioritization

Influence	Lower Impact	Higher Impact
Higher	**Collaborate to maintain confidence** Indirect stakeholders pay attention to the finished project outcome, rather than the process of completing it. Indirect stakeholders concern themselves with things like pricing, packaging, and availability.	**Invest in, as critical, significant and influential** Primary stakeholders have the highest level of interest in the outcome of a project because they are directly affected by the outcome. They actively contribute to a project. These types of stakeholders include customers and team leaders.
Lower	**Monitor and inform** Direct stakeholders are involved with the day-to-day activities with a project. Employees can be considered direct stakeholders as their daily tasks revolve around projects at a business.	**Maintain effective liaison** Secondary stakeholders also help to complete projects, but on a lower, general level. These types of stakeholders help with administrative processes, financial, and legal matters.

- Provides active two-way communication (listen and feedback).
- Results in the sharing of meaningful insights that have an impact.
- Requires follow-through of commitments given.
- Considers the varying needs of different stakeholders.

Chief audit executives could establish an audit dashboard for stakeholders who are being audited by establishing a centralized portal to track the progress of the audit and respond to related communications. The portal would boost collaboration throughout the audit engagement by allowing invited users involved in the audit process an opportunity to assign requests, communicate on minor observations, and monitor the progress of the audit. The main features of the portal would include:

- Workflow – auditors and engagement clients would utilize a dynamic information request feature to keep track of inquiries, monitor the status of documentation sought, and track open requests.
- Centralized communication – provide the free-flow of information between auditors and engagement clients to enhance efficiency by eliminating data-gathering silos and avoid the risk of lost or duplicated requests and misplaced documentation.

- Project management – allow auditors and engagement clients to work collaboratively in real time and to provide notifications of changes.
- Accessibility – deliver a web-based dashboard that is readily accessible whenever needed.

Boards and audit committees should determine how the business leaders are managing stakeholder relationships, and can gain preliminary insights by asking five focused questions[3]:

1. Is there a documented program to facilitate two-way interaction with key stakeholders and the public?
2. Is the program reviewed annually, or when there is a significant change to the nature of the organization's business or its key processes?
3. Is information about an entity's functions, key policies and practices, and governance structure freely available? – e.g., published on the web – additional to the annual report.
4. Is there a complaint handling policy and procedure and are these publicly accessible and easily understood?
5. Are there prompt responses and actions towards complaints and grievances?

Inspire Innovation and Improvement

Setting the Scene

Innovation and improvement come at many different levels, from flair by an individual, through to structured departmental or entity-wide innovation strategies.

I was always encouraged when I saw individual auditors embracing innovative practices. One of my favorites was observing an auditor undertaking what appeared to be a routine review of maintenance charges. It was a safety requirement for the rail organization to paint yellow stripes about two feet from the platform edge so customers would know not to cross the line into a dangerous area close to fast-moving trains. The yellow lines needed to be repainted every few years as passenger movements dulled the effect. The organization had outsourced this painting work, and paid a standard rate based on the total length of all the platforms at each station. While the cost for each station was reasonably modest, the overall cost was more significant with a network of hundreds of stations, and the ongoing nature of the work. Invoices were calculated based on the total

[3] "Governance Lighthouse", Audit Office of New South Wales. https://www.audit.nsw.gov.au/our-work/resources/governance-lighthouse (Sourced 13 July 2020).

length of the platforms in yards, multiplied by the contracted dollar rate per yard, plus taxes.

The auditor hired a perambulator (surveyor's wheel or measuring wheel) and went onsite at several railway stations to independently calculate the length of the platforms. He found errors because the length of the platforms had changed due to modifications, or some platforms were no longer used but the asset records had not been updated. The auditor helped to reshape the organization's control environment, and his work resulted in a significant refund.

******

Upon taking on the chief audit executive role at the ATO, it was apparent that each team across different sites was running as a separate discrete silo. A standardized audit methodology was not in place, with reporting outputs being presented in inconsistent formats. The approach was confusing for the audit committee and internal clients.

We needed to inspire innovation and improvement across the internal audit activity as nothing would change if we tackled it in isolation or if we sat back and passively expected things to evolve.

We established an innovation and improvement forum under my sponsorship and chaired by one of my direct reports to demonstrate an active commitment to innovation and improvement. The forum was established with blended representation from each audit team, geographic location, and levels of seniority. The forum members at the auditor-level were selected based on their talent, creativity, and potential, and they were combined with more senior, experienced and hardened practitioners.

The aim of the innovation and improvement forum was to facilitate the timely identification and consistent implementation of agreed changes to internal audit practices that support the activities and objectives described in the internal audit charter. Recommendations of the forum were reached through consensus, which was achieved by having frank, open, respectful, and timely discussions, with final decisions on changes resting with me (or for less significant changes, one of my direct reports).

We established clear parameters for the forum upfront with well-defined terms of reference that covered the forum's purpose, governance arrangements, management of relationships, justification for establishment, membership, roles, responsibilities (chair, secretariat, members), delivery mechanisms, administration (quorum, resources, meeting frequency, calendar, records management, communication and escalation arrangements, conflicts of interest, charter review), and approval arrangements.

The forum captured and addressed ideas raised by the internal auditors and their teams then developed them through a collaborative approach. This ensured fully-developed innovations were brought forward to me that were then consistently applied to the whole of the internal audit activity.

To ensure the forum had credibility and never became a "black hole" where ideas were sent to never again see the light of day, we established our expectations for the forum's performance and outcomes that were measured and reported periodically, including:

- Timely consideration of ideas, innovations, and improvements.
- Effectiveness of the outcomes and outputs based on feedback from internal audit stakeholders.
- Length of time issues and opportunities remained on the issues register.
- Confidence that internal audit stakeholders had in the decision-making process.

Internal auditing standards require chief audit executives to develop and maintain a quality assurance and improvement program that covers all aspects of the internal audit activity (standard 1300); the forum delivered innovation and improvements while providing clear evidence of conformance with this standard.

******

Internal auditors at the Asian Development Bank are also embracing opportunities for innovation and improvement through enhanced digital skills. They are currently using technology, including drones, and artificial intelligence (AI), to conduct better audits. Examples include[4]:

- Using drones to track on-the-ground progress of building projects, such as new roads and transmission towers under construction in Kalimantan Indonesia, which saves auditors from having to travel to remote sites in person. It also helps to monitor the progress of larger areas, with drones providing a bird's eye view.
- Using natural language processing (a way of teaching computers to make sense of and analyze a written document) to check that key covenants in a contract are reflected in their system. The tool reads a document, compares it against what is in the system and points out any differences. The time for completing this process for a single loan has been slashed from around two hours to seconds. The technology equips the auditors with the precise terms when they audit projects without the need to refer back to the agreements.
- Using an AI technique to check that all payments are processed according to established rules. For example, the software checks

[4] Yun Xuan Poon, "How ADB is using AI to refine audits - Interview with Hock-Chye Ong, Auditor General at the Asian Development Bank," *GovInsider* (20 May 2020).

that the person initiating a payment cannot then give approval for it, and that the transaction has proper confirmation before it goes through.
- Using machine learning to identify risk areas more accurately by setting parameters based on rules; exceptions are raised for items not meeting the rule which narrows down the areas for which auditors need to conduct more in-depth checks.

What It Means for Business

Well-considered innovation and improvement can help to deliver strategic objectives by reinvigorating a business, creating new value, yielding a competitive advantage, boosting growth, and lifting productivity and performance. This could result in new revenue opportunities, or boost revenue through existing channels, and may drive efficiencies that save time, money, or both, leading to higher profits.

Business innovation typically falls into several different types, such as[5]:

- Product or service – developing new products or services, enhancing existing products or services, or introducing technology.
- Process – improving operational processes such as financial systems, human resource management, internal methodologies, and information and communications technology (ICT).
- Marketing – how products or services are promoted and the channels used to distribute them.
- Business model – revising the structure of a business or developing strategic relationships with suppliers, distributors and customers.
- Disruptive innovation – discussed in Chapter 3.

Innovation *refers to changing business processes, adapting the business model, improving the workplace, or creating more effective processes and products. This could mean implementing new ideas, creating dynamic products or improving existing services. Innovation can be a catalyst for the growth and success of the business, and can help it to adapt and grow in the marketplace.*

While innovation and invention are closely linked, they have differing characteristics. An invention is an entirely new creation (such as the original telephone) whereas innovation typically applies an existing concept, practice, or technology in a new way (such as a cell phone), or applying

[5] "Innovation", https://www.smallbusiness.wa.gov.au/business-advice/innovation (sourced 11 July 2020).

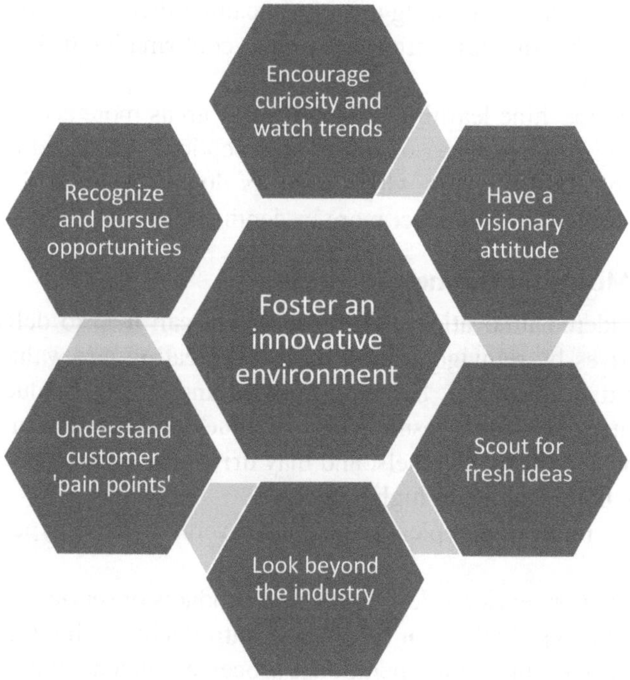

EXHIBIT 8.6 Features for fostering an innovative business environment.

new technology to an existing product or process to improve upon it (such as a smartphone).

Business leaders need to take calculated risks to position the business to adapt to change and respond to new opportunities. They need to foster innovation, and can do this by[6]:

- Encouraging staff to provide ideas and be creative.
- Rewarding innovative ideas and thinking.
- Seeking feedback from customers and other stakeholders.
- Building innovation into the organization's strategic and operational planning.
- Investing in the resources that promote innovation.
- Undertaking research and development activities.

Common features for fostering an innovative business environment are illustrated in **Exhibit 8.6**.

Business leaders who are driving a strategy of innovation need to establish a repeatable process to generate, test, and develop ideas that can

[6] Ibid.

potentially lead to innovations. The first step is typically to articulate ideas around key areas before moving through discovery then onto development and delivery. That is:

- Create and record ideas then undertake a preliminary evaluation as to whether the ideas could deliver value.
- Test the veracity of the ideas through pilot programs or proofs of concepts, and further evaluate the likelihood of value creation.
- Scale the ideas before moving them into production and integrating them into normal business operations.

Business leaders need to recognize that innovation can potentially be a costly endeavor that does not always deliver a return on investment. Even ideas that are expected to succeed could fail on some occasions because stakeholders (e.g., employees, customers, partners, or others) might not embrace the new ways of operating.

Boards and audit committees should seek to understand how innovation is fostered within the business environment. They should also ensure that the work of governance, risk, compliance, and assurance specialists does not detract from well-founded innovations.

Recognize Good Performance Outcomes

Setting the Scene

Soon after joining the ATO we developed a staff engagement strategy aimed at nurturing existing talent and shaping a performance culture. The strategy included a range of initiatives illustrated in **Exhibit 8.7** and these included staff newsletters, team-building activities, and community outreach. The success was assessed, in part, through trends in the periodic staff satisfaction surveys, which were monitored and reported in the internal audit balanced scorecard (see KPI measure "internal auditor workforce satisfaction" in **Exhibit 6.6**).

Prior to me commencing, the efforts of staff in the internal audit area were not being adequately recognized or rewarded. While a publicly funded organization is limited in the remuneration (extrinsic rewards) it can offer, there were opportunities for intrinsic rewards that we identified through collaboration with our staff and then promoted well. These included:

- Actively engaging staff in nominating colleagues for entity-wide recognition awards.
- Linking performance enhancement ideas and rewards programs.

EXHIBIT 8.7 Staff engagement strategies.

- Recognizing staff achievements in a monthly Chief Internal Auditor electronic newsletter.
- Introducing the prestigious Chief Internal Auditor Medal and awarding it annually to a select individual.

The CIA Medal was an important innovation that was introduced to recognize an individual's commitment to continued professional development, teamwork, and innovation. The six recipients during my five years at the ATO represented diversity perfectly with a mix of people at all levels in the structure, and across genders, generations, ethnicity, and disability. The diversity was not a deliberate creation, rather it was a recognition that everyone was treated equally.

The CIA Medal was presented at a team meeting or, in some cases, at a whole-of-team conference, and was then showcased in the organization's weekly electronic all-staff newsletter. The CIA Medal meant a great deal to the recipients, with one commenting on my retirement:

> On a more personal note, receiving the CIA Medal from you in 2010 meant a great deal to me and is certainly the highlight of my career to date. I thank you very much again for that honor, as well as for all the other acts of kindness you have shown me (and I can recall there are many of those). It really reminded me of how privileged I am to have

exceptionally skilled leaders and colleagues who have brilliantly good-natured dispositions and personal values, while unwavering in their professionalism.

******

Things moved quickly in the lead-up to my retirement when a non-management level staff member advocated for the establishment of the perpetual "Bruce Turner Citizenship Award" in my honor (discussed in Chapter 10). The suggestion was agreed by the local executive leadership team, with criteria established for nominees to be assessed on their:

- Support and active participation in local events.
- Championing of the site, while supporting the organization's vision and corporate values.
- Active involvement and encouragement of colleagues in site initiatives and opportunities.
- Mentoring of others, and consistently adding value above their immediate role.

When I attended the retirement function of the 2013 recipient, I was chuffed to hear that one of her proudest achievements in her long and successful career was to be awarded the Bruce Turner Citizenship Award. The sentiment emphasized to me how important it is to recognize good citizenship efforts through personal recognition like this. This is another example of the benefits of intrinsic rewards.

What It Means for Business

Setting personal goals for staff underpins an integrated performance management process. It ensures the alignment of the staff's personal goals to their divisional and organizational goals and objectives. Effective goal-setting requires business leaders to:

1. Align individual goals to organizational and divisional strategies.
2. Establish meaningful goals that are clear, measurable, and achievable.
3. Equip managers with the necessary skills and provide them motivation to establish goals.
4. Provide sufficient time for managers and staff to develop and agree goals.
5. Set goals that are commensurate with the staff member's capability.

In a four-stage performance management process (as illustrated in **Exhibit 8.8**), the individual's performance appraisal considers the outcomes achieved against the goals set at the start of the process. In turn,

EXHIBIT 8.8 Typical elements of a performance management process.

the appraisal outcome feeds into the staff member's proposed professional development activities and will influence any intrinsic and extrinsic rewards.

The establishment of individual goals is an iterative process between the manager and staff member. The aim is to identify the specific results that the individual is required to achieve to help the division (and ultimately the organization) achieve its objectives. Depending on the organization's human resources policies, the goals may well be a combination of work specific outcomes, and personal development needs.

In effect, over a typical 12-month cycle, the staff member's performance goals are discussed and agreed, they take action to achieve their goals, their performance is appraised, and the goals are refreshed and, where appropriate, performance improvements are identified.

Despite management's best endeavors, not all staff are equal in their performance; **Exhibit 4.7** illustrates how staff could be assessed across five different categories. Chapter 4 focuses on steps for dealing with poor performance, and for maintaining professional development.

The rewards element of a performance management process is important as compensation alone provides limited motivation. Business leaders need to consider a combination of both intrinsic and extrinsic rewards, noting:

- Extrinsic rewards include money, bonuses, special gifts, and other benefits.
- Intrinsic rewards relate the value staff derive from their work (see **Exhibit 8.9**); it is an outcome that gives an individual personal satisfaction for a job well done.

In a changing work environment, there is a stronger expectation for intrinsic rewards such as work-life balance; career advancement opportunities; training and certification support; exposure and visibility in important meetings; public recognition of achievements; and mentoring or coaching opportunities. The importance of these factors will change depending on gender, generational, and cultural drivers. The priorities will also be weighted higher at different stages of the staff members life, corresponding to external interests and family demands.

EXHIBIT 8.9
Examples of intrinsic rewards and other factors as motivators

- Loyalty, appreciation, and recognition
- Personal growth
- Participation in decision-making
- Greater job discretion
- Challenging and interesting work
- Exposure/visibility in important meetings
- Constructive feedback
- Regular, open communication
- Training and certification support
- Mentoring and coaching arrangements
- Job security and workplace stability
- Working conditions for work/life balance
- Flexible working arrangements, such as:
  - Options for working remotely
  - Working part-time
  - Alternative hours
  - Job share
  - Support for career breaks

When business leaders understand the intrinsic drivers for their workforce and apply them in the reward structure, they derive benefits for the organization, such as:

- Improved employee morale, motivation, and productivity.
- Being an employer of choice.
- Reducing employee turnover and absenteeism.
- Reducing employment costs.
- Attracting staff that they may not have otherwise appealed to.

Business leaders have a responsibility – both individually and collectively – to maintain a highly motivated, productive and well-equipped workforce. This should be underpinned by:

- An employee engagement model tailored for their workplace that reflects what motivates the different staff across the workforce.
- A suitable rewards system for staff that extends beyond compensation to encompass both intrinsic and extrinsic rewards, and aligns to the vision, strategic direction, and plans of the organization.

Manage Customer Complaints Well

Setting the Scene

We completed an audit of complaints management reporting at one commercial organization as part of a broader review of the reporting of non-financial information. The organization's annual report contained very detailed analysis and commentary on complaints which were being received across multiple reporting channels. We confirmed the integrity and completeness of complaints data through five primary channels and several smaller channels.

As we explored further, we noted that there was one primary complaints channel that had been forgotten in the collating of data, and it represented about 20 percent of all complaints. Despite the organization's best endeavors of open and transparent complaints reporting, the information was seriously flawed and misrepresented the true position … and had done so for several years. Management reviewed the data capture processes and strengthened accountability to ensure meaningful complaints reporting in the future.

******

At another organization, the executive team discovered a serious backlog of complaints that were not being addressed. There were many thousands of unaddressed complaints, most of which were long-dated. In effect, the complaints were falling into a black hole, so customers complained again with no reply, multiplying the stakeholder angst. The way complaints were being handled in practice was contrary to the commitment given to stakeholders in the customer service charter (the importance of these charters was discussed in Chapter 2).

We worked with management to provide guidance to a project team on the steps required to address the root cause of the problem. Incremental changes saw the backlog cleared over several months, and enhanced case handling arrangements were established, coupled with credible themes-based reporting to the executive team.

******

The twenty-first century has brought the effective management of customer complaints into sharper focus. This has been partly in response to whole industry sectors that simply ignored the legitimate complaints of their customers, or downplayed them. Chapter 2 reflected upon the findings of independent enquiries, including:

- Major quality and safety shortcomings across the aged care industry.
- Alarming and unconscionable conduct that ignored basic standards of honesty in the financial services sector.

A separate independent prudential enquiry into a major bank highlighted the importance of reporting on customer complaints to the board and executive committee in line with better practice peer organizations.[7] The report noted that the large volume of information on customer complaints was not fully utilized in its analysis, with only 3.4 percent of all complaints reviewed to find systemic issues; the report commented that, "Internal

[7] "Prudential Inquiry into the Commonwealth Bank of Australia", April 2018, 45.

audit assessed that this may cause (the organization) to miss significant insights in systemic issue analysis."[8]

What It Means for Business

Boards need to understand how their organization stacks up in terms of meaningful metrics and analysis of complaints, and key report-enabling elements.

> ***Complaint management*** *describes the constructive handling of customer complaints within an organization. It provides a framework for evaluating criticism in a systematic and orderly manner, and is used to create a positive stakeholder impact. A primary aim is to resolve the issue that prompted the customer's criticism in a way that ultimately strengthens customer loyalty and improves the quality of products and services.*

A customer service charter articulates the rights of customers in terms of standards of quality, issues, complaints, feedback, privacy, and conflict resolution (see **Exhibits 2.4** and **2.5**). Organizations should first focus on maintaining quality control over its products and services so that the number of complaints is minimized.

When customers do have complaints to raise, then the process should be simple and accessible. The elements of a typical complaints process are illustrated in **Exhibit 8.10**.

Analyzing an organization's customer complaints arrangements can be revealing, and provides useful insights that should be shared with the board and audit committee. For organizations with well-formed complaints management arrangements, it can help to pinpoint areas that might require focus by business leaders; it can also guide the focus and efforts of governance, risk, compliance, and assurance specialists. For organizations with immature complaints management practices, there might be opportunities for the internal audit function to highlight better practice arrangements.

Well-run businesses have arrangements that ensure the customer voice is heard in their decision-making forums and product design; these organizations don't just focus on short-term, aggregate customer satisfaction scores. Their reporting to the board and executive committee includes meaningful metrics and analysis on customer complaints. For instance:

- Trends observed in customer complaints (both volume and topic).
- Sophisticated customer metrics, including sentiment across social media platforms.

[8] Ibid.

EXHIBIT 8.10

Elements of a typical complaints process

Contribute to a positive customer experience	
Deliver quality products and services and fulfil the customer service charter	Maintain quality control over goods and services so that complaints are minimal.
Simplify the complaints lodgment process and make it easily accessible to customers	Have accessible and easy-to-use customer feedback mechanisms, that encourage dissatisfied customers to first turn to the organization before venting their dissatisfaction on social media networks. Organizations can positively address complaints when a customer's justified criticism is first reported.
Ensure that the initial contact is positive	Do everything possible to make the customer feel that they are in good hands when they submit a complaint. Trained complaint-handling staff must be well- equipped to accept criticism, and make the dissatisfied customer feel their opinion matters.
Clearly design the process	Complaint management requires clearly defined structures, accountabilities and responsibilities. There should be no doubt as to which feedback is directed to which departments. Management should monitor complaints.
Carry out direct actions	Actions should be taken immediately and directly after contact with the customer, with precise action determined depending on the circumstances of the individual cases (e.g., price discount or product exchange); options should be determined beforehand. Complaints and their responses often point to longer- term quality assurance considerations which should also be addressed.
Leverage complaints to improve the quality of goods and services to drive long-term improvements to company processes	
Analyze feedback	All customer complaints must be evaluated with regard to the content of the customer's feedback and their intention. Management needs to determine patterns, set appropriate priorities, and implement improvement measures.
Audit management	Complaint management should be subject to internal audits periodically. The aim is to minimize the risk of a negative complaints handling culture developing, and to potentially identify opportunities to optimize complaint handling processes.
Issue reports	Management should initiate the appropriate enhancements identified in internal audit reports.
Use of collected information	Data collected through complaint management will often tell a story. These constructive insights provide points of reference for quality assurance that can ultimately contribute to improvements in production and service performance.

- Systemic issues observed in customer complaints that could result in regulatory breaches or group-wide reputational damage.
- Individual material customer complaints that may result in adverse regulatory or reputational damage; these reports include the complaint, its cause, remediation plan, and periodic updates on whether remediation actions have been closed or whether deadlines have been extended or delayed.

The key report-enabling elements include:

- Tying customer complaints to other sources of data to identify broad systemic issues, and operational and compliance risk issues.
- Investing in data and analytics to analyze complaints data, for example by product, business line or geography.
- Maintaining "sensitivity guidelines" that prompt escalation to a high-priority complaints team, including visibility of complaints from customers with extreme negative experiences and/or involving complex issues.
- Focused resolution of the tail of extreme examples of poor customer experience.

Serious customer complaints pose reputational risks to organizations; though they might represent a small portion of overall complaints they could potentially affect many customers with an extremely negative experience.

Boards and audit committees are increasingly interested in complaints management, and are seeking quarterly complaints reporting trend analysis and key actions being taken.

MAINTAIN FOCUS WHEN UNDER ATTACK

Setting the Scene

I endured a horrid experience in one organization, when I was subjected to a series of allegations of wrongdoing over a period of two years. The allegations were totally unfounded and covered a range of claims, which can be split into the following themes:

• Secondary employment	• Misuse of assets (car)	• Rorting of travel claims
• Misuse of information	• Leaving work early	• Reserving car parking spots
• Corrupt recruitment practices	• Corruptly changing reports	• Bullying and harassment

The organization's policy, quite appropriately, required the investigation of all allegations of wrongdoing raised against senior executives. So, the allegations were investigated … and I was cleared. None were ever substantiated, which didn't surprise me as there was never any substance; all of the allegations were untrue, mischievous, frivolous, and vexatious.

There were robust controls over every process that was the subject of allegations and there was rigorous adherence to these controls, including higher-level approvals in line with organizational policy (i.e. secondary employment which related to a developmental role on an audit committee; travel claims), some were related to negotiated conditions of my employment contract (i.e., motor vehicle; parking), my authority as a chief audit executive (authorized use of information; amending audit reports that were founded on flawed analysis; recruitment in line with HR policy), compliance with safety and fatigue management policies (i.e., leaving interstate office before dusk after working until midnight the evening before to avoid wildlife hazards for a long drive home), and others were in response to dealing with poor performance (bullying and harassment).

Despite knowing I was innocent of every allegation, it was an unsettling period. Finding all the help I needed to contest the allegations was difficult, even though the organization had many policies and procedures covering ethical requirements, raising allegations, and investigation approaches. However, it was extremely difficult to locate meaningful and helpful information for me, the respondent; that sort of information was virtually nonexistent, and what was there seemed to be hidden away amongst other drab corporate policies, seemingly put there as an afterthought.

In hindsight, it is clear that I was being undermined, my integrity was being questioned, and the allegations were intended to destabilize the change agenda. Unfortunately, several of my direct reports and trusted allies were also directly impacted when allegations of wrongdoing were raised against them. It was clearly the second phase of an orchestrated resistance agenda. Those allegations were also investigated and found to be untrue; none were substantiated.

By unexpectedly switching places through my story of despair, I realized that respondents to allegations needed some help too … through a charter of rights. I championed the concept and it was supported by the audit committee and the CEO.

Fortunately, the internal audit leadership team remained focused on the change agenda, notwithstanding the personal despair and distractions of being under attack. Together, we persevered and managed to establish a highly effective internal audit practice by applying the ABCs of being attuned, balanced, credible.

What It Means for Business

Engaged and capable employees underpin the success of most organizations. It is difficult to quantify the precise financial impacts when innocent employees are the subject of allegations of fraud, corruption, misbehavior, and other wrongdoing, but the potential cost can be significant in terms of both bottom-line impacts and employee turnover costs. Global research shows that about 60 percent of allegations of wrongdoing against employees are unsubstantiated.[9] It is even more difficult to measure the impact on an innocent employee's mental wellbeing.

The investigation of allegations of fraud or wrongdoing can have long-term detrimental impacts on an organization and innocent employees if the process is not consistently handled in a well-defined, fair, equitable, and effective manner. The availability of a charter of rights can minimize the risk of lost productivity through employee disengagement and de-motivation when there is no basis to the allegations; it can also help to preserve the mental wellbeing of innocent employees.

A ***charter of rights*** *draws together in a single "ready reckoner" document all of the information that respondents to allegations of wrongdoing may require. It is written in an easy to understand "plain English" style, so that it meets the needs of its target audience and is made available to persons being investigated as soon as they are notified of the allegations. It is also readily available on the organization's intranet site. It is intended to be used for "routine" investigations of fraud, corruption and other wrongdoing within an organization; it is not intended for situations where criminality is suspected or where law enforcement agencies are involved (or likely to become involved).*

Well-designed charters of rights reflect the organization's corporate values, and demonstrate its commitment to providing procedural fairness and due process to respondents. They benefit both employees and workplaces by clearly articulating and making available to all employees the safeguards in place for all respondents of fraud and other wrongdoing. Notably, the charter of rights will:

1. Provide clearly articulated investigation and support arrangements that help to:
   a. Minimize lost productivity through an innocent employee's disengagement and de- motivation when there is no basis to allegations raised against them.

[9] Bruce Turner, *Introducing a Charter of Rights for Employees Being Investigated* (Sydney: Institute of Internal Auditors Australia, 2020), 2.

   b. Avoid employee turnover costs which result from innocent employees who became disenchanted following unsubstantiated allegations of wrongdoing.
   c. Preserve the mental wellbeing of employees who are the subject of investigations.
2. Demonstrate commitment to proper handling of allegations of fraud or wrongdoing which consequently:
   a. Avoid long-term detrimental impacts on an organization and its employees as the process is consistent, well-defined, fair, equitable, and effective.
   b. Enhance an organization's credibility when defending appeals against sanctions (for breaches of the code of conduct) through the courts and other industrial relations avenues.
3. Provide a comprehensive and useful "ready reckoner" for respondents that:
   a. Demonstrate procedural fairness to the courts and other review processes where disciplinary action occurs.
   b. Emphasize management's commitment to effective communications throughout the course of an investigation.
   c. Outline how management manages workplace allegations and complaints.
   d. Articulate the communication channels and support that is available.

Governance, risk management, compliance, and audit professionals are encouraged to champion the development and roll-out of charters of rights within their organizations. This should complement steps taken to shape good investigations governance (discussed in Chapter 7). Establishing a charter of rights involves a five-step process, as illustrated in **Exhibit 8.11**.

A critical step is to determine the content of the charter of rights, which could include the following elements:

- Develop a design (see **Exhibit 8.12**).
- Outline why the charter has been introduced, how it will operate, how it supports a robust complaints and allegations system, and how it aligns to the organization's values.

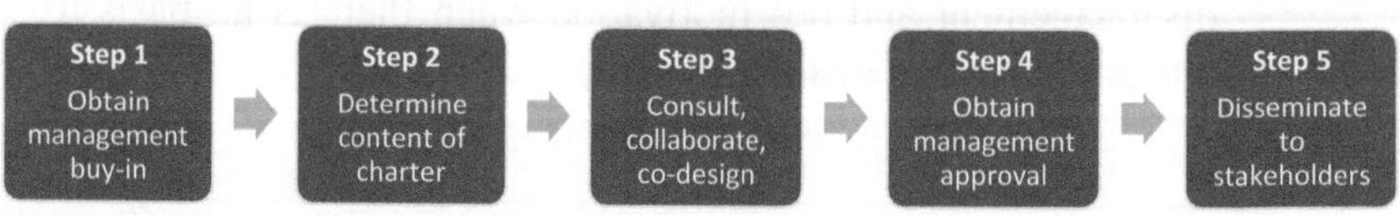

EXHIBIT 8.11 Five-step process for establishing a charter of rights.

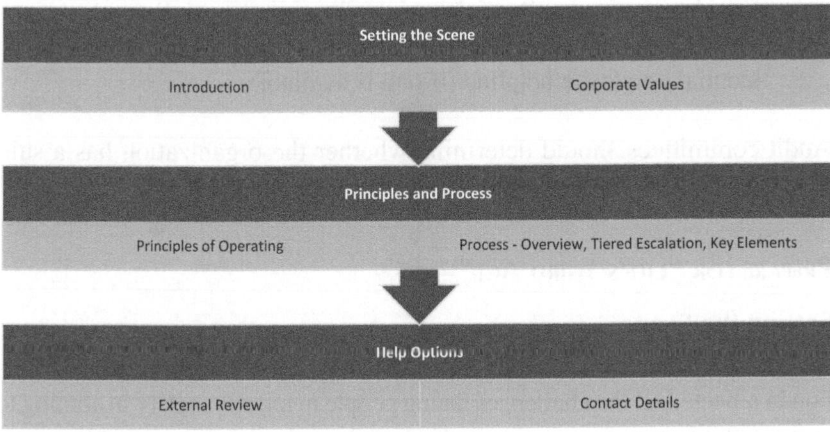

EXHIBIT 8.12 Example design of a charter of rights.

- Restate the values, and particularly reinforce the values that relate to areas of integrity (for instance, being ethical, fair, professional, open, accountable, and lawful).
- Provide firm commitments and information on areas such as principles of natural justice, commitment to approach all allegations with an open mind and without prejudging them, undertaking to acknowledge and resolve all complaints expeditiously, commitment to informing the respondent where an allegation has been raised against them (unless exempted because of potential criminality).
- Provide a high-level overview diagram of the process, including the channels for submitting allegations, then the distinct phases for logging, assessing, investigating the allegations, and the final decision-making phase.
- Provide commentary on the tiered escalation process for handling allegations that reflects (at one end) how issues of a serious, sensitive or significant nature are addressed, and encourages (at the other end) the handling of low-level localized issues as close to the source as possible.
- Provide answers to common questions that respondents might have about the process for dealing with allegations, such as "what can I expect if an allegation is made about me," "are outcomes always reviewable," "what does frivolous and vexatious mean," "what happens when a process is finalized or resolved," "what will I be told about the outcome of a process," "what happens when a process is concluded?"
- Outline the options for sourcing an independent review of adverse investigation outcomes through both internal and external channels.

- Provide contact details of the human resource specialists who can provide assistance, including details of an external specialist confidential employee helpline (if one is available).

Audit committees should determine whether the organization has a suitable charter of rights or similar arrangement in place.

Prepare for "Life's Third Act"

Setting the Scene

As she approached her senior years, Academy Award-winning actress Jane Fonda reflected on the challenges facing people in today's society in coming to terms with life expectancy. Noting that people in the developed world are now living, on average, 34 years longer than during their grandparents' generation.

Jane Fonda mused about what sexagenarians and beyond are supposed to accomplish in the time that remained, referring to it as life's third act (one's early life and schooling reflect the first act, and their working career the second act).

******

During my working career, I had thought that retirement in about 2010 would give me the opportunity to do a range of different things through the next stage of my life. In the end, I spent an extra couple of years working, retiring in 2012.

I had carefully chosen each new role over the decade 2000 to 2010 to broaden my knowledge, skills, experience, and reputation. In fact, the fruits of my efforts over an extended period of time were recognized through some notable awards in the mid-2000s, including:

- Presented with the Bob McDonald Award for audit professionalism. This was a national award for significant contributions to the profession, and is the highest honor that can be conferred on an internal auditor by the Institute of Internal Auditors in Australia.
- Presented with a Penrith City Wall of Achievement Award for championing good governance. This was a local award from my home city for successfully influencing the efficient, effective, and ethical operation of organizations critical to the local community.

My audit committee chair at the ATO was supportive of me taking on an audit committee role at a local council so that I could further develop my governance, risk and assurance skills. I was then offered a couple of other audit committee roles, including as chair. I found these to be highly valuable learning experiences because I was exploring the internal audit outcomes and outputs from the other side of the table (discussed further in

Chapter 9). These experiences helped me to do my "day job" as ATO chief audit executive even better because I gained a stronger understanding of the dynamics, areas of interest, and questioning techniques of audit committees. Their polish rubbed off on me.

By the time I retired, I had clarity on what I would do, and had the "street cred" to be offered interesting roles on boards and audit committees.

With more time to smell the roses in retirement, I established by blueprint in the form of a retirement plan founded on the acronym FLOWERS – Family, Leisure, Overseas, Writing, Events, Roles, (and other) Stuff. This allowed me a much more balanced perspective than I had when working in a fulltime executive role. It was especially nice to be able to spend more quality time with my family – weekly family dinners, working together on home improvement projects, and watching over the pre-schooler grandchildren one day a week (our "Adventure Thursdays", morphed into "MysTOURy Mondays", and then "Fundy Mundys" (fun-day Mondays) with each of the grandchildren) and sharing new experiences with the grandchildren from art galleries to zoos; enjoying hobbies, creativity, and cultural activities; traveling to different parts of the world and across my home country; giving back to the profession through voluntary technical writings; representing my profession and family at special community events; taking on new roles on boards and audit committees, and as a mentor, coach, presenter, and ambassador; and fitting in other special tasks as they arose (e.g., genealogy). Of course, when retiring, your partner's expectations need to be discussed, agreed, and factored into the planning (e.g., reallocation of household chores to better share the workload; getting the balance right between companionship and providing personal space / freedom).

Often when credible leaders retire, they receive many offers of things to do. The most important word in retirement is "No," otherwise retirement will end up being even more busy professionally than a fulltime executive role. My FLOWERS plan helped me to determine when I should say "Yes" in accepting a fresh opportunity by weighing up the offers against what I wanted to do, and to maintain a good balance overall.

There needs to be a great deal of variety to stimulate the mind in retirement. So, typically, no two days are the same, as illustrated in **Exhibit 8.13** in a snapshot of a week in the life of an active retiree. The other 51 weeks in the year are likely to be structured differently, and that's part of the beauty of spreading over half-a-million minutes across a year to different activities. An advantage of board and audit committee roles is that there is not a constant time commitment (day-in and day-out), and in non-peak periods there can be a gap of up to six weeks between all of the board and audit committee meeting commitments; this provides reasonable opportunities for travelling throughout the year while fulfilling all commitments (intermediate digital contact, including circulating resolutions, can be handled remotely through board portals or secure emails).

EXHIBIT 8.13
A week in the life of an active retiree

	Monday	Tuesday	Wednesday	Thursday	Friday	Weekend
Family	✓MM					✓FD
Leisure	✓XT	✓SO	✓XT	✓XT		✓SO / XT
Overseas		✓PB				
Writing				✓WB		✓WB
Events		✓WR		✓DS		
Roles	✓AR	✓MS	✓BM		✓AM	
Stuff			✓HH	✓GR	✓HH	✓GD

Legend:
AM = Audit committee meeting
BR = Read board pack week before
GD = gardening and mowing
MM = MysTOURy Monday
SO = Social outings
AR = Reading audit committee pack
DS = deliver speech
GR = genealogy research
MS = provide mentoring session
WB = writing book (hobby)
BM = Board meeting (at night)
FD = Family dinner (Sunday)
HH = household chores or pay bills
PB = prepare USA trip photo book
WR = watch professional webinar
XT = various: beach trip, dining out, reading novel, shopping, sporting event, television, walking, watching movies

What It Means for Business

Research suggests that retirement is one of the ten most stressful life events. Retirees can struggle with their new identity after defining themselves over many decades in relation to their careers. They need to establish a purpose and new routines, pursue their interests, look for ways to stay active, focus on their health and well-being, and involve themselves in activities that help to structure their day.

When people are considering retirement, they often reflect on relaxing, spending more time with the grandchildren, catching up on chores around the home, playing golf, watching movies, attending sporting events, and enjoying lots of travel (among other things). I always challenge them to think about what they are going to do in the second and subsequent years of retirement.

There are 525,600 minutes in a year, so retirees need to accommodate having much more flexible time during life's third act than they were used to having at their disposal as long-term employees. And retirees will need intellectual rigor and challenges in their life.

People at all levels need to imagine the new phase of their lives as they approach and move into retirement. When they are approaching retirement, they should develop a holistic retirement plan that extends well beyond financial parameters. And this should start a year or two before the proposed exit date. Financial retirement planning should be determined decades earlier.

Individuals need to have clarity of the retirement they want, by:

- Defining their retirement objectives.
- Establishing their financial retirement plan and goals based on their current financial position and the income required in retirement.
- Determining the best course of action for transitioning into retirement.

Retirees also need to factor in changes in their spending patterns in retirement that will likely to change over the three typical phases of retirement, notably:

- Phase 1 refers to the initial "care-free" period of retirement where retirees tend to focus on travel, spending time with family and friends, and enjoying a relaxed lifestyle. During this phase, the retiree's health and wellbeing and that of their partner remain strong, and their income needs are generally well accounted for in the planning process.
- Phase 2 shifts to the "quieter" years when the retiree's health starts to decline and they (or their partner) experience some level of disability and/or a decline in their level of activity which leads to a reduction in spending.
- Phase 3 is essentially the "frailty" years when retirees experience a more severe level of disability and may need help with daily living activities. During this phase (which can account for up to a quarter of retirement years) more is likely to be spent on aged care needs.

According to research, a male retiree aged 65 has a life expectancy of 84.6 years (a female is 87.3 years); the male retiree could be expected to spend 9.2 years in in the "care-free" period, 7 years in the "quieter" years, and

EXHIBIT 8.14

Change in retiree activities through the three phases of retirement[11]

What to Expect	Phase 1 – Carefree	Phase 2 – Quieter	Phase 3 – Frailty
Time	More time for leisure, travel, and family	More passive activities, travel close to home	Restricted mobility, limited activities
Work	Part-time work	Unpaid volunteer work	Reduced ability to work
Finances	Increased spending on leisure, but majority still save money	Increased spending on health	Increased spending on health and aged care
Housing	Housing upgrade	Housing down-sizing or modifications	Retirement village or nursing home (residential aged care)

3.4 years in the "frailty" years.[10] A retiree's activities change as they shift through the three phases of retirement as illustrated in **Exhibit 8.14**.

Soon after retiring, while they still have wherewithal to do so, retirees should consider putting in place appropriate legal structures so their interests are protected by someone they know and trust once they reach the frailty stage or otherwise lose their functionality or capability (e.g., though a stroke or dementia). These could include:

- Establishing a "power of attorney," which gives someone they trust the authority to act for them in specific (or all) legal or financial matters.
- Appointing an "enduring guardian," who is someone they trust to make lifestyle, health, and medical decisions for them when they are not capable of doing this for themself. The enduring guardian can make decisions such as where the retiree will live, what

[10] Assyat David, "The reality of three phases of retirement," 26 September 2018. https://www.firstlinks.com.au/phases-retirement-frailty-years/ (sourced 10 July 2020). Note that life expectancy varies across nations and ethnic groups. The figure cited is for an Australian male and is intended to be illustrative. Of the 44 developed nations of the Organization for Economic Co-operation and Development (OECD), countries like Monaco, Japan, and Singapore have the highest life expectancies; Canada and the majority of western European counties are similar to Australia; and the USA is generally lower except for Asian-Americans.

[11] TJ Ryan, "The Three Stages of Retirement Preparation," 4 December 2015 https://www.canstar.com.au/account-based-pensions/what-are-the-three-stages-of-retirement/ (sourced 10 July 2020). Modified slightly. Intended to be indicative and general in nature; users should seek their own professional financial and retirement advice.

services they are provided with at home and what medical treatment they receive.
- Executing a "will" or updating an existing will, which clearly sets out the retiree's wishes for the distribution of their assets and care of loved ones after their death. Having a clear, legally valid, and up-to-date will is the best way to help ensure that their assets are protected and distributed according to their wishes.

******

Business leaders need to recognize the impact of such a significant change on their staff, then support them in achieving a smooth transition to retirement, and into life's third act. In some cases, staff transitioning to retirement may wish to reduce their working hours to, say three or four days a week. Others may require opportunities outside the organization that will set them up for a board or audit committee role, or a part-time or volunteer role in a not-for-profit organization.

The lives of retirees are often enriched (especially in phase 1 of retirement) when they are able to give back through sharing their experiences, teaching others, and inspiring excellence. Governance, risk, and assurance specialists who leverage these opportunities (often at little to no cost) contribute to the development of the next generation of specialists while enriching the third act of retirees.

Business leaders have an opportunity to establish alumni arrangements so that retirees can stay connected with the organization, and share their wisdom with continuing staff so they leverage a rich source of ideas, insights, and perspectives. This can be achieved through direct engagement with continuing staff through options illustrated in **Exhibit 8.15**, recognizing that:

- Retirees usually have strong technical skills so they are well-placed to deliver either classroom training or one-on-one instruction on topics for which they have expertise. The technical training is delivered based on a gap analysis undertaken by business leaders or governance, risk, and assurance specialists. It frees up management from delivering training themselves and allows them to focus on strategic issues in the knowledge that staff development is being handled competently and expertly.
- Retirees trained and accredited in coaching may be willing to provide this as a service to help emerging executives achieve their development objectives and ultimately unlock their potential. Coaching uses a highly structured, objective-driven approach, that leverages insightful analysis. The coach acts as a sounding board and nurtures strategic development, so that, over the longer term, those being coached gain self-awareness and clarity of personal and professional goals.

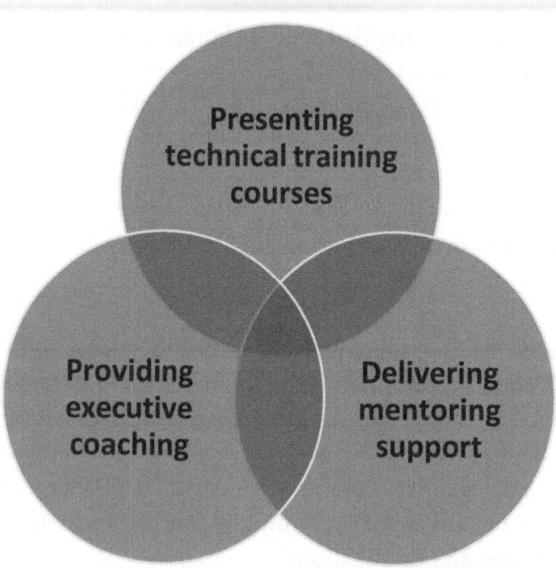

EXHIBIT 8.15 Leveraging the expertise and experience of retirees to boost staff development.

- Retirees are equipped to deliver mentoring support through constructive and frank advice and by collaborating and sharing insights with high potential and developing people. The continuing staff acquire knowledge and skills, build business acumen, develop their careers and learn how to operate in a challenging environment. Mentoring focuses on the issues of the day and achieves incremental professional development.

Retirees will often provide training, coaching, or mentoring at a moderate cost (or, in some cases, without charge) as a means of staying connected, investing in the future of the organization, paying forward to the next generation, and maintaining intellectual rigor and challenges in their life.

CHAPTER 8 – TEN CLOSING REFLECTIONS

- Boards, audit committees, and business leaders should expect the internal audit function to add value to the business, and they should initiate transformation action should the function become tired and not function at an optimal level.
- Governance, risk, compliance, and assurance specialists should maintain professional outreach strategies to connect with professional leaders, and practitioners from outside

their entity, so they avoid becoming too inward-looking, gain insights on innovations, and keep abreast of emerging risks, hot topics, and better practices.

- Boards and audit committees should determine how the business leaders are managing stakeholder relationships, recognizing that stakeholder engagement programs deliver improved business outcomes by promoting effective two-way communications.
- Boards and audit committees should seek to understand how innovation is fostered within the business environment, and they should also ensure that the work of governance, risk, compliance, and assurance specialists does not detract from well-founded innovations.
- Business leaders should maintain a highly motivated, productive, and well-equipped workforce underpinned by an employee engagement model and a suitable rewards system that aligns to the vision, strategic direction, and plans of the organization.
- Boards need to understand how their organization stacks up in terms of meaningful metrics and analysis of customer complaints, and the associated reporting.
- Boards and audit committees should seek quarterly complaints reporting that include trend analysis and insights on key actions being taken.
- Governance, risk management, compliance, and audit professionals should champion the establishment of charters of rights within their organizations, to reflect corporate values and demonstrate the organization's commitment to providing procedural fairness to respondents of allegations of wrongdoing (engaged and capable employees underpin the success of most organizations, and 60 percent of allegations of wrongdoing against employees are unsubstantiated).
- Individuals approaching retirement need to establish a purpose and new routines, pursue their interests, look for ways to stay active, focus on their health and well-being, and involve themselves in activities that structure their day; a well-considered retirement plan is crucial.
- Business leaders need to recognize the impact of retirement on their staff, then support them in achieving a smooth transition to retirement; they should particularly consider opportunities like alumni arrangements so that retirees can stay connected with the organization, and share their wisdom, ideas, insights, and perspectives with continuing staff.

International quality award

The StateRail Internal Audit Team (now covering RailCorp) was officially recognised for its professionalism and dedication to continuous improvement in May.

The Institute of Internal Auditors (IAI) international chairman, Bob McDonald, presented the prestigious international Commitment to Quality Improvement Award to Bruce Turner, Director Audit and Investigations Unit, who accepted the award on behalf of RailCorp.

The award has been in existence since the 1990s recognises organisations that are committed to providing quality internal audit services. Twelve prestigious winners across the world received the award in 2003, and our Internal Audit team is only the second organisation in Australia to be recognised in this way.

On receiving the award, Bruce Turner said the award not only acknowledges the professional work of the Internal Audit team, but also the commitment and dedication by the Board, executive and senior management to improving the entity's Corporate Governance standards.

"These efforts have resulted in management and front-line staff across RailCorp gaining a better understanding of risks and controls associated within their roles," he said.

In presenting the award at an Audit Executive Network meeting in Sydney, Mr McDonald emphasised the importance of Internal Audit functions and having staff with professional qualifications who completed their work in accordance with professional auditing standards. He cited our Internal Audit team as a good example of what can be achieved.

Neil Adams, Chairman NSW Chapter of IAI (centre), with RailCorp Internal Audit staff Tom Woodbridge (left), Bruce Turner, Christina Phillips and Siri Thongsiri.

Transforming any business function requires vision, focus and a lot of hard-work. The successful transformation of the internal audit activity at StateRail gained international recognition with the presentation of a "Commitment to Quality Improvement Award" through the IIA-Global in May 2004. Bruce (second from left) with members of his hardworking internal audit leadership team Tom Woodbridge, Christina Phillips, and Siri Thongsiri; the IIA New South Wales State Chapter Chairman Neil Adams is in the centre. (Photo: Personal collection (from StateRail staff newspaper).)

Working within the business is a critical success factor for any governance role. Bruce as Head of Audit and Risk at Integral Energy Australia facilitating a business continuity management workshop with operational and corporate executives from across the company. His risk manager Julian Gaillard is seated with dark tie. (Photo: Personal collection (from *Inside Integral* staff newspaper September 2006).)

Internal auditors need to maintain professional outreach if they are to develop professional capability, and keep abreast of changes in the profession, stakeholder priorities, environmental shifts, and new technologies. Bruce is a regular conference presenter and is pictured at the IIA-Australia SOPAC Conference in Melbourne 2007. (Photo: Simon Woo (used with permission).)

Internal audit derives great strength from the meaningful and consistent support of the chief executive. Bruce is pictured with Australia's Commissioner of Taxation Michael D'Ascenzo AO at the ATO's inaugural internal audit conference in 2007 themed "from good to great." Bruce regards Mr D'Ascenzo as his "best ever" chief executive. (Photo: Simon Woo (used with permission).)

Public sector auditors are driven in part by a desire to minimise waste and mismanagement to maintain funding for education, health, law and order, and other public services. Bruce with the Mayor of the City of Penrith Greg Davies receiving a Wall of Achievement Award in 2008. (Photo: Penrith City Council (used with permission).)

Governance, risk, compliance and audit professionals need to embrace broader leadership roles. Bruce delivered the introductory address at the 20th anniversary celebration of the ATO Penrith office in 2010. Pictured with David Bradbury (local politician and Federal Assistant Treasurer), and former Deputy Commissioners for the Penrith site Ted Withers (ATO alumni) and Bruce Quigley (then ATO Audit Committee Chair and Second Commissioner). (Photo: Personal collection.)

Professional roles can be very demanding, but we should all have the strength and focus to "never give up." Bruce with Australia's first ever Winter Olympics gold medallist Stephen Bradbury; they were the keynote speakers at the World Computer Congress in Brisbane in 2010. (Photo: Personal collection.)

Bruce Turner (right) receives his award from Bob McDonald at the recent Institute of Internal Auditors conference.

BRUCE WINS PRESTIGIOUS AUDIT AWARD

THE ATO'S CHIEF INTERNAL AUDITOR RECENTLY RECEIVED THE PROFESSION'S HIGHEST NATIONAL HONOUR FROM THE INSTITUTE OF INTERNAL AUDITORS (IIA).

Chief Internal Auditor Bruce Turner was recently awarded the 2008 Bob McDonald Award in front of more than 600 local and international delegates at the Institute of Internal Auditors premier South Pacific and Asian Audit Conference.

Bruce received the award for his outstanding contribution to the internal audit profession over many years.

Performance counts! Henry Ford is quoted as saying, "You can't build a reputation on what you are going to do". Bruce was the 2008 recipient of the "Bob McDonald Award," which is the highest honor that can be conferred by IIA- Australia on an internal auditor. Bob McDonald OAM was the first Australian to hold the position of Chairman of the IIA Global Board of Directors (2003-2004). (Photo: Personal collection (from ATO staff newsletter).)

Rewarding and recognising staff performance is fundamental to inspiring high morale. Auditor Priyadharshini (Priya) Mahadevan (front right) after receiving the annual Chief Internal Auditor Medal for 2008 from Bruce with members of the New South Wales audit team. (Photo: Personal collection.)

Good, honest, dedicated, loyal and capable people help you to achieve sustainable success and champion corporate values.

Above: With Executive Director Steve Dardo and Penrith Site Coordinator Nicole Preissl who provided exemplary support in shaping and leading the ATO's Penrith site leadership efforts. Pictured at Bruce's retirement function after presenting him with the "Mr Clever" teeshirt. (Photo: Personal collection.)

Left: With Executive Director Suzy Stamatonikolos who was an outstanding deputy and professional colleague to Bruce throughout his five years at the ATO. (Photo: Personal collection.)

A business vision becomes reality when it is a natural part of the team's conversation. The ATO internal audit vision was to be recognised as a "world class" internal audit practice, and this was ultimately confirmed over several years by independent assessments. Bruce with members of his ATO internal audit team after his retirement announcement; he is holding the "World Class Chief Internal Auditor" goblet the team presented to him. (Photo: Simon Woo (used with permission).)

It is important to establish a retirement plan well in advance of finishing up. Bruce had a rousing farewell when he retired from the ATO (and fulltime work) in 2012 and reflected on his FLOWERS retirement plan. Pictured here with his family, Robert, Bonnie, Nicole, Sally, Bea, Lucy, Jacqueline, Elina, Elijah and Glen. (Photo: Personal collection.)

Part 3

Shaping the High-Level Agenda

Key message: Success comes from keeping the big vision in sight, fueling your vision with perseverance, then embracing your unique talents.

"Bruce, I am writing to express my thanks to you for the duration of your tenure on the Board. You have brought a level of professionalism and quality to the operation of our Board that have made it more effective and up to the mark.

I have always appreciated your special blend of diligence and respect and goodwill that shines through in everything you do and say. I am also grateful for your warm personal support that is consistent and hugely helpful."

Emeritus Professor Stephen Leeder
Chair, Western Sydney Local Health District Board
December 2016

9 Positioning Yourself for the Other Side of the Boardroom Table

Gravitating towards board positions can be a daunting proposition. These opportunities rarely arise by chance; it takes effort and preparation for board roles to come to fruition. Governance, risk, compliance, and assurance professionals have somewhat of a head start, as their unique skills and experiences align with some of the base skills required for boards. There are similar challenges in retiring from fulltime employment; professionals can't just step off the treadmill and hope to maintain their balance, so transitioning in retirement demands well-considered planning. This chapter showcases an effective planning approach to underpin preparing oneself for board roles and/or meaningfulness in retirement; it starts with envisaging the "vision," articulating practical steps, applying a memorable formula (Family, Leisure, Overseas, Writing, Events, Roles, Stuff [FLOWERS]), and even monitoring the progress. Everyone needs to remember the teachings of Dr Stephen Covey (1932–2012) who once said, "To achieve goals you've never achieved before, you need to start doing things you've never done before."

PERSONAL STORY

I have always been a firm believer that every individual needs to add something new to their CV every year to continue to flourish professionally. This reflects the adage that *to achieve goals you've never achieved before you need to start doing things you've never done before.*

This can be attained through completion of post-graduate studies, gaining a professional certification, completing a contemporary training course, taking on a new role, shifting to a different entity, experiencing a different industry or sector, applying new ways of working, or investing in the development of others (e.g. mentoring or coaching).

When I became interested in assuming board roles, I first recognized that these roles are sought after and require well-considered preparation and planning. Boards are typically looking for a blend of experience, skills, qualifications, and personal attributes as illustrated in **Exhibit 9.1**.

EXHIBIT 9.1 Ingredients for securing a seat in the boardroom.

These requirements are further unpacked in **Exhibit 12.4** which provides an example of the typical content of a board composition matrix.

Individuals aspiring to move to the other side of the boardroom table need to take steps to broaden both their technical and specialist expertise, and their product and industry knowledge. **Exhibit 9.2** provides examples of how I was able to progressively craft a rich tapestry of skills and experience.

In an article "6 steps to getting board-ready," the Chartered Professional Accountants Canada reflects that, "Board service is a journey that begins long before your first board position. Turn your mind to what you can do to prepare early in your career, so that when the opportunity arises, you are well positioned to obtain a board role."[1] The key steps are illustrated in **Exhibit 9.3**.

The key insights from this phase of my story are:

- Work well with the board.
- Find the right board.
- Make the transition.
- Stay connected.
- Maintain health and wellbeing.
- Pay it forward.
- Reflect on the journey periodically.

CONTEXT

There are a number of interconnected elements that people can embrace to secure a role on the board and, where this coincides with life's third act, achieve meaningfulness in retirement. **Exhibit 9.4** illustrates some of these elements, which are founded on knowing what boards need, understanding your personal motivations, being fit for the role, and maintaining meaningful conversations that aid the process.

---

[1] *Six Steps to Getting Board-Ready,* CPA Canada, https://www.cpacanada.ca/en/business-and-accounting-resources/strategy-risk-and-governance/corporate-governance/publications/six-steps-to-getting-board-ready (Sourced 10 October 2020).

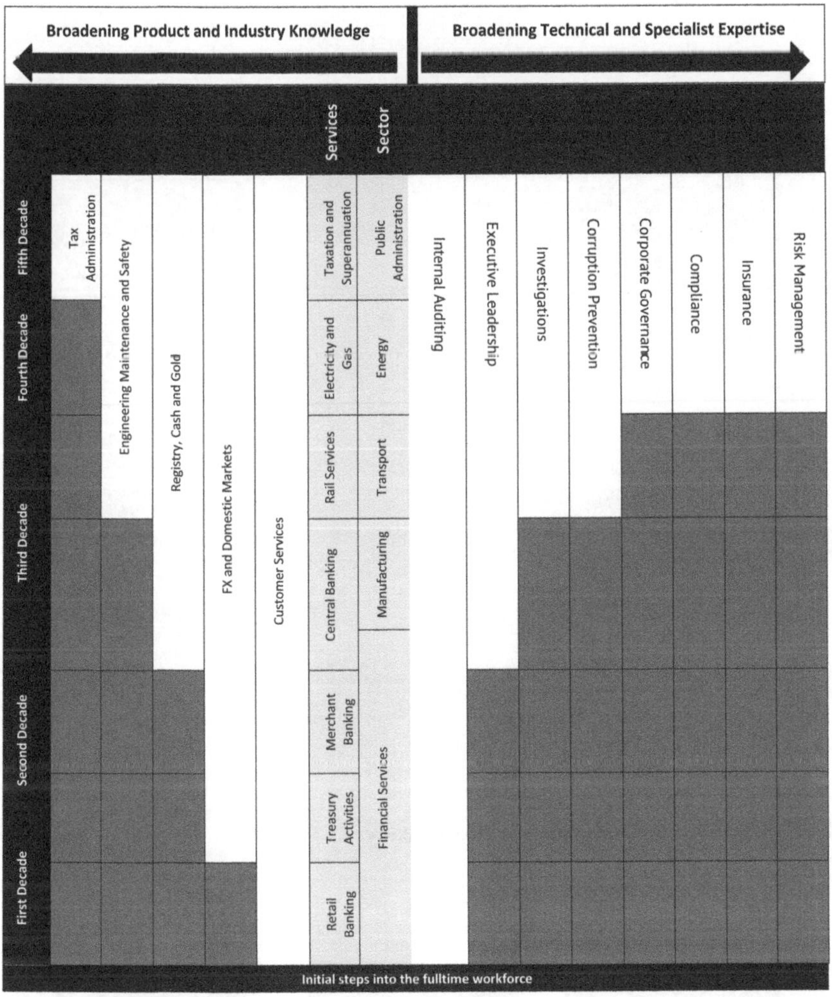

EXHIBIT 9.2 Crafting a rich tapestry of skills and experience.

KEY TAKEAWAYS AND DEEP DIVES

Work Well with the Board

Setting the Scene

Business leaders, and governance, risk management, compliance, and assurance specialists will often have periodic interactions with the board through routine reporting or by presenting occasional updates. When interacting with the board, it is important to communicate in a language they understand.

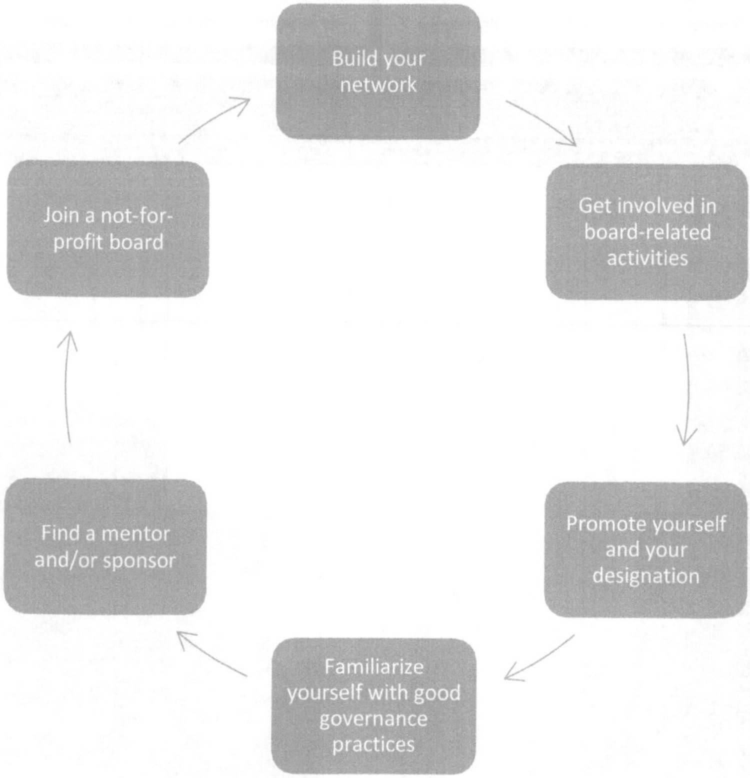

EXHIBIT 9.3 Steps for getting board-ready.[2]

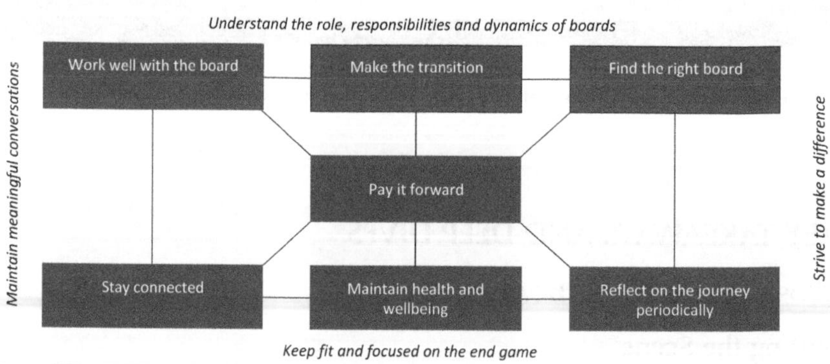

EXHIBIT 9.4 Securing board roles and meaningfulness in retirement.

[2] Ibid.

At one organization, I received advice from the audit manager of serious issues that could have a multi-million-dollar impact on the organization. A major information systems development contract had been established with a local company with limited capital, and no parental support. The information systems development was strategically important and time-critical, and the shortcomings that had surfaced were outside the organization's defined risk appetite. As the chief audit executive, I deemed the shortcomings to be serious enough for me to promptly alert the CEO and chair of the audit committee.

I arranged to meet with each of them the next morning (notwithstanding their tight schedules, they truly provided me with unfettered access), and I asked the audit manager to provide me with some bullet points on a page by the end of that day so that I could brief them appropriately in the morning. At that stage I only had the very comprehensive narrative, which was much too detailed for these briefings.

At the end of the day, I was given a "summary" which was about eight pages long. It was totally useless! I spent the night reading through and comprehending the full report, and then dissected it into key themes which I captured in bullet points on a single page. Both briefings went extremely well the next morning, and the CEO and audit committee chair were grateful that the matters had been identified and brought to their notice. The responsible managers were brought to account, and high-level discussions with executives at the parent company of the third party service provider resulted in a satisfactory resolution.

But the situation highlighted to me that further education was required for audit managers and others in the team on reporting techniques, and how to work well with business leaders and boards, including communicating with them in a language and style that they understand. These and other stakeholders are more likely to understand what is being reported to them when the people preparing the reports take the time to frame their communication within the context of the organization's vision, values, mission, strategy, objectives, and risks. It can be helpful to introduce the concept of a three-inch report to shape the thinking around how best to report.

The Three-Inch Report *is a great way for people reporting to the board to sharpen their messaging skills. One business leader reflected on a time when he had to report his observations to a three-star general at a military facility. There were limited resources during an operation involving a coalition of 34 countries. Consequently, the general provided guidance to all his direct reports on how they were to bring problems to his attention each day. He required all* *problems or challenges to be written on 3-by-5-inch index cards. With some effort and creativity, the leaders were able to condense their matters to fit on the index cards. This inspired innovative ways to produce streamlined reporting, sped up the reporting process, and improved their timeliness.*[3]

It was clear to me, that working well with the board requires business leaders and governance, risk management, compliance, and assurance specialists to understand their needs and expectations through effective engagement strategies. This ultimately leads to an effective working relationship by:

- Meeting the needs and expectations of the board consistently.
- Garnering support for proposed or ongoing programs.
- Identifying emerging risks, trends, and issues through the eyes of the board.

Meeting stakeholder expectations is discussed in Chapter 3 and establishing meaningful stakeholder communications is discussed in Chapter 8.

What It Means for Business[4]

When dealing with a board, it is important to understand its purpose for being, which is usually captured in a board charter or the organization's constitution or other establishing documents. The six common purposes of a board involve: Setting policy and direction; monitoring operations for compliance and mission; representing the organization; serving as strategy partners; keeping records for the organization; and developing current and future leaders.

Business leaders build relationships of trust with the board when they communicate openly and transparently. Conversely, trust between the board and business leaders can be diminished when the business leaders attempt to "control" the messaging and avoid leaning into full transparency. In the latter case, these business leaders are more likely to be pushed out of the organization, whereas the business leaders who build trust are more likely to move on from the organization at a time of their choosing.

Investing in the relationship between business leaders and the board is pivotal to success. In the best-case scenario, the business leaders who build trust with the board are well-placed to weather the inevitable difficult

---

[3] Richard Chambers, Lessons Learned on the Audit Trail (Lake Mary, FL: Internal Audit Foundation, 2014), 184–185.

[4] Insights in this section were gleaned from a Coaching for Leaders Podcast with Dave Stachowiak and Denise Hinden episode 432, "How to work with your board," https://coachingforleaders.com/how-to-work-with-a-board/ (sourced 21 August 2020).

times. Effective relationships will help business leaders get past the fear of sharing bad news with the board, and helps to position the board as a vital sounding board or thinking partner.

A risk for business leaders and board members is that the board can become somewhat disconnected from the organization when lots of things happen between meetings, as is often the case. While business leaders live and breathe within the organization each and every day, board members typically spread their expertise across many different organizations and only come together once every month or two. So, business leaders should take the time to reset the context regularly. For instance, there will be matters presented to the board that have been considered elsewhere (such as at an executive committee or audit committee meeting) and the CEO or business leader presenting the item needs to share the different points of view so the board recognizes the context in which the decision is to be made.

Business leaders need to be particularly cautious of making assumptions about what board members want to know. Five common mistakes for matters being considered by the board are:

- Failing to deliver the context and big picture strategic perspective.
- Not being sufficiently transparent or inclusive.
- Providing insufficient time to work through or discuss critical or complex strategic matters.
- Not being mindful of what board members carry forward from meeting to meeting, therefore failing to move the conversation forward based on what came before.
- Failing to take the temperature of board members before the meeting, perhaps as a result of not investing sufficient attention to managing conversations with individual board members.

Business leaders also need to recognize that board members typically look for strategic opportunities or to solve problems, whereas conversations with peers are often at the more tactical level.

When business leaders meet one-on-one with board members, they should communicate what has happened in conversations with other board members to help keep things moving forward.

There may be times when the member of a board or board committee is not contributing effectively. This calls for tough discussions between the board chair (perhaps in concert with the CEO for independent members on board committees). It could well be that their contribution would be greater if they were shifted onto something where they have a greater interest. These situations need to be handled thoughtfully, with candor.

Boards and business leaders alike should recognize three cornerstones of success:

- Developing an effective relationship between the board and business leaders. The organization is more likely to achieve its vision and realize its strategic initiatives where strong relationships exist. The relationship needs to be reaffirmed periodically (at least annually) and as opportunities evolve.
- Establishing and maintaining good board meeting practices. These are more effective when reports presented to the board are engaging and stimulate interest, where board members truly understand the different sides of the issue, and the boardroom conversations generate questions for which there may be no ready answer.
- Maintaining good board processes for the identification, recruitment, and cultivation of board members that delivers a well-balanced and experienced board cohort.

The relationships between board members and business leaders can be nurtured informally, perhaps over a cup of coffee. Business leaders get to know the board members, what interests them, where they want to be involved, and their concerns. Through these periodic interactions board members often cement their role as strategic thinking partners, and provide informal mentoring support that contributes to the overall success of the organization.

For governance, risk management, compliance, and assurance leaders there is often a natural link to at least one of the board members, and that is the relationship that they should invest in to help them frame their thinking. For instance, these natural links form between the chief audit executive and the audit committee chair, or between the chief financial officer and the finance committee chair. As an extension, there might be a board member who is passionate about sustainability which provides a natural link for the leader of the organization's environmental compliance activities.

Find the Right Board

Setting the Scene

I liked the meaning behind the adage that *a good company delivers excellent products and services, and great company does all that and strives to make the world a better place.* I embraced it as my aspiration to make the world a better place. It helped that my favorite motor vehicle since my childhood was a Ford; I still drive a Ford these days, a Ford Mondeo.

Taking on a board role was a natural progression for me, so when the time was right, I reflected on my personal drivers – to make the world a better place – to determine the natural fit for my capabilities, experience, interests, and personal vision. It was important to maintain meaningfulness through these pursuits (unpacked further in the section on maintaining health and wellbeing).

The Institute of Internal Auditors was my "go to" professional body for most of my career, so it seemed a natural fit when I weighed up the options for my first board role. Through the work that they do, particularly in the public sector, internal auditors ensure that business leaders remain focused on the public good (i.e. delivering value or benefits to all members of society); when public sector organizations maintain effective controls, there is likely to be less waste and more effective use of money that, ultimately, boosts the funding for essential frontline services like health, education, law and order, and public transport.

As board opportunities arose, I reflected on what I wanted to achieve, then considered five key questions to ensure the potential board roles were the right fit for me at the right time:

- Am I comfortable in the expertise I can bring and the time I can commit?
- Do I understand the role I will be expected to play on the board?
- Do the expectations of the board match what I believe I can contribute?
- Does the board expect me to help solve a problem; if so, what, and am I comfortable doing so?
- Can I make a real and sustainable contribution?

I also recognized the importance of getting a feel for the other directors and their approach to business. As a relatively conservative risk-taker, I needed to ensure that I was compatible with the personalities on the board, and recognized that an aggressive, entrepreneurial, profit-centered board would not suit my nature.

For each board opportunity I made an effort to get to know the board chair and other directors. In addition to meeting with the board chair and CEO to discuss the board dynamics, I researched the profile of each of the board members by reviewing their biographies in the annual report, looking at their career history where I could (e.g. LinkedIn), undertaking an Internet search, and informal reference checking through professional contacts and personal network.

What It Means for Business

The first step for people wishing to secure a role on the right board is to understand what they are personally striving to achieve.

The second step is to do their homework upfront, by reviewing information about the organization's operations. This is typically available in the organization's annual reports, website, media releases, and corporate documents. For publicly listed companies, it is also prudent to undertake a company search of public records (e.g. to determine details of directors, share price history, company announcements etc.). The annual report provides insights about the organization's operations, competitive position, challenges, and opportunities. In turn, the published financial reports may reveal any potential "red flags," including financial problems, unusual accounting techniques, and audit qualifications.

The third step is to obtain recent management reports, where possible, to determine whether the organization has sufficient cash (or access to funding) to pay its commitments. For instance, the organization's solvency can be determined by reviewing liquidity and other financial ratios, such as current and liquid ratios; net asset position; cash at bank and on deposit; trade debtors (and aging); and trade creditors (and aging). This step is vital because the financial position of organizations can deteriorate very quickly, and the true position might not be reflected in the financial reports from a year or so ago because of the time lag. An example of the swift change of an organization's financial position that lead to significant financial uncertainties is discussed in Chapter 12, within the section for managing CEO succession planning.

Fifteen questions to ask before joining a board:[5]

For the board chair, CEO, and company secretary

1. What can you tell me about the business?
2. What is the current financial position, including cash, liquidity and solvency?
3. What legal and regulatory environments does the company operate in?
4. What is the quality of the information I will be provided with?
5. What can you tell me about the board?
6. Why does the board need a new director and what is it looking for?
7. Who are the shareholders, members, and stakeholders?
8. Who holds the power on the board?
9. What are the board rituals and routines (e.g. location, length and style of board meetings, and boardroom seating arrangements)?
10. Do board members have unfettered access to the company secretary?

[5] "Joining a board," Australian Institute of Company Directors (originally sourced from: Finding the Right Board for You – 10 Questions to Ask Before Joining a Board, CPA Australia). http://www.companydirectors.com.au/director-resource-centre/publications/company-director-magazine/2000-to-2009-back-editions/2007/november/joining-a-board (Sourced 11 August 2020). Extensively modified.

11. Are there any unresolved tax issues, litigation, or any unresolved issues or disagreements with tax officials, regulators, or auditors?

To ask yourself

12. Why am I interested in taking this directorship and what do I want to achieve?
13. What can I contribute?
14. Do I have the capacity to do the job?
15. Will I be taking on responsibility for things that leave me with unacceptable personal liability or reputational risks?

Board chairs and CEOs need to attract talent onto the board to maintain the strongest possible team. They should therefore be open, honest, and transparent about the strengths and challenges for the board, and be willing to answer questions that potential board members pose. Steps for the board chair to establish and maintain a skills-based board are discussed in Chapter 12.

For people pursuing board roles, it is important to undertake due diligence in finding the right board, however there might still be a few unanticipated shocks that surface at the first (or an early) board meeting; some examples are interspersed in Chapter 12.

Make the Transition

Setting the Scene

I was fortunate that when I was ready to step-up, I had a reasonable understanding of the workings of board and audit committees through my leadership roles in internal audit, governance, risk management, and compliance. This set me up for a reasonably smooth transition from a business leadership role onto the board. I had to let go of the typical business leadership responsibilities to take on the typical board responsibilities illustrated in **Exhibit 9.5**.

It was also important that I brought my own ideas onto the board, some of which were shaped from watching things from the sidelines rather than as a fully-fledged participant on the playing field. As Dame Joan Sutherland has said, *"You can listen to what everybody says, but the fact remains that you've got to get out there and do the thing yourself."*

About a year after I had joined one board, I heard the board chair talking to one of the new directors who had been appointed in the latest round after the retirement of a longstanding board director. The conversation went along the lines that the board chair would wait about nine to twelve months before appointing the new board director to one of the board committees, as there was much to learn about the organization. I reflected on my much shorter transition, having been thrust onto the board audit

Board	Business Leaders
Sets and monitors the organization's direction.	The CEO leads the business leaders in keeping with the board's direction.
Board responsibilities include:	Responsibilities include:
- Setting values, vision, mission, business objectives, and strategic planning goals	- Maintaining customer relationships
- Choosing the CEO	- Making operational decisions
- Approving major policies	- Making operational policies
- Making major decisions	- Keeping the board well-informed
- Overseeing performance	- Educating the board
- Serving as external advocate	- Delivering to the board well-developed recommendations and opportunities

EXHIBIT 9.5 Transitioning of responsibilities from a business leader to the board.

committee as chair at my first meeting! So, it dawned on me that there are two sides to making the transition to a board or board committee role – the board chair has to see you as being ready for greater responsibility, and you have to have confidence in your experience and capability to fully embrace the new challenges and drive the agenda.

What It Means for Business

The board sets the organization's key strategic direction and major decisions, and monitors their implementation by management. In turn, audit committee activities are informed by the overarching strategies and provide oversight of the associated governance arrangements.

Boards will typically develop structural arrangements that suit their circumstances and create governance frameworks that enable the organization to achieve its vision, maintain its values, and pursue its business objectives and ultimate success. In some jurisdictions, the governance environment is such that it encourages boards to design their governance structures and frameworks under an "if not, why not" regime.

One of the most significant challenges for business leaders, governance, risk management, compliance, and assurance specialists, and others making the transition onto the board or a board committee (like the audit committee) is to embrace the concept of "nose in, fingers out."

There should always be a clear distinction between the obligation of a governing body and board committees to stick their nose in an organization's governance matters, but to keep its fingers away from management's responsibilities to run the organization on a day-to-day basis. Boards and audit committees are expected to ask challenging and meaningful questions, but must always keep their hands-off operational activities, so they do not blur their independent oversight role. There may be exceptions to this approach; for instance, in some companies (more so in the United States) this could involve executive directors or executive chairs rather than non-executive directors.

> ***Nose in fingers out*** *refers to the distinction between the obligation of a board and board committee to stick its nose in an organization's governance matters, but to keep its fingers out of the management of the organization. A board committee is expected to ask challenging and meaningful questions, but committee members must keep their hands-off operational activities, so they do not blur their independent oversight role.*

Another challenge for people transitioning to a board or board committee role is to understand that (unlike former executive or management roles they might have held) they have no inherent authority or executive power. Any material enquiries made by board members of business leaders and, conversely, by business leaders of individual board members should primarily be channeled through the board chair and CEO. The two common exceptions will be:

- Where the board chair and CEO permit open communication between individual board members and business leaders, typically for an authorized board-related task.
- Between the chairs of board committees and the relevant business leaders responsible for those functions, on matters within the scope of those functions.

A successful transition is more likely to occur when there is a clear understanding of roles, delegations, and boundaries which allows both the director and business leaders to respect the responsibilities, contributions, and expectations of the other party. This should complement the behavior of the director in courteously and respectfully listening to the business leaders with an open but constructively challenging mind to allow management to make its contribution with confidence and clarity of viewpoint, and without undue interference, constraint or trepidation.[6]

[6] "Relationship between the board and management," Australian Institute of Company Directors https://aicd.companydirectors.com.au/-/media/cd2/resources/director-resources/director-tools/pdf/05446-3-10-mem-director-gr-rel-board-management_a4-web.ashx (sourced 1 September 2020).

Stay Connected

Setting the Scene

In 2001 (when our children had reached adulthood or late teens) my wife and I established an annual *Turner Family Newsletter* that we circulated to our extended family and friends with our Christmas cards in December each year. In addition to staying in contact, it was a reminder to the people who played an important part in our lives when we were young that their efforts were appreciated and would never be forgotten. Of course, we strive to maintain contact through the year, but capturing the whole story in one place is often a little more informative and can be more readily shared; and we know that the family newsletters are passed around the extended families of the recipients, which is nice.

The recipients of the Christmas newsletters extended across people of different generations and relationships as illustrated in **Exhibit 9.6**.

Others have picked up the Christmas newsletter concept over the years, and we love reading their stories. Alas! with social media now booming, I'm not sure how much life there is left in our annual newsletter. Sadly, many of the older generations are no longer living, but while they remain, I aim to continue the practice, as I know it means a lot to them. It is also useful for my own children and grandchildren to capture these stories for our descendants, given that letter-writing is becoming a lost art.

The nature of some of the relationships with my professional associates and former workmates is that even though some years (or in some cases decades) may pass, we are always ready to help where we can, should the need arise. The relationships never really diminished, it was more that the busyness of life meant we took different paths, especially as our children were growing up.

My family arranged a surprise party for me in 2015 to celebrate my appointment as a Member of the Order of Australia in the Queen's birthday honors. It was a special occasion, and they tracked down people that I had worked with at every organization for the preceding 45 years. The planning was so well considered and concealed; I had no inkling until I arrived at the venue! For many of these treasured colleagues we had stayed connected in some way or another across the decades.

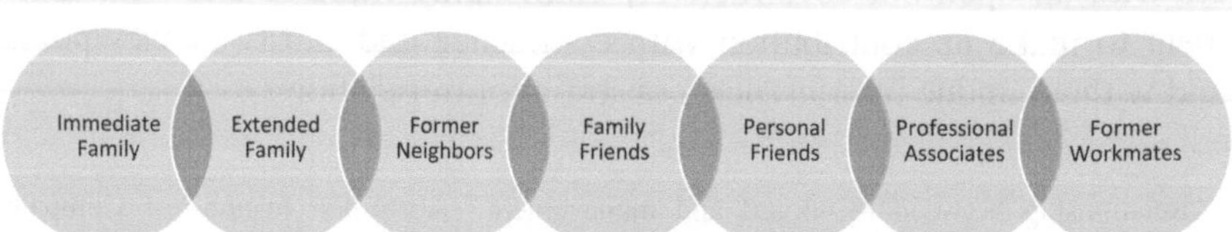

EXHIBIT 9.6 Staying connected with a mix of people.

What It Means for Business

Inevitably, business leaders who reach the top of the corporate ladder will have less interaction with the rungs below and those they serve. While the responsibilities of business leaders change as they move into more senior roles, their level of responsibility is broader and they need to rely on competent leaders below them to run more of the daily operations. This is necessary structurally, otherwise business leaders could potentially get bogged down in day-to-day logistics and end up burning the time and energy they need for the responsibilities of the position they currently hold. There are, however, ramifications if they don't make an effort to stay connected.

It is also important for business leaders, governance, risk management, compliance, and assurance specialists to leverage techniques like intelligent conversations to stay connected with employees, customers, stakeholders, their peers in other organizations, professional relationships, and others with whom they have dealings. For those folk aspiring to take on board and board committee roles, intelligent conversations help them to grow and connect, ultimately positioning themselves for opportunities that could arise.

*An **intelligent conversation** is one where people gain knowledge from the people with whom they are speaking. When business leaders establish intelligent conversations as a regular part of their lives, they will continuously learn from the people they encounter.*

Business leaders usually make it to the top because they know how to get others to do what needs to be done, and they are attuned to the needs and expectations of their customers and other stakeholders. While their leadership role requires them to look to the future, they also need to take the time to look over their shoulder to make sure their team is informed, motivated, and feel valued, and that their stakeholders continue to be well-served.

Part of the job as a business leader is to stay informed, so effective communication skills are imperative. When business leaders remain cloistered in their office, they run the risk of being kept out of the loop of important information, which can ultimately adversely impact on the effectiveness of their work and the health of the organization. Staying connected helps the business leader to recognize shifts in corporate dynamics at the grassroots level.

Staying connected is also essential for the health and wellbeing of the business leader, as they need to remain purposeful in their career to remain engaged and effective. Staying connected as a leader helps to engender a deeper sense of purpose; they need to remember where they came from, why they do what they do, and what it's all for? But they need to be

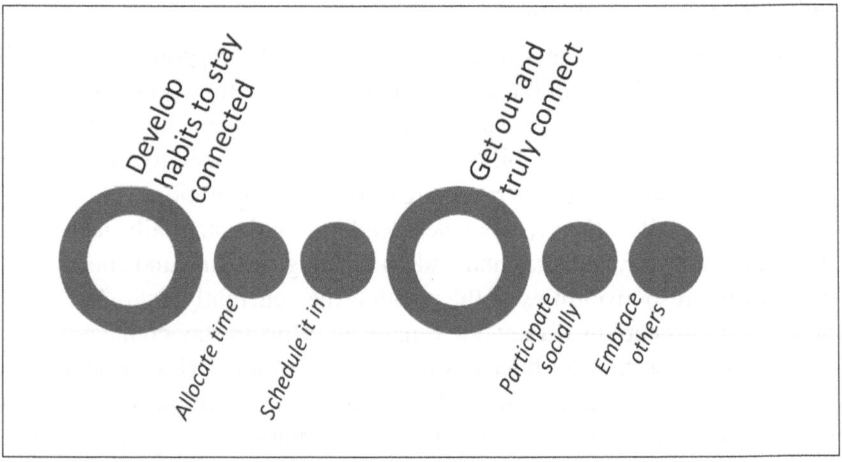

EXHIBIT 9.7 How business leaders can stay connected.

proactive in making the effort to stay connected, with examples of steps they can take illustrated in **Exhibit 9.7**.

Maintain Health and Wellbeing

Setting the Scene

When we are young, we can sometimes take our health for granted. As an example, few people in their 20s think of the consequences as they relish in themselves and self-indulge. A person's metabolism influences the longevity of their lives, but metabolisms do slow down with age. People who maintain a well-functioning metabolism through a balanced diet are typically able to survive longer.

When I attained senior management roles in my 30s, my employers usually encouraged their senior executives and other critical employees to undertake an annual medical examination. The cost was paid by the employer, and the results were confidential between the doctor and the employee. The checks were extensive, and included consideration of:

- Presenting symptoms (i.e. cardiovascular, respiratory, alimentary, Genito-urinary, central nervous, limbs and joints, skin).
- Past medical history (i.e. illnesses, operations, accidents, vaccinations, family medical).
- Allergies.
- Bodily functions (i.e. weight, appetite, eating habits, bowel habit, micturition, sleep, medication).
- Social activities (i.e. smoking habits, alcohol, physical activities).

- Physical examination (i.e. general condition, height, weight, cardiovascular [pulse, blood pressure, heart sounds, murmurs, peripheral pulses], respiratory system [i.e. sinuses, ears], alimentary system [mouth, Valsalva, abdomen]).
- Genito-urinary system.
- Central nervous system (eyes, ears, reflexes).
- Investigations (hematology, biochemistry [including cholesterol], serology, urinalysis, chest x-ray, lung function, ECG exercising, eye testing, audiometry).

The results of the annual medical examinations were pivotal to me gaining a reasonable level of health literacy and sharing these insights with my staff. Health literacy is important to maintaining health and wellbeing in the workplace.

The organizations I worked for typically established a range of health programs to complement the medical examinations. Health promotion is a process that is crucial to creating awareness, and ultimately in enabling people to increase control to improve their health. Health promotion involves a range of things that help to boost health literacy, including health policy, environmental improvements, workplace health and safety, minimizing risk behaviors, improving protective behaviors, creating supportive environments and networks for people as well as providing access to health care. The aim is to increase the power individuals have over their own health and remain mentally-health aware.

Organizations are best served when they focus on health literacy issues that are most meaningful to many people. For example, where employees or their families have been affected by a health issue – such as cancer, or diabetes, or heart disease – these situations can be used to guide the organization's health literacy efforts; an employee survey in January could be used to determine which causes or events the employees have a preference to support during the year. Alternatively, an onsite health check could be arranged to provide business leaders with an overview of the primary health risks of their workforce, allowing them to tailor future health-awareness initiatives.

Health providers in many jurisdictions produce a health-works calendar that captures a range of national and international health-awareness events, providing hundreds of ideas to inject energy and enthusiasm into an organization's wellness program. The aim is to choose one or two days each quarter for a health-awareness event, and do them really well. These events can bolster existing physical and mental health activities or give them more meaning. There are universal topics that can be used to promote physical fitness or mental health goodness during the workday, such as walk to work day (October) or world compliment day (March).

One of the health initiatives that I personally promoted each year was the Step-tober 10,000 steps challenge (held in October). At the ATO, we established internal audit Step-tober teams across each of the four sites where I had staff, and I offered small prizes for different categories. It was a fun event each year, notwithstanding the interstate friendly rivalry. We tracked the number of steps and announced the progress each day. On some days during Step-tober, after a long day in the office, I would be driving home in the evening from Canberra (about 200 miles), and would stop at the mid-point to walk around the service center for about half-an-hour to achieve my 10,000-step target for the day. After which I would resume the drive home.

***The 10,000 steps challenge** is a simple, flexible, and fun workplace health and wellbeing initiative where workplace team members are challenged to achieve 10,000 steps each and every day of the challenge. The steps are counted and the winning team is the one that reaches the destination on a virtual map first, or the one that accumulates the most steps over a predetermined time period (usually between four to eight weeks). The daily target was set based on international research that indicates that if people complete 10,000 steps per day, they dramatically reduce their risk of developing a number of lifestyle illnesses and diseases such as obesity, type 2 diabetes, cardiovascular disease, and some cancers.*

Most people are keen to pursue a happy and healthy retirement (or semi-retirement) when they reach the retirement age and are ready for it. When the lifestyle-changes upon retirement and in the lead-up are ill-considered, there is a significant risk to meaningful retirement longevity.

What It Means for Business

Organizations benefit from an investment in the health and wellbeing of employees through improved productivity, optimal engagement, high morale, improved employee recruitment and retention, reduced absenteeism, and camaraderie among workers.

People who maintain their physical health are better-equipped to perform at work because they feel better, have more energy, are usually in a better mood, feel more relaxed, and sleep better.

Physical activity or exercise can improve the physical health of employees, both immediate and long-term. Health benefits include reduced risk of a heart attack, better weight management, lower blood cholesterol levels, lower risk of type 2 diabetes, and some cancers, lower blood pressure, lower risk of falls, lower risk of developing osteoporosis (by having stronger bones, muscles, and joints), and better recovery from periods of hospitalization or enforced bedrest.

Maintaining one's emotional well-being also provides physical health benefits by reducing stress and the related negative impacts on the body, while allowing people to lead more active lifestyles and potentially boosting their immune system to help protect against diseases. Mental health is discussed in greater depth in Chapter 10 in the section on focusing on mental health. Boards should seek to understand the programs that business leaders have in place to maintain the health and wellbeing of employees. For instance, does the organization meet the cost of annual medical checks for business leaders and other critical employees; does the organization provide annual influenza vaccine shots; is access available to guided-assistance or support programs outside the workplace; is there a wellness program (e.g. 10,000 steps team challenge, provision for siesta naps, healthy lunch and snack initiatives, etc.); and, is there sponsorship of fitness activities (e.g. sports team, or gym memberships)?

The board or audit committee should also monitor trends in employee sick leave, and understand the story behind any adverse statistics (in reviewing sick leave trends, there may be employees with serious illnesses, such as those undertaking cancer treatments, that need to be accounted for separately so as to not distort the true trends for occasional sick leave-taking by disengaged employees).

Pay It Forward

Setting the Scene

Throughout my career, I have been blessed by the many people who have supported me in my endeavors, with no expectation for anything in return. I have called out some of these people in Chapter 1, the postface (the formative years), and in the acknowledgements (24 legends who inspired me). In reality, these people are just the tip of the iceberg, as my career trajectory owes itself to many of my past colleagues who have invested in my growth through a genuine interest, kind word, role modeling, or sincere compassion. In turn, I have maintained a commitment to paying it forward myself, and have encouraged my closest colleagues to embrace a similar philosophy in striving to make the world a better place. The break-out box below reflects one of my proudest moments as a business leader.

The Brisbane River broke its banks in January 2011 and a wave of brown water inundated the city in the biggest floods to hit Queensland's capital city since 1974. About 40 km (25 miles) south west of Brisbane, the city of Ipswich was flooded when the Bremer River broke its banks inundating the central business district and 1,000s of houses, with 38 people losing their lives. The leadership team at the Australian Tax Office in Penrith wanted to do something to aid the Ipswich recovery effort; the ATO also had an office in Ipswich. As the senior site executive, I welcomed the idea and supported the initiative.

Our staff teamed up with their peers at the Penrith City Council, coordinated with the state rail operators to sponsor the cost of the 1,000 km (620 miles) train trip, and in collaboration with the state recovery coordinator determined an area that needed assistance. Our team of 40 made the 24 hour train trip to Ipswich and spent a few days investing their own time in cleaning up a horse-riding center. Many children gained enjoyment from horse-riding, though the center was a lower priority from a strategic recovery perspective. Through the team's voluntary efforts, the horse-riding center re-opened many months earlier than it would have, helping to put smiles on the faces of the children.

The genuine efforts of the Penrith team set the bar high for other corporate business leaders, and cemented the site's reputation as one that reflected "the joy of life."

For people interested in paying it forward, all it takes is the first step. Work out what and how you want to pay it forward, then determine your best options. Once the first step has been taken, it is amazing how one activity can lead to many more opportunities to share one's insights and influence increasing numbers across the world. As an example:

- The Institute of Internal Auditors Australia produced a special edition journal in March 2012 to mark its 60th anniversary. I wrote an article *The ABC of Professional Practice – Delivering What the Audit Committee Really Needs*, that was well-received.
- In his regular blog[7] Norman Marks (who was a chief audit executive and chief risk officer at major global corporations for more than 20 years) commented, "Bruce Turner, an

[7] Norman Marks blog, 26 March 2012, "Fine article on the ABC of a Professional Internal Audit Practice" https://iaonline.theiia.org/blogs/marks/2012/Pages/Fine-Article-on-the-ABC-of-a-Professional-Internal-Audit-Practice.aspx (Sourced 18 August 2020).

experienced and respected head of internal audit (CAE) has written a fine piece for the initial issue of the IIA– Australia Journal. ... While I can't share the entire piece ... I would like to share some of the highlights." He concluded by remarking, "I repeat: the value of article is easily more than the cost of buying the Journal."

- The article was selected to be presented at a session of the 2012 South Pacific and Asia Audit Conference (SOPAC – the premier internal audit event in the region) which I duly did.
- The SOPAC conference session was also well-received, and I was ultimately invited to present a modified-version (suitable for global delegates) at the Institute of Internal Auditors International Conference held in Orlando, Florida, United States of America in July 2013.
- The editor-in-chief of the *Internal Auditor Magazine* (International Edition) attended the above conference session and asked me to write a piece for the magazine which I did, translating my original article into content suitable for an international audience and calling it *Delivering Value to the Audit Committee – the ABC's of Success.* It was published in the December 2013 issue of *Internal Auditor.*
- For the above article I was the recipient of an "Outstanding Contributor" award from the *Internal Auditor Magazine* for 2014. The article was "... cited for its outstanding quality, clear presentation of ideas, practicality, and relevance to the continuing practice of internal auditing."
- Next, I reworked the content for an article in the *Internal Auditor Middle East Magazine* of June 2014 which they titled, *Scoring goals ... a veteran chief audit executive shares his game-plan for adding value and meeting stakeholder needs.*
- No doubt, the one original piece of work on the ABCs of auditing morphed into numerous other opportunities, though the above points provide useful examples of the ripple effect.

Pay it forward *is an expression that covers the situation where a person who has received a gift, a deed, a nice thing, or an act of kindness doing something kind for someone else, a third-party beneficiary (i.e. someone other than the person who did the initial good deed). While the concept is over a century old (some suggest it was coined by Lily Hardy Hammond in her 1916 book "In the Garden of Delight"), it is an oft-used expression in the 21st century.*

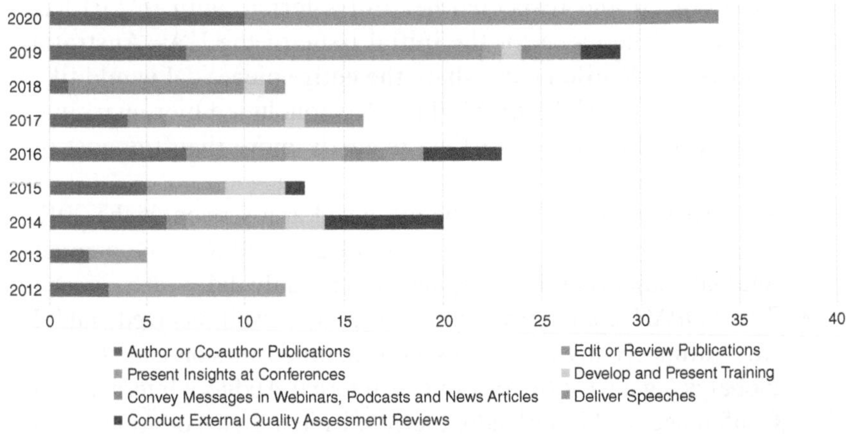

EXHIBIT 9.8 Paying it forward in retirement – snapshot of author's activities.

How you pay it forward will ebb and flow through one's life as illustrated in **Exhibit 9.8**. Sometimes the nature and number of these activities in life's third act will be dictated by opportunities, and others will be influenced by availability. For instance, there is less time to undertake discretionary activities when you are travelling extensively overseas in retirement; on other occasions you might accept an overseas speaking engagement and build a vacation, an adventure, or a cruise around it.

What It Means for Business

Some business leaders support employee initiatives to pay it forward, which can create the ripple effect. For instance, employees could serve community members at a local soup kitchen; support a monthly charitable cause; put together care packages for homeless individuals or other community members; clean up litter, plant trees, or otherwise beautify local parks or outdoor areas; serve as a lecturer or guest speaker at a local university or college; or, support the Red Cross in a blood drives collection. The opportunities are only limited by imagination.

There are also many opportunities for business leaders to pay it forward themselves or on behalf of the organization. Examples include, lend expertise to a non-profit organization; donate the organization's own products or services to a good cause; establish a long-term partnership with a charitable group that is consistent with the organization's mission; sponsor a local youth sports team; allow local students to shadow a business leader to learn more about business; sponsor a local event; establish a community garden; or, donate old computers to local schools when the organization upgrades its obsolete personal desktop and laptop computers (where they are still of value for teaching).

> ***Meaningfulness*** *refers to the quality of being useful, serious, or important, and reflects the importance of contributing to something beyond yourself, such as connecting with others and helping them.*

People who find opportunities to pay it forward will often build meaningfulness in their lives. As a result, they are more likely to enjoy their work, to be more productive, and feel committed to their employers and satisfied with their jobs. **Exhibit 9.9** highlights four steps that people can pursue to find real meaning in their lives.

Meaningfulness comes from several constructs:

- Coherence (how people understand their life).
- Purpose (the goals that people have for their life).
- Significance (the sense that people's lives are worth living, and that life has inherent value).[8]

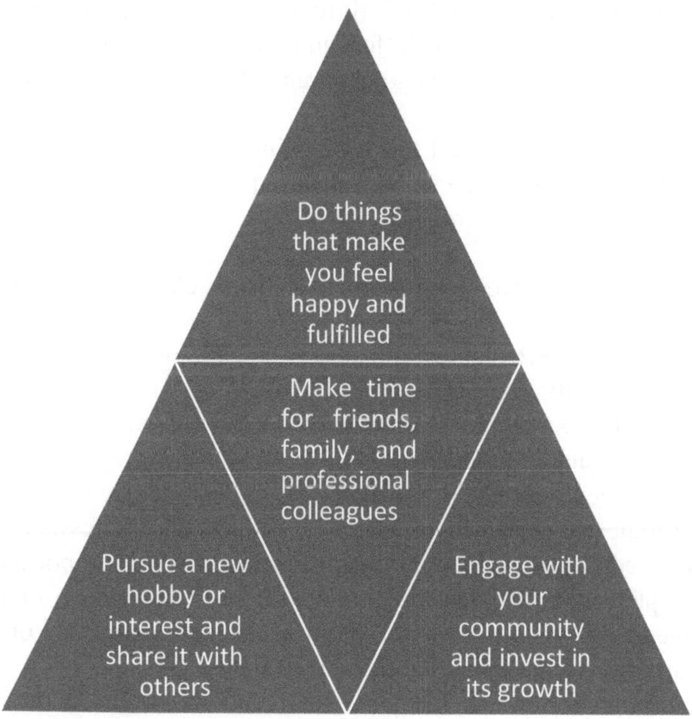

EXHIBIT 9.9 Four steps to finding meaning in life.

[8] Alicia Nortje, "Realizing your meaning: 5 ways to live a meaningful life," 7 July 2020. Citing Reker and Wong (1988). https://positivepsychology.com/live-meaningful-life/ (Sourced 20 August 2020).

Some studies have concluded that helping others improves social interaction, distracts people from their own problems, and ultimately improves self-esteem and competence.[9]

Employees who perceive their work to be purposeful and meaningful typically exert more effort, and highly-productive older workers who feel fulfilled at work will often seek to postpone their retirement.

Boards should encourage business leaders to support pay it forward opportunities that align with the mission of the company and are compatible with the corporate values.

There are many different ways that people can pay it forward and this can occur at any stage of a person's career. We delve further into the examples of this in Chapter 10, when we focus on how we can make it count through philanthropy.

Reflect on the Journey Periodically

Setting the Scene

I envisaged my "vision" for "life's third act" as I entered that phase of my life, and captured a memorable formula using the acronym FLOWERS (Family, Leisure, Overseas, Writing, Events, Roles, (and other) Stuff) that I discussed in Chapter 8.

As in the business world, I saw little point in having a vision and a plan if I didn't monitor the progress. So, I made a point of capturing the journey through stories. As an example:

- For the "FLO" we captured many of these elements through our storytelling, newsletters, photoalbums and photobooks.
- For the "WERS" I established a log along similar lines to **Exhibit 9.10**, and summarized the activities in the chart similar to **Exhibit 9.8** to record occasional events where I had the opportunity to share my insights.
- My curriculum vitae (CV, which is Latin for "course of life") was periodically refreshed to reflect changes to my professional history, education, skills, and achievements. This is important, as people recommending you for board, audit committee or other roles will typically give you a quick call seeking a copy of your current CV; and they often need it straight away.

Another of my interests is genealogy, so I have taken the opportunity to record my journey to date in a number of ways as illustrated in **Exhibit 9.10**.

[9] Mike Gonyea, "Importance of helping others." https://oureverydaylife.com/aggressive-behavior-in-adults-4635517.html (Sourced 20 August 2020).

Bruce and Bea The Formative Years to 1977	Bruce Turner Retirement Reflections First 5 Years to February 2017	The Turner Family History The First 2 Decades of the Twenty-first Century
Charts the early story of Bruce and his wife Bea born on different sides of the world (Australia and The Netherlands respectively) through to when they met and ultimately became engaged in 1977. Contains a pictorial record that combines photos, artifacts, memories, and stories. Produced in 2017 to commemorate the fortieth anniversary of their engagement.	*Reviews the activities pursued by Bruce in his first five years of retirement against each of the seven elements of his FLOWERS retirement plan. Captures the story through photos, artifacts, and statistics. On the whole, illustrates a well-balanced retirement journey with relatively equal representation of each of the seven elements.*	*Storybook with blend of photos, commentary, a timeline of key family events and an amalgam of the annual 'Turner Christmas Newsletters' (mentioned in 'stay connected' section of this chapter) that chart the family wrap for each year from 2000 to 2020. It also captures a few lead-in stories from the 1980's and 1990's to provide context.*

EXHIBIT 9.10 Examples of personal storytelling.

These short storybooks have been produced and distributed to my family for their personal records.

What It Means for Business

It doesn't matter which stage your career has reached or whether you're in life's second or third act (mentioned in Chapter 8), every individual needs to add something new to their CV every year to continue to flourish professionally. It's not just about adding something new, it's also vital to tell the story so that others can pick up on what you've accomplished in your life's work (i.e. academic formation, publications, qualifications, etc.).

A starting point is to maintain a log of your professional activities (like publications you've produced, public forums you've participated in, or specialist activities you've undertaken) along the lines of **Exhibit 9.11**. It's amazing what you forget if you don't maintain a structured and disciplined approach to your personal recordkeeping. These logs are useful when you are fronting up for your annual performance appraisal, or preparing yourself for a new job or board opportunity.

Armed with the information from the log, business leader aspirants are better-positioned to reflect on their journey through stories or anecdotes. This approach works best when the story is credible and accurate, and is more likely to engage the brain in a deeper way than facts and figures alone.

Business leaders who reflect on their personal journey periodically and capture their memories, motivate others, make conversations more interesting (and sometimes exciting for others), and ultimately strengthen relationships. Storytelling focuses on the human side of life, so people engage better through good memorable stories; powerful stories are more likely to inspire others and stick longer in their mind.

Part 1 - Details of Occasional Events on Governance, Risk, Compliance, Control, Assurance and Leadership				
Event	Organization	Date	Activity	Topic
<Details>			*<Color-coded as per categories in part 2>*	

Part 2 - Summary of All Completed Activities as at <Date>								
Year	Publications		Public Forums				EQAR	Total
	Author or Co-author	Edit or Review	Present at Conferences	Develop and Present Training	Develop and Deliver Webinars or Contribute to Podcasts and News Articles	Deliver Speeches	Conduct external Quality Assessment Reviews	
<Year 1>	*<Number>*							
<Year 2>	*<Number>*							

EXHIBIT 9.11 Summary of sharing insights at occasional events. *Notes:* 1. Each "activity" in part 1 is color-coded. The color-coding corresponds to the activities in part 2 (which are shown as light-grey boxes in the exhibit but different colors in practice). 2. The content for each year in part 1 can be separated by including a "year" row separator.

Boards, in turn, need to carefully construct the story of the organization's journey, and they do so through regular publications, on the website, and in the published annual report. Board chairs and business leaders invest considerable energy and effort in capturing the story of the organization. Individuals should embrace a similar approach.

CHAPTER 9 – TEN CLOSING REFLECTIONS

- Boards and business leaders should recognize organizational success comes from developing an effective relationship between themselves, establishing and maintaining good board-meeting practices, and maintaining good board processes for the identification, recruitment, and cultivation of board members.
- Individuals wishing to secure a role on the right board need to understand what they are personally striving to achieve, look for suitable matches, and do their due diligence or homework upfront.
- Business leaders, governance, risk management, compliance, and assurance specialists, and others making the transition onto the board or a board committee (like the audit committee) need to embrace the concept of "nose in, fingers out."

- Board members making material enquiries of business leaders should primarily be channeling these through the board chair and CEO (likewise, when business leaders communicate directly with individual board members).
- Business leaders, governance, risk management, compliance, and assurance specialists should leverage techniques like intelligent conversations to stay connected with employees, customers, stakeholders, and others with whom they have dealings.
- Individuals aspiring to take on board and board committee roles can use intelligent conversations to help them to grow and connect, ultimately positioning themselves for opportunities that could arise.
- Business leaders should make sensible investments in the health and wellbeing of employees, which will reap returns through improved productivity, optimal engagement, high morale, improved employee recruitment and retention, reduced absenteeism, and camaraderie among workers.
- The board or audit committee should monitor trends in employee sick leave, and understand the story behind any adverse statistics.
- Business leaders and individuals should look for opportunities to pay it forward; this will often build meaningfulness in their lives and result in them enjoying their work, being more productive, feeling committed to their employers, and being satisfied with their jobs.
- Every individual needs to add something new to their CV every year to continue to flourish professionally, and they need to tell the story so that others can pick up on what they've accomplished in their life's work (i.e. academic, publications, qualifications, experience, etc.).

10 Making It Count through Philanthropy

Professionals who establish a strong personal brand and a high level of credibility have an opportunity to champion societal-changing pursuits. Storytelling in all its guises can often be more powerful than financial philanthropy alone. This chapter considers several practical examples, such as paying it forward through coaching and mentoring, actively addressing gender diversity, opposing violence against women and children, and promoting health, wellbeing, and employment initiatives for the under-privileged … and it also calls-out the lost opportunities when professionals maintain a narrow and shallow focus. We get a sense of the difference between being good and great through the eyes of businessman Bill Ford Junior who said, "A good company delivers excellent products and services, and great company does all that and strives to make the world a better place."

Entity Profile and Role

Entity and Role:	Various as shown in Chapters 11 and 12.
Timeframe:	The Fifth Decade.

PERSONAL STORY

While I am charitable by nature and keen to help others, I am cautious about the registered charities I support financially. I accept it costs money to run a charitable organization, and some of the higher-rated charities generally spend at least 75 percent or more on their programs, which means that more of the money raised goes to causes that people want to support. Media reports have suggested that some charities spend as little as 4 percent on their programs (clearly a "fail").

I am more inclined to support charities that are transparent and reasonable on fundraising efficiency, and report on financial efficiency and financial capacity performance metrics (discussed later).

The are many philanthropic opportunities that I have had the privilege to participate in over the years involving financial contributions. My four personal favorites have provided people with wonderful opportunities for personal growth without unacceptable "administration costs," these include:

- Working-a-day-for-kids (all administration was provided voluntarily and 100 percent of money raised reached the needy).

- Sponsoring the travel, accommodation, and other costs for someone from a developing South Pacific nation to attend an international conference in Sydney (100 percent of money was used for the purpose intended, and was matched by a free conference registration provided by the conference organizer).
- Playing a part in the launch of a health board's first-ever bursary program aimed at providing individual staff with financial support to further their education and training pursuits (again a direct contribution to the bursary recipients).
- Donating the family electric organ to the local primary school (the thrill of the school principal when collecting the instrument was electrifying).

But the focus of this chapter is on non-financial philanthropy; doing the things directly that improve the professional wellbeing of individuals and help to shape a better society. This is often aided by the brand that a person has developed.

The key insights from this phase of my story are:

- Understand your personal brand.
- Shine the light on domestic violence.
- Focus on mental health.
- Deliver mentoring and coaching.
- Improve Indigenous health and wellbeing.
- Provide storytelling that is meaningful.
- Volunteer to help others.

CONTEXT

An important outcome of developing a personal brand that is well-regarded and highly-respected is that you have an opportunity to extend your influence well beyond your day job. **Exhibit 10.1** illustrates how these elements can come together to make meaningful differences, recognizing that people will identify and pursue different personal preferences and interests.

KEY TAKEAWAYS AND DEEP DIVES

Understand Your Personal Brand

Setting the Scene

Individuals need to nurture a personal brand consistent with their personal values and personality. When I first started fulltime work as a 16-year-old, my parents arranged for me to buy a suit from the local Webber's

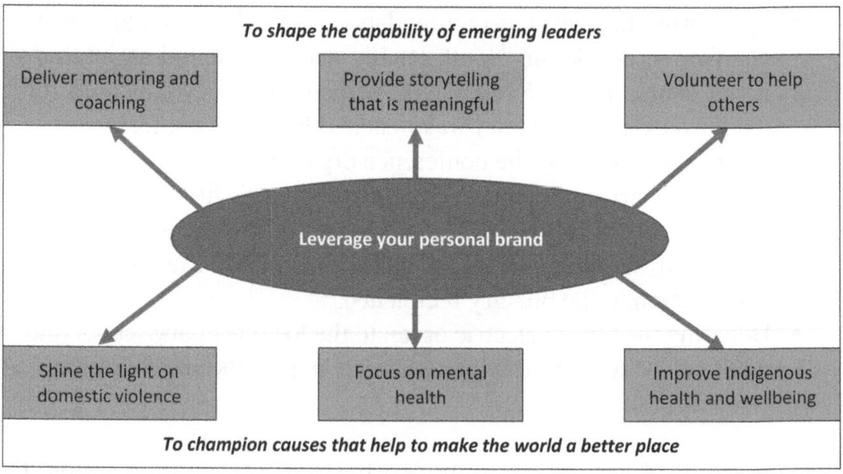

EXHIBIT 10.1 Leveraging your personal brand to shape capability and champion causes.

Menswear store. I duly complied, and each week I diligently paid part of my wages to Mr. Webber to repay the cost of the suit. Of course, I was the best-dressed junior banker ever, as no-one apart from the bank manager wore a suit, and he did so only very occasionally. If nothing else, my supervisors were impressed with my professional attire. And being well-dressed helped build my confidence, inspiring me to always present myself professionally.

Appearance, though important, is but one factor in shaping a personal brand. The personal brand is really founded on the areas where everyone says a person excels. As a young banker I had to listen to others to get a sense of how they perceived my attitude, capability, personality, quirkiness, dress sense, conduct, behavior, and communication skills. My regular performance-feedback sessions helped me to paint the picture, and I could then modify my behavior to change any perceptions that didn't align to how I wanted management and the workplace to see me.

There are no rules for creating a personal brand, and it will constantly evolve and change. It is, in effect, a project that takes a lifetime.

Success in activities that I've pursued has resulted in the achievement of numerous work-place, academic, and civic awards over the years. While few people are motivated by awards, they are an important ingredient in building a personal brand of professional credibility. This is illustrated in **Exhibit 10.2**.

In the lead-up to my retirement, a non-management level staff member advocated for the local office to establish the perpetual "Bruce Turner Citizenship Award" in my honor (reflected upon in Chapter 8). This aligns

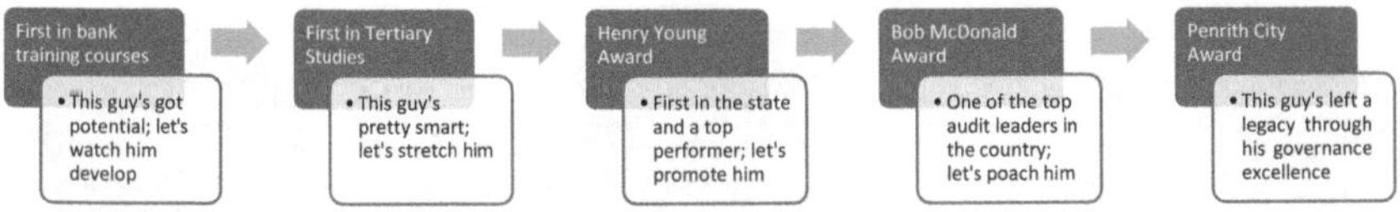

EXHIBIT 10.2 Example of an evolving personal brand.

nicely with my personal brand and opens up opportunities for storytelling; it also reflects my substance as a person. The honor is presented annually at the Australian Taxation Office in Penrith, which was employing up to 1,400 people during its peak operating period each year. The award recognizes the people who operate the engine-room of the business, with the criteria ensuring it is open to anyone from the basement to the boardroom; anyone can nominate or be nominated regardless of role, seniority, or years of service. Each year I present the award, I am asked to deliver an address related to the recipient's achievements. This has enabled me to speak on a range of topics including embracing change; social and business cohesion; business process improvement; how one person can make a difference; health and wellbeing of the Aboriginal community; innovation; mentoring; and retirement planning.

My personal brand has helped me to leverage opportunities to help make the world a better place through my philanthropy efforts.

What It Means for Business

A person's brand is what differentiates them from other people. It helps a person to promote themselves to gain opportunities, to influence others, and to attract the best talent by being an employer of choice.

A personal brand reflects the person's uniqueness; that is, the unique skills, experience, personality, dress sense, and other softer attributes such as their conduct, behavior, spoken and unspoken words, and attitudes. It answers the question, *how would you portray your personal story to others*?

The starting point in establishing a personal brand is to consider how you want the world to see you. Then determine the current perception that people have of you, which you can do through interviews, performance reviews, personality assessments (e.g. Myers-Briggs), through 360° reviews (involving your boss or key clients, peers, and support staff), or other approaches that facilitate frank and honest feedback. The difference between how you want to be seen and how you are currently perceived reflects the developmental opportunity (or gap), which you should then develop an action plan to address. This is illustrated in **Exhibit 10.3**.

Personal branding is the ongoing process of developing and maintaining a reputation, and nurturing the perception others have of you.

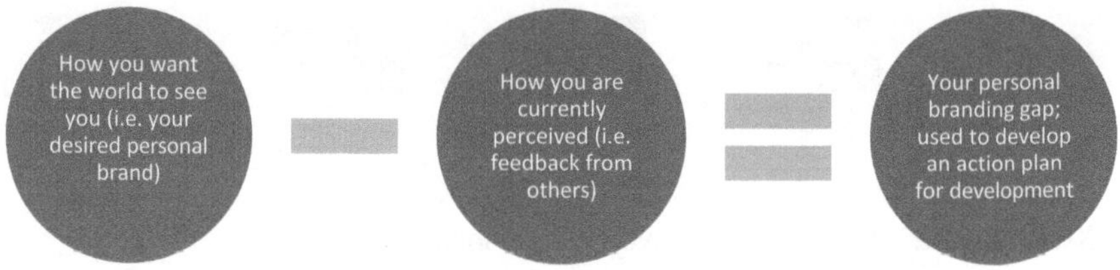

EXHIBIT 10.3 Overview of personal branding analysis.

The perception that stakeholders have of you will be determined by how they perceive your personal brand. Establishing meaningful stakeholder communications were discussed in Chapter 8.

Most people who deal with me in a business environment will see me as very patient, and I have heard them comment, "he has the patience of a saint." That is their perception. However, I am a naturally impatient person, keen to push things forward as quickly as possible; I've just had to learn how to curtail that natural instinct.

Ten critical elements of personal branding are illustrated in **Exhibit 10.4**.

Shine the Light on Domestic Violence

Setting the Scene

Just recently as I was helping my daughter at her home and showing her how to do things, I reflected that my father was rarely at home and didn't really teach me anything, except practical risk management … stay out of trouble, keep your head down, and stay out of the way! While the level of violence in our home was less than at some other households in our neighborhood, we always lived under the *threat* of physical punishment. My parents had a leather strap about 2 yards long and 2 inches wide that was used to dish out punishment (so risk avoidance was the preferred approach). But sometimes the consequences were not fair, rational, or predictable. By way of example:

- When I was in sixth grade, I attended the weekly boys club run by the local church (it was a bit like the Boy Scouts but had a religious element). One winter night when the event finished around 7:00 p.m. my father was not there to pick me up. I waited. And waited. Then the news came through that one of the other boys had been struck by a car crossing the road a few 100 feet away, and an ambulance had been called to take him to hospital. By 7:45 p.m. it was clear that my father had forgotten to collect me. It was dark. The place had been locked up and the lights turned out, and one of the leaders offered to drive me home. There were no phones. A dilemma. What to do? Of course, when I was dropped

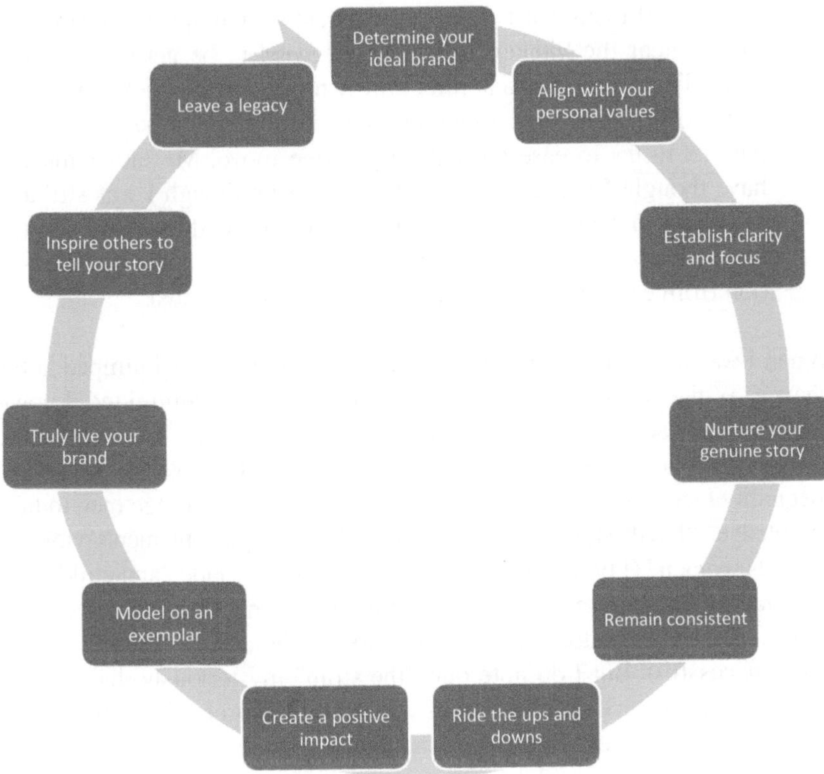

EXHIBIT 10.4 Ten critical elements of personal branding.

home my father wasn't there. He came in a few minutes later and was angry that I'd wasted his time and caused him some angst because it might have been me who was hospitalized and I should have waited. The consequences were severe.

- One of my siblings had done something wrong when I was in my early teens (I can't even recall "the crime," though it was nothing significant) and my father was furious. He wanted to know who the culprit was. He lined up the four older children (including me) and belted each one in turn until one of us confessed. After a few rounds, I could see this was not going to end well (my sharpened risk-management reflexes), so I stepped forward and said, "it was me." And, surprisingly, that was the end of it, and I was told not to do it again! I then fronted my mum and said that I was innocent but just wanted to stop the carnage. I knew who the culprit was but never threw them under the bus; and they forever remained quiet about the incident (as did I).

- In my mid-teens (just before my parent's final split), I heard a ruckus near the kitchen and things seemed to be getting out of hand. There had been a hammer thrown through the back window and broken glass was strewn everywhere. I stepped between my parents to try to ease the tension. Wrong move! My father must have thought I was going to go for him (even though I was still a scrawny kid, half his size). He hit me, and I fell to the ground. I lay motionless and my father abruptly left. But I'd prevented the situation from escalating (by pretending to be unconscious).

When I was asked to become a White Ribbon Ambassador I jumped at the chance. White Ribbon Ambassadors are described as "committed, knowledgeable and active men who recognize the importance of men taking responsibility and being part of the solution to end the violence, abuse and inequality faced by women." An important step is to encourage men to take the pledge, "I will stand up, speak out and act to prevent men's violence towards women" (I broaden the words at the end to include "and children").

I was well-versed in some of the common violence-minimization techniques (i.e. those I adopted during my youth, though they hadn't always been successful). But I do note that "the strap" mysteriously disappeared before the younger kids in the family felt the full force of the instrument (fortunately, I was never caught on that one!).

In recent years I have delivered speeches to local schools and others to get the message through early. I have also delighted in attending the annual "walk against domestic violence" with dignitaries, police, and members of the local community, usually accompanied by my son and/or daughter, and occasionally a grandson.

What It Means for Business

Domestic violence is prevalent in every society in the world, and is not confined to any particular class, culture, or religion. Indicative global estimates (based on media reports) show that one in three women will be subject to violence in her lifetime, including physical, sexual, psychological, emotional, and economic harm or abuse; and, alarmingly, four in ten of all women murdered globally have died at the hands of their intimate partners.

Domestic violence does not just occur in low-income families (as myth would have it). Rather, domestic violence can happen in families that are either rich or poor, and can occur in any home setting including urban, suburban, and rural. It also can be spread across all racial, religious, and age groups.

There are a range of steps that business leaders can take to promote the message that violence, abuse, and intimidation are unacceptable behaviors, and to promote the message that people at all levels are expected to stand up, speak out, and act to prevent such behavior in the workplace and at home.

These steps can include policies and procedures (e.g. bullying and harassmcnt) that addrcss workplacc wrongdoing, training that hclps managers to identify the indicators of employees dealing with domestic violence or abuse, and confidential employee helplines so there is an expert available to provide advice.

Part of my role as a White Ribbon Ambassador has been to encourage men to take action in respect to domestic violence, to show their respect for women, and do the right thing. Some of the key messages include:

- Listening and believing women who are in need, and treating them as equals.
- Reflecting on and changing the unacceptable behavior of men.
- Disrupting other men's violence towards women and children.
- Promoting good practices on "how to be a man" and how men should act.
- Talking to young men about the signals they send based on what they watch, the media they use, and the respectful relationships they maintain.

Of course, men can also be the subject of domestic violence, especially those who identify as gay, bisexual, and transgender. Organizational policies should be designed to protect people of all persuasions.

Focus on Mental Health

Setting the Scene

When I was growing up, I could never understand why my mother spent pretty much *every* day in bed, even when friends, family, and neighbors would visit. Though she did often get up to cook the family dinners. Pretty much all of the household chores were shared between my sister Jennifer and me; our younger siblings were six to fifteen years younger. So, from the age of about eight (and for much of the ensuing decade), Jennifer and I would complete most of the household chores each and every day. My sister would also often "deputize" for mum in looking after the younger kids.

Mum was a good person, but the events of her early years had long-lasting consequences – by age 15 she had lived through the Great Depression, the Second World War, the death of both of her parents, and the loss of all her adult teeth through a cycling accident.

In her later years (well after I had reached adulthood) she became more active and had a regular routine of heading out to meet other seniors to have a chat, play cards, read together, watch shows, participate in community raffles, and "invest" some money on the poker machines. She also became an active member and volunteer of the women's auxiliary and cardiac support group, and I was thrilled to see this activity and her enjoyment.

It was only in later years that I found out that my mother had suffered depression for much of her adult life. No doubt this was exacerbated by her extended and frequent periods of physical illness (including open heart surgery). She ultimately fought back from the adversity of her early years, then the depths of depression and ill health to achieve wide-ranging recognition for her volunteer work in the community. What she ultimately managed to achieve is a lesson and an inspiration for others.

Throughout my adult years I have seen the detrimental effect, as mental health issues reared their ugly head with family, friends, and colleagues. Some have been treated in specialist medical facilities. Sadly, several have taken their own lives. And alarmingly there were clusters of suicides at local high schools through the school-years of my children, so we were ever-vigilant for their wellbeing.

Suicide *is the act of intentionally causing one's own death. Mental disorders – including depression, bipolar, schizophrenia, anxiety, alcoholism, and substance abuse – are risk factors. Sadly, while I was writing this chapter, I received the news that my cousin Judee, an experienced and accomplished nurse, had passed away. She had taken her own life.*

My roles on the boards of health entities during the last decade have helped me to contribute to the discussion, debate, and consideration of options for advancing mental healthcare. But there is still a long way to go.

Sometimes an ***act of kindness*** *can help people to reignite a passion which, in turn, can help them cope better with the ups and downs of life. A few years ago, I was preparing a presentation for an international conference, and wanted to get some photos to provide a better balance to the messaging. I thought a fun way to do so would be to arrange a photography competition with my immediate family, with a few prizes to be awarded at Christmas lunch when we would all be together. We had invited some friends along who would otherwise be alone on Christmas day, and therefore asked if they also wanted to participate in the photography competition. I identified a few themes and categories as the basis for judging, and basically any photo I used in the presentation would win one of the eight categories. In the end the winners were spread across different age groups* *(including my children, their partners, my grandchildren, and one of our guests). The overall winner (based on a popular vote of those at lunch) was one of our guests who had been struggling with life's challenges. It turned out, he rediscovered his passion for photography and in the years since we've seen many of his wonderful scenic shots which have taken him out of his home into the wider natural landscape. A win/win all round!*

What It Means for Business

Mental health disorders represent one of the leading causes of ill-health and disability worldwide. Media reports (citing the World Health Organization) indicate that one in four people in the world will be affected by mental or neurological disorders at some point in their lives, with around 450 million people globally currently suffering from such conditions.

Boards and business leaders need to take mental health in the workplace seriously. An organization can have extensive obligations under the law where a worker acquires or aggravates a mental illness, as a result of their work. This can involve compensation and rehabilitation.

When organizations invest wisely in organizational strategies for the identification, support, and confidential case-management of workers with mental health, they typically generate improved productivity (i.e. increased work output and reduced sick and other leave).

Maintaining a safe and healthy workplace is good for business in other ways, because it can help to:

- Reduce staff turnover.
- Minimize the cost of staff absences.
- Better leverage investments in training.
- Avoid litigation and fines for non-compliance.
- Boost staff loyalty.
- Minimize staff stress levels.
- Comply with health and safety laws.
- Improve morale.

Business leaders have an obligation in most jurisdictions to identify workplace practices, actions or incidents which have the potential to cause or exacerbate mental illness within the workplace, and they should take meaningful action to eliminate, minimize, or manage these risks.

Staff have the right for business leaders to handle their mental illness in a similar manner as would any other illness or health concern. Mental health challenges can be triggered by challenging life events, many of which are not permanent. There should never be a situation where staff feel there is stigma attached to their mental health condition.

Business leaders can take proactive steps within their workplace in consultation with medical professionals. Examples include:

- Establish an employee assistance program that provides counseling and mental health support, and ensure staff are aware of its availability and how to use it.
- Provide training for managers in either a tailored session or part of a broader course on how to spot and deal with signs of stress, fatigue, anxiety, or depression in the workplace.
- Have HR include information in the staff handbook on how to handle mental illness in the workplace.
- Provide information, facts, and resources to staff in the workplace on mental health.
- Encourage staff to share their feelings with their manager or a colleague when they are experiencing a difficult time at home, or are feeling overwhelmed at work.
- Establish HR policies that empower managers to help their employees balance their workloads, embrace a healthy work-life balance, and avail themselves of flexible working arrangements.

The recovery or improvement of staff experiencing mental health is aided when organizations maintain a balanced and caring culture where people feel they matter.

Deliver Mentoring and Coaching

Setting the Scene

When I completed the research for a previous book for team leaders, the most often cited professional development opportunity that people either promoted the need for or wanted was mentoring. Daylight was second! Business leaders should encourage their people to establish a mentoring arrangement, either through their organization's internal training offerings, or through a professional association.

I have been a mentor through the mentoring programs for professional associations throughout the past decade or so (a role I continue to fulfil). I've also provided mentoring support for emerging leaders undertaking post-graduate studies at university. In addition to sharing insights directly with leaders and emerging talent, the approach often challenges me and helps to refresh my thinking on a range of topics. When the match is good (as it usually is), I find it incredibly enjoyable, enriching, and energizing.

I do set clear expectations upfront for those I am asked to mentor. Six key obligations I place on them:

- Respect and value my time, as I have many other things I could otherwise be doing.
- Take responsibility for scheduling mentoring sessions at regular intervals (usually three to four weeks).
- Where necessary, manage upwards as I don't have personal staff to keep everything on track.
- Before each session identify a topic (or more) that you'd like to focus on and let me know so I can give it some prior thought.
- Be on-time always, come prepared, complete all agreed actions, and listen … really listen.
- At the conclusion of each session provide a recap on the discussion, the outcomes, and the actions.

In some circumstances the mentoring arrangements do not always work out, despite one's best efforts. I remember one person I was mentoring who was keen to secure a promotion. We had many discussions and I offered many ideas, and I always heard, "Oh yes, I do that already." Every single time! It got to the stage where I thought, well you obviously don't need me. A lack of meaningful listening inhibited the individual's development … and the promotion was not forthcoming, in part because the things I'd suggested were never really adequately addressed.

I've also seen mentoring programs implemented with great gusto and then they fail because of a lack of professionalism and follow-through. In more than one instance, I have been matched with an "emerging talent" who is required to contact me (under the rules of the scheme) to set up the first meeting, but they never have the time to do; these arrangements usually fail. As I see it, I'm offering up my time and expertise so the onus is on the mentee and the organization arranging the program to follow-through.

I have also had the opportunity to informally mentor board chairs and CEOs through the unique insights I can bring into their businesses based on my experience across other sectors. Mentoring of senior leaders is a powerful and influential means of improving business operations. As an example:

- In a letter to me on his retirement, one CEO reflected, "These contributions (improvements and mentoring), and others, are laudable but above all you modelled behavior of uncompromising professionalism and generosity in sharing your expertise with others. This included me. I have referred to you many times as one of my important teachers. You are a standard that I will attempt to measure myself against."

- In a letter upon his leaving an organization, another CEO commented, "... thank you for the leadership and clear advice you have provided me with ... through some very challenging circumstances. It has been critical for me to be able to seek independent advice and test my views with someone I hold in the highest regard. ... I could not have wished for a better mentor."
- In one organization, I used to have informal sessions with the board chairman for a year or so after being appointed to his board, and he concluded his letter to me on his retirement by saying, "You have brought a level of professionalism and quality to the operation of the board that have made it more effective and up to the mark. I have always appreciated your special blend of diligence and respect and goodwill that shines through in everything that you do and say. I am also grateful for your warm personal support that is consistent and hugely helpful."

While one never goes the extra mile through mentoring for any other reason than it's the right thing to do, it's gratifying to hear that these efforts are well-regarded. Discretionary efforts like informal mentoring often inspire senior leaders to try *to achieve goals they've never achieved before, by starting to do things they've never done before* (a salient aspiration originally conveyed by Dr Stephen Covey).

I have also achieved accreditation as an executive coach. When I completed the coaching course, I identified three personal goals:

- Mind and body in sync.
- Audit leaders on the main stage.
- Stress levels in the green zone.

The focus on these goals helped me, by addressing things that I didn't realize needed some attention. By paying greater attention to my health and wellbeing, and by encouraging my direct reports to take a more prominent role in forums (i.e. by me stepping back a little as the sole "face of internal audit"), I ultimately reduced the instances and frequency of stress. It also reinvigorated the fun side of work.

Through executive coaching I have enjoyed interactions with many highly-regarded people who have subsequently been elevated into more senior roles. They achieved promotions based on their personal capability and performance, though, in some cases, the executive coaching helped them to successfully fulfil their developmental goals and navigate perceived blockages in their career path.

What It Means for Business

Mentoring and coaching are powerful developmental tools when harnessed well by business leaders. I have seen organizations invest in the development of its people to become mentors and coaches, then fail to meaningfully monitor the return on investment.

The course to achieve coaching accreditation typically involves an intensive program spread over a couple of weeks. Given there are usually around a dozen senior executive or executive-level participants, the salary cost alone for the participants is notable.

Only those who compete the course successfully achieve formal accreditation. It follows, that business leaders then need to fully leverage this resource; they should not put senior people through an intensive coaching course and then not follow-through by tasking them to actually coach.

There are quite distinct differences between mentoring and coaching. Some key features of each are illustrated in **Exhibit 10.5**.

Mentoring

Mentoring is a relatively straightforward concept – an experienced and credible person shares their wisdom to advise or train someone else (usually younger or less experienced) through an informal professional relationship during a sustained and pre-defined period of time.

These days there are many types of mentoring approaches, including:

- *Group mentoring* uses an expert to facilitate a series of developmental team sessions focused on a specific issue, such as effective communication techniques, customer service, or leadership development.
- *Project mentoring* leverages an expert who is brought in to provide expertise to a specific project, such as a higher-risk infrastructure development, business restructure, marketing campaign, or a product launch.
- *Reverse mentoring* involves a lower-level employee providing insights to managers and leaders (e.g. a business manager tasked with developing a product launch wants to engage younger consumers who understand modern telecommunication channels, including social media).
- *Flash mentoring* uses a speed-dating type format.

This section focuses on *traditional one-on-one mentoring* where mentors and mentees are paired for a period of time and given the opportunity to work together without a defined agenda. The primary aim is to drive the personal growth of the person being mentored (i.e. the mentee) by shaping new skills, knowledge, and understanding. It usually provides

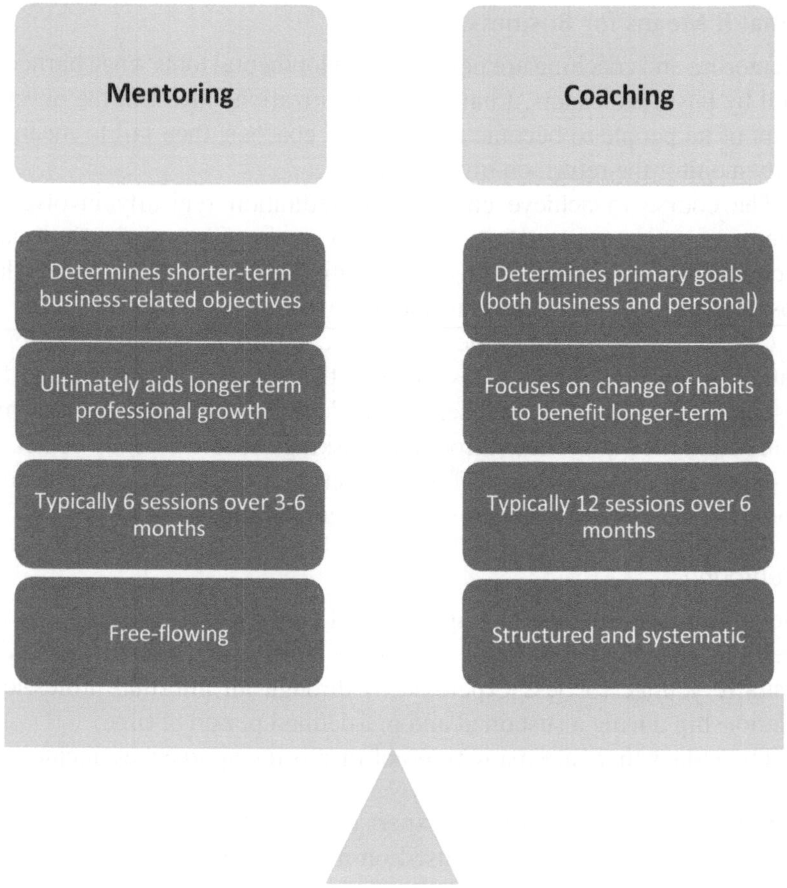

EXHIBIT 10.5 Differences between mentoring and coaching.

a rich learning and development experience for both mentees and mentors. Mentors typically have a semi-charitable or social-capital objective in becoming involved, through which they pass on their experiences and learnings to someone who will benefit from their sharing from a work, career, and professional perspective.

Within the business or professional environment mentoring increases retention; boosts employee or member engagement, loyalty, and satisfaction; assists with onboarding; and provides a competitive advantage when the labor or professional membership market is tight.

A well-designed and credible mentoring program helps to support an individual's personal and professional growth and develop future leaders by:

- Building or sharpening business acumen.
- Challenging traditional thinking.

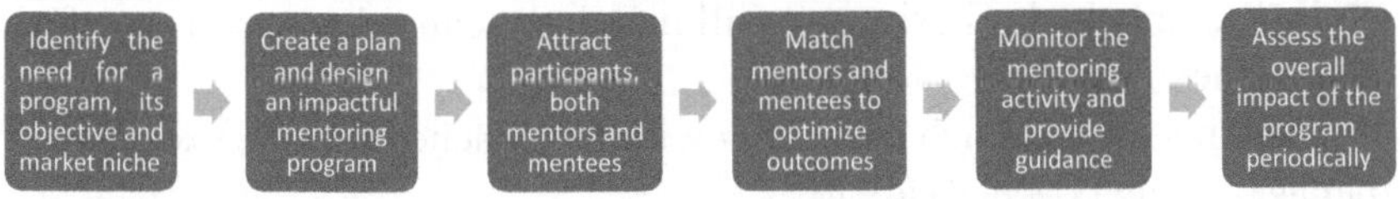

EXHIBIT 10.6 Structuring a mentoring program.

- Imparting new skills.
- Sharing organizational and professional knowledge.

Mentoring programs within the business, at universities, and through professional associations are usually developed through a structured approach as illustrated in **Exhibit 10.6**.

For individuals keen to participate in an established mentoring program (as either a mentor or mentee), it is important to watch out for or research opportunities. The HR department or professional association will usually offer assistance.

Coaching

Executive coaching typically involves the completion of an intensive multi-staged training course to prepare the coach for the task. There are accredited colleges and registered training organizations that deliver the training.

The training course starts with the *what* of coaching, providing an orientation to the program, and the theory of coaching. It then focuses on developing the base skills needed to be an effective coach, including:

- Challenging the way that people think.
- Developing active listening skills.
- Providing tips on direct-communication techniques.
- Helping coaches to establish trust and familiarity.
- Shaping more powerful questioning techniques.
- Modeling new ways of thinking.

Once the first stage of the course has been completed, the training then focuses on the *how* of coaching. This includes establishing coaching relationships and the techniques for generating insights, drawing out areas of focus, identifying three primary goals, developing strategies to achieve the goals, designing actions to reach the goals, and creating new habits. Practical insights cover how to manage coaching sessions and how to ultimately close-out the coaching relationship.

Where coaches are established within a business environment, executives within the business either nominate or are nominated for executive coaching. A central area, such as HR, will assess all nominations against established criteria, and will match the candidates with appropriate coaches.

The aims of the coach in dealing with the coachee (i.e. the executive or manager being coached) are to:

- Provide a sounding board and personal resource.
- Inspire the coachee to be their best.
- Believe in, encourage, and support the coachee.
- Be there for the coachee.
- Keep everything discussed confidential.

The coach and coachee will meet initially for a "trial session" to ensure they are compatible and can work together effectively. This is an opportunity for the coach to establish credibility and trust, and for the coachee to understand how the program works as well as their rights, responsibilities, and obligations.

Once the coaching relationship is cemented, the next discussion between the coach and coachee will go through a list of questions that might seem a little invasive, so the establishment of trust upfront is paramount. The coach is trained to stretch and challenge the coachee, and the questions are designed to draw out areas requiring focus. The questioning will span areas like work, time management, performance, health, finances, relationships, and other personal areas. This process helps them to collectively determine the priorities and needs of the coachee, and isolate three primary goals (two of the goals are typically business focused, and the third could be of a personal or familial nature).

With several pithy goals established, the coach and coachee will develop a set of strategies for each goal. Over a dozen hour-long coaching sessions, the coach and the coachee will work towards the goals step-by-step identifying specific shorter-term actions for the coachee to pursue, and developing new habits along the way. Setting the agenda for a coaching session is important, and an example is illustrated in **Exhibit 10.7**.

Agenda for Coaching Session
1. Focus on the session; clear everything else 2. Discuss the context for the session 3. Recap on the three primary goals and their inter-relationships 4. Discuss each of the three goals, and their strategies and actions; agree new actions 5. Assess any other actions from prior session 6. Session closeout

Session Close-out
1. Establish next coaching session date and time 2. Recap on insights from the session 3. Reflect on points to be covered next session 4. Summarize agreed actions for next session - <Action / expected outcome / target date> - <Action / expected outcome / target date> - etc.

EXHIBIT 10.7 Typical construct of a coaching session.

Effective executive coaching can deliver powerful results. Previous participants reflect that they have benefitted in any number of ways, including:

- Setting better goals and sticking with them.
- Thinking more clearly.
- Making better decisions.
- Becoming more focused.
- Developing new ways of thinking and working.
- Improving communication skills.
- Becoming more motivated.
- Having less (adverse) stress.
- Producing outstanding results.
- Feeling greater satisfaction in the workplace.
- Achieving surprising workplace outcomes.
- Boosting self-confidence and sense of purpose.

In one of my initial coaching sessions in a decentralized national operation, I established that the coachee was troubled that he had never met his "manager once removed" (i.e. his boss's boss). He felt she was getting mixed messages about his contribution and capability. I knew her well, so we rectified that issue without fuss or fanfare to gain a quick win, and the leader gradually recognized the coachee as one of her stars. We broadened the related goal to "boost positioning" as the coachee was so focused on delivering business outcomes he had never invested in his personal brand. He was so successful in achieving this goal, he has since been elevated into the senior executive ranks.

Another emerging leader who was highly regarded was getting swamped with work beyond her capacity, and she was working increasingly long hours. She was clearly getting "burnt out," and this was affecting her performance and her family life, so we established a goal to "learn the right way to say no." She formed fresh habits that didn't offend others, willingly sharing her expertise without getting drawn directly into the activity for which others were responsible.

Many coachees have reflected that they enjoyed the process more than they expected, the new habits stay with them for a long time, and they find value at many levels, often in unexpected areas. Examples of the primary goals established for some coachees are illustrated in **Exhibit 10.8** against three common elements, leadership, stakeholders, and personal growth. These are intended to be illustrative.

Improve Indigenous Health and Wellbeing

Setting the Scene

In writing this section, I acknowledge and pay my respects to the traditional custodians of the lands, and of elders past, present, and emerging.

MEANING OF INDIGENOUS PEOPLES

Indigenous peoples are ethnic groups who are the original or earliest known inhabitants of an area, in contrast to groups that have settled, occupied, or colonized the area more recently. In some regions, they are also known as First peoples, First Nations, Aboriginal peoples, Native peoples, or autochthonous peoples.

Example: American Indians are the Indigenous peoples of the United States, except Hawaii and territories of the United States. The term Native Americans is broader, including American Indians and extending to Native Hawaiians and Alaskan Natives of different ethnicities.

Only later in life did my family find out about its roots with the Gamilaroi people, 1 of the 4 largest Indigenous nations in Australia. The connection is through my maternal bloodlines.

When she was a kid, my mother spent several years during the Great Depression living in a country town in regional Australia called Walgett … Gamilaroi country. Mum taught our mob to respect the culture, and customs of "the first Australians," the Aboriginal peoples. And throughout my youth I had a wonderful, caring, and inspirational life coach and teacher in Uncle Jim Jackson (my great uncle). He was a "jack of all trades" and about 60 years my senior. He taught me carpentry, painting, gardening, and landscaping. His grandmother, Nancy Clarke, was a Gamilaroi woman, though we didn't know it back then. Times were very different!

Aboriginal people are one of the world's oldest continuous cultures. And by the accounts of some experts they are the oldest. In his award-winning book "Dark Emu" the author, Bruce Pascoe, draws on the journals and

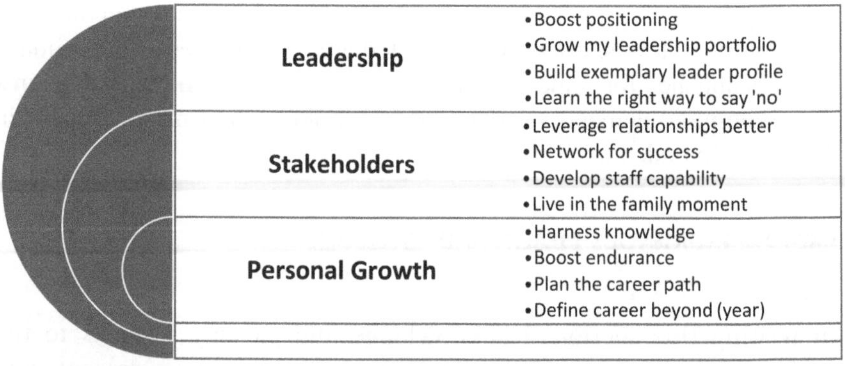

EXHIBIT 10.8 Examples of primary coaching goals.

diaries of explorers and colonists to share the story of the sophisticated, settled, innovative practices Aboriginal people used to care for "mother-earth" or Country ... the land, sea, and air. He reflected (in part):[1]

- They were not merely hunter-gatherers ... they built dams and wells; planted, irrigated, and harvested seed; preserved the surplus and stored it in houses, sheds, or secure vessels; understood the soil and how to keep it moist and fertile; used productive fishing techniques; created elaborate cemeteries; and manipulated the landscape.
- Most of the grains they cultivated were gluten free, and didn't require heavy chemical supplements for their successful cultivation.

Some of the policies of past governments have been detrimental for Aboriginal peoples. This has resulted in unanticipated consequences, including most notably:

- Their life expectancy is significantly lower than the non-indigenous population, with a gap of more than ten years.
- Their unemployment rate is more than three times greater than the non-Indigenous unemployment rate (17.1 percent, compared to 5.6 percent).

A decade ago, the Council of Australian Governments (i.e. the coalition of all governments at the national, state, and territory levels) agreed to six targets aimed at closing the gap in Indigenous disadvantage in the areas of life expectancy, health, education, and employment, and these targets are complemented by state priorities. However, progress has been well short of needs and expectations at all levels of government.

Because it is the right thing to do, I developed a keen interest in actively promoting and helping to shape programs that support the health, well-being, and employment of the Aboriginal peoples. And one of the most tangible steps I have been able to take at all my organizations over the last decade is the development of a reconciliation action plan, which is regularly monitored and assessed at a board level.

What It Means for Business

Numerous studies have highlighted that the lack of cultural competence within government agencies, organizations, and service providers is a major barrier to disadvantaged Indigenous people accessing much needed support. Business leaders need to consciously stand up against epistemic

---

[1] Bruce Pascoe, *Dark Emu*, Magabala Books Aboriginal Corporation, Broome (2018).

violence and ensure that their organization's policy, practices, and culture avoid othering.

Epistemic violence *sits at the core of the process of othering marginalized groups. It is not a type of physical violence, rather, it is exerted against or through knowledge and is said to be a key element in any process of domination. It is, in effect, people being prevented from speaking for themselves about their own interests because of others claiming to know what those interests are. It is tied to a concept introduced to postcolonial studies, and is accredited to an Indian scholar, Gayatri Chakravorty Spivak.*

Othering *is a pattern of exclusion and marginalization. In the workplace it is usually an invisible form of prejudice that bars people outside the dominant culture from accessing opportunities.*

Across the world, for all nations with Indigenous people, a culturally safe organization should acknowledge cultural diversity with appropriate policies, procedures and practices, and include cultural knowledge and awareness in all aspects of the planning, delivery, and evaluation of its services.

Media reports reflect that American Indians still suffer economically, and have employment rates far below those of others, despite strides taken to recover from a long history of subjugation.

Leaders of culturally sensitive organizations across the world are encouraged to take clear actions to promote "reconciliation" and improve the health, wellbeing, and employment opportunities for Indigenous communities. They can do this by setting a dedicated course for action in a guided, structured, and evidence-based process (i.e. a reconciliation action plan).

A ***reconciliation action plan*** *is a formal statement of commitment to reconciliation with Indigenous peoples. This is achieved by developing respectful relationships and creating meaningful opportunities with Indigenous staff and, in its broader context, the wider Indigenous community. In doing so, it helps in advancing the five dimensions of reconciliation: Race relations, equality and equity, unity, institutional integrity, and historical acceptance.*

These plans are not about Indigenous people doing the work and bridging the gaps. Rather, the planning is about all people from the boardroom and throughout the organization focusing their efforts. In particular, business leaders are expected to influence individuals and teams to commit to bridging the gaps, make the effort, build the relationships, show respect and work with opportunities with Indigenous peoples, and a commitment to following through with actions that are meaningful for Indigenous people.

"Reconciliation is hard work – it's a long, winding and corrugated road, not a broad, paved highway. Determination and effort at all levels of government and in all sections of the community will be essential to make reconciliation a reality," according to the wisdom of Karen Mundine mentioned in the reconciliation action plan for Wentworth Healthcare Limited (one of the boards I sit on).[2]

Provide Storytelling that Is Meaningful

Setting the Scene

People traditionally pass knowledge from generation to generation by telling engaging stories. We grew up hearing stories (perhaps through bedtime fairytales or family stories at occasional get-togethers) so we often think in stories because they inspire us and fuel our emotions. For most people, stories are much easier to remember than simple facts.

When my children and grandchildren were young, I enjoyed reading them books … but they seemed to enjoy made-up stories even more, especially when they were depicted as the heroes. My storytelling transitioned from the kids' bedrooms into my business and professional world. I enjoyed the creativity, and still do.

Well before the digital age, my wife and I recorded our family highlights through thousands of photos organized (mainly by my wife) into hundreds of paper-type albums. Over recent years, we have prepared glossy hardcover photobooks to record special occasions. These include historic photographic collections that celebrate anniversaries and special birthdays, through to notable vacations and trips. I also consolidated the individual *Annual Turner Christmas Newsletters* from the last 20 years into a single photobook volume for each of our children's families. When our grandchildren started school (after we'd minded them one day a week since they were toddlers), we even prepared a photobook for each of them as they "graduated" from homecare to capture the A-Z of our weekly activities; they were so proud when we presented them with their own personal book at a special whole-of-family family dinner together with a framed certificate. The photo albums and photobooks have proven to be wonderful props

---

[2] Wentworth Healthcare Limited, *Innovate Reconciliation Action Plan June 2018 – June 2020*, (2018) https://www.nbmphn.com.au/Resources/Programs-Services/Aboriginal-Health/Wentworth-Healthcare-Limited-Innovate-RAP-v3.aspx (sourced 25 September 2020). Citing Council for Aboriginal Reconciliation.

to inspire conversations with our adult children and our grandchildren. They also record part of the family history.

The concept of storytelling can be used in a business, professional, or personal environment. This includes meetings, team briefings, informal stakeholder-engagement sessions, business reports, books, journal articles, and in conference presentations.

In several organizations I became the "correspondent" from my work area to the staff newsletter, which enabled me to share messages, stories, and "happy snaps" to people across the organization. I did this in collaboration with my colleagues. While the editors were often reticent at first to accept me as a correspondent (with the misconception that governance, risk, compliance, and assurance topics seemed unappealing), the stories were usually well-received and we became embedded in the process.

What It Means for Business

Storytelling is a special way of sharing ideas that engage an audience or stakeholders and make something clearer. Done well, it is an art aimed at enhancing the enjoyment, retention, and understanding of a message conveyed skillfully – often subliminally – in an entertaining way, perhaps using props.

Regardless of the business or professional setting (or even at home) I've found a few critical success factors, notably:

- Reflect on your life experiences and memories to find ideas to illustrate the message you wish to convey. Follow through, even if you feel vulnerable because the stories reflect upon struggles or barriers you overcame.
- Consider your audience and choose the best approach that will resonate with your audience. Be clear on the moral or message you are aiming to impart.
- Maintain honesty in your stories and keep them relatively simple and straightforward, as too much detail can be distracting from the key message. Some embellishment is okay if it is to add a sense of fun, excitement or intrigue.
- Don't disparage, undermine, or embarrass someone else in telling the story. It is not necessary, and people rarely enjoy the reputation of someone else being trashed.
- Take a chance on storytelling, and start with a small group where you feel comfortable and secure (such as with your own team). As you gain experience and hone your techniques, expand your horizons. Practice leads you to perfection.
- If you establish your authenticity through storytelling, people will be inspired and will want to follow your lead, even if it involves changing the business environment in which they are invested.

It's a relatively small step to take to share your stories with a national and global audience once you've mastered the storytelling approach and established a reputable personal brand. You can do this through personal delivery (e.g. podcasts, webinars, conferences, adult education, training courses, mentoring, and coaching) or through your writing (e.g. articles in professional journals, stories in your organization's staff newsletter, chapters of books, books).

Volunteer to Help Others

Setting the Scene

There are many community groups, sporting clubs, youth entities, and welfare groups that rely on volunteers to operate. In addition to boosting the health and wellbeing of people in the community, these forums play a vital role in joining people together and ultimately sparking the flame that lights up the community as a whole. My mother was recognized with a civic award for her volunteer work with the local women's auxiliary and the cardiac support group. Similarly, my wife was recognized in 2019 as a "Legend of the Nepean" (our local region) for her voluntary work in life coaching and other endeavors.

I have served the internal auditing profession over the last decade through voluntary roles on the board of the Institute of Internal Auditors Australia and as the chair of its audit committee. I also had the honor of sitting on the global public sector committee for the Institute of Internal Auditors Global (including 2014–2015 as its international chairman). All of these roles drew on my broad business experience and expertise to invest in the next generation of professionals.

I have found that I can directly help in the development of emerging and experienced leaders, and advance the profession by sharing my experiences. Since 2012, I have embraced storytelling by authoring more than 40 publications (books, white papers, practice guides, guidelines, and articles), co-authoring an additional 15, and reviewing and editing another 40. Hopefully, the profession and the community more broadly are richer from having these leading practices recorded and made readily available.

Throughout my career I have enjoyed hosting delegations from other nations throughout the Asian Pacific Rim that are keen to learn about contemporary governance, risk management, compliance, and assurance techniques. These delegations are often attracted to large exemplar organizations where I worked – like the Reserve Bank of Australia and the Australian Tax Office – and the senior leaders of those organizations helped to achieve tangible outcomes in the region through their explicit support for these initiatives. It is especially rewarding when these nations leverage the ideas they gleaned from the visits and implant them in their own countries.

In other parts of this book I've reflected on other voluntary pursuits (including coaching and mentoring, my work as an anti-domestic-violence ambassador, and my advocacy for Indigenous health, wellbeing, and employment). Hopefully others will be inspired to find their own niche where they can make a difference, then reach out to convert the idea and opportunity into something tangible.

What It Means for Business

People have different life experiences that influence what, when, and how they contribute to society more broadly. The circumstances for some will limit these opportunities.

Consequently, people will contribute to society at different stages of their lives. And their options for contributing will be dictated by their personal interests. For instance, some people will opt to coach local sporting teams, others will become missionaries in developing nations, others will immerse themselves in charitable fundraising, while others will leverage their skills to invest in the development of others.

When considering helping or donating money to charitable entities, there are measures that can assist in determining whether the ultimate contribution to charitable programs is reasonable. These include:

- Fundraising efficiency (i.e. how much was actually spent to raise each $1).
- Financial efficiency performance metrics, including percent of total functional expenses spent on:
  - Programs and services,
  - Management or general costs, and,
  - Fundraising.
- Financial capacity performance metrics, including:
  - Program expense growth over the last three to five years,
  - Ratio of liabilities to assets, and,
  - Working capital ratio.

The process for determining philanthropic options is illustrated in **Exhibit 10.9**. The measures outlined above would be used to consider the performance metrics of a charitable entity.

There will be situations where management pursues team-building through charitable pursuits. This could involve packing food hampers for the needy at Christmas, serving food at kitchens for the homeless, or participating in a local or national "clean-up" the environment day. The process depicted in **Exhibit 10.9** can also be used in those situations.

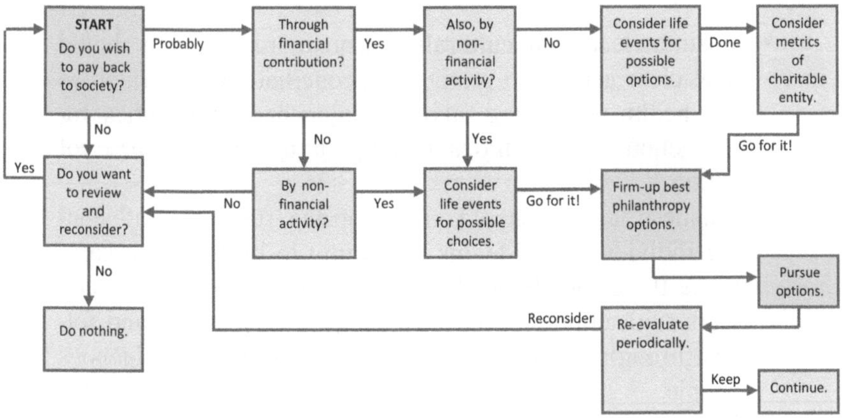

EXHIBIT 10.9 Process for determining philanthropic options.

CHAPTER 10 – TEN CLOSING REFLECTIONS

- Individuals should nurture a personal brand that is consistent with their personal values and personality.
- Business leaders should take steps to promote the message that violence, abuse, and intimidation are unacceptable behaviors, and emphasize that people at all levels are expected to stand up, speak out, and act to prevent such behavior in the workplace and at home.
- Business leaders should establish policies and procedures (e.g. bullying and harassment) that address workplace wrongdoing, training that helps managers to identify the indicators of employees dealing with domestic violence or abuse, and confidential employee helplines so there is an expert available to provide advice.
- Boards and business leaders need to take mental health in the workplace seriously, and invest in organizational strategies for the identification, support, and confidential case-management of workers with mental health.
- Business leaders should encourage their people to establish a mentoring arrangement, either through their organization's internal training offerings, or through a professional association.
- Business leaders can achieve powerful performance-boosted results (for themselves or their employees) where the organization establishes effective executive coaching arrangements.

- Business leaders in culturally sensitive organizations should take clear actions to promote "reconciliation" and improve the health, wellbeing, and employment opportunities for Indigenous communities through a dedicated course of action.
- Business leaders should take a strong stance in influencing individuals and teams to commit to bridging the gaps, make the effort, build the relationships, show respect, and work with opportunities with Indigenous peoples, and follow through with actions that are meaningful for Indigenous people.
- Business leaders are encouraged to embrace storytelling as a powerful way to share ideas that engage an audience and make things clearer; storytelling is used in business, professional, or personal environments, including meetings, team briefings, informal stakeholder-engagement sessions, business reports, books, journal articles, and in conference presentations.
- Individuals wishing to contribute to society will do so at different stages of their lives based on their personal interests and the approach that suits them; those considering charitable donations can look to a range of measures to determine reasonableness, including fundraising efficiency, financial efficiency, and financial capacity performance metrics.

11 Holding Court at the Audit Committee Table

Audit committees and the internal audit activity have a symbiotic relationship, with chief audit executives deriving their organizational strength from a powerful audit committee. This chapter considers the steps for establishing an effective audit committee with a credible membership, appropriate mandate, meaningful performance reporting, a continuous improvement philosophy, and a willingness to champion leading practices … and it also highlights the challenges in managing situations when the principles of the audit committee member and organization are not in alignment, and the difficult decision to release a chief audit executive for wrongdoing. The powerful sentiments of José Ugaz, (Chair Transparency International, 2016) should be a constant reminder for all who sit around the audit committee table as to their broader civic responsibilities, "In too many countries, people are deprived of their most basic needs and go to bed hungry every night because of corruption, while the powerful and corrupt enjoy lavish lifestyles with impunity."

Entity Profile and Role

Sector:	Spanning the private, not-for-profit, and public sectors (across the three tiers of government in Australia: federal, state, and local government).		
Industry groupings:	Central government, customer services, environment, finance, health, professional services, transport, telecommunications, various regulatory authorities, and the supreme audit organization.		
Entities:	Twenty-five distinct entities.		
Metrics of entities – spread of entity sizes:	*Small* 40 percent of entities Entities with annual expenditure less than $25 million.	*Medium* 20 percent of entities Entities with annual expenditure less than $400 million but over $25 million.	*Large* 40 percent of entities Entities with annual expenditure greater than $400 million.
Primary role:	Audit committee chair (56 percent of entities) and independent audit committee member (44 percent).		

Main responsibilities:	Provide independent assurance and advice to the governing body on the organization's governance processes, risk management, compliance, and control frameworks, and its external accountability obligations. Includes review and overview of internal controls, risk management, corruption, and fraud prevention, external accountability (including the financial statements), applicable laws and regulations, internal audit and external audit.
Timeframe:	Since 2007 and continuing. The end of the Fourth Decade, then through the Fifth Decade.

PERSONAL STORY

Coincident with me commencing my role as chief audit executive at the Australian Taxation Office (ATO), I was appointed to my first audit committee role. It was at Wyong Shire Council which was situated on the central coast of New South Wales north-east of my home, and involved a 155 mile (250 km) four-hour return trip for each of the six meetings held annually.

After I presented one of my annual audit committee reports for the Wyong Shire Council at a public meeting the local press reported, "Chair of council's independent (audit and risk) committee, and one of the pre-eminent auditors in Australia, Bruce Turner, delivered his annual report last week. He commented positively on the committee and the governance framework of the council with improvements in auditing and risk management in all areas."[1] My attendance at the council's public meeting and the subsequent media reporting was an important step for public sector audit committees to deliver transparent reporting to the community.

I gained my second audit committee role in 2010, as chair of the audit committee for the Department of Premier and Cabinet. The department is one of the most significant government entities in Australia's most-populated state, New South Wales, with responsibility for leading the state's public sector to deliver on the government's commitments and priorities.

When I was appointed to this audit committee, the former Deputy CEO at StateRail then held a similar deputy role at the Department of Premier and Cabinet. I have little doubt that she was influential in my merit-based appointment, given the outcomes my team and I achieved at StateRail, coupled with my work ethic, skills, expertise, experience, and leadership credentials. Under the government policy, I was "pre- qualified" as an audit committee chair and independent member (achieved through a rigorous vetting process by an expert panel with firm criteria). I completed

[1] "Positive result for council activities," Central Coast Express Advocate, 1 February 2013, 15.

the maximum eight-year term on the audit committee, and it was the most fulfilling experience.

My first two audit committee roles were the catalyst for many other such roles over the ensuing decade. They also provided me with opportunities to develop an audit committee training course, to mentor aspiring audit committee members, to prepare related technical papers (including one focused on skills-based audit committees), and, more recently, to write a book on *Powering Audit Committee Outcomes*.

Audit committee roles can sometimes be quite challenging, and there will be times that chairs need to address difficult situations and take well-considered positions. A couple of examples follow.

******

In one organization where I was chairing the audit committee, we received allegations that a chief audit executive had been "spying" on the governing body, the audit committee, and senior executives by monitoring their emails for no proper or authorized purpose. The chief audit executive was well-regarded professionally and claimed to be conducting an investigation. However, an independent assessment determined that there were no authorized internal auditing or investigative activities being undertaken, and therefore the monitoring activities were outside the approved internal audit charter and the stated independent authority. The chief audit executive was ultimately terminated from the organization because of findings of breaches of organizational privacy, technology and digital surveillance policies, and serious breaches of the trust of the position.

******

I opted to stand down as audit committee chairman from one public sector entity following changes announced by a departmental secretary because the changes didn't "feel right." After an objective assessment I believed the changes would have a profound detrimental effect on the organization's governance, risk, control, and compliance arrangements, and its external accountability obligations. I did not believe I could continue to provide the CEO with relevant and timely advice, as the changes meant the CEO would not have direct control of critical legislated activities and functions (such as finance, environmental, work health and safety, and other compliance obligations), nor its people who influence the culture and how the corporate values are applied. The changes had been imposed on the CEO and he did not support them; he ultimately left the organization. Another audit committee member also resigned.

I detailed the reasons for my resignation in a letter to the CEO, government minister, and departmental secretary expressing my view that effective statutory accountability-setting requires a clear, direct, and

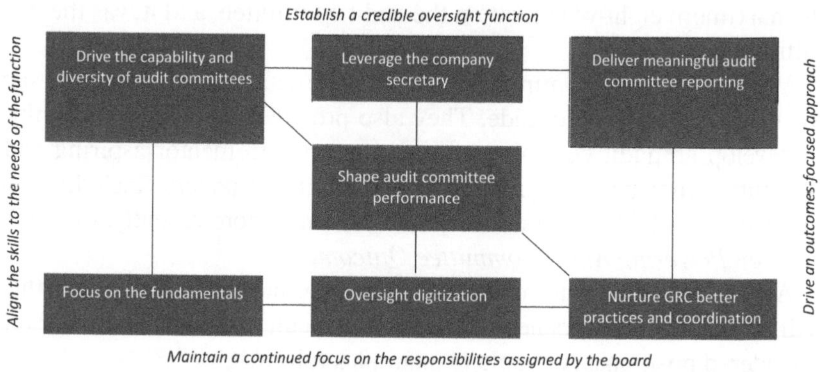

EXHIBIT 11.1 Shaping a strong audit committee performance.

unambiguous single point of responsibility and oversight, and, in my view, the changes announced represented an unacceptable risk to government and the associated public sector leadership. Subsequent events validated my assessment and decision to stand down.

The key insights from this phase of my story are:

- Drive the capability and diversity of audit committees.
- Leverage the company secretary.
- Deliver meaningful audit committee reporting.
- Focus on the fundamentals.
- Shape audit committee performance.
- Nurture GRC better practices and coordination.
- Oversight digitization.

CONTEXT

Audit committees provide the eyes and ears for the board and do much of the heavy-lifting in respect to oversighting the organization's governance, risk, compliance, and assurance activities. There are a range of factors that help to shape a high-performing audit committee, with some of these elements discussed in this chapter and illustrated in **Exhibit 11.1**.

KEY TAKEAWAYS AND DEEP DIVES

Drive the Capability and Diversity of Audit Committees

Setting the Scene

Recognizing that audit committees were an increasingly critical stakeholder group for governance, risk, compliance, and internal audit specialists, the board of the Institute of Internal Auditors in Australia identified the need in 2014 to develop a suitable audit committee training course. With my growing reputation as an audit committee chair, I was engaged to develop the course and present the course for the initial intake of participants.

*An **audit committee** is a committee of the governing body (such as the board of directors where the organization has one) with its objectives clearly defined and documented in its charter, and its efficiency and effectiveness measured by reference to its objectives. An independent audit committee is fundamental to good governance. The internal audit activity (through the chief audit executive) will typically report functionally to the audit committee.*

Participants rated the quality of the initial course highly, with 100 percent satisfied with the overall learning experience. There were also 100 percent ratings for each of the secondary rating categories including that the content was relevant, the course met their objectives, the course was well structured, the materials supplied supported their learning, and they satisfied with the facilitation of the course. Since it was developed, the course (with periodic updates and refreshes) is run regularly across Australia and throughout parts of Oceania by a number of different facilitators and continues to provide a quality learning experience. It has also been tailored for specific organizations and run for their audit committee, and in some cases has been tailored and run for similar regional organizations.

The learning objectives of the audit committee training course were to:

- Equip audit committee chairs and members and those that support them with contemporary skills and tools to undertake their roles to high level.
- Enable them to drive exemplary governance practices that help their entity to manage its affairs efficiently, effectively, and ethically.
- Position them to help the CEO and governing body to achieve their vision and deliver the business or statutory objectives.

What It Means for Business

The board sets the organization's key strategic direction, makes major decisions, and monitors the implementation of strategies by management. The audit committee's activities are informed by the organization's overarching strategies. In oversighting good governance, the audit committee should apply the concept of "nose in, fingers out" which means the audit committee should oversight management but should not try to do management's job.

*The **board** refers to the body of persons or officers having ultimate control of an organization. In the private and for-purpose sectors this would usually be the board of directors, whereas in the public sector this could be the board (e.g. for a government trading enterprise), department head where there is no board (e.g. secretary, director general, chief executive), or the local council (within local government).*

Contemporary audit committees should comprise an appropriate mix of people, typically at least three members, with skills and experience relevant to the organization's current and future operations, and including an independent non-executive chairman, non-executive directors, and independent members (but not the chairman of the board or governing body).

Audit committee charters and government policies on the qualifications of audit committees should expressly state the minimum requirements. As an example, audit committee members should collectively develop, possess, and maintain, skills and knowledge including:[2]

- Suitability to the specific needs of the organization.
- Extensive knowledge of governance and financial management.
- Exceptional financial literacy, including the ability to understand and appropriately interrogate financial statements.
- Understanding of organizational objectives and responsibilities.
- Functional and operational knowledge of risk management; performance management frameworks; internal audit; external audit; financial management; accounting; internal control frameworks; governance (including planning, reporting, and oversight); business operations; legal and compliance frameworks.
- Capacity to ensure the integrity of the decision-making of the audit committee, including a willingness to constructively challenge management practices and information.
- Unwavering professionalism and ethical behavior which exemplifies the desired culture of the organization and its corporate values.

---

[2] "Internal audit and risk management policy for the NSW public sector: TPP15-03," NSW Treasury Policy and Guidelines Paper. https://arp.nsw.gov.au/assets/ars/f79e35043d/TPP15-03-Internal-Audit-and-Risk-Management-Policy-for-the-NSW-Public-Sector.pdf (sourced 21 July 2020). Modified. The skills and qualifications cited in this chapter remain relevant, although the 2015 policy was updated in December 2020 and is now called the "Internal Audit and Risk Management Policy for the General Government Sector: TPP20-08".

Additionally, there are other specific attributes to be considered when appointing an audit committee chair, including:

- Leadership qualities and the ability to promote effective working relationships in complex organizations.
- An ability to communicate complex and sensitive assessments in a tactful manner to CEOs, senior management, chief audit executives, and the board or governing body.
- A well-founded understanding of the principles of good organizational governance and accountability, including financial reporting, internal audit operations, selection and review of chief audit executives, and risk management standards and principles.

*A **charter** is a formal document (in the form of a mandate) approved by the board that defines the purpose, authority, and responsibility for the audit committee (in this case), and for other independent areas that support the board, including the internal audit function.*

The board should first determine and define in an audit committee charter, policy or skills matrix the minimum skills needed on the audit committee (e.g. accountant, lawyer, business leader), then identify other governance and industry skills that are desirable. A skills-gap analysis will substantially influence these needs, and will help to achieve a well-balanced audit committee that meets the needs and expectations of both the board and audit committee chair.

The board or governing body can use an audit committee skills matrix (see **Exhibit 11.2**) as the basis for selecting audit committee members. This involves five key steps:

1. Establish the current strengths of the audit committee members and the situation once audit committee members complete their terms of appointment (i.e. skills that need to be replaced when they step off).
2. Assess the audit committee charter and the organization's strategic agenda to determine the ideal audit committee appointee based on appropriate considerations, such as governance expertise, professional and industry expertise, personal attributes, and diversity.
3. Use steps 1 and 2 to develop or update an audit committee skills matrix.
4. Determine the unique skills and experience new audit committee members are expected to bring onto the committee, then prepare a suitable advertisement to optimize candidate interest.
5. Undertake a skills-based selection process using the audit committee skills matrix to differentiate between candidates.

EXHIBIT 11.2
Example of an audit committee skills matrix

				Audit Committee Current Members and Candidates				
	Current	Require	Comments	1	2	3	4	5
Governance – must have extensive knowledge and experience								
Strategic thinking								
Strategic financial skills with exceptional financial literacy and the ability to understand and interrogate financial statements								
Risk and compliance expertise								
Corporate governance								
Commercial acumen								
Ability to lead the board or audit committee								
Previous board or audit committee experience								
Professional and industry skills – to deliver overall balance of complementary skills								
Related industry/sector experience								
Relevant CFO experience								
Relevant CAE experience								
Relevant CRO experience								
Corporate lawyer experience								
Practical ICT experience including cyber risks								
Skills in strategic priority areas, including digital								
Advanced understanding of stakeholder engagement concepts								

Personal attributes and behavioral qualities – to be demonstrated and validated
Integrity/ethics and modelling organizational values
Effective listener/communicator/strategic questioner
Unwavering professionalism, ethical behavior, commitment
Influencer and negotiator
Critical and innovative thinker
Transformational leadership
Willingness to constructively challenge management practices and information
Capacity to ensure integrity of audit committee decision-making

Diversity – to be considered as a secondary consideration for overall balance of audit committee membership
Age
Gender diversity
Cultural diversity
Geographic location
Employment diversity

Source: Developed by author based on research and practical examples.[3]
Note: More detailed descriptions should be developed for each skill area.

[3] Also used in Bruce R Turner, *Powering Audit Committee Outcomes*, 2020 (Exhibit 3.3).

The audit committee skills matrix remains a "living document," and can be used in future audit committee appointments once it has been reviewed and refreshed. Circumstances might dictate the inclusion of other priority areas identified by the board, such as disaster management following the events of 2020/21 (including once-in-a-generation global pandemic, wild fires, and flooding).

The audit committee chair in conjunction with the CEO and company secretary (or equivalent) should ensure there is a formal induction process for audit committee members to acquaint them with the organization and its operations, including the values, vision, mission, strategies, business objectives, policies, and the audit committee's role and responsibilities. Additionally, they should ensure audit committee member succession arrangements are managed to ensure continuity and ongoing corporate knowledge, including staggering the terms of committee membership, limiting the number of years a person can serve on the committee, and transparency of the committee appointment process.

Leverage the Company Secretary

Setting the Scene

In my experience, the company secretary provides the foundation for an effective board and the board committees including the audit committee. People who are appointed to the role of company secretary need to operate at a consistently high level. They should be capable, understand the position requirements, and have completed higher education (e.g. relevant professional qualifications with ideally current accreditation with a professional association such as chartered secretaries, governance institute, company directors).

> *The **secretariat** is a function performed by a team of people working seamlessly together for a common goal in supporting the effective administration, meeting coordination, and minute-taking of the board and board committees. It is usually headed up by the **company secretary**.*

Within the private sector, there are more rigorous arrangements for appointing the company secretary. As a consequence, the company secretary typically demonstrates the full mastery and polish to underpin the board and board committees they service.

The public sector is starting to reap the benefits of appointing people with similar attributes to a company secretary to develop and drive the professionalism of the secretariat function. The public sector entity's governing body (i.e. board where there is one, council, CEO, secretary, or director general) is increasingly recognizing that the secretariat function is no longer a simple administrative role that anyone can do.

References within this section to *company secretary* are intended to also cover the secretariat function in the public and not-for-profit sectors; the term is intended to reflect a higher-order secretariat (regardless of the specific title of the role).

When the company secretary delivers services that are efficient, effective, seamless, disciplined, and clear, the board and audit committee (and other board committees) are better-positioned to operate at a strategic level that achieves the organization's objectives and complies with its legislative and regulatory obligations. Conversely, the work of the board and its committees is hampered when the papers and reports processed through the company secretary are inconsistent and reflect poor quality standards.

In some of my early audit committee meetings, I was delivered audit committee packs containing between 800 and 1,000 pages. This level of detail is unnecessary and unacceptable. It is almost impossible to process that amount of information in less than a week, then discern the key points and have a strategic discussion. The company secretary should have strict safeguards in place to ensure that audit committee papers are short, sharp, and succinct; a style guide is crucial as a first step, and "policing" the style guide becomes the second important step.

A ***style guide*** *is a set of standards developed and distributed by the company secretary for writing, formatting, and designing papers and reports provided to the audit committee. It establishes standard style requirements to improve communication by ensuring consistency both within a document, and across multiple documents. The style guide may require certain best practices in usage, language composition, visual composition, typography (i.e. how typing is arranged to make the writing legible, readable, and appealing when displayed, including typefaces, point sizes, line lengths, line-spacing, and spacing), and orthography (i.e. writing conventions including norms of spelling, hyphenation, capitalization, word breaks, emphasis, and punctuation). It sets out standards for common content, such as the agenda name and number, recommendation, related strategies, risks, key issues, and discussion.*

The distribution of the audit committee pack through traditional manual processes is cumbersome, costly, and inefficient. Over the last decade, the vast majority of the boards and audit committees that I have been involved with have shifted to a board portal (and those that haven't already plan to do so soon). In addition to making the access, navigation, and transport of audit committee papers more timely, secure, and simpler, it has had the added benefit of reducing the vast amount of storage space that audit committee packs were taking up in my home office.

*A **board portal** is an electronic tool that facilitates secure digital communication between members of a board of directors and across its board committees, including the audit committee. Where organizations do not use a board portal, the dissemination of board and board committee papers is usually a manual process.*

What It Means for Business

The company secretary plays a vital role in supporting the effectiveness of the audit committee by monitoring compliance with the audit committee's mandate (contained in its charter or terms of reference), administering the affairs of the company, managing the business of the audit committee, and coordinating the timely completion and dispatch of the audit committee agenda and audit committee pack. All audit committee members should have full and unfettered access to the company secretary.

The company secretary provides the critical interface between the audit committee and business leaders, and acts as an important link between the audit committee and the business. The company secretary will usually coach business leaders so they understand the expectations of, and value brought by, the audit committee.

Within the private sector, the board technically appoints the company secretary so it is appropriate that they report to the chair of the board. Within an audit committee context (and irrespective of which sector they are operating in), the primary purpose of the company secretary is to serve the audit committee, through its chair, and to focus heavily on audit committee performance. The common skillsets required by a company secretary are illustrated in **Exhibit 11.3**.

Effective company secretaries can support the audit committee by focusing on six primary success factors which are illustrated in **Exhibit 11.4** and expanded upon in **Exhibit 11.5**.

The company secretary should develop and maintain a secretarial handbook (i.e. policies and procedures for the secretariat). This will provide the guidance necessary to deliver an efficient, effective, seamless, disciplined,

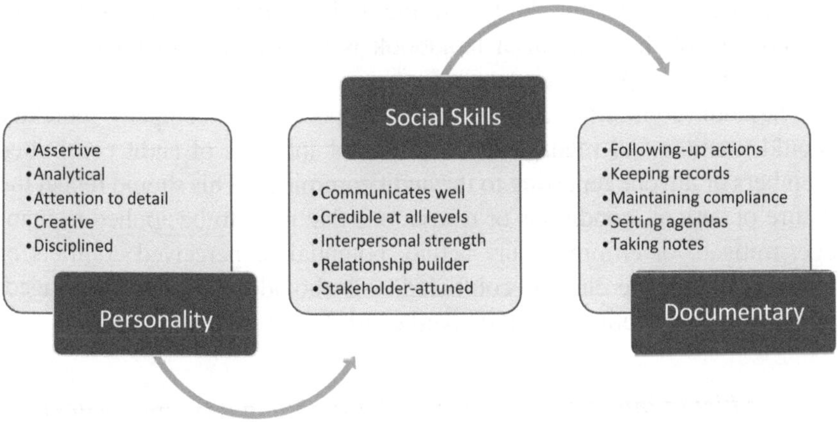

EXHIBIT 11.3 Common skillsets required by a company secretary.

EXHIBIT 11.4 Primary success factors for the company secretary.

Fulfil Primary Success Factors of a Secretariat
▪ Understand the business – organization's vision, strategies, objectives, values, priorities, governance, risk management, compliance, assurance and related regulatory and government's policies. ▪ Maintain reporting discipline – use a consistent style guide and templates for meeting papers, train business areas in its use, provide for a clear decision, link the paper to the corresponding element of the audit committee charter, police the style guide (e.g. number of pages, font type and size, format). ▪ Leverage efficient distribution channels – ideally, maintain a secure and effective board portal and establish settings that suit the audit committee's needs. ▪ Keep audit committee well-informed – agree forward meeting dates a year in advance, keep the member'scalendars updated, maintain a listing of terms of appointment for audit committee members. ▪ Communicate with audit committee regularly – schedule regular catch-ups with audit committee chair, ensure audit committee chair knows who is in the room when meeting is underway, provide water and refreshments. ▪ Stick to agreed times – agree meeting agenda with audit committee chair, avoid changes to timings without audit committee chair's agreement.

Structure Meetings Well	Control Meetings	Wrap-up Meeting Effectively
▪ Know the role, responsibilities, obligations and scope of audit committee charter ▪ Develop and maintain annual work plan for audit committee ▪ Establish an audit committee timeline ▪ Maintain an audit committee meeting planner ▪ Develop a financial statement work plan in consultation with CFO	▪ Design a work flow summary ▪ Use a secretariat meetings checklist ▪ Prepare a meeting agenda that aligns to the audit committee's responsibilities and calendar ▪ Develop a run sheet for audit committee chair ▪ Maintain a guide for presenters and provide to them upfront ▪ Manage conflicts of interest	▪ Record minutes in a fashion that supports the audit committee ▪ Ensure action items are recorded correctly in line with the intent of audit committee members ▪ Update action tracking (actively follow-up action items to meet due dates; escalate delays to CEO) ▪ Develop 'five key takeouts' (or similar) at end of each meeting to facilitate the chair's briefings

EXHIBIT 11.5 Content of a secretarial handbook.

and clear secretariat for the board and audit committee. An example of the content of the secretariat handbook is summarized in **Exhibit 11.5** together with the primary success factors.

The audit committee chair with the support of the company secretary should monitor and manage the conflicts of interests of audit committee members or anyone reporting to the audit committee. This should reflect the nature of actions, conditions or restrictions that need to be applied to manage, mitigate or eliminate any actual, potential or perceived conflicts of interest. Where the chair is conflicted, this should be similarly managed, perhaps in consultation with the board chair if not reasonably resolved.

> *A* ***conflict of interest*** *refers to any relationship that is, or appears to be, not in the best interest of the organization. A conflict of interest would prejudice an individual's ability to perform his or her duties and responsibilities objectively. For instance, this could involve a person who has two relationships that might compete with each other for the person's loyalties, such as loyalty to an employer and also loyalty to a family business.*

The audit committee chair should establish key performance indicators (KPIs) for the company secretary so there can be no misunderstandings about performance expectations. For example, the following KPIs could help to achieve positive trends:[3]

KPI-1 – percent of papers delivered on-time (at least seven days prior to the audit committee meeting).
KPI-2 – audit committee satisfaction level of the quality of papers (based on discussion or quarterly survey).
KPI-3 – percent of papers submitted by management that did not require secretarial rework (rolling average).
KPI-4 – reduction of volume of papers by 25 percent within 12 months (from a base of <number of> pages).

Deliver Meaningful Audit Committee Reporting

Setting the Scene

The true value of an audit committee is reflected in how it translates its thought leadership into meaningful contributions to the achievement of

---

[3] Bruce R Turner, *Powering Audit Committee Outcomes* (Lake Mary FL: The Internal Audit Foundation, 2020), Chapter 4.

the strategies and objectives of the organization. The audit committee outcomes should be tracked and reported formally to the board in an annual audit committee report. While the audit committee will report to the board incrementally throughout the year, it is the annual audit committee report that draws the efforts and outcomes together in a consolidated form.

An early success when I took on the chairmanship of audit committees was to strengthen the committee's reporting to the board or other governing body to make it more relevant and meaningful. The format I developed for a streamlined two-page (one sheet of paper) audit committee annual report was well- received:

- The head of one agency commented, *I have been a CEO of other organizations with independent audit committee members and this style of annual report is the best that I have received.*
- The company secretary at another entity also commented favorably, *really love the format – very readable and easily digested; would like to take the format of your report to the board sub- committee secretariats as an example.*

The format of the audit committee annual report was shared with others, and was subsequently applied across many public sector entities in the state, and was featured in an audit committee training course.

An audit committee annual report should reflect the personality of the board and its needs, and would typically include:[4]

- An overview of the outcomes delivered by the audit committee in relation to the organization's strategies, objectives, and the management of key risks and associated controls.
- An overall assessment of the entity's risk, control, and compliance framework, including details of any significant emerging risks or legislative changes impacting the organization.
- A summary of the entity's progress in addressing the findings and recommendations made in internal and external audit reports.
- Details of meetings, including the number of meetings held during the relevant period, and the number of meetings each member attended.
- A profile of each of the audit committee members (typically 500 to 750 words in length for each, and often accompanied by a professional "headshot" photo).

[4] Bruce R Turner, *Powering Audit Committee Outcomes* (Lake Mary FL: The Internal Audit Foundation, 2020), Chapter 12.

What It Means for Business

Audit committees rely on chief audit executives to share their insights based on the approved internal audit plan. This is achieved primarily through internal audit reports and reports on the status of audit recommendations, coupled with informal conversations between the chief audit executive and the audit committee chair.

But there are many other vital contributors to the audit committee, with the following examples discussed in Chapter 7:

- High level reporting on open and completed investigations.
- Periodic assurance on ten action steps that shine the light on an organization's values of integrity.
- Periodic assurance from the chief audit executive that core enterprise risk management elements are in place and operating as intended.
- Regular risk reporting covering strategic risks, operational risks, project risks, infrastructure risks, risk-based scenario analysis, and emerging risks (in some organizations this might be handled by a separate risk committee).
- Commentary on the organization's lived corporate culture and the overall control environment, including insights on emerging trends and risks.
- Clear and complete compliance reporting, together with periodic analytical assessments.
- Information from business leaders periodically on the status of all policies and procedures, so they can be assured that the policies and procedures are being reviewed and updated in line with the scheduled review dates or when significant changes to obligations are externally-imposed.
- Commentary on how the organization's business continuity activities fit together, how effective they are, whether they are likely to be successful if a need arises to stand them up, and whether the customer experience sits at the heart of decision-making.
- An annual insurable risk report on the organization's insurance practices and arrangements.

Further, collaborative reporting (discussed later in this chapter) provides an overall conclusion or opinion on the outcomes of all of the work of the governance, risk, compliance, and assurance specialist areas.

The audit committee annual report consolidates other periodic reporting provided to the board through other regular reporting, such as the minutes of the meetings, dialogue between the audit committee and board chair, five key takeout summary, and board presentations (discussed under the "optimize communication between the board and board committees" section in Chapter 12). The audit committee annual report captures the essence of the committee's operations, and can ultimately provide trends over three to five years. It is a vital record that aids in the onboarding of new board and audit committee members, and is useful for regulators.

The style and content of the audit committee annual report (introduced in this section under "setting the scene") will evolve over time, and will be influenced by the quality of the audit committee chair's input to the board throughout the year.

Where robust reporting to the board is maintained throughout the year, especially for smaller organizations, the audit committee annual report can be condensed to one-page, with the following features:

- Foreword – provides context including references to the committee's mandate (in its charter).
- Membership and attendance – this section reflects the current membership and changes in the composition over the year, and records the number of meetings each audit committee member attended against the number they were eligible to attend. It helps to demonstrate engagement.
- Compliance with charter – reflects the outcome of a self-assessment by the audit committee, with the chair asserting the mandate remains consistent with the strategic direction of the organization, the committee addressed all duties listed in its charter, its composition matches the requirements of its charter, it has operated in compliance with its charter, and it has adhered to its delegated authority. It also comments on the positive interactions maintained with the board.
- Continuing areas of focus – captures a few areas that are in train or will be progressed during the ensuing year (for example, this could relate to the review, refresh, and rollout of the risk appetite statement).
- Qualitative assessment – this is the meat of the report, and provides comments on the challenges, highlights, and outcomes for the year.

Further insights on audit committee reporting are covered later in this chapter under shaping audit committee performance, and in Chapter 12 which discusses optimizing communication between the board and board committees.

The audit committee chair should be proactive in working with the company secretary and collaborating with the board chair on the breadth, depth, frequency, and mix of reporting provided by the audit committee to the board. There will be instances where boards know they need something more in terms of audit committee reporting, but do not always know what this could look like. This is an area where the audit committee chair can be instrumental in designing an appropriate reporting suite.

The length of the annual audit committee report will depend on the level of engagement between the audit committee and board throughout the year, and whether the audit committee is at the evolving or mature stage. A one or two-page report is appropriate for mature audit committees, but more extensive reporting will be necessary for evolving audit committees with little (or no) interaction with the board.

Focus on the Fundamentals

Setting the Scene

As a corporate lending audit specialist in the late-1980s, I was fascinated by the collapse of a merchant bank that operated independently and nearly bankrupted both its parent bank and the state that ultimately owned it. Notably:[5]

- Tricontinental Holdings Limited (Trico) was formed as a merchant bank in 1978.
- The State Bank of Victoria (SBV) was a statutory corporation of the state of Victoria in Australia, and initially acquired a 25 percent interest in Trico which was increased to 100 percent by the mid-1980s.
- Trico operated with a high degree of independence from the SBV until problems surfaced in the late-1980s relating to its lending activities, liquidity, and corporate management.
- Trico's bad and doubtful debts increased to $A1,712 million in 1990, and the rapid escalation of its inability to pay its way was financially disastrous for both SBV and the state of Victoria.
- Just as SBV had accepted responsibility for meeting the obligations of Trico, so too the state government had accepted statutory and commercial responsibilities to support SBV.
- The state government sold SBV to the Commonwealth Bank of Australia in late-1990, with the sale proceeds enabling the state government to cushion the impact of Trico's actual and potential losses upon the finances of the state of Victoria.

[5] Developed by the author from media reports and a Royal Commission report into the Tricontinental Group of Companies; intended to be illustrative. Also referred to Hugo Armstrong and Dick Gross, *Tricontinental: The Rise and Fall of a Merchant Bank* (Melbourne University Press, Carlton, 1995).

The Trico collapse highlighted to me the importance for boards and audit committees to get the fundamentals right in terms of organizations to which they don't have direct control but do have ultimate financial or reputational exposure.

******

In 2007 an independent review was conducted of internal audit[6] capacity in an Australian state public sector, which found varying levels of internal audit performance, internal audit not mandated, uneven capacity, opportunities for improving internal audit effectiveness without increasing direct costs, and, importantly, the increasing trend in the private sector toward greater independence of audit and risk committees not being mirrored in much of the public sector. The 2008 report was the catalyst for strengthening the government's policy arrangements the following year, including the establishment of world leading-practice audit committee arrangements.[7] The principles of the policy aim to ensure:

- The agency has a risk management framework in place that supports the agency to achieve its objectives by systematically identifying and managing risks to increase the likelihood and impact of positive events, and mitigate the likelihood and impact of negative events.
- The agency's internal audit function provides timely and useful information to management about the adequacy of, and compliance with, the system of internal control; whether agency results are consistent with established objectives; and, whether operations or programs are being carried out as planned.
- The agency head receives relevant and timely advice on the agency's governance, risk and control frameworks and its external accountability obligations from an independent Audit and Risk Committee with appropriate expertise.

Each of the principles are expanded upon through the more detailed core requirements of the policy.

---

6 "Performance review: Internal audit capacity in the NSW public sector," Department of Premier and Cabinet New South Wales, final report 2008.

7 "Internal audit and risk management policy for the NSW public sector: TPP15-03," NSW Treasury Policy and Guidelines Paper. https://arp.nsw.gov.au/assets/ars/f79e35043d/TPP15-03-Internal-Audit-and-Risk-Management-Policy-for-the-NSW-Public-Sector.pdf (sourced 21 July 2020). Issued in 2015 as an update to the original 2009 policy. The 2015 policy was reviewed coincident with the time of writing this chapter, and was ultimately reissued in December 2020 with cosmetic updates but no substantial changes as "Internal Audit and Risk Management Policy for the General Government Sector: TPP20-08".

What It Means for Business

The board will determine the role, objectives, scope, and composition of the audit committee based on the organization's vision, values, and tone at the top. And at a secondary level the role will be influenced by standards, guidance, and legislative and regulatory requirements. An effective audit committee will do a lot of the heavy lifting within its mandate to enable the board to spend more time on other matters.

The audit committee should be established in a way that it assists the board fulfill its corporate governance and oversight responsibilities, and facilitate decision-making in areas including corporate reporting (i.e. external financial reporting, the directors' report, and annual report); external audit; internal audit; internal control; compliance; ethics and organization culture; fraud and corruption. And in some organizations, risk management.

The audit committee chair plays a key role in ensuring the committee has an appropriate mandate with a credible membership, meaningful performance reporting, a continuous improvement philosophy, and a willingness to champion leading practices. The chair should also promote and facilitate open communication between the board and senior management, governance, risk, compliance, and assurance specialists.

*The **scope of the audit committee** is defined in its charter and typically (i) focuses on the integrity of financial reporting; (ii) oversees the organization's risk and assurance activities including external audit, internal audit, risk management, internal control, and compliance; and, (iii) liaises with the board (or governing body), internal and external auditors and management.*

The audit committee charter should clearly articulate boundaries, if any, (that is, areas "in scope" and "out of scope") to make clear the audit committee's role in monitoring or oversighting subsidiaries, associated or controlled entities that are not under the organization's absolute control, and entities that are otherwise controlled, jointly controlled, or significantly influenced. Some examples of where scope boundaries could be blurred if not clearly defined include:

- A merchant bank subsidiary of a commercial bank that has its own governing board that sets its strategic direction, and lending and investment policies (such as the Trico and SBV example in this section).
- A joint venture established by a manufacturing company with an overseas scientific organization to produce a substrate used in the primary manufacturing process.

- Several smaller independent agencies within a central government agency cluster, including a supreme audit organization, corruption watchdog, and ombudsman.
- A performing arts and entertainment center operated with substantial local council funding contributions and operating in a council-owned dedicated arts center that has a separate board consisting of citizens, councilor representatives, industry experts, and performers.

An important role for the audit committee is to oversight and support the internal audit function, which is the only independent and objective area within organizations that reports to the audit committee. The audit committee should establish effective functional reporting lines for the chief audit executive. The reporting lines should be captured in both the audit committee charter and the internal audit charter.

In practice, the chief audit executive will typically have a dual reporting line to ensure independence, with functional reporting to the audit committee, and administrative reporting to the chief executive (or a delegate at a senior level) as illustrated in **Exhibit 11.6**. The audit committee chair should complete or contribute to the formal performance assessment of the chief audit executive each year.

Under the chief audit executive's dual reporting lines:

- Functional responsibilities include approving the internal audit charter and forward audit plan, reviewing audit reports, monitoring reports on the follow-up of audit recommendations, and approving the internal audit budget and resource plan. The audit committee will also be involved in the hiring, compensating, performance assessing, and (in rare cases) removing the chief audit executive.
- Administrative reporting responsibilities include human resource administration, technical and corporate support, approval of

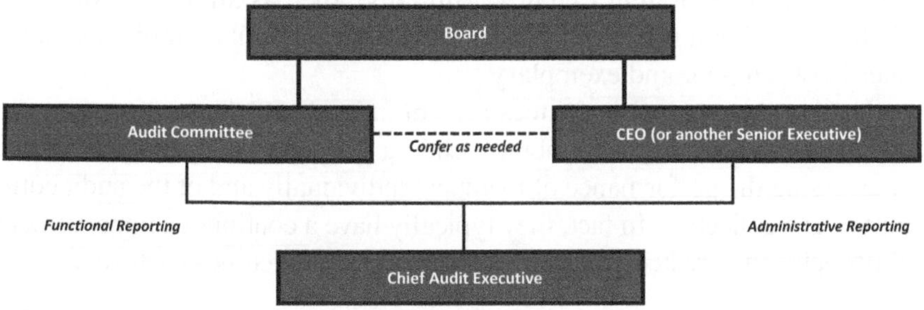

EXHIBIT 11.6 Typical duel reporting lines of the chief audit executive.

financial transactions within budget but outside the chief audit executive's delegation, support in executive forums, and assuring the audit committee that there are no inappropriate scope or resource limitations.

A publication from the Chartered Institute of Internal Auditors UK and Ireland called *What Every Director Should Know About Internal Audit* discusses ten ways to get the most from internal audit.[8] These include:

1. Evaluate the need for internal audit where it does not exist.
2. Assess and approve the internal audit charter (terms of reference) and review regularly.
3. Ensure a close working relationship with the chief audit executive, promoting effective formal and informal communication.
4. Assess the resourcing of the internal audit function.
5. Monitor the quality of internal audit work, both in-house and external.
6. Evaluate, approve, and regularly review the risk-based annual internal audit plan.
7. Oversee the relationship between internal audit and centralized risk monitoring.
8. Ensure the collective assurance roles of internal audit, other internal assurance providers, and external audit, are coordinated and optimized.
9. Assess internal audit findings and the breadth and depth of internal audit reports.
10. Monitor management implementation of internal audit recommendations.

Shape Audit Committee Performance

Setting the Scene

Having attended several hundred audit committee meetings over the last 20 years as a chief audit executive (initially), then as an audit committee chair or member it is clear that the performance of audit committees gravitates between poor and exemplary.

The best-run audit committees are committed to delivering against the approved charter and they embrace leading practices. They are not fearful of assessing the performance of members individually and of the audit committee as a collective. In fact, they typically have a continuous improvement philosophy and are keen to evolve their work and outcomes each year.

---

[8] What Every Director Should Know About Internal Audit (Chartered Institute of Internal Auditors UK and Ireland, 2013).

Audit committees should at least self-assess their performance each year, and communicate the consolidated results to the board. As they mature, the audit committee assessment in larger organizations will seek input from other stakeholders including the CEO, company secretary, chief audit executive, chief financial officer, chief risk officer, the external auditors, and other regular attendees.

A further step-up can be achieved where the audit committee annual assessment applies a 360-degree feedback approach (also known as multi-rater feedback, multisource feedback, or multisource assessment).

The audit committee chair should use the results of the self-assessment to provide feedback to each audit committee member individually, and the committee as a whole. The audit committee should identify a small number of improvement opportunities to progress over the ensuing year.

High-performing audit committees will usually embrace the "mature" features of audit committee reporting to the board outlined in Chapter 12.

I have considered a dozen features of successful audit committees and captured them in the pie illustrated in **Exhibit 11.7**. These features can, of course, vary according to the maturity of the audit committee, but do generally set apart the poor and exemplary performing audit committees. Even audit committees that are not operating at an optimal level can achieve sustainable improvements that drive them to an exemplary level when they bake each piece of the pie into one solid pastry.

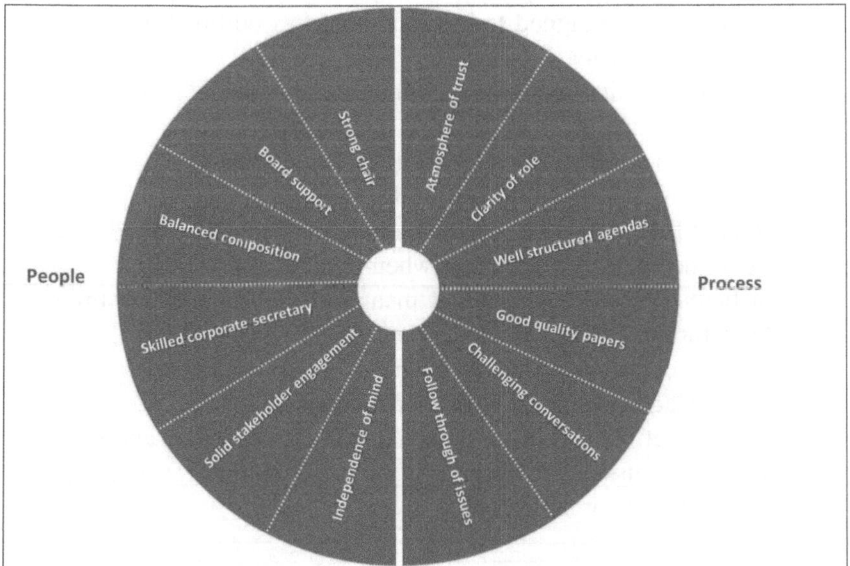

EXHIBIT 11.7 Ingredients for audit committee success – slices of the pie.

What It Means for Business

Audit committees are required to fulfil their responsibilities to many different stakeholders, with differing needs and interests. As an example:

- The board will be interested in leveraging audit committee outcomes as will the CEO.
- The CEO and business leaders will be interested in gaining insights from the audit committee as will the board at a strategic level.
- The chief financial officer will be focused on delivering financial credibility as will other business leaders for their discrete areas of responsibility.
- The chief audit executive and external auditor will be focused on providing independent opinions to the audit committee, and they will expect the audit committee to support them in fulfilling their independent mandates.

It can be useful for the audit committee chair to articulate the expectations of audit committee members. As a starting point, they would generally be expected to:[9]

- Establish effective and meaningful relationships with stakeholders and maintain professional dealings with them.
- Contribute to fulfilling the fiduciary, oversight, strategic, and governance tasks assigned to it by the board as outlined in the audit committee charter.
- Attend all audit committee meetings and the annual general meeting (if a company).
- Attend the board's annual governance and strategy retreat when invited (usually the audit committee chair).
- Prepare fully for audit committee meetings, and for attendance at board meetings as a presenter when invited.
- Participate knowledgably and meaningfully at audit committee deliberations inside and outside meetings.
- Ask appropriate questions of business leaders, and insist on receiving satisfactory answers to all pertinent questions.
- Listen carefully and bring personal skills, experience, and knowledge to discussions regarding the strategic challenges and opportunities for the organization.

---

[9] Richard Leblanc and James Gillies, *Inside the Boardroom* (John Wiley and Sons Canada Ltd, Ontario, 2005), 86–87. Modified and tailored for contemporary audit committees.

- Work constructively with audit committee colleagues including the chair.
- Encourage discussion of key issues.
- Introduce relevant items for discussion that are not on the agenda (say, in general business).
- Initiate meetings with the audit committee chair and/or members to discuss critical issues.
- Exercise mature business judgment, not emotion, in discussion of issues.
- Refrain from interfering in the day-to-day responsibilities of the CEO and business leaders.
- Be available when needed for consultation and advice.
- Comply with the organization's code of ethics and/or code of conduct.
- Act with integrity and high-ethical standards, and model expected behaviors.

Nurture GRC Better Practices and Coordination

Setting the Scene

Over the years I have witnessed situations first-hand where governance, risk management, compliance, and assurance specialists have accepted things at face value, when they should have challenged the situation. In some cases, flaws in reporting were obvious, if just a little common-sense was applied or if there was meaningful collaboration between the different governance, risk management, compliance, and assurance functions. Several examples follow:

- As a chief audit executive, I was reviewing the draft audit report on a recruitment review. The review had concluded that established internal controls were being met (i.e. conformance lens). While I trusted the audit process and the capability of the auditors performing the audit, the conclusion seemed at odds with reality, where I thought the organization's recruitment processes were relatively poor. I asked the team to revisit the review and spend a little more time looking at the recruitment process by expanding the audit scope to consider recruitment through a performance lens. Unsurprisingly the results were different. There were many shortcomings, including the organization was not attracting good quality external candidates, the processes were inefficient and took too long so candidates pulled out, candidate care was inadequate so the preferred candidates were choosing other offers, and none of the KPIs for effective recruitment were being met. Recruitment processes were actually failing badly, even though all of the paperwork was properly completed, signed off, and approved within delegation.

- There have been occasions where reporting of KPIs has been flawed, even though the compliance reporting of these performance measures (in line with the service-level agreement) suggested that the organization was doing a good job. In one rail organization, the reported KPIs regularly demonstrated the standards for carriage cleaning were consistently being met. When we conducted an internal audit, we found that the work was only being partially completed, partly because the average age of the cleaning staff was mid-70s, despite it being a very physical activity. We looked behind the KPI reporting, and reviewed the state of the carriages after cleaning was reported as completed, and found that many tasks, and in some cases whole carriages, had been skipped.
- At one audit committee we reviewed the routine risk report and found that residual risks relating to the privacy and confidentiality of customer information were assessed as strong, even though serious security breaches were reported in another part of the audit committee pack. The people in the respective risk and compliance (breach reporting) areas were obviously not talking with each other (the breach had occurred a month earlier, prior to the reporting cut-off).
- At another audit committee a significant spike in the number of investigations was baffling for a particular theme, and those results were at odds with the information contained in risk management and compliance reports within the audit committee pack from the previous meeting. When the audit committee challenged the situation, the investigators reviewed the source of their data and found that it was flawed, as it double-counted matters that had been referred to other areas to assess. The investigations coordination group (mentioned in Chapter 6) illustrated the value of ensuring that the respective investigation efforts were coordinated, didn't interfere with each other, allowed systemic issues to be determined and actioned, and produced intelligence on emerging themes that informed the communications strategy for corruption prevention. The group helped to ensure the completeness and integrity of the regular investigations.

It is also important when undertaking onsite visits to actually look around. There have been numerous occasions when I've been in the public chamber of a business office and noticed outdated certificates of registration, compliance certificates, licenses, and the like; these were certificates and notices well past their expiry dates. It not only looks unprofessional but, in some cases, it is not fulfilling specific compliance requirements to display the current certificates and notices in a public area.

The impactful words of José Ugaz (at the start of this chapter) highlight the effect of corruption on people when they are deprived of their most basic needs and go to bed hungry. The critically acclaimed 2019 miniseries ***"When they see us"*** *reminds us of how widespread injustices can be, and their effect on the lives of so many others. The Netflix miniseries tracks the "true life" story of five boys (aged 14 to 16) following the 1989 rape and assault of a jogger in Central Park, New York, USA. The boys were falsely accused, coerced into giving false confessions, were prosecuted and found guilty, forced to do time for crimes they did not commit, and, eventually, exonerated when their convictions were vacated in 2002. Governance, risk management, compliance, and assurance specialists need to bear these types of stories in mind when doing their work, as their efforts ultimately help to prevent a lived culture where injustice is allowed to prevail. The tenacity of the five boys (now men) continues to inspire me – I'd like to acknowledge Kevin Richardson, Antron McCray, Yusef Salaam, Korey Wise, and Raymond Santana.*

What It Means for Business

Governance, risk and compliance (GRC) together with assurance arrangements help to identify and manage situations that can impact an organization's ability to achieve its objectives. The success of these arrangements is founded on the support of the board and business leaders; sufficient funding, staffing, and technology resources; and, the clear definition of the organization's purpose, objectives, and goals.

Boards need to determine whether the essential features of an effective governance, risk management, compliance, and assurance framework are in place, as illustrated by **Exhibit 11.8**. The board should leverage the collective analysis and management of these activities, and their interaction with the business, as well as internal and external factors. This is an oversight role that the board can delegate to the audit committee.

The audit committee should monitor the effectiveness of governance, risk management, compliance, and assurance arrangements to be satisfied with the coverage of potential threats, compliance with legislative and regulatory requirements, and optimal management of the organization. Particular attention to be given to the following steps:

- Ensure business leaders support the work in line with the board's expectations and its risk appetite statement.

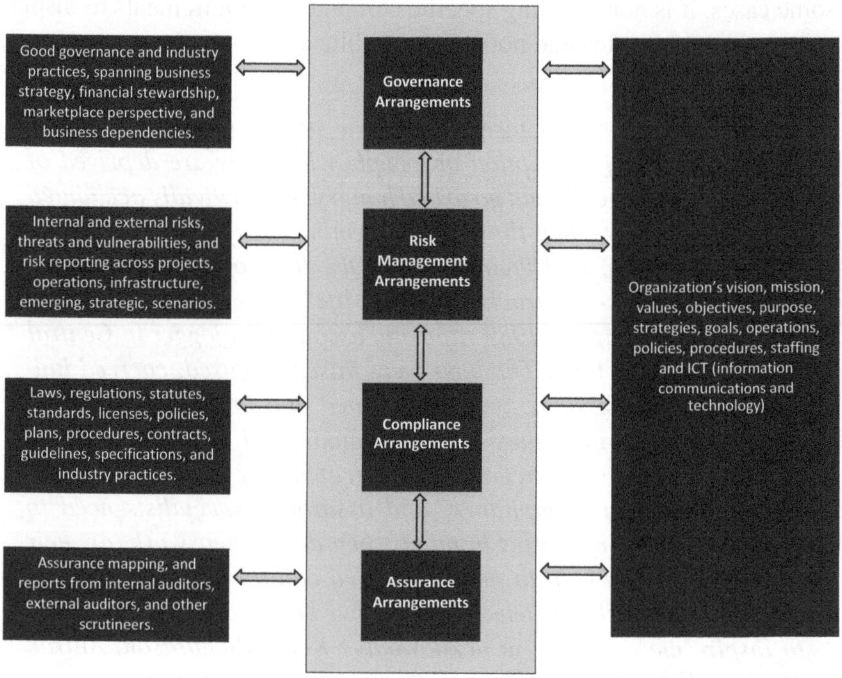

EXHIBIT 11.8 Basic governance, risk management, compliance, and assurance framework.

- Establish entity-wide arrangements for governance, risk management, compliance, and assurance, ensuring all components are addressed in an easily-understood framework (see **Exhibit 11.8**).
- Assess the current environment against industry leading practices, including risk, and regulatory requirements.
- Provide sufficient funding for governance, risk management, compliance, and assurance arrangements, and establish appropriate financial budgeting arrangements.
- Establish and maintain effective resourcing across each of the disciplines, taking into account the professional credentials, certifications, and experience of staff.
- Align the arrangements against the organization's business goals, objectives, and values from numerous perspectives, including financial, investment, competitive position, reputation, new product development, and employee development.
- Maintain effective communication with stakeholders, including periodic briefings with business leaders on significant insights, and frequent meetings with governance, risk management,

compliance, and assurance specialists to ensure they all remain in sync with the overall goals of the arrangements.
- Deliver training and education briefings for employees and business leaders on governance, risk management, compliance, and assurance arrangements, both holistically and singularly.
- Undertake periodic audits of the governance, risk management and compliance arrangements and ensure they are functioning as designed and fulfilling their purpose (the internal audit arrangements are the subject of periodic independent reviews under professional auditing standards; standard 1300).
- Inspire continuous improvement, and adopt suitable automated governance, risk management, compliance, and assurance software applications, and other tools that can streamline activities.

Boards and audit committees should encourage and expect audit, risk, compliance, and assurance professionals to embrace a collaborative reporting approach (the breadth of assurance reporting to the audit committee is illustrated in **Exhibit 3.8**).

***Collaborative reporting** is an approach whereby audit, risk, and compliance specialists work together on analyzing trends and patterns in their collective work to deliver greater value to the audit committee and management through consolidated insights and assurance on the overall state of the organization's risk and control environment.*

Collaborating with others through combined assurance (sometimes referred to as integrated assurance or coordinated assurance) is a way for all assurance providers to work together to align their assurance processes so that the audit committee and business leaders are given insights on governance, risk management, compliance, and control arrangements from a comprehensive holistic perspective. This helps to provide consistent messaging, is more efficient, provides a common view of risks, and delivers more effective oversight.

The combined assurance approach draws together work undertaken by different work areas within an organization (including internal audit) to consolidate into a collaborative report the opinions and insights on a topic of interest to the audit committee. For instance, the combined assurance report could paint the picture on the organization's security culture by consolidating insights from the different assurance areas on topics like cybersecurity, privacy of personal information, penetration testing, information and technology governance.

Oversight Digitization

Setting the Scene

When I was writing this chapter, one of the close family friends of my parents, Ken (Dave) Dibden, passed away aged 93. He was a single man with no children of his own. He worked with my father on the railways in the mid-1950s where they completed a "fitter and turner" apprenticeship together. Ken worked on the railways until he retired after 44 years, whereas my father moved around a lot. When I was about 18 months old, Ken needed a place to stay for 6 months and my father offered him a bed at our home. Ken ultimately lived with my family as a boarder for 58 years. In preparing for his funeral and writing the eulogy (as I am the executor of his estate), it struck me how few photos we could find of Ken throughout his life; this was partly because he tried his best to avoid being photographed. But his early life was a different time and there were fewer photos of people.

Ken was a keen tourist and visited many remote sites around Australia on his annual sojourns, often travelling by motor car and occasionally by long-distance train. He took many scenic and railway-related photos during these adventures, capturing the images on photographic slides (i.e. specially mounted individual transparencies – using reversal film or slide film – intended for projection onto a screen using a slide projector). As a young child, I recall fondly the occasional slide shows where Ken would show us his latest collection of scenic images on the wall, using a rather clunky slide projector.

As our children were growing up my wife and I accumulated many photographs at different stages of their development, capturing birthdays, vacations, and other memorable moments. We have about 10,000 photos (i.e. photo print, which is a physical copy of a photograph printed on paper or other materials) spread throughout over 50 carefully structured and labelled photo albums … all in hardcopy. At the time, we were probably at an extreme level with the size of our photographic collection. Over the years, our children and now their children often pull out a few albums and browse through the happy snaps recalling memories and stories of the time.

Digitization has impacted people at a personal level in many ways, and will continue to evolve. Nowadays we have digital photography, and this is made easier (and cheaper) through the ready availability of cameras on smart phones and other digital equipment. And my wife and I take about 10,000 photos a year of our grandchildren and other occasional moments! What a headache it becomes to sort all the images into digital photo collections … but we can now watch the images on the wall using a more modern and streamlined slide projector!

> ***Digitization*** *is the process of converting analog signals or informa tion from a physical format into a digital format that can be understood by computer systems or electronic devices. In this format, information is organized into binary data that computers and many devices with computing capacity (such as digital cameras and digital hearing aids) can process. It can be used to convert an original or source record to digital format through scanning or photographing the source record. When this process is leveraged to improve business processes, it is called* ***digitalization****. The results of this process are called* ***digital transformation****.*

The objectives of an organization might lead it down the path of digitization. As an example, legislation in some jurisdictions requires information to be accessible to the public by requiring government agencies to make certain information freely available; encouraging government agencies to release as much other information as possible; giving the public an enforceable right to make access applications for government information; and restricting access to information only when there is an overriding public interest against disclosure. The government agency responsible for the collection and storage of public records in my home state houses records dating back to 1788 (i.e. European settlement in Australia), with historical records now being digitized, transcribed, and made available through many collections online for browsing and searching. This has made genealogy searches possible from people's homes.

What It Means for Business

An organization's digital initiatives were discussed in other chapters, including Chapter 3 (digital innovation) and Chapter 5 (business transformation). But there is another lens … the digitization of existing records, such as analogue audio and video recordings. The common reasons for digitization relate to the organization[10]:

- Facing difficulties in providing access to existing resources, as the devices to read them are no longer widely available in the organization or elsewhere (for example, record players or VCRs).
- Having existing analogue resources that are becoming fragile or being degraded by poor storage conditions, the passage of time or overuse, threatening their accessibility.

[10] State Archives and Records Authority of New South Wales, "Digitisation of analogue audio and video," https://www.records.nsw.gov.au/recordkeeping/advice/digitisation-of-analogue-audio-and-video (sourced 28 July 2020).

- Wanting to improve the recordings (e.g. digitally enhance them or improve indexing of the recordings), and therefore improve search and retrieval.
- Wanting to make them more readily available by providing the potential for online delivery.
- Wanting to create new versions of the recordings, e.g. tailor them for other uses.
- Aiming to leverage the advantages of digital over analogue methods of recording and playback, such as:
  - The binary code of digital audio and video can be read by a computer. Therefore, computers can be used to edit the data (e.g. remaster to enhance sound and visual quality), and to create new effects. Analogue signals only play what was originally recorded as it was recorded.
  - Digital media is non-linear (or non-real time), so it can be edited and played back starting at any point.
  - Digital information does not degrade and lose quality with repeated use (like tapes or record albums do). They may be copied repeatedly without loss.
  - Groups of numbers can be compressed by finding patterns in them, meaning the same information can be stored more efficiently.

The board's role in an organization's digitization efforts is very much strategic in nature, and such efforts should be in line with the board's vision, mission, strategy, and risk appetite. The board should approve any strategies for digitization (including digitization of existing records) and effectively oversee the transformation, by focusing on the strategic plan, risks, and opportunities, and the change management program.

*A **post-implementation review** (PIR) is often conducted after completing a project to evaluate whether project objectives were achieved. The reviews help to determine project effectiveness, identify lessons learned for future projects, and establish if the organization attained optimal benefits from the project. The reviews typically are undertaken by business leaders or independently by the internal audit team.*

The board should monitor implementation of digitization strategies – perhaps through the audit or risk committee – to ensure that the investment results in long-term value for the organization, then seek and consider a

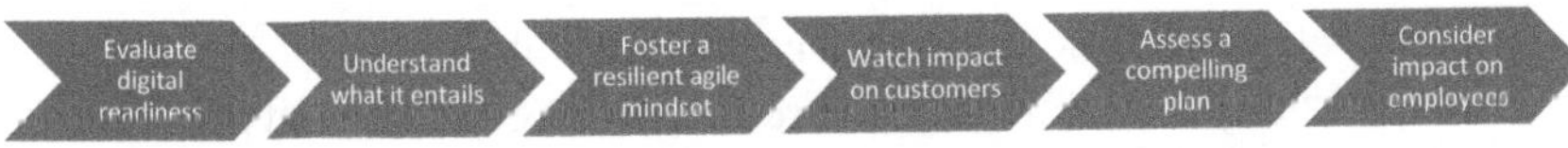

EXHIBIT 11.9 Board's oversight of digitization.[12]

post-implementation review. Boards need to understand the goals of the digitization and how they link to the organization's strategy; ensure that business leaders develop a plan to address the main risks and opportunities; determine how employees are likely to embrace the digitization initiatives; ensure the right talent strategy is in place; and, set metrics for success to determine whether the digitization efforts are taking hold. Key features of the board (or audit committee) oversight of digitization are illustrated in **Exhibit 11.9** and then discussed.

There are six important areas of focus for boards in oversighting digitization within their organization, and this can be delegated to the audit committee to assess and monitor. Boards and their audit committees need to be satisfied that:[13]

- Business leaders have prepared the organization to compete in the digital age, and understand the level of digital know-how across the organization. A well-developed digital strategy will only reap value if the organization is digital-ready.
- Business leaders and company directors are committed to developing digital familiarity and literacy themselves, and ensure they have access to digital-savvy experience.
- They maintain effective oversight of the organization's digital journey, perhaps by establishing an innovation committee with technology, digital, and transformation experts as members. Other options include appointing directors with the requisite technology expertise, or engaging outside advisers to inform the board with relevant perspectives.
- People and culture have been factored into the decision-making as they are the keys to successful digitization.
- Business leaders have established effective digital leadership, enhanced the digital capabilities of its people, created a corporate culture that incentivizes and empowers creativity and innovation, and maintained effective communication.
- Sufficient agenda time is allocated to discussing the organization's digital opportunities, innovation strategy, and culture, and encouraging open discussion on direction and progress.

---

12 National Association of Corporate Directors, "Oversight of digital transformation: Insights from active directors," https://blog.nacdonline.org/posts/oversight-digital-active-directors (sourced 28 July 2020).

13 Ibid.

- Innovation-specific metrics have been established to reflect how the strategy is performing, the return on investment, and the effectiveness of digital culture and capabilities.
- Adequate assurance is obtained from business leaders on the customer experience and competitive advantage, with reports to be provided should problematic data strategy and legacy infrastructure issues arise (e.g. technical debt).
- Business leaders have established and executed plans to deal with business disruption and transformation, covering technologies, new products and services, strategic supplier and distribution channel partners, and changes in the business.
- There is a clear and coherent strategy to address worker dislocation, displacement and impacts, and they should be kept apprised of progress.

CHAPTER 11 – TEN CLOSING REFLECTIONS

- The board should establish an audit committee skills matrix to select audit committee members so as to achieve a well-balanced audit committee with a blend of skills and experience that meets the needs and expectations of the board and audit committee chair.
- The audit committee chair with the support of the company secretary should monitor and manage the conflicts of interests of audit committee members or anyone reporting to the audit committee.
- Company secretaries should be capable, understand the position requirements, have completed higher education, and must operate at a consistently high level.
- The company secretary should provide the guidance necessary to deliver an efficient, effective, seamless, disciplined, and clear secretariat for the board and audit committee; a secretarial handbook typically provides the foundation.
- Audit committee chairs are responsible for ensuring the audit committee has an appropriate mandate with a credible membership, meaningful performance reporting, a continuous improvement philosophy, a willingness to champion leading practices, and open communication with the board and senior management.
- Audit committee chairs should ensure the audit committee delivers against the approved charter, embraces leading practices, and maintains a continuous improvement philosophy.

- Audit committee performance should be assessed at least annually, with the consolidated results reported to the board; ideally the assessment will apply a 360-degree feedback approach.
- The audit committee should produce an annual audit committee report to the board; the report should complement and consolidate periodic reporting provided to the board through other regular reporting, such as the minutes of the meetings, dialogue between the audit committee and board chair, five key takeout summary, and board presentations.
- Boards and audit committees should encourage and expect audit, risk, compliance, and assurance professionals to embrace a collaborative reporting approach that delivers insights on those areas from a comprehensive holistic perspective.
- Boards should approve the organization's digitization strategies and effectively oversee the transformation (including strategic plan, risks, and opportunities, and the change management program), then monitor implementation, and consider a post-implementation review to ensure that the investment results in long-term value for the organization.

Further reading: *The book I wrote on* ***Powering Audit Committee Outcomes*** *(Internal Audit Foundation, 2020) takes a deeper dive into the changing governance, risk, compliance, and assurance landscape, and provides ideas on current and emerging audit committee requirements.*

12 Boardroom Conversations

Boards benefit enormously from having membership diversity, with experienced and talented auditors now being appointed to boards to complement the expertise of professors, doctors, accountants, lawyers, engineers, and others. Professionals from governance, risk, compliance, and assurance backgrounds add an extra dimension to the boardroom's balance. This chapter explores contemporary thought leadership to discuss foundation elements for boards, mentoring, succession planning, blend of board skills, performance management, ties between the board and board committees, and stakeholder engagement … and it also highlights challenging boardroom discussions around financial and governance failings, and the difficulties in managing serious allegations of wrongdoing against another director. The perspectives of Dr Anne-Maree Moodie (Australian corporate governance professional and company secretary) are critical, "Boards must ensure that succession planning for the board is aligned with the future strategic direction of the company, so that the board, the senior management team and shareholders are confident that the collective skills of the board are at all times appropriate, and are being refreshed regularly."

Entity Profile and Role

Sectors:	Spanning the public, private, and not-for-profit sectors.		
Industry groupings:	Health and professional services.		
Entities:	Several distinct entities.		
Metrics of entities – spread of entity sizes:	Small 33 percent of entities Entities with annual expenditure less than $25 million	Medium 33 percent of entities Entities with annual expenditure less than $400 million but over $25 million	Large 33 percent of entities Entities with annual expenditure greater than $400 million
Primary role:	Member of the board (non-executive board director).		

Main responsibilities:	Ensure the organization's prosperity by collectively directing its affairs, while meeting the appropriate interests of its shareholders, members, and other stakeholders. Provide strategic leadership and stewardship to safeguard the future well-being of the organization through leadership, enterprise, integrity, judgment, and highest standards of corporate governance. Play a key role in establishing the vision, mission, and values; setting strategy and structure; delegating to management; and exercising accountability to shareholders and being responsible to relevant stakeholders.
Timeframe:	The Fifth Decade (since 2012 and continuing).

PERSONAL STORY

During the twilight of my working career I put my mind to what I would do in retirement. I had established well-rounded skills in governance, risk management, compliance, and assurance during my career, so I was well-positioned to take on a board role in addition to the audit committee roles I had already secured.

The roles I held at the Australian Taxation Office in the five years prior to my retirement helped to sharpen my strategic thinking (the performance side of the business equation), and I gained valuable experience in having strategic conversations with people at all levels within the organization. The Australian Taxation Office had an exemplary strategic-planning approach which was driven by a clear vision, well-founded objectives, strong values, commitment to its clients through a taxpayer charter, and effective leadership from the Commissioner and the executive team.

To ready myself for potential board roles, I completed board training courses through the Australian Institute of Company Directors and the Ministry of Health. The training modules covered a range of topics, including governance roles and duties; role of the director and the board; board meetings and governance; financial management and reporting; financial statements for directors; assessing company performance for directors; strategy, performance, and risk; strategic role of the director; issues in governance and clinical governance; activity-based management; and, organizational culture.

My first board role was as a volunteer on the board of the Institute of Internal Auditors in Australia, and I assumed that role soon after I first retired. It was a professional association with global ties, and I had been a member for about 30 years, so I understood its objectives and knew most of the executive team in Australia. The Institute of Internal Auditors was established in 1941 and has more than 200,000 members across the world from 190 countries.

My primary motivation for joining the Institute of Internal Auditors Australia board and subsequent boards was to drive high-level initiatives that resonated with me. It was a good way to give back. It also enabled me to leverage my specific knowledge and expertise to make a real difference to the operations of the organizations.

My various board roles have provided rewarding learning experiences and intellectual challenges. As my board roles typically served different industries than I had specialized in, I had to quickly become accustomed to the vagaries of the industry and its competitive landscape so as to make well-considered contributions. I also had to reshape my thinking processes to consider things more holistically and to grasp the breadth of topics handled by boards. The richness of my board experiences also helped me to contribute even more effectively in my audit committee roles. There is a great deal of cross-fertilization on boards, with fresh ideas permeating around the boardroom table, reflecting the diverse skills and expertise that boards have individually and collectively.

The key insights from this phase of my story are:

- Maintain a skills-based board.
- Embed the corporate values.
- Shape the organizational strategy.
- Understand the lived culture.
- Oversight business performance and conformance.
- Optimize communication between the board and board committees.
- Manage CEO succession planning.

CONTEXT

The board has primary responsibility for the overall governance, strategic direction, performance, and conformance of the organization and for delivering outcomes in line with the organization's vision, values, objectives, goals, and customer commitment. There are a range of essential ingredients that shape an effective board, including the fundamentals for success, clarity of direction, a values-based culture, and knowing how the business is really operating; these elements are discussed in this chapter and illustrated in **Exhibit 12.1**.

KEY TAKEAWAYS AND DEEP DIVES

Maintain a Skills-Based Board

Setting the Scene

When I retired, one of my early decisions was to accept a voluntary position on the board of the Institute of Internal Auditors in Australia, which

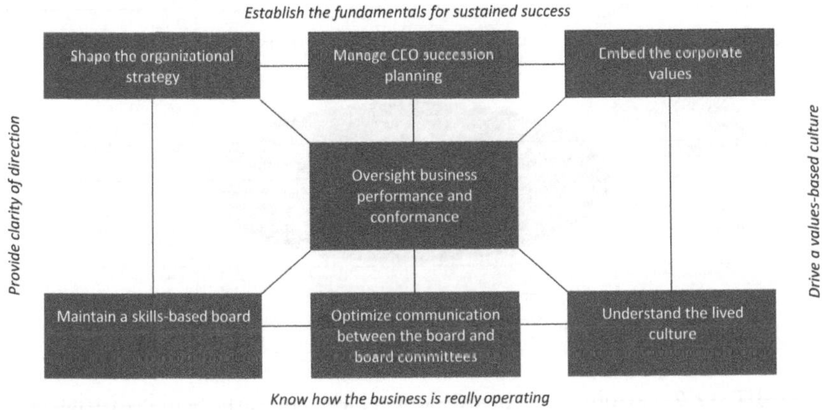

EXHIBIT 12.1 Essential ingredients for oversighting business performance and conformance.

coincided with the institute's 60th anniversary year. It was a great way to learn the ropes as a board member while sharing my expertise in business, governance, risk management, compliance, and assurance. I simultaneously assumed the chairmanship of the board audit committee.

A couple of years later I was appointed to a remunerated position on the board of a health district, as I had gained board experience and "knew" the health district having chaired its audit committee for several years. The district had five hospitals that delivered healthcare to more than 900,000 residents across 120 suburbs. In 2015–2016 the district handled 175,000 emergency department presentations, had almost 180,000 admissions, conducted 43,000 surgeries, handled over 10,000 births, provided 220,000 dental services, and provided 50,000 vaccinations at high schools (amongst other healthcare activities).[1]

Around the boardroom table there were five professors, two doctors, two lawyers, the CEO, company secretary, and me (see depiction in **Exhibit 12.2**). It was a diverse skills-based board that served the organization well. The professors and doctors had diverse skills, spanning general practice, primary healthcare reform, academia, surgery, obstetrics, and gynecology, renal and transplant specialist, and medical research and education. The lawyers, too, specialized in different fields.

My first board meeting seemed a little daunting. I was overwhelmed at the talent in the boardroom, and was uncertain what impact I would have. Dame Anita Roddick (British Businesswoman and Founder of the Body

[1] Western Sydney Local Health District, 2015–2016 Year in Review.

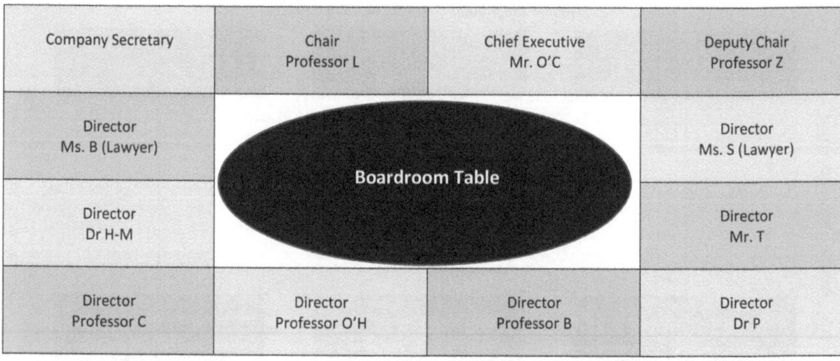

EXHIBIT 12.2 Around the boardroom table – an early health district board meeting.

Shop) once commented, "If you think you're too small to have an impact, try going to bed with a mosquito (in the room)." I was warmly welcomed and made to feel at ease. And I soon learned that the skills and experience that I brought to the table helped to boost the overall capability of the board. I quickly gained the trust and confidence of my boardroom colleagues and did influence a range of fresh governance initiatives (some of which are showcased in the "understand the lived culture" section).

It struck me that the board gains its strength from all of the individual pieces contributing equally to deliver the strategies and objectives of the organization. With diversity of skillsets comes a range of differing ideas, and the conversations around the boardroom table typically translate into the best solutions and opportunities for the organization.

With the half the board members scheduled to complete their maximum terms within the next 18 months, I was appointed chair of the board nominations committee to manage the refresh and reassess the skills needed for the board of the future. We developed the terms of reference, in consultation with the board chair, and these were approved by the full board. The terms of reference included a requirement to produce a Board Composition Matrix (referred to as a Skills Matrix in some organizations).

What It Means for Business

Stable boards with experienced, committed, and longstanding board members are well-positioned to understand the organization's mission, vision, values, objectives, and strategies. However, there will be times when boards need to inject new blood to represent the changing business environment and community attitudes, as well as the emerging needs and interests of the organization's owners or members.

Changing the board composition is not a simple task, and it requires a carefully considered strategic approach to create the board of the future.

Board members should have staggered terms so the board composition changes incrementally, and the refresh of the board should never be sudden in nature or involve wholesale changes.

The composition of the board is determined by who is on the board, the unexpired term, the board's current skills mix, and the skills mix required by the board of the future. Both structural and cultural issues need to be factored into the assessment, with board effectiveness depending on the right mix of skills and experience. Board composition requirements differ between organizations and are influenced by:

- The size of the board.
- Legal requirements (e.g. organization constitution, mix of executive and non-executive directors).
- Director competencies (i.e. current and future, alignment of skills to strategic direction).
- Terms of office for directors (i.e. maximum terms, unexpired terms of current appointments).
- The structure of the organization's shareholding or membership.
- Succession planning (including cultural fit with board, time to become an effective contributor).

Further reading: The National Association of Corporate Directors (NACD) report ***Fit for the Future*** *reflects on "... leading boards into the future and about positioning boards to help their companies meet the challenges of the future. It argues that the pace and scale of change require different modus operandi ... a new approach involving greater speed of decision making, proactive behaviors, adaptability, and innovation." (Full name of report released in 2019 – The Report of the NACD Blue Ribbon Commission: Fit for the Future – An Urgent Imperative for Board Leadership).*

The board should be considered as a whole unit, in which each individual director makes their own contribution; no single director is likely to possess all the competencies and skills required for the board (nor should they be expected to have them). Prior to reappointing, nominating or appointing individuals as directors, the board should:

- Assess the competencies and skills each incumbent director possesses.
- Determine the competencies and skills the board, as a whole, should possess.

- Consider personalities and behavioral types that impact boardroom dynamics.
- Assess the integrity, ethical standards, and other character traits of incumbent and potential directors, and their fit with the expected board culture.

Many boards utilize a board composition matrix to systematically assess the skills, diversity requirements, and other attributes of the board in the future.

A ***board composition matrix*** *(also called a skills matrix) sets out the mix of skills and diversity the board currently has or is looking to achieve in its membership. The process of creating the board composition matrix provides a means to consciously reflect on whether the boards' skillset is aligned to the organization's strategy and industry, or whether there is presently a skills deficit on the board. It also helps to identify whether there will be a gap in the future as circumstances change.*

There are typically five steps required when developing a board composition matrix (an example of which is contained in **Exhibit 12.4**), and these include:

- Obtain examples of the skills matrix used by other boards and use these as the basis for developing a draft board composition matrix that fits the peculiar needs of your organization.
- Establish the criterion that are most appropriate for your organization and include them in a board composition matrix summary. Include specific requirements for the organization as well as other common elements. The aim is to provide a structured assessment tool that applies a strategic lens (it will be backed up by detailed supporting documentation).
- Develop a board composition matrix aide memoir once the criteria have been agreed.
- Support the high-level matrix by developing (i) a detailed-level assessment of current board composition and skills, (ii) an assessment of skills required for the "board of the future," and (iii) schedule of approved terms and options/intentions of incumbent board members. See **Exhibit 12.3**.
- Consider and gain board approval for the content of the board composition matrix, paying particular attention to the criterion, priority factors, the priority element *number of board members*, and ultimately the assessment factors including priority, timing, opportunity, and timeframe which will to be populated after the board composition assessment.

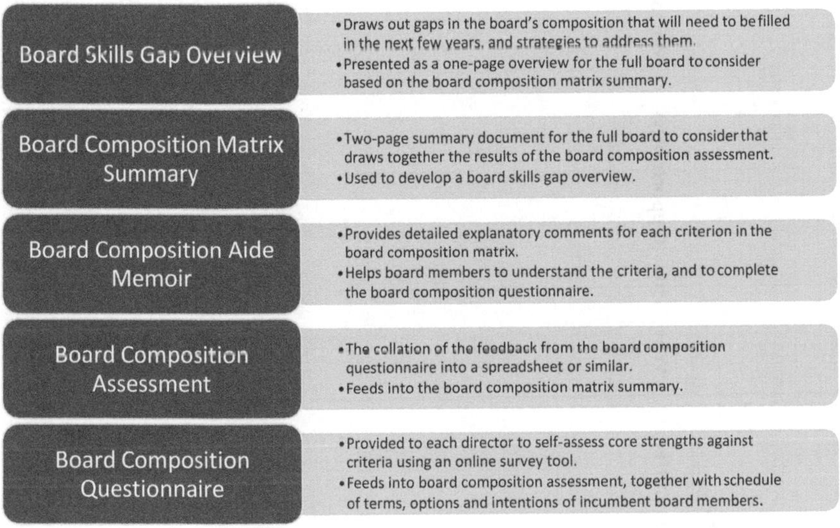

EXHIBIT 12.3 Tools and techniques used in board composition assessment.

Note: Steps flow from the bottom of the diagram to the top.

In some cases, the board might not have the right candidates to directly satisfy its "priority" requirements and may need to consider "buying in" those attributes for specific purposes.

In the example board composition matrix (**Exhibit 12.4**), the board started the conversation about the skills they would require in the future (regardless of the current skillset) and formed a view on the skillset requirements. Once the skillsets were established, the priority of those skills were ranked by both the proportion of board members requiring the skills, and secondly by the timing for when the skills needed to be brought on board. Recognizing that the board had insights on the performance and contributions of members of board committees, they identified potential pathways from those committees (in this case from the audit and risk, finance, and investment board committees). They were then able to plot how the opportunities might arise, for example:

- Director C retires in six-months, let's start the process now to secure potential director X from the board's investment committee to fill an identified skills gap related to a significant building development scheduled to commence soon.
- The term of our legal specialist director Y has twelve-months to run, but we need to have at least a six-month transition period, given the specialist skills held by just one director, so we will advertise the vacancy in three months.

EXHIBIT 12.4
Board composition matrix example

Part 1 – Determining Board Skills Mix – *How we identify and fill gaps for the 'board of the future'.*

What (Criteria)	Priority	Pathway (Committee)	Why / How (Opportunity)	When
1.1 – Skills				
Governance, risk management, control, and compliance	A:	Audit & Risk		
Board leadership (potential as Chair of Board or Board Committee)	C:			
Performance monitoring (financial and non-financial KPIs)	B:	Finance		
Strategic mindset (critical and innovative thinker)	B:			
Community and stakeholder engagement	B:			
1.2 – Industry Specific				
<To be added>				
1.3 – Business and Financial Management Experience				
New ways of working (transformational leadership)	C:			
Commercial (workforce transformation; operational expertise)	C:			
Financial management	C:	Finance		
Infrastructure development (large capital projects)	C:	Investment		
Legal specialist (priorities: health, safety, security, privacy)	D:			
Strategic marketing (branding; industry lobbying; public relations)	E:			
1.4 – Specialist Experience - Current Priority Areas				
Digital transformation (big data; AI; cyber control; ICT)	D:			
<More to be added>				
Part 2 – Considering Board Diversity – *How we get the right balance.*				
2.1 - Demographics				
Community representation (geography, understand community)	B:			
Generational diversity	D:			

(*Continued*)

EXHIBIT 12.4 (*Continued*)

Board composition matrix example

What (Criteria)	Priority	Pathway (Committee)	Why / How (Opportunity)	When
Gender mix (at least 40% of each gender)	B			
Other (ethnicity, culture, faith)	D:			
Part 3 – Exploring Critical Selection Criteria – *How we select the right people.*				
Other consideration: Actual, potential or perceived conflicts of interest.				
3.1 – Board Experience				
Previous Board role and/or completed formal directorship training	B:			
3.2 – Knowledge of the Business				
Through a Committee of the Board	C:			
<Others to be added>				
3.3 – Personal Behavioral Attributes				
Commitment and dedication	A			
Integrity (ethics)	A			
Strong contributor (influencer, questioner, team player)	A			
Thought leader	B:			
Willingness to attend community and business events	A			

Legend for 'priority':

Number of Board members:

A = All

B = Between 40% and 60% of Board members

C = Several

D = At least one

E = Considered as opportunities arise

Timing (i.e. 'when' column):

a = Immediate need

b = Within twelve months

c = Within two years

d= Considered as opportunities arise

- The board chair retires in 18 months and the chair of the audit and risk committee has the capabilities to assume the role of board chair, so let's bring him/her onto the board as soon as practicably possible.

Embed the Corporate Values

Setting the Scene

Well-founded values should underpin behavior and decision-making from the boardroom to the mailroom (or its equivalent in today's business world). The values need to be reinforced, as we can sometimes lose sight of what the values really mean for us.

> ***Corporate values*** *refer to the operating philosophies or principles that guide an organization's internal conduct as well as its relationship with its customers, partners, shareholders, and other stakeholders. They guide the behavior of business leaders and staff and help them strive toward a common goal.*

During my first day at the Australian Taxation Office, I met with the Commissioner Michael D'Ascenzo as part of my induction. He shared with me his insights on the area that I was charged with transforming and reflected that the staff in the team were good people who needed the strategic direction he knew I could provide.

During the conversation he spoke frankly and passionately about things like consultation, collaboration, and co-design; when I reflected later, I recognized that these words (and others he had used) were part of the corporate values. The Commissioner was living the values, incorporating them as part of his conversations with others, inspiring a strong values-based culture, and setting a strong tone at the top.

Fast forward a decade, and it struck me when I was interviewed for the role on the board of Wentworth Healthcare Limited and for the audit committee at Penrith City Council that the corporate values were printed on the glass walls of the entry foyer as people came into the respective organizations. And in both organizations, I was impressed when the respective organizational leaders instigated conversations with me about the importance of their corporate values.

For anyone aspiring to board or audit committee roles, it is important to establish whether corporate values are truly embraced within the organizations at all levels or are simply statements that seemed like a good idea when they were formulated though they have since been allowed to gather dust.

What It Means for Business

The corporate values should encapsulate what your business stands for and its underlying philosophy; they should sit at the core of every business.

Corporate values typically reflect the behaviors that will deliver the organization's vision (discussed in Chapter 2). The corporate values gain real meaning and life when the staff are involved in their development, and when they are explicitly aligned with the organization's vision (its reason for being).

Once the board has determined the corporate values, the business leaders will develop a compendium (illustrated in **Exhibit 12.5**) to set out the general principles that will guide the behavior of all employees of the organization, the third parties with whom it has dealings, and the board.

Given its broader fiduciary and other responsibilities, the board will usually establish a separate board code of conduct to capture the values and principles that define the standards of behavior of members of the board and associated committees. The primary audience is the organization's board of directors. The code will reflect how the board will set the tone at the top. The board members are also expected to embrace the organization's code of ethics and code of conduct.

The statement of business ethics articulates the expectations of third parties in conducting the overall business relationship and dealing with

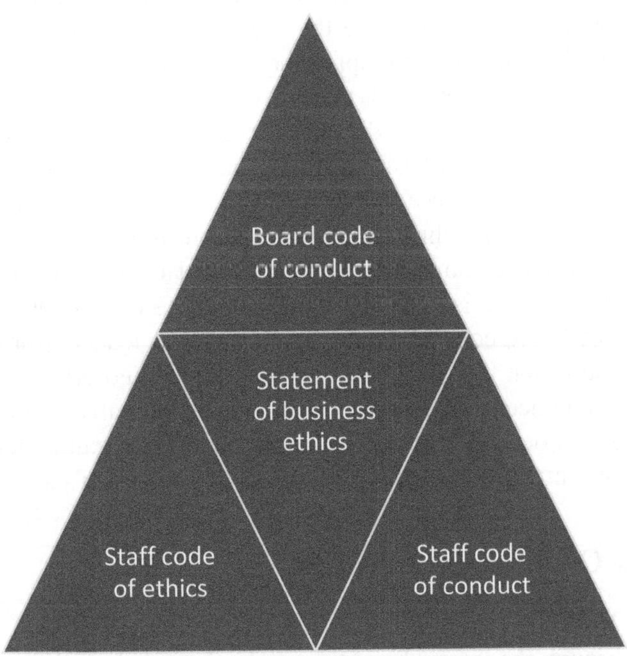

EXHIBIT 12.5 Disseminating the values.

staff. Its primary audience is third party suppliers, contractors, consultants, tenderers, joint venture and alliance partners, and other external parties.

The concept of a statement of business ethics evolved because contemporary business models increasingly involve third parties, with external supplier costs now representing one of the most significant lines of expenditure for an organization. As such, an organization's commitment to fairness and ethical values needed to be documented and disseminated to all third-party suppliers of goods and services.

While organizations might use the phrases code of ethics and code of conduct interchangeably, there are fundamental differences; the code of ethics provides the philosophical perspective while the code of conduct provides real-life application. Notably:

- A code of ethics is a principles-based guide that sets out the corporate values, describes the organization's obligation to its stakeholders, and helps staff to conduct business honestly and with integrity (it can also take the form of a value statement).
- A code of conduct is a subset of the code of ethics and describes the manner in which employees are expected to implement the code of ethics.

Some organizations will choose to combine the code of ethics and the code of conduct into a single document and call it either the code of ethics or the code of conduct. They articulate the organization's expectations of staff conduct and the sanctions that apply for wrongdoing.

Each of these documents needs to be developed in consultation with the concerned stakeholders (i.e. board directors for the board code of conduct, third parties for the statement of business ethics, and staff for the code of ethics and code of conduct). Governance, risk, compliance, assurance, and HR professionals are usually consulted throughout the development phase, trade unions (for staff code) and audit committees may also be asked to provide their input.

The roll-out phase is critical for each of these documents. The board chair (for the board code of conduct) and business leaders (for the others) need to ensure that the documents are communicated effectively to their respective audiences, and that the values are periodically reinforced.

All of these documents are typically placed on the organization's website (internet and intranet) and referenced in the organization's annual report.

SHAPE THE ORGANIZATIONAL STRATEGY

Setting the Scene

Coming through the internal auditing ranks, I was relatively strong on the conformance side of the board's strategic focus, and, in a sign of those times, had less involvement in the performance side. As the internal auditing profession evolved and as I moved into more senior roles, I was increasingly involved in strategic planning from a broader perspective; it enabled me to showcase my talents on the strategic performance side of the equation. I enjoyed the interactions as I was clearly contributing effectively and meaningfully.

Of course, determining the organization's strategies and disseminating the strategic messages to the staff are complementary activities. The Commissioner at the Australian Taxation Office was keen to ensure that its 25,000 staff at all levels had a clear line of sight between their role and the related strategic initiatives. All senior executives were tasked with sharing the key messages at "road-shows" covering all of the 70 sites spread across Australia.

The roadshow at one of the organization's largest sites in Parramatta was co-hosted by the Second Commissioner Jennie Granger and me. Rugby league football is the premier sport along Australia's eastern states. Parramatta has a major rugby league team as did my home site of Penrith; and the Second Commissioner followed another team, South Sydney. Recognizing the importance of storytelling in capturing the attention of the audience, I bought three scarves, one representing each of the Parramatta, Penrith, and South Sydney teams. My wife cut the scarves in half and sowed each half together so there was one scarf representing the three teams. During the roadshow I presented the scarf to the Second Commissioner, showing the cardinal red and myrtle green colors of her beloved South Sydney. Of course, when she unrolled the scarf to put it on it revealed all three teams, and the audience burst into laughter. It was a fun moment but proved to be memorable. The strategic messages resonated with the staff.

When I visited the Second Commissioner in her Canberra office some weeks later, the scarf was proudly adorning her visitor's lounge chair. No doubt many a story had been told. It was also a subliminal reminder about the Penrith office. Jennie relocated to London in 2012 to assume the role of Director General HM Revenue and Customs, a role she held for nearly five years. In a pretty neat twist, she took the scarf with her to adorn her London office!

Having cut my teeth on strategic planning in my executive roles, I have enjoyed the opportunities to more directly contribute to the strategic direction of organizations while sitting on various boards. I really value the richness of the conversations at the board retreats, and love seeing each of the board directors sparking off the ideas of our colleagues to arrive at the best strategic solutions and opportunities. Given my background, I often look at things from a different perspective or have fresh insights to contribute to the conversations; it confirms that my thought leadership is truly adding value, which helps to build my confidence around the boardroom table.

What It Means for Business

A well-shaped organizational strategy enables the board to respond to changing market conditions, ensure management's focus on the most important long-term initiatives, achieve performance targets, deliver greater value, boost employee efficiency, sustain competitive advantage, drive continued success, grow the revenue, and maintain or shrink expenses.

*An **organizational strategy** is the sum of all the actions an organization intends to take to deliver the vision and mission through the achievement of long-term objectives and goals in line with the corporate values. Together, these actions make up an organization's strategic plan.*

The organizational strategy is brought together into a consolidated strategic plan that the board develops in consultation with the CEO and business leaders to provide management with clear directions that help them to deliver upon the vision, maintain corporate values, position the organization, compete successfully, satisfy customers and other stakeholders, achieve good business performance, and maintain sustainability.

A SWOT analysis is a common starting point as it leads to fact-based analysis, fresh perspectives, and new ideas. The key steps for developing and communicating the organizational strategy are illustrated in **Exhibit 12.6**.

*A **SWOT analysis** is a framework that considers the strengths, weaknesses, opportunities, and threats of an organization in the context of its vision, mission, values, and objectives. The SWOT analysis provides a realistic, fact-based, data-driven input to strategic planning by evaluating internal and external factors, the competitive landscape, changing community attitudes, and current and future potential.*

Once the organizational strategy has been determined and converted into a strategic plan, the board needs to assign responsibility to the CEO for actioning the strategic initiatives. In turn, the CEO needs to develop a business plan that allocates strategic initiatives across the business leaders who leverage it to establish their operational plans. The board should recognize that strategic initiatives span more than one year, and this should be factored into

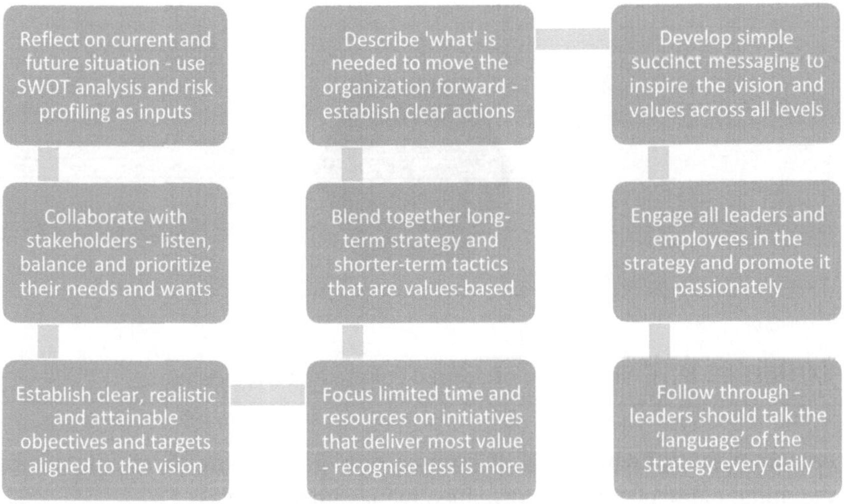

EXHIBIT 12.6 Key steps for developing and communicating the organizational strategy.

the KPIs to be achieved by the CEO over the ensuing year, and the lead-in for longer-term initiatives to be delivered in the second year.

Communication strategies should be pursued so all employees understand how their role contributes to the overarching strategies, and the related activities or actions should be incorporated into employee performance agreements. Chapter 8 discussed the importance of recognizing good performance

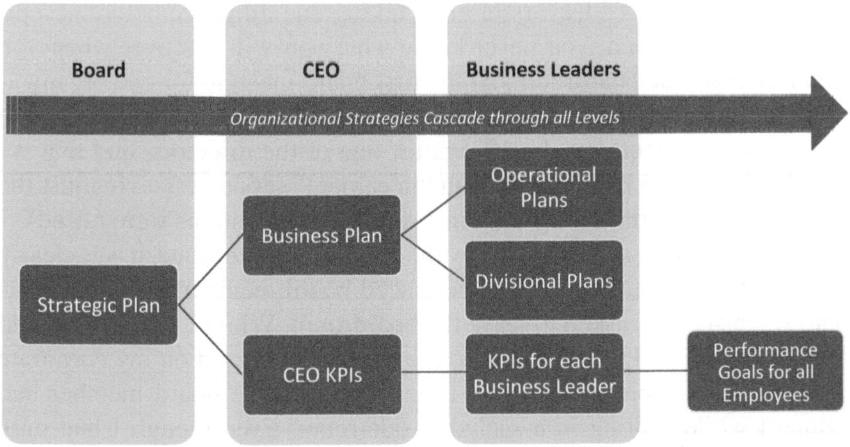

EXHIBIT 12.7 How the organizational strategy cascades through the organization.

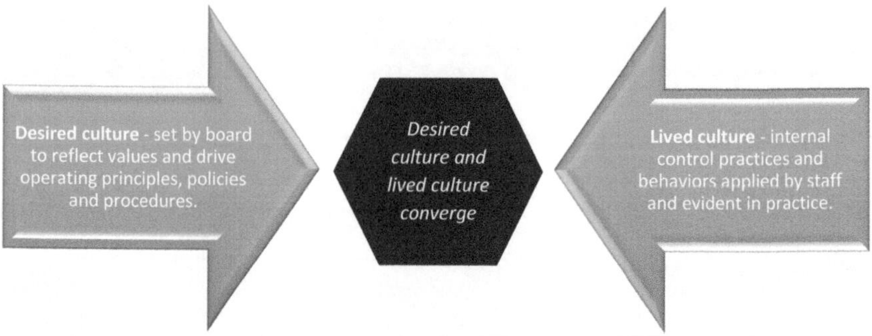

EXHIBIT 12.8 Convergence of desired culture and lived culture.

outcomes, with **Exhibit 8.8** illustrating how goal setting represents one of the initial elements of a performance management process.

The board should monitor the progress in achieving the organizational strategy, and CEOs are often required to establish a traffic-light based performance dashboard that is reported to the board on a quarterly or half-yearly cycle. The strategic plan is typically refreshed each year, often at the board's strategic planning retreat. The CEO should then present a complete picture of the progress, and their annual performance assessment undertaken by the board chair in consultation with the full board will reflect the achievement of strategic outcomes and other KPIs.

Understand the Lived Culture

Setting the Scene

Despite one's best endeavors in undertaking due diligence before accepting a board position, you never know what you will discover when you initially enter the boardroom. At my first board meeting for one organization, the chair alerted the board that serious allegations of wrongdoing had been made by operational staff against one of the directors, and that we would discuss the matter during an "in camera" session involving just the directors (except the director against whom the allegations were raised).

While the approach proposed by the chair was appropriate, it was clearly an unsettling moment for the experienced board member (a septuagenarian) when she was asked to leave the boardroom. While I thought I would be well-positioned to contribute to the discussion (based on my corporate investigations experience), I was eager to ensure the board member had support while waiting in a secluded side-room. Even though I had only just met her, I offered to sit with her while the board discussed the matter.

We chatted for perhaps an hour before being called back into the boardroom. The matter related to allegations of bullying and harassment, and the board member conceded that she did push hard for what she wanted, and some people might see her manner as abrasive. I did have a chance to review and provide input to the next steps of the assessment and investigation processes in separate discussions with the board chair. The matter was independently investigated over subsequent weeks. The board was apprised along the way, and informed of the outcome upon conclusion of the investigation.

While it was difficult to deal with serious allegations of wrongdoing against another director so early in my term, it highlighted the value of having solid governance arrangements, clearly communicated values, a board code of conduct, and a commitment to having the desired culture and lived culture in sync.

When I was appointed to the board of another organization, the board chair arranged for me to meet with him in private, each month, as he was keen to leverage the experience that I had in larger well-governed organizations. It was a good way to exchange views on the lived culture of the organization, and to share ideas for setting a strong tone at the top and for enhancing board processes that would help to evolve an already strong board culture.

We had many such conversations, and he followed through on the meritworthy ideas at subsequent board meetings. These resulted in a range of fresh initiatives being introduced as entity-firsts, including:

- Development and implementation of a statement of business ethics (for third party suppliers).
- Creation of a stakeholder relationship-management program and associated policy and procedures.
- Development and implementation of a board charter with a complementary board manual/induction guide.
- Refinement of the board performance assessment process, aligning it to the board charter.
- Strengthening formal and informal communication channels between the board and board committees through a focused reporting process, complemented by committee chairs attending board meetings on rotation.
- Establishment of a risk appetite statement for the organization and associated policy framework.
- Determination of a revised risk reporting model to extend from strategic and operational risks to project, scenario analysis, and emerging risks.
- Development of a reconciliation action plan.
- Implementation of a revised acknowledgement of country arrangement (in a sign of respect to Indigenous peoples) prior to board

meetings that involves storytelling by board members on a rotational basis (rather than just making the standard statement).
- Developing a board composition (skills) matrix with an aide memoir and associated supporting templates.

What It Means for Business

The foundations for delivering for business success were illustrated in **Exhibit 2.2**, and reflect that board sets the desired culture, though it is staff that determine the lived culture (as shown in **Exhibit 12.8**).

The board and audit committee should have steps in place to gain assurance that the lived culture is consistent with the desired culture (**Exhibit 2.3** illustrates some ways for the board, audit committee, and business leaders to monitor the culture).

EXAMPLE – DESIRED CULTURE AND LIVED CULTURE

The board of a railway company might identify a culture of safety as being critical to its operations. This is the desired culture.

As part of its safety precautions, the business leaders install a "dead man's handle" in all its trains; this is a specially constructed lever that acts as a safety device by shutting off power when it is not held in position by the train driver. Train drivers dislike the lever and place a block of wood to hold it in place. This reflects the lived culture.

Alas! the gap between the desired culture and lived culture only came to light after a train accident that resulted in multiple fatalities when the train driver had a heart-attack, and the control designed to minimize the risk of this very event had been deliberately disabled (that is, there was a block of wood holding in place the "dead man's handle").

The audit committee has a critical role to play in enabling the board to understand the lived culture by:

- Ensuring there are robust systems, policies, and processes maintained to support ethical behavior and other corporate values, underpinned by effective performance and accountability arrangements, and strong organizational governance.
- Determining the steps taken by business leaders to align the organization's strategy and culture, and embed the values across the organization.
- Gaining insights from business leaders (at least annually) on the level of staff engagement and the strengths and weaknesses of the organization's lived culture.

- Undertaking periodic site visits and field trips to connect with operational staff and observe business operations and risks "on the ground."
- Arranging for the chief audit executive to include an assessment of the organizational culture in the internal audit plan; then assessing the results of the internal audit assessment and monitoring the implementation of recommendations arising.

Oversight Business Performance and Conformance

Setting the Scene

Anyone aspiring to a board position should recognize that the role extends well beyond attending board meetings and reading all the associated board papers. These activities outside of the formal board meetings are absolutely imperative, and provide the cornerstone for monitoring the organization's performance and conformance.

During my four years on the health district board there were many other activities assigned (with no additional remuneration). As an example, these included:

- Out of session representational activities, such as attendance at public meetings, strategic planning workshops, annual board conference, quality awards, and staff meet and greet sessions.
- Member of a joint redevelopment board with the adjoining children's hospital.
- Board working group leader for a board refresh.
- Board working group leader for risk management improvement.
- Chair of the board nominations committee.
- Championed, reviewed, and contributed to the development of a range of critical board governance publications.

Boards and audit committees should never try to understand the organization's performance, conformance risks, and its lived culture by sitting around the boardroom table in the central business district. They should not just hear about things but should see them firsthand.

Effective boards will arrange site visits and field trips periodically to gain an appreciation for how the organization really operates and the on-the-ground risks.

If a board visited a site that stored ammonium nitrate, a combustible material, it is likely that board members would ask many questions about the potentially catastrophic risks, the security and safety arrangements, and regulatory obligations. How combustible is the material? What is being stored nearby? Are there sprinklers or fire retardant in the warehouse? Is the material checked regularly? How capable and aware are the staff and their supervisors? Are emergency protocols documented and understood? What are the regulatory requirements? How do we know we are compliant? and so on. It is possible that being armed and alert, the board members would order immediate risk-mitigation strategies if the identified risks were outside the board's risk appetite.

The disaster story below (based on media reports) illustrates the serious consequences of inadequate risk-mitigation arrangements and governance failings.

Site visits and field trips undertaken by the board are educational for the board members, and spark conversations that shine the light on risks from a holistic enterprise perspective. These visits allow board members to connect with staff and avoid potentially catastrophic incidents that impact on the organization's performance and conformance outcomes, not just for the organization but for the nation and its economy as a whole.

APOCALYPTIC DISASTER IN LEBANON[2]

In August 2020 a mega-blast tore through the city of Beirut, the capital of Lebanon, killing hundreds of people and injuring many thousands.

The explosion occurred when 2,750 tonnes (6.1 million pounds) of ammonium nitrate ignited. For scale, the bomb used by the Oklahoma City bomber in 1995 that killed 168 people was 2 tonnes (4,500 pounds) of ammonium nitrate, which is a fertilizer that can also be used to fuel bombs. The nuclear- like explosion had massive consequences, notably:

- Total destruction of the Port of Beirut (the city's largest port) and 1.5 km around it.
- Widespread and severe damage all over the city; heavy damage within 5 km, and reported damage up to 10 km away.
- About 300,000 people left homeless.
- The boom was heard 200 km away.
- Severe disruption to the nation's medical and other supply chains, as nearby warehouses were flattened.

---

[2] Prepared based on various media reports 6, 7, and 8 August 2020. Intended to be illustrative, and no aspersions are intended against those responsible and accountable for managing the warehouse or its content.

- Silos were destroyed that hold the nation's grain reserves and other food.
- Repair bill estimated to be $28 billion.

The ammonium nitrate was reported to have been stored in a "decrepit" and "rundown old warehouse" since it was seized by government authorities in 2013.

The Beirut disaster was one of the world's biggest-ever peacetime explosions.

WHAT IT MEANS FOR BUSINESS

The business awareness triangle (**Exhibit 12.9**) illustrates four features for how individuals understand and cope with typical business situations.

- Development, implementation, monitoring, and reporting of business strategy.
- Financial stewardship, spanning financial statements, metrics, asset management, cash flow, and bottom- line influences; collectively, financial acumen.

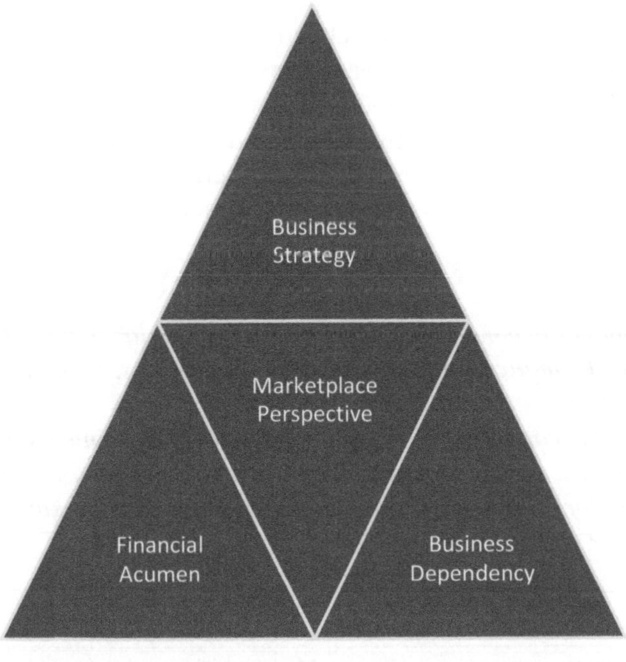

EXHIBIT 12.9 Business awareness triangle.

- A marketplace perspective, encompassing the value proposition, knowing customers and competitors, understanding marketplace trends, and innovation.
- Grasping the business interdependencies, through a big-picture focus, understanding the impact of decisions on others such as operations, manufacturing, service providers, and the supply chain.

Boards need business leaders, governance, risk, compliance, and assurance specialists to help them with their performance and conformance endeavors, notably:

- Business strategy – will the overall direction and strategy of the organization ensure its sustainability and prosperity, meet the interests of shareholders, customers, other stakeholders and the community, and ensure CEO succession.
- Marketplace perspective – do we understand the changing needs of stakeholders, and is this reflected adequately through the organization's vision, values, objectives, and priorities of the strategic planning suite.
- Business dependency – can you help to discover things the board did not know concerning areas such as emerging issues and risks; trends, systemic issues, and reporting themes; culture of the organization; and the efficiency, effectiveness, and ethics of operations.
- Financial acumen – are we discovering issues and opportunities for delivering value to the business and helping management to achieve business objectives through documented enterprise risks (both current and emerging), and information on the organization's governance, risk management, and financial compliance arrangements.

A common dilemma for boards is to get the balance right between their ***performance and conformance*** *obligations. Conformance is oriented to the past and the present and involves monitoring and supervising compliance (inward looking) and providing accountability (outward looking). Performance is future oriented and involves strategy formulation (outward looking) and policy making (inward looking).*[3]

[3] These elements are based on the Tricker Model which was developed in the 1980s by Dr Robert Ian Tricker.

Optimize Communication Between the Board and Board Committees

Setting the Scene

In my early days as an audit committee chairman, there seemed to be minimal communication expected by the board (or other type of governing body). It seemed to be an obvious gap, and I set out to bridge the gap by taking proactive steps. In my view, audit committees and other board committees should do a lot of the heavy lifting for the board, so the board should expect timely and meaningful feedback.

While the board did receive and note the minutes of audit committee meetings, there seemed to be very little appetite to ask questions or understand the true story of what transpired. This needed to change, so for each audit committee I arranged to meet with the board chair (or governing body where there was no board in place) to encourage them to support my efforts in optimizing two-way communication between the board and board committees. With their agreement, I set out to initially share with the board the key takeouts soon after the audit committee meeting, and simultaneously stressed upon the board my need to better understand the board's perspective on the strategies, objectives, goals, and risks of the business.

While the board chair (or governing body) was unsure of the value of these interactions at first, they grew to understand the benefits. Then the board welcomed additional layers of feedback, as these gradually evolved to ultimately include:

- A five key takeout summary after each audit committee meeting.
- A periodic balanced scorecard to report on progress against the key performance indicators (KPIs) of the audit committee each half-year.
- Formal quarterly meetings with the board chair.
- Attendance (as audit committee chair) at board meetings each quarter.
- An audit committee annual report presented to the full board (which could include a compliance assertion).
- Attendance at the board annual strategic planning retreat (for at least part of the activity).
- Attendance annually at a public meeting (for a local council).

Once this level of advanced audit committee reporting became "business as usual," the same reporting concepts were rolled-out to all other board committees.

The dialogue between board committees and boards for which I am involved is now considerably stronger, which has enhanced the board's

Standing committees	Ad hoc committees
Audit	Research (for a specific function)
Compensation	Major infrastructure development
Nominations and governance	People (during restructuring)
Risk management	Major events

EXHIBIT 12.10 Examples of board committees.

awareness and appetite for the organization's governance, risk management, compliance, and assurance arrangements. The enhanced reporting has also helped the board to better understand the importance of having a strong, independent, professional, and well-resourced internal audit function.

What It Means for Business

Boards typically establish board committees (see examples in **Exhibit 12.10**) when there are issues that are too complex or numerous for the whole board to handle. These could be standing committees that exist year-round (for ongoing, major activities) or short-term ad hoc committees (that cease when the activities are completed).

Board committees are crucial in the age of innovation and transformation, with board members facing increasingly complex challenges in overseeing corporate culture, strategy, and risk oversight, while often having to change their business models as a consequence of radical advances brought about by the digital revolution and the need for strong cybersecurity protection.

Board committees do a lot of the "heavy lifting" for the board, leveraging the expertise, time, commitment, and diversity of the committee members. While they operate at a board level (and not a staff level), they do not supplant the responsibility of each board member. Committees will have a clearly defined mandate (in the form of a charter) which may require them to recommend policy for approval by the entire board.

These board committees portray various functions that service the full board, and the summary is not intended to provide a complete list or to suggest that all of these committees should exist. It is ultimately up to the board to determine which committees should exist and what they should do.

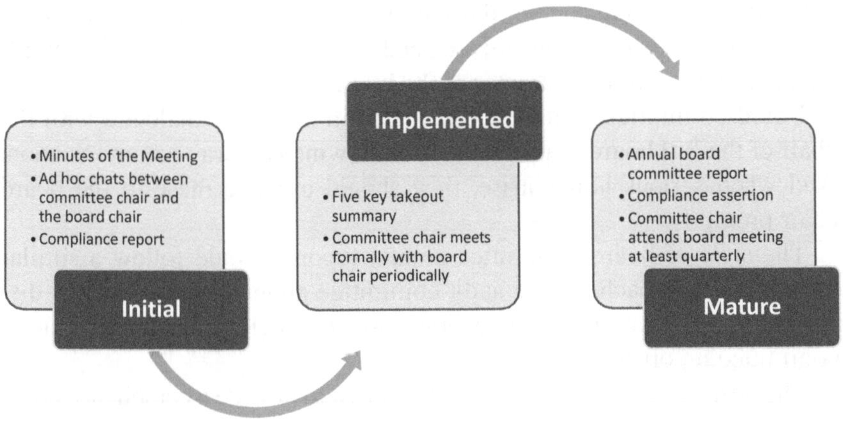

EXHIBIT 12.11 Maturity of board committee reporting to the board.

Board committee chairs (and deputy or vice chairs) are required to lead the committee in translating the board's goals for the committee into meeting agendas, work plans, and reporting mechanisms. Committee chairs are often (but not always) board members as a means of providing a direct reporting channel between the board committee and the full board. Regardless of whether or not the committee chair is a board member, well-functioning boards expect board committees to report to each board meeting on the committee's work since the past board meeting.

Meaningful board committee reporting to the board ensures timely and consistent messaging, so the board committee's main priorities of interest are elevated in a structured and well-considered way. While the board committee will usually produce minutes of its meetings, as the maturity of its reporting shifts through the different stages illustrated in **Exhibit 12.11** it adds on different layers of reporting to tell a more fulsome story.

The depth and breadth of board committee coverage makes it difficult to discern the most important takeouts from the detailed minutes of the meeting. The introduction of a five key takeouts summary helps to paint a clearer picture for the board based on the opinions of board committee members. The takeouts are determined collaboratively by the board committee at the end of the meeting, and the committee chair will usually allocate five or ten minutes on the agenda to facilitate a recap. Experienced committee chairs will often prepare in advance some jottings to facilitate the conversation, then enhance these at the end of the meeting to accord with the views of the committee.

The board committee chair or a representative from the board or council who sits on the board committee can use the five key takeouts summary to share the important narrative at the next board meeting (or the local council, other governing body, or head of the government agency where no board exists). Of course, the number "five" is indicative and can be adjusted upwards or downwards depending on the scale of board committee operations and the character of the board.

Board committee chairs should maintain a regular dialogue with the chair of the full board to promote a free-flowing two-way communication. And when serious issues arise, they should escalate these to the board chair promptly.

The style of board committee annual reports should follow a similar format and approach for the audit committee annual report that was discussed in Chapter 11 in the section covering "deliver meaningful audit committee reporting."

The board committee will often be required to provide a compliance assertion to the full board each year, with the board committee chair asserting that the committee mandate is consistent with the strategic direction of the organization, the committee addressed all duties listed in its charter, its composition matches the requirements of its charter, it has operated in compliance with its charter, and it has adhered to its delegated authority. The compliance assertion reflects the outcome of a self-assessment by the board committee.

Some boards may require a more comprehensive compliance report from the board committee, depending on the maturity of governance arrangements. The compliance reports are structured in a way that the board committee duties and responsibilities are listed in one column, then succinct narrative or bullet points are added in an adjoining column to depict how successfully the board committee fulfilled those responsibilities and duties. The full compliance report would usually only be required for new, less-mature or developing board committees, and would transition across to a compliance assertion once the full board had confidence in how the board committee was fulfilling its duties and responsibilities.

Manage CEO Succession Planning

Setting the Scene

I learned very early in my time on the board that CEO succession planning is an important aspect of the board's role (and some would say one of the most crucial responsibilities because, as the leader of the management team, the CEO's contribution cannot be undervalued).

Within a few months of joining the board of the Institute of Internal Auditors Australia, the CEO retired after 14 years at the helm. The organization was in the midst of a significant transformation and did not have clear succession arrangements.

The institute's dilemma was not uncommon. Data reported from a Stanford research initiative on "The Board's Critical Role in CEO Succession Planning" revealed only 51 percent of boards can name the successor CEO and 39 percent say they have zero internal candidates, even though the CEO turnover rate ranges from 9 to 14 percent globally each year.[4]

I was asked to assume the role of interim executive director to maintain liaison with the board and steer the ship until a longer-term CEO appointment could be made. I filled the role for a few months on a part-time basis. An experienced executive then assumed an interim CEO role fulltime until a more permanent CEO appointment could be made.

It was a challenging time for the institute with boardroom discussions centering on significant financial uncertainties, with accumulated losses totaling $603,000 for the prior two years, and members' equity (net assets) dipping to $53,000 by end-2012. The chair of the board reflected on the difficulties in the institute's annual report, "…a number of factors lead to some tough decision-making by the Board. The CEO made a formal announcement about his retirement; a number of staff resigned; a review of all business activities indicated that some tightening on expenditure was necessary and that our income generating activities were faltering. As a result, some staff vacancies were not filled, two positions were made redundant and all expenditure was subject to close scrutiny."[5]

The board ultimately appointed Peter Jones as CEO in April 2013, and he has proven to be an inspired choice, combining strategic and conceptual thinking with personal attributes of vision, motivation, energy, resilience, and leadership capability. Peter is a highly capable and experienced executive and came with an extensive background and successful track record in professional services, peak professional organizations and government that allowed him to operate with a vision shared with the board to achieve optimum business outcomes and implement sound business plans in executing strategy and goals.

The institute's financial situation improved off the back of a leaner national office team, focused leadership, strong board oversight, refreshed strategies, and strong financial stewardship.

It was an important lesson for me in understanding the importance of CEO succession planning, so that, as a board, we would always ensure there was a clear path forward in the short, medium, and longer term to cover the loss of the CEO. It also opened my eyes about the importance of balancing strategic initiatives with financial stewardship.

What It Means for Business

Effective succession planning means there will always be a talented and properly trained business leaders or specialist operatives who can take over

---

[4] "The board's critical role in CEO succession planning" (2020). https://pgs.brushpic.org/library-articles-3/boards-critical-role-succession-planning/ (Sourced 11 August 2020). Statistics intended to be indicative; not separately validated.

[5] Institute of Internal Auditors – Australia Annual Report 2012, Presidents Report, 1–2. https://www.iia.org.au/sf_docs/default-source/membership/Final_-_Annual_Report_2012.pdf (Sourced 11 August 2020).

to ensure the sustainability of an organization. It recognizes that critical roles are hard to fill, so boards need to be ready to respond to both planned (e.g. retirement) and unexpected (e.g. early ill-health retirements or career change) departures.

Critical roles may be at the board, CEO, C-suite, business leadership roles of any ranking, highly specialized roles, or crucial operations positions. Succession planning ensures that each vacancy of a critical role will be passed on to an appropriate person who has the skills, maturity, and motivation to take the place of departing leaders.

***Succession planning** is a strategy for passing on leadership to an employee or group of employees to ensure that the business continues to run smoothly after its most important people move on to new opportunities, retire, or pass away. It involves preparing employees so that they develop skills, knowledge of the business, and a holistic understanding of the organization, its vision, values, objectives, risks, and strategies.*

Boards are required to manage CEO succession so that there is a clear path forward in the short, medium, and longer term in the absence of the CEO. Boards will often delegate responsibility for CEO and other succession planning to the board nominations and governance committee (or its equivalent) and require it to make recommendations to the full board.

The establishment of a formalized succession plan provides benefits for the board, in that:

- Business leaders recognize that there are opportunities for their personal advancement which can lead to a higher-level performance, empowerment, and job enrichment.
- The board's commitment to succession planning means that business leaders are more likely to mentor employees to transfer knowledge and expertise, producing a new generation of leaders.
- Business leaders are better-positioned to keep track of talented employees so that positions can be filled internally when opportunities arise.
- The organization becomes an employer of choice as people recognize that it plans for future opportunities and invests in career development.
- Business leaders and employees are better able to live the company values and drive its vision.

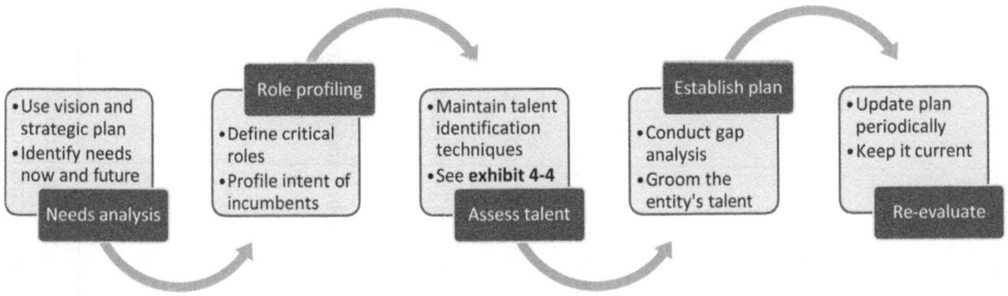

EXHIBIT 12.12 Five key steps for succession planning.

- Shareholders of publicly traded companies are more likely to retain the company's stock when the CEO retires and is replaced by a well-respected successor.

Not everyone can step up to the CEO level and handle the myriad competing demands. So, even where there seems to be a clear successor, it is important for the board to test other business leaders who might have the potential to handle the CEO role.

While this section focuses on the CEO succession planning, a similar process can be applied to other critical roles. There are typically five key steps to succession planning as illustrated in **Exhibit 12.12**.

In the short to medium term, there may be either planned or unplanned CEO absences (e.g. annual leave or illness) that need to be catered for, and the board should have clear options on who may be best-placed to fill the CEO role during these times. For short to medium term absences, the succession arrangements should identify the person or persons who were able to undertake the CEO duties during their absences and the training requirements undertaken and/or proposed for the business leaders identified, including attendance at board meetings, compilation of board papers, and gaining experience in external-facing engagements.

The board, through the CEO, should make it clear to business leaders that opportunities to work at a higher level are provided to ensure the organization's continued growth; where business leaders are not interested or capable of doing this, then it might be necessary for the board or CEO to recruit higher-level executives. In some circumstances, the CEO's duties might be split between two business leaders for short-term absences.

For a permanent CEO replacement, it could well be that the new CEO is appointed from outside the organization through a global search. This is one of the four common types of models for longer-term CEO succession planning solutions. The board could also consider options like appointing a chief operating officer, establishing a horse race, or utilizing an inside-outside model. The four common options are illustrated in **Exhibit 12.13** together with their respective merits.

EXHIBIT 12.13
Common types of CEO succession planning models[6]

Appoint an external candidate	Appoint and assess a chief operating officer	Establish a 'horse race'	Inside-outside model
Board recruits an external candidate from the market	*Board promotes a leading candidate to the position of chief operating officer (COO)*	*Board promotes two or more internal candidates to high-level operating positions to compete to become CEO*	*Board develops internal talent and simultaneously evaluates external candidates*
Advantages			
Tends to have proven experience as CEO More freedom to make strategic, operating, cultural changes	Board observes performance before promotion Scope of position is customized to entity needs Executive gains experience interacting with board, analysts, and shareholders	Board observes performance before promotion Board does not commit to preferred candidate in advance Executives develop specific skills needed to succeed	Internal candidates develop new skills and experiences Levels field between internal and external candidates External validation assures board that best CEO is selected
Disadvantages			
Less familiar with entity Leads to disruption among operations and staffing Board has not evaluated performance first-hand Leadership style might not translate to entity's culture	Adds more complexity to organization decision making Responsibilities need to be clearly defined and differentiated from CEO Risk of becoming "lifetime COO" if left in role too long	Highly public and might bring unwanted media attention Creates internal factions that advocate favored candidate Precipitates a "brain drain" when losers resign	Requires significant planning and oversight Breakdown in process can lead to erosion of trust

6 "CEO succession planning," Stanford Business Graduate School, Corporate Governance Research Initiative, https://www.gsb.stanford.edu/sites/gsb/files/publication-pdf/cgri-quick-guide-07-ceo-succession-planning.pdf (Sourced 11 August 2020). Tabulated, slightly modified and consolidated.

CHAPTER 12 – TEN CLOSING REFLECTIONS

- Board chairs should recognize that boards gain their strength from all of the individual board members contributing equally to deliver the strategies and objectives of the organization through the diversity of ideas.
- Boards should develop and utilize a board composition matrix to systematically assess the skills, diversity requirements, and other attributes of the board in the future.
- Boards should establish (and periodically reinforce) well-founded corporate values in collaboration with stakeholders, and these values should underpin the behavior and decision-making across the organization.
- Boards should develop an organizational strategy in consultation with the CEO and business leaders and use this to establish a consolidated strategic plan to provide clear directions for delivering upon the vision, maintaining corporate values, positioning the organization, competing successfully, satisfying customers and other stakeholders, achieving good business performance, and maintaining sustainability.
- The board and audit committee should have arrangements in place with governance, risk, compliance, and assurance specialists to gain assurance that the lived culture is consistent with the desired culture.
- Individuals aspiring to board positions need to recognize that the role extends well beyond attending board meetings and reading all the associated board papers, with activities outside formal board meetings providing the cornerstone for monitoring the organization's performance and conformance.
- Boards should arrange site visits and field trips periodically to gain an appreciation for how the organization really operates and the on-the-ground risks.
- Boards should expect meaningful reporting from the audit committee and other board committees so the main priorities and insights of the respective board committees are elevated in a structured, well-considered, timely, and consistent manner.
- Boards (perhaps through the board nominations and governance committee or its equivalent) should manage CEO succession as a priority so that there is a clear path forward in the short, medium, and longer term in the absence of the CEO.
- Board chairs and CEOs should recognize the critical roles beyond the CEO that may include board, C-suite, business leadership, highly specialized roles, or crucial operational positions and embrace succession planning so vacancies of any critical roles will pass on to appropriate persons with the skills, maturity, and motivation to take the place of departing leaders.

There is a symbiotic relationship between Chief Audit Executives and the audit committees to whom they report functionally. Pictured in 2012 with three of the ATO's four most senior executives Bruce Quigley (left), David Butler, and Jennie Granger. Bruce Q (initially) and Jennie were exemplary audit committee chairs who provided tremendous unwavering support for Bruce and the ATO internal audit function. (Photo: Personal collection.)

All business leaders need to develop public speaking skills to facilitate presentations in many different fora and in locations across the world. Bruce speaking at an ATO event in 2012. (Photo: Personal collection.)

Investing in the growth and development of others through executive coaching and mentoring requires dedicated effort. With Executive Director Claire O'Neill who Bruce mentored through her post-graduate studies. He is proud to see Claire to realise her potential and ultimately rise to the senior executive level. (Photo: Personal collection.)

Representing Australia at the IIA Global Council meeting in Dubai United Arab Emirates in 2014. (Photo: Personal collection.)

Mayor of the City of Penrith Ross Fowler OAM (left) with Bruce and his family in 2015 at a council reception in his honour after being appointed a Member of the Order of Australia in the Queen's Birthday Honours. The Queen approved the institution of the Order of Australia in 1975 for according recognition to Australians for achievement or meritorious service. (Photo: Penrith City Council (used with permission).)

An organization's alumni network helps individuals enormously to maintain professional connections following retirement. Bruce (third from left) attending a function as part of the ATO Penrith alumni network with Australia's then Tax Commissioner Chris Jordan AO (center) and other ATO executives in 2017. (Source: Personal collection.)

The Board of Western Sydney Local Health District in 2017. (Source: Western Sydney Local Health District annual report.)

With Wentworth Healthcare CEO Lizz Reay and Aboriginal Artist Vicki Thom in 2019 after giving an address to launch the entity's initial Reconciliation Action Plan (RAP) for the "first Australians"; at the centerpiece of the photo is the RAP artwork used in the publication. (Photo: Wentworth Healthcare Limited (used with permission).)

Sending a strong civic-minded message that domestic and family violence is not okay. Joining the mayor (front with hat), other local dignitaries, police, community members, and daughter Jacqueline (obscured) in the walk against domestic violence hosted by Penrith City Council in November 2019. Bruce is in a black cap behind the mayor's right shoulder. (Photo: Penrith City Council (used with permission).)

Part 4

Postface

Key message: It's important to remember where you came from and learn from the past, while focusing on where you need to go, how you'll get there, and being mindful of the legacy you'll leave.

"Bruce – On behalf of the global internal auditing profession I am thrilled to congratulate you on your prestigious award as a Member of the Order of Australia, for your significant contributions to public administration through contributions to governance and risk management practices, and to the profession of internal auditing.

I am grateful for you representing our profession so well. As a champion for internal auditing you have helped raise awareness about the value that practitioners bring to their organizations and communities. You have delivered outstanding service to the Institute of Internal Auditors and to your community, and so it is fitting that you are recognized with this national honor. Thank you for your distinguished contributions to the profession."

Richard F Chambers
President and Chief Executive Officer
The Institute of Internal Auditors, USA
June 2015

13 The Formative Years

OPENING ONE'S EYES TO THE OPPORTUNITIES

A person's professional and personal journey is influenced from their formative years where they learn life skills, develop personal values, make social connections, gain an appreciation for others, and – for some – develop a desire to help those in need. This section provides a brief overview of the author's preteen experiences in dealing with the quandaries of others who were supposed to be nurturing him (family, friends, and neighbors), including some of the drivers of their problematical behaviors including marital dilemmas, mental and physical health challenges, violence, alcoholism, and infidelity. It also reflects on the people – the angels amongst us – who were truly influential in showcasing the positives in life that opened his eyes to the opportunities that we all have if we have the good sense to embrace them. Dame Anita Roddick (1942–2007) once reflected on what we would now call our personal brand when she remarked, "Whatever you do, be different. If you're different, you will stand out."

PERSONAL STORY

My father apparently saw my mother, quickly fell for her, and then pursued her even though he lived an hour or so away from mum's hometown of Penrith. He was a most charming young man with a steady job, a lovely smile, and an attractive set of teeth. Mum ultimately agreed to go out. They married a couple of years later. He seemed like a good catch.

I was the second of five children with an age span of 15 years between my older and younger sisters. Growing up, I enjoyed reading, tennis, badminton, board and card games, backyard cricket, and kicking the football around. I watched a little television but preferred to be outside. As a keen supporter, I followed my local first grade football team, the Penrith Panthers.

I provided some reflections in Chapter 10 about my family's challenges with mental health and domestic violence. Notwithstanding those challenges, I had a very fortunate upbringing with a roof over my head, medical treatment when required, sufficient clothing and bedding for warmth, and food on the table. We also had a supportive and close-knit extended family around us, wonderful family friends, and caring and considerate neighbors.

My father did not drink (he was a teetotaler) and did not smoke. He had many jobs after completing his apprenticeship as a fitter and turner. These included prison warden, state police, petrol pump fitter, federal police, pest control, cash register mechanic, warehouse supervisor, and foreman (several different factories), wildlife service, then a public servant within housing commission and Valuer-General agencies. He was unemployed for several years during the 1970s.

My father's main hobby was caged birds, and he had many large aviaries full of a variety of parrots, finches, budgerigars, and canaries (amongst others). He used to enter his best stock at bird shows and won many trophies and ribbons.

My mother was a "stay-at-home mum," and we were very comforted to have her there to greet us after school every day. We were always well provided for. She ensured that we experienced a religious upbringing, and arranged for us to attend Sunday School every week. Mum taught us to mind our p's and q's.

If I may be blunt for a moment, my father was a charming man and had many fine qualities, but he was a selfish man, with a bad temper, and was rather brutal in dishing out punishment (as described in Chapter 10). He was not a constantly violent man but had flashes of temper. My dad and I exchanged letters occasionally when he worked out in the country at a tin mine (Tullabong), when I'd started high school. He was a man who did unfathomable things. For instance, on the day of the christening (baptism) of my brother Jon, when mum had invited family and other guests over to celebrate, he decided it was a great day to paint one of the rooms in the house, causing quite a ruckus (it was the *only* time I ever saw him painting).

By the late-1960s and early 1970s home-life was particularly tumultuous. Dad had found joy with other women. Mum probably knew that she was losing him, and the squabbling became more frequent, louder, and scarier. Heaven help anyone who got in the way, as I managed to do from time-to-time in my teens as a protector for Mum. It was a difficult time for all of us, and we still carry the mental scars to this day.

One of my greatest regrets is that my father didn't teach me anything of any consequence when I was growing up. Even simple things like mowing and gardening (my neighbors), painting (my mother's elderly uncle, Jim), carpentry (school), electrical circuitry (my father's friend, Ken), mechanical stuff (my father-in-law, Albert), parenting and homecare (my wife, Bea) … but mostly I was self-taught, and as a perfectionist that can be rather challenging. I had little interest in my father's caged bird hobby, probably because it was a daily chore to feed and water them during his extended absences!

My father was rarely at home, and my parents endured several separations prior to the final split when I was just about to turn 16 (my younger siblings were then 10, 8, and 2); my parents ultimately divorced in 1977. Surprisingly, against his lawyer's advice, my father signed the unencumbered family home over to my mother so that she and the younger children would always have a safe and secure place to live; he was always quite a unique man, and you could never predict what he would do.

Mum's friends, neighbors, and relatives were a steady influence for us, especially when she found herself to be a single mum with five children. We were blessed to grow up in Union Road in Penrith. You can't choose your neighbors, but we were so fortunate to have as ours, the Dysons, Rickwoods, Rees, Placketts, and others. Close by were lifelong family friends, the Whitcmans and Bootles.

I was acutely aware of the strength of the "neighborhood network" as people genuinely cared for those in need, whether it was the result of violence, alcoholism, infidelity, unemployment, or insufficient money to put food on the table. I still send Christmas cards and an annual family newsletter to the few surviving members of the neighborhood just to let them know they will never be forgotten; one in particular, Jean Dyson, who was a nurse, has continued to care for others even though she is herself a nonagenarian (i.e. in her 90s) and we still often exchange messages.

It was a curious way that I had secured my first job (discussed in Chapter 1) just after I had completed my final School Certificate exams; I passed all subjects with credit. I was in two minds about whether I would continue to complete my Higher School Certificate (year 12), with the intention of then embarking on accounting studies. But the prior two years had been rather tumultuous at home, so I opted to join the workforce as a mere lad of 16 years and 1 month. I ultimately completed tertiary studies in accounting, then completed further studies in banking, and ultimately gained a range of global certifications (discussed in Part 1).

Industrial tensions between employees and employers were high during the 1970s and employee strikes were commonplace. My father had been unemployed for long periods during this time, with significant impact on my family. When I was in my late teens, bank employees were considering strike action and arranged a town hall meeting to discuss the options. It was at full capacity, and I was determined to stand my ground, opposing any strike action. I was determined that my personal values would not be compromised. After all the speakers finished, a motion was put forward to strike (or so I thought that was what they were saying). I voted against the motion, and was one of a handful to do so. I was proud to have withstood "peer pressure" to follow my beliefs. I heard the next day that there was just a handful of people who voted to strike (gulp) which was overwhelmingly defeated by the majority of union members.

I know that my father had other families (he was married several times and also had other long-term relationships), and that there are half-brothers and step-brothers and step-sisters who I have never met. But the acrimonious split between my parents meant that these relationships were never really possible. Dad was 73 when he passed away, and I delivered the eulogy, though there was a 25-year gap in our relationship with occasional albeit minimal contact (largely his choice) through that time.

My mother was a constant in my life until her mid-80s, when she moved 220 miles north to be closer to my three sisters, at that time her health was faltering. Until then, she lived just five minutes or two miles away from my home. Mum endured extended and frequent periods of physical illness during our life, from her "crookback" to her problematic "ticker." My little branch of the family enjoyed having her join us for special events and our regular Sunday night family dinners. This allowed my five older grandchildren to get to know their Granny G, their great grandmother.

Mum was nearly 87 when she passed away, and I delivered the eulogy. I started by reflecting on her passing, "Mum slipped away quietly, peacefully and without fanfare on Monday at the local club. Well kinda … except for the hundreds of people who were at Club Taree when she had her 'funny turn', the dozens of people who rushed to her aid, the sirens and flashing lights of the ambulance and fire-truck that came to transport her to the hospital as quickly as possible. Of course, in the end, it wasn't to be."

Mum was the youngest of eight siblings, and all our aunts, uncles, and cousins played an important part in our lives. The family had good genes, with my aunt Lylie living until 102 and uncles Bob and Keith into their 90s. Mum proved to be the last one standing in her family … the last of her generation.

The key insights from this phase of my story are:

- Leverage your curiosity.
- Evaluate and pursue potential career growth opportunities.
- Remain motivated.
- Present oneself professionally.
- Invest in personal professional growth.
- Stay mates for life.
- Fix it if it's broken.
- Leave a legacy.

CONTEXT

When taken together, the key insights from this phase of my story are illustrated in **Exhibit 13.1**.

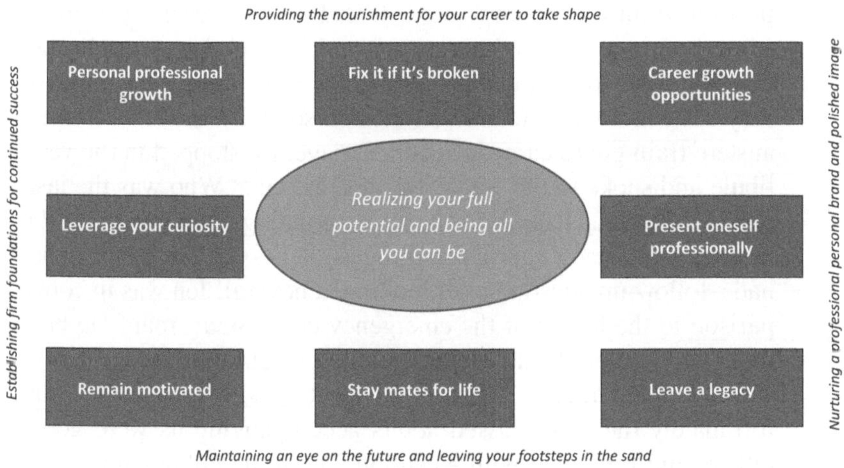

EXHIBIT 13.1 Steps for realizing your full potential.

KEY TAKEAWAYS AND DEEP DIVES

Leverage Your Curiosity

I had a natural curiosity as a child, and my inquisitiveness got me into a spot of bother on numerous occasions as I tried to come to grips with how things worked. As an example:

- I was an early walker … initially. When I was a toddler (about ten months old) and starting to walk more confidently, I pulled a kettle full of boiling water onto myself when I was investigating the steam. While I have no memory of the incident, I'm informed that it proved to be a rather painful experience. After six months of recovery, and with burn scars on my neck as evidence of my adventure, I was finally fit enough to resume my exploration.
- By age 4 I was a confident explorer. So, when my mother took me into the "big city" of Sydney when she had a medical appointment, I took the opportunity to look down at the trains … it only took a little effort to squeeze my head through the bars of the balustrade. Alas! I hadn't quite worked out my escape plan, and my head got stuck. My mother left me and went for her appointment (I'm assured her friend stayed), while the fire-brigade was called to rescue me.
- At age 10 I had a little brother, Jon, who was six years my junior. We were on a neighborhood excursion to the zoo on a fancy country train. I took my brother to the toilet, and my curiosity got the better of me. While waiting in the bathroom, I was tempted to

pull the train's emergency cord. It had a swift result! The train screeched to a halt, and alarms started blaring. Everyone in the carriage was wondering what was happening, and I was comfortably back in my seat (Jon had followed soon after) when a rather austere train guard came into our carriage. He stopped in the vestibule and spoke to the whole carriage asking, "Who was the last one in the toilet." I answered honestly, pointing out it was my little brother Jon. I hadn't anticipated the astuteness of the guard, who had a follow-up question after looking at how tall Jon was in comparison to the height of the emergency cord. Smart man! He had me. I hadn't seen the notices mentioning a $200 fine for wrongful use of the emergency alarm (equivalent to $1,650 in 2020), but fortunately the embarrassed adults accompanying us were good talkers and I escaped with a caution. For some unknown reason, this was our last neighborhood adventure.

As I moved through the banking and then internal auditing ranks, I used my curiosity to understand a process from cradle to grave. Then when I was supervising other auditors, my quality review didn't just focus on the documented work (i.e. audit evidence), I was keen for the auditors who provided the assurance or identified weaknesses to illustrate what they had done and how they reached the conclusion.

As an example:

- A central bank processes banknotes through high speed counting, sorting, and verification machines to identify counterfeit and poor notes (amongst others), and then the machines automatically destroy poor-quality banknotes by shredding. The residual shreddings then make their way through a clear pipe, are secured, and are ultimately used for recycling. I would ask the auditor a myriad of questions like, (i) what would happen if the shredder blades were disabled; (ii) where does the pipe go; (iii) what if the pipe was diverted; (iv) where do the shredded notes end up; (v) show me where the recycling bins are kept. By the end of the quality review I would understand the process well, and also get a good sense of the capability of the auditor who conducted the work.
- At a rail passenger organization, I was curious about on-time running statistics (one of the KPIs reported daily), and had my team explore the process. I was keen for the checks and balances to be assessed at every stage of the process, even though the final sign-off and uploading controls were strong. And of course, at the data capture stage which was performed manually there were serious weaknesses that meant the end result was seriously flawed.

> *My **natural curiosity** proved to be a godsend in the end. A half a century after my visit to the zoo it was no surprise when Australia's Commissioner of Taxation Michael D'Ascenzo wrote to me and said, in part, "You impressed us all with your expertise, professionalism, dedication to people and YOUR ABILITY TO EMBRACE AND QUICKLY COME TO GRIPS WITH THE MANY DIFFERENT AND DIFFICULT CHALLENGES PRESENTED TO YOU." (EMPHASIS added). My natural curiosity aided my career enormously and is a trait associated with many successful auditors.*

Individuals with natural curiosity or inquisitiveness should be encouraged to explore the possibilities, as they will often challenge the status quo to deliver innovative opportunities and solutions for business.

EVALUATE AND PURSUE POTENTIAL CAREER GROWTH OPPORTUNITIES

At high school, science was my least favored subject, and I achieved inconsistent results (notwithstanding my school reference noting science as one of my best subjects). I had a great teacher (Mr. Corcoran) for three of my four years at junior high school, and passed all of my exams with him as my teacher. We connected, and I learned well, even though it was not an area that interested me much. In the third year, I had two different science teachers who had different teaching styles that I struggled to connect with; I failed pretty much every science exam that year and was ultimately relegated to lower classes. Fortunately, I rebounded the following year under Mr. Corcoran's guidance, achieving a superior grade to many of the students in the higher classes. My experience with science heightened my awareness of creating the right environment for growth and having compatibility with those supporting those efforts.

Strong business leaders weave professional growth into their culture to create an environment where people want to grow and where there is often an aversion to excessive order. When people do the same thing over and over again, they maintain order, but that can ultimately result in no growth which leads to stagnation or negative growth. Ironically, growth typically occurs in a state of discomfort, so some level of disruption needs to occur within the workplace for growth at that level (examples include different work, a new learning situation, a different boss, or a new attitude).

People have different ways of defining what they want from their career growth depending on their aspirations and goals. This growth will change as people progress through their career and life; people will have a different level of excitement for their second, third, and fourth roles

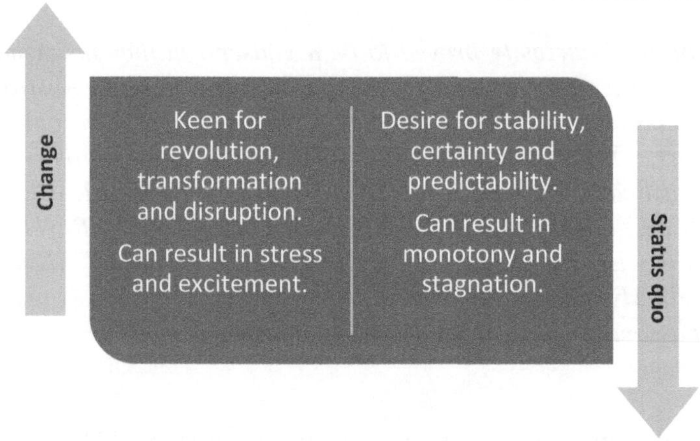

EXHIBIT 13.2 Conflicting career growth ideals.

compared to their very first job and paycheck. Some people will be seeking change, whereas others are more comfortable maintaining the status quo (as illustrated in **Exhibit 13.2**).

While I personally felt more comfortable in a stable work environment, I recognized that I developed more skills when I was stretched and was forced to adapt and change. With a reputation for getting things done, many tasks were passed on to me even if it resulted in an uneven distribution of work, but I sucked it up and successfully established a strong and diverse skill-set. During the second half of my career I was employed as an "agent of change," and my success was measured against the delivery of a transformation agenda. My early business teachers had set me up well to succeed.

On every occasion I took on new opportunities throughout my career (whether by choice or forced upon me) I was actually ready for the change and, in hindsight, every career move I made was perfectly orchestrated. With the benefit of experience, my mindset shifted to one of "change is good" when I evaluated and pursued potential career growth opportunities. In some ways I was lucky with my choices, in others I had put in the hard yards and was ready to step up. The results of those changes were discussed during the early chapters of the book.

Remain Motivated

At the most basic level, people are motivated to do something to satisfy their basic needs (e.g. food, shelter, and clothing), and these behaviors are directed by their motivation. People devoid of motivation are doomed to fail in life and at work. People's motivation to excel in a hobby or profession typically comes from within. While it is largely inherent, it can be also inspired by outside factors.

Within business, motivation underpins the success of most organizations. It requires a motivated workforce. Motivation and inspiration usually go hand-in-hand. Inspiration is something innate. People are drawn to a vision or goal through a strong sense of purpose; typically, the drive to shape or deliver something that will make a difference, not just to their life but to the world (the importance of inspiring others was discussed in Chapter 5).

Successful business leaders recognize that motivation can wane over time if it is not nurtured and refreshed. They make conscious efforts to shape a motivated and highly productive workforce that delivers value to the business and its customers. People's motivation is influenced by a wide range of factors including life satisfaction across the course of one's life, generational differences, and unique gender needs. Extrinsic rewards (such as money, bonuses, and special gifts) provide limited motivation. The common motivators are more likely to be intrinsic rewards (that is, the value derived from work).

> ***Life satisfaction factors*** *influence a person's motivation as they move through different age groups. Through the normal course of life, a person's life satisfaction changes and is typically affected through seven major life events: Leaving the parental home, marrying or moving in with a partner, childbirth, separation from a spouse or live-in relationship, becoming empty nesters, retirement, and widowhood. A person's life satisfaction is reported to decline from the age of 15 to the mid-30s, then stabilizes for the next 15 years, before beginning to improve from the early-50s until the late-60s.*[1]

Business leaders need to shape a work environment to satisfy the changing needs of their people. Employers of choice typically present a greater range of relevant and meaningful intrinsic rewards such as work-life balance, career-advancement opportunities, training and development, and public recognition of achievements (further examples are contained in **Exhibit 13.3** and are mirrored in Exhibit 8.9).

Intrinsic rewards drive outcomes that provide individual personal satisfaction, often derived from a job well done. The importance of these factors will change depending on gender, generational and cultural drivers. The priorities will also be weighted differently at other stages of the person's life, corresponding to external interests and family demands.

---

[1] Bruce Turner, *GREAT Ways to Motivate Your Staff: Shaping an Audit Team that Adds Value and Inspires Business Improvement* (Altamonte Springs, FL: Institute of Internal Auditors Research Foundation, 2016), 15.

EXHIBIT 13.3
Examples of intrinsic rewards and other factors as motivators[2]

- Participation in decision-making.
- Greater job discretion.
- Challenging and interesting work.
- Exposure in important meetings.
- Constructive feedback.
- Individual recognition in front of peers.
- Visibility as part of team recognition.
- Regular, open communication.
- Training and certification support.
- Mentoring and coaching arrangements.
- Job security and workplace stability.
- Working conditions to provide work/life balance (such as flexible working arrangements).
- *Examples of flexible working arrangements:*
    - *Options for working remotely.*
    - *Working part-time or job share.*
    - *Alternative hours.*
    - *Support for career breaks.*

Internal auditors are increasingly encouraged to utilize contemporary agile auditing techniques and to shift into previously out-of-scope areas like assessing the corporate culture. As the profession continues to evolve, boards, audit committees and business leaders will be expecting even more. I believe one of those new areas of focus will be assessing the motivation within and across the organization.

Case in point *– Curijo is a majority Aboriginal owned and controlled company headquartered in the Australian Capital Territory. The company provides mainstream services including consultancy, strategic insights, and capability, together with unique offerings around Aboriginal affairs. The company uses a Motivational Maps® tool under license to develop motivational map profiles.*[3] *It involves a simple online survey of employees to determine what motivates each individual or team, and how motivated they are. The concept recognizes that a person's happiness and success at work are partly determined by whether or not their core motivations are being met.*

The Curijo approach helps senior management to:

- *Respond to increasing pressure to understand workplace culture and staff well-being, especially for employees working remotely or online.*

[2] Ibid, 28. (Slightly modified).

[3] Information on Curijo and the Motivational Maps® tool have been used with permission.

- *Target interventions appropriately, that are fit for purpose and specific for the individual, team, and organization.*
- *Understand how well the workforce is aligned to strategic factors such as planning and direction, speed of change, resilience, and overall motivation.*
- *Determine themes, issues, problems, and gaps at organization, team, and individual levels that are reported with appropriate recommendations.*

Individuals need to take ownership of their own motivation (notwithstanding the climate that can be created by business leaders). Where their motivation is waning, they need to do something about it; perhaps something different, like a new activity, a course of study, a cause to help others, a new hobby, or even a change in jobs. Looking back through my career and life, I can see that I have constantly reinvented myself and this has continued to feed my naturally high levels of motivation.

While writing this book, I completed one of the motivational mapping questionnaires through Curijo, and they provided me with a detailed report with a one-on-one debrief. It is a powerful research-based approach that aligns nicely with the need for business leaders to understand and nurture the culture of their organization. Each contributing survey participant receives an individual report almost immediately upon completion.

My individual report assessed my level of motivation as being in the "optimal zone," sitting at 100 percent (which occurs in about 1 in 45 assessments). An excerpt from the report at the higher-level follows.

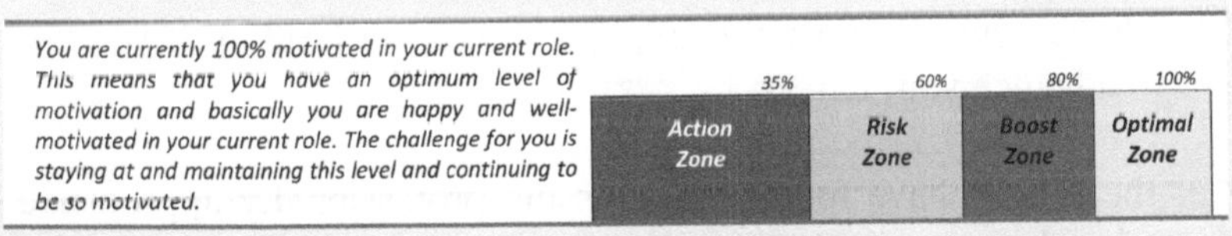

The specialist coach then drills down into potential actions to address opportunities for improvement. People sitting in the "action zone" typically require urgent and specific support, as this level of motivation could point to mental health challenges, whereas people in the risk zone need firm ideas on how to improve.

The specialist coach also leverages and reports to business leaders the consolidated results and recommendations at the team and organizational levels to identify potential hotspots, including conflicting levels of motivation and potential strategy-disrupting motivations between discrete areas of the business.

Present Oneself Professionally

Banking was seen as a prestigious employer in the 1970s, so my parents arranged for me to buy a suit from the Webber's Menswear store before I started my first job (as mentioned in chapter 10). Being well-dressed helped build my confidence and inspired me to always present myself professionally.

The way you dress typically reflects the way you feel. In a business setting, first impressions are critical, so it is imperative that people present themselves in a professional well-dressed and well-groomed manner. Clothes should be neat, well-fitted, clean, and pressed. And men (in particular) should polish their shoes and tuck in the shirt. Avoid looking lazy and unprofessional, and maintain an effective tone of voice and good body posture.

Like products in the grocery store, people are judged by their overall packaging. A few tips:

- Take care in your appearance, as it will influence the impression you make (positive or otherwise).
- Focus on the substance of introductions and the quality of conversation, as the impressions you leave can affect your longer-term success and achievement.
- Avoid letting a shabby purse or briefcase detract from your overall appearance, as these accessories offer clues to your professionalism, success, and personality.
- Do not allow your appearance to undermine the image of your employer.
- Model your attire after exemplars at the next level up if you wish to advance your career.

Over the years I have found that dressing professionally appropriate has put me in a better mental space, underpinned my self-respect and composure, and ensured I remained focused and productive.

Business leaders should also put sufficient thought into their office environment so that it presents as a stylish, functional, organized, and professional office space. It is easy to get overwhelmed with work that clutters the workspace; however, the clutter can become an eyesore visually and will often adversely impact productivity. It can create a bad vibe to other employees and visitors by leaving an impression that you have a messy and disorganized mind. For many people their workplace is often a symbol of whether or not they feel valued by the business.

The use of videoconferencing is booming and it is also important to present oneself professionally in a virtual meeting space. There are a few basic rules to follow:

- Dress properly. Business-related videoconferences should be regarded as formal settings. As a representative of your business unit or organization, you should never act or dress in a way that would be inconsistent with the corporate values, or would jeopardize the company brand. It is okay "to do a newsreader" and dress sartorially from the waist up.
- Set the right environment. Select an appropriate venue, so that it looks professional. Remove any potential distractions prior to the videoconference, and clear any obstacles or distractions in the line of sight of the camera. Where possible keep children and pets away. I've seen a bedroom in the back of one videoconference with dirty clothes spread across the bed. In another, I've seen a scantily dressed person walking in the background. And in another, unrestrained dogs nearby causing distraction with their constant barking.
- Maintain focus throughout the videoconference at the same level that you would if you were attending in person. Avoid checking your inbox, reading articles, typing, or looking at something else. Pay close attention when people are speaking and always keep your eyes on the camera.
- Understand the technology requirements (e.g. stable internet connection, appropriate videoconferencing services and software, awareness of conferencing features, testing of video and audio beforehand), security needs (e.g. private or controlled internet, take precautions before sharing your screen), and the meeting structure (e.g. be organized and punctual, have an agenda, consider compatible time zones, mute when not talking, mute other devices like the cellphone).

Invest in Personal Professional Growth

Our personal growth starts from our early months, when we learn a language, then develop our reading, writing, and arithmetic skills. We continue to learn things throughout our life. As children we learn many life skills from our parents, siblings, family, friends, and neighbors. Some of the more common examples of life skills are illustrated in **Exhibit 13.4**. These provide a useful baseline for parents to consider, though they are illustrative in nature as children can learn at a different pace depending on their personal and family circumstances.

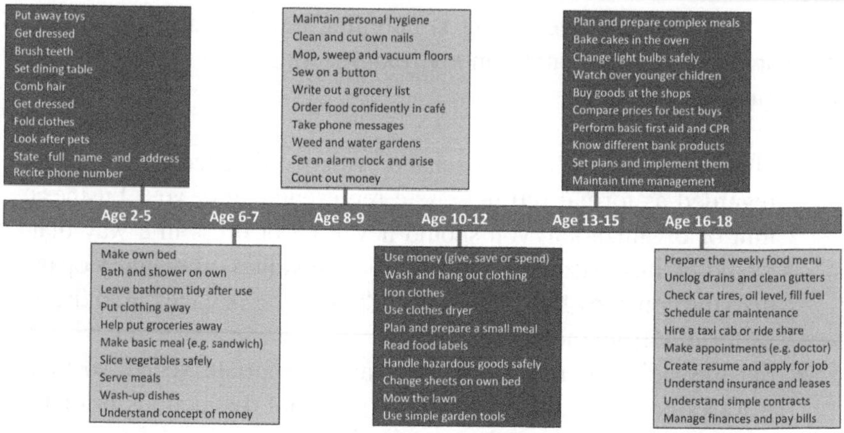

EXHIBIT 13.4 Examples of life skills developed through until adulthood.

It is sometimes surprising that well-educated graduates, scholars, and cadets joining an organization through an entry-level employment program (see **Exhibit 1.2**) have not been taught many of these basic life skills. Supervisors need to watch out for any significant gaps in these expected life skills, and provide nurturing and support to help them learn.

Young and old alike need to consider their preferred personal professional growth expectations, then assess their goals against their career progression to determine and plan the steps to close the gap. A simple process is illustrated in **Exhibit 13.5**. Where the organization has a Professional Development Plan (PD Plan), then it is useful to incorporate meaningful developmental needs from that into the professional growth plan (professional development was discussed in Chapter 4).

Personal professional growth *refers to the improved outcomes achieved through the development or better use of talents and skills. It should not be confused with professional development – growth is the outcome, whereas development refers to the process or input that leads to the growth.*

There will be times where people feel they are stuck in a rut and are not growing professionally. They should take steps to address the situation before they hit rock bottom. The key is to be emotionally attuned to know when they are approaching the crossroads.

It is important to recognize that your personal professional goals will often be quite different to those of your managers, as your focus will usually be broader. This will vary according to the stage of your career and

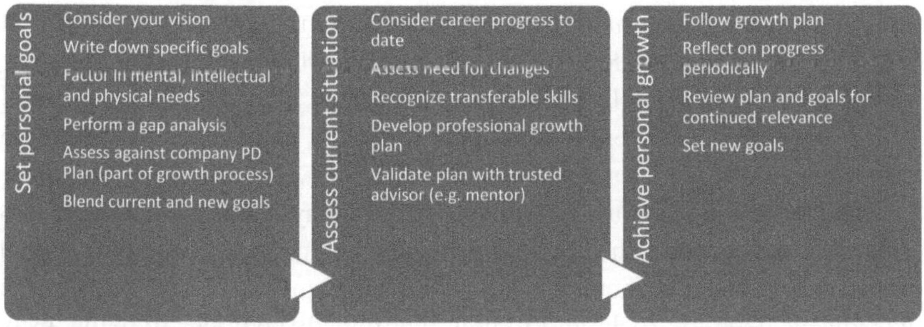

EXHIBIT 13.5 Example of professional growth planning.

your personal aspirations. For instance, an accountant wanting to move into academia within five to ten years might well be working to pay their way through post-graduate university studies while gaining valuable practical financial experience; their personal goals will not reconcile with the organization's PD Plan initiatives that might well focus on maintaining current and deep knowledge of technical accounting standards.

Stay Mates for Life

In mid-1974 we had a new junior banker commence. A young lady named Bea Waayer, a couple of years younger than me. We became good mates and often had lunch together, playing cards, going for a walk, or just chatting.

One busy Friday when I was a teller, I was serving a local businessman. He was depositing a large sum of cash and I was engrossed in counting the money. Bea popped up behind the teller's box and mentioned to me that her father was in front of me. With a long queue of over a dozen people I looked down the line to work out which customer was her father, still puzzled. Then she said right in front of you. I looked at the next few customers in the line and none looked quite right. Then she said … you're serving him!

Of course, I went bright red and they both had a good chuckle. I had served the guy in the past, and he seemed a bit clumsy in counting his cash. It was not uncommon for him to have less cash than what he had recorded on the deposit slip. It could be a hundred dollars, or a few hundred (relatively large sums back then), and he would always whip it out of his wallet when you informed him of the error. It was only later that I found out he enjoyed "testing" the tellers to see how good they were. Fortunately, I always passed the test!

Anyhow, that was the day that I officially "met" Albert Waayer. I doubt that he would ever have guessed it at the time that I would marry his daughter a few years later in 1978. Albert had been a very protective father, but he warmed to me and gradually allowed Bea some freedom. He would ultimately become an important father figure throughout the next decade, until his passing in 1985 at age 60. The loss was sudden, unexpected, and devastating. He had been a wonderful teacher, role model, and support. Fortunately, all of my children (and all of his other grandchildren) had the opportunity to meet their Opa before he passed away, albeit not for long enough.

My work as an auditor has taken me to many different places across Australia and around the world, and I have spent much time away from home. It has been difficult because I am naturally a "home body." Bea has always been my rock, and I know that my "difficulties" in being away from home pale behind the challenges she has had to navigate. On my first trip to London in 1985 I was away for a month, and Bea was at home with three children aged five, three, and one. Later trips combined the audits of London and New York and meant I was away for six weeks. My first trip to New York in 1986 coincided with the release of Paul Hogan's movie blockbuster Crocodile Dundee that made about $US 330 million at the box house; Bea and I watched the movie upon my return, and it was quite special reflecting on the landmarks that I'd seen a few days earlier that were depicted in the movie.

Bea and I initially got to know each other when we worked together (she made me look good) and that gradually transitioned into a strong friendship before we started dating. We have both grown a lot throughout the four decades together while developing broader interests and nurturing our family. We have navigated the natural challenges throughout the journey and still enjoy each other's company. She remains my best mate for life.

Everyone needs someone to support them and their endeavors, and put meaning into what they do.

Fix It if It's Broken

I grew up in a three-bedroom weatherboard home with eight occupants. The two boys and an uncle in one room, the three girls in another room, and my parents in the third room. The configuration changed occasionally, and part of a back verandah was converted to sleeping quarters at one stage when the family was a bit older.

The home had two toilets, one in the bathroom and a second in the external laundry, undercover just outside the back door. For most of the time I lived in my parent's house the laundry toilet could not be used, as it had malfunctioned. It was never fixed. So, the inside toilet was often in great demand. I look back now, and realize that to fix the laundry toilet would have required a quick trip to the hardware store to secure a few parts (there was a hardware store a mere 100 yards from our front door), then maybe a couple of hours work. Of course, an alternate approach would have been to call out a plumber and pay them a moderate sum.

As I grew into my early teens I shifted into a van in the backyard. It was the back of an old Allen's sweets truck that my father had secured for a good price. An extension cord (probably not in accord with government regulations) provided power for a light and a radio. I'd learned carpentry at school, so I reconfigured the inside with my uncle to provide secure sleeping quarters. At first, I did enjoy the peace and quiet. Unfortunately, when it rained the roof would leak. After prolonged rain the carpet would be soaked, and an unpleasant odor would emerge. And I would hear drip … drip … drip throughout the night. Even now, I find dripping water to be quite disturbing. Despite repeated promises, over many years, my father never did repair that roof. It was beyond my capability (despite repeated efforts), and I never had sufficient pocket money to fund a repairer. When I started work, I moved back into the house onto a small corner of the back verandah (which adjoined the kitchen and was a thoroughfare to the outside). The van was abandoned.

A wooden paling fence separated my parent's property from the adjoining neighbors, the Rickwoods. It was quite a long fence, over 225 feet, and was quite old. Many of the palings and the support poles had rotted away, so the fence fell into disrepair and stood that way throughout my youth. It was an eyesore. The fence was eventually replaced many years later when the Rickwoods had left, and a new apartment building was constructed.

One thing that these incidents (and others) impressed upon me was the importance of fixing things when they became broken. And to do so quickly. Even during our early marriage when funds were scarce, my wife and I always maintained a separate budget for repairs and maintenance. When something stopped working or broke down, we repaired it. Our family home has always been well cared for and remains in good shape four decades after we moved in.

During my time sitting on government audit committees, I am astonished at the level of maintenance backlogs across public assets. There seems to be greater enthusiasm for public officials to cut the ribbon, uncover a plaque, and appear in photos than there is to actually invest in the maintenance of these very same assets. It is important for boards, audit committees, and business leaders to maintain effective strategic asset arrangements, and these should include strategic asset planning, asset registers, logging of maintenance and repair needs, including asset quality on the risk register, and initiating remedial action when necessary, especially when the asset condition falls outside the board's risk appetite level.

Business leaders and their people also need to remain alert to the breakdown of personal relationships, with the aim of fixing them swiftly and appropriately (Chapter 2 mentioned the need for meaningful arrangements for managing complaints, and stakeholder management and communications were discussed in Chapters 3 and 8).

Leave a Legacy

Members of my mother's family (the Ausburns) have lived in the Nepean district ever since John Ausburn came to Penrith in the mid-1800s … some 160 years ago. Penrith was a very different place at that time and its population was just a few 1,000 people. John Ausburn's ancestry now extends to at least seven generations, with a continued family presence (including my own). A local historian (Betty Hargreaves) recognized the Ausburns as *one of the pioneering families that contributed enormously to the growth, prosperity and heritage of Penrith.*

I was well aware that the generation of Ausburn's born in the 1921 to 1930 decade had left an enduring legacy for the Nepean District, particularly with respect to football (Ken), rowing (Bob), and the local hospital (Bon). The Ausburns were visionary pioneers who took many of the first steps that left a rich footprint for the Nepean community to enjoy today, and they helped to lay the foundation for some of the district's greatest celebrations including the 2000 Olympics (rowing) and one of Australia's most successful sports brands (Panthers).

So, I lobbied through the local council to the Geographical Names Board for the family and its legacy to be officially recognized by the naming of a park or reserve in their honor. It was a long and time-consuming process, but in September 2016 the government gazetted the Ausburn Reserve in Emu Plains, near the western bank of the Nepean River.

The local Mayor hosted the official opening of the Ausburn Reserve in March 2017. Rubbing shoulders with local dignitaries were over 100 members of the Ausburn clan who had come from all points of the compass, including interstate and overseas, for the event.

The Mayor and I delivered speeches, and my mother joined the Mayor in cutting the ribbon. Mum had made the six-hour trip especially for the event. She was in her element. It was a very proud moment. She mixed with her immediate family, nieces and nephews, friends and dignitaries. Sadly, it was the last time I (and many others) saw her as she suddenly and unexpectedly passed away some weeks later. But what a farewell it had been!

Leaving a legacy *means making a contribution to future generations. For some people, leaving a legacy is important for them to feel that their life mattered. For others, it is simply being remembered for what they want to be remembered for, such as a tangible achievement, being a champion for a cause, or for being a good parent espousing strong values.*

EXHIBIT 13.6 Five ways to craft a legacy.

People will leave a legacy in different ways. And many who do so are quiet achievers (like the Ausburns) who do what they do because it is the right thing. They don't seek or expect gratitude.

It was at a management training course at the turn of the century that I was challenged to think about the legacy I would leave. All of the participants were required to write their own eulogy, as a way of thinking about what it was we wanted to be remembered for at the end of our lives. It was a challenging and somewhat emotional exercise and sharpened ones thinking.

Business leaders of today would benefit from the clarity of completing a similar eulogy exercise. Several ways of crafting a legacy are shown in **Exhibit 13.6**.

A person's legacy stays in the hearts and minds of other people and is shared through the stories they tell about you. US statesman Benjamin Franklin (1706–1790) is quoted as saying, "If you would not be forgotten as soon as you are dead, either write something worth reading or do something worth writing."

CHAPTER 13 – TEN CLOSING REFLECTIONS

- Individuals with natural curiosity or inquisitiveness should be encouraged to explore the possibilities, as they will often challenge the status quo to deliver innovative opportunities and solutions for business.
- Business leaders should weave professional growth into their culture to create an environment where people want to grow, recognizing growth typically occurs in a state of discomfort or disruption in the workplace.
- Individuals need to take ownership of their own motivation, and if it is waning, they need to do something about it like a new activity, a course of study, a cause to help others, a new hobby, or even a change in jobs.
- Individuals should present themselves in a professional well-dressed and well-groomed manner with effective tone of

voice and good body posture, in recognition that first impressions are critical and the way they dress typically reflects the way they feel.

- Business leaders should put sufficient thought into their office environment so that it presents as a stylish, functional, organized, uncluttered, productive, and professional office space.
- Individuals should seek to understand their preferred personal professional growth expectations, then assess their goals against their career progression to determine and plan the steps to close the gap.
- Individuals need someone to support them and their endeavors, and put meaning into what they do.
- Boards, audit committees, and business leaders should maintain effective strategic asset arrangements that ensure asset conditions don't fall outside the board's risk appetite level.
- Business leaders and individuals need to remain alert to the breakdown of personal relationships, with the aim of fixing them swiftly and appropriately.
- Individuals should challenge themselves to think about what it is they want to be remembered for at the end of their lives and the legacy they will leave, as this will provide meaningfulness and influence the way they behave.

14 And We Told You So ... the 2020s

GLOBAL CONNECTIONS

Governance, risk, compliance, and assurance professionals have often experienced push-back, been ridiculed, or challenged by management and other stakeholders when emphasizing the importance of good business practices like business continuity management, crisis management, balance sheet management, cash reserves management, capacity management, telecommunications bandwidth, and chain supply certainty (amongst others). The 2020 coronavirus (COVID-19) has reshaped the business and societal landscape like never before ... because the world has never been so connected as it is today through travel, telecommunications, social media, and supply channels. This section will draw out some of the lessons for governance, risk, compliance, and assurance professionals ... and for boards, audit committees, and business leaders! During challenging times, I often reflect on the wisdom of Henry Ford (1863–1947) who said, "You can't build a reputation on what you are going to do."

PERSONAL STORY[1]

We approached 2020 with great hope for the new decade. By the end of 2019, large parts of Australia were experiencing a severe drought. However, hope was born out of predictions that rain would come over the ensuing year that was sufficient to fill the depleted dams and give hope to the drought-stricken famers.

But the hope faded slightly in the first week of January 2020 when a heatwave hit the eastern states of Australia. On one day in early January, my hometown of Penrith was reported as the hottest place on earth when it recorded a new high of just over 120 degrees Fahrenheit (i.e. 48.9 degrees Celsius).

Then the wildfires that had been lingering throughout December, suddenly burst out of control over the Christmas/New Year period ... in every

[1] The statistics contained in this section were collated by the author from various media reports throughout 2020. The statistics have not been independently verified and are intended to be illustrative of the challenging period.

state of the largest island on earth. The mega-wildfires spread further and further over days and weeks with seemingly no end in sight. Local firefighters were supplemented by 668 personnel from New Zealand, Canada, and the United States, and almost 6,000 firefighters from other Australian states. The horror bushfire season continued through the early months of 2020, with devastation reported daily on the news bulletin. The shock and sadness overriding the community was palpable; somebody was either affected directly by the wildfires or knew somebody who was.

In the end, the wildfire devastation was unprecedented, with the media reporting:

- More than one billion animals were killed.
- So many koalas were lost, they are likely to be elevated from a vulnerable species to endangered (koalas are a type of marsupial unique to eastern and south-eastern Australia).
- 24.2 million acres (9.8 million hectares) were burned.
- 3,048 houses were lost.
- 33 human fatalities were the direct result of the fires, including 9 firefighters.
- Estimated property losses of $A1.9 billion.
- About 80 percent of Australians were exposed to smoke during the wild fires.
- Smoke indirectly claimed almost 450 lives, resulted in almost 4,700 people being hospitalized for asthma, heart, and lung problems, and caused billions of dollars of health costs.

The rain finally came in February 2020. It helped bring the wildfires under control. Then it rained … and rained … and rained. The large dams around Sydney that had been depleted to just 42 percent full, suddenly filled to over 80 percent capacity within a few days. But the rain didn't stop and many areas that had been destroyed by wildfires just weeks earlier were now severely flooded.

***Warragamba Dam**, south-west of Sydney, is one of the largest domestic water supply dams in the world, supplying water to more than 5 million people. It stores around 80 percent of Sydney's water, with its storage lake being four times the size of Sydney Harbour. The dam was sitting at just 42 percent capacity in February 2020, with tight water usage restrictions in place. By August 2020 the dam had reached 100 percent capacity, representing the most rapid six-month surge in the water level since the 1960s.*

What a start to the year! It couldn't get any worse. Then whispers of a global pandemic surfaced and started getting louder by March 2020. The whole world was suddenly in crisis as COVID-19 played havoc with our lifestyles and economies across the world. I was suddenly reminded of the storytelling of my parents-in-law, and the restrictions they had endured in the Netherlands (northwestern Europe) during the depression and war years. Reality hit!

The key insights from this phase of my story are not on the disasters that have occurred, but on how they have sparked innovation, broken through barriers, and inspired new ways of working. These disastrous events have increased our focus on the wellbeing of others, and reinforced the importance of fundamental risk management basics like business continuity and crisis management. The deep dives include:

- Embrace crisis management.
- Maintain a pandemic plan.
- Pursue red tape reduction.
- Sustain the supply chain long-term.
- Consider risks to sovereignty.
- Maintain professional connections.
- Watch out for others in need.
- Position yourself to step from one level of leadership to another.

******

The events of 2020 sparked a fresh look at risk management, and the operation of business. Integrated disaster and recovery arrangements have been pursued to improve resilience.

Australia is the driest inhabited continent in the world, and the widespread drought that was endured for several years leading into 2020 was said to be the most severe on record, and as bad as it gets according to meteorologists. Federal and state governments have been spurred on to boost water storage capacity to safeguard local communities, with risk-mitigation announcements made in early-2020 for:

- Construction of the first new dam to be built in the state of New South Wales for over 30 years, in the north-west of the state.
- Enlarging the capacity of an existing dam by 50 percent in the mid-west of the state.
- Building a new pipeline to sure-up water security for country towns and drought-affected farmers.
- Removal of temporary earthwork dams (known as "block banks") from Australia's third-longest river system (the Darling River, at 915 miles, or 1,472 km) to ensure the flows, or "first flush," help to restart the parched river and bring fresh life to it.

The Australian wildfires of 2019/2020 saw a fresh response to risk management, with the media reporting:

- More than 2,000 satellite dishes will be installed across Australia to maintain critical communications if phone lines are lost.
- Purchase of two new aircraft to map "at risk" fire grounds and deliver warning messages to the community much earlier.
- Secure more stable fire trucks that are less likely to roll-over in rough terrain.
- Improve face masks, helmets, and other safety equipment to boost personal protective equipment available to frontline fire fighters.

The global COVID-19 pandemic saw lock-downs, state border closures, and other social-distancing restrictions being put in place, and many people working from home. Even organizations with mature and largely effective business continuity and crisis management arrangements had to refresh and strengthen their arrangements, following practical operational failings, to incorporate more intense and widespread digital solutions, and boost the available bandwidth.

There have been many other profound changes across the world in a short period of time. For instance, residents of India could see the towering peaks of the Himalayas for the first time in 30 years after a significant drop in pollution (the Himalaya mountain range in Asia separates the plains of the Indian subcontinent from the Tibetan Plateau, and has many of earth's highest peaks, including the highest, Mount Everest). The media also reported the following:

- 92 percent increase in lunch food delivery and 76 percent for breakfast.
- 82 percent increase in parcel delivery of alcohol products.
- 70 percent surge in internet demand when work and school went online.
- 50 percent increase in television audiences compared to last year.
- 50 percent plummet in demand for petrol.
- 48 percent fewer commuters, as many people transitioned to working from home.

The most profound changes from the COVID-19 response involved the swift loosening of red tape requirements by governments, which would normally take many years to implement. These changes were inspired by the need to support economic activity. Examples include:

- Allowing construction sites to operate on weekends and public holidays (previously restricted).

- Doubling the "tap and go" (contactless) maximum payment limits at the checkouts.
- Permitting round-the-clock grocery operations (rather than regulating store opening times).
- The adoption of audio-visual link options for witnessing affidavits, statutory declarations, and other legal documents.
- Lifting restrictions to make it easier for food trucks and dark kitchens to be established and operate (note - dark kitchens sell meals exclusively through delivery and are also called virtual kitchens, cloud kitchens, ghost kitchens or delivery-only restaurants).
- Authorizing the bottling of tap beer and allowing it to be sold to the public (it contains fewer preservatives and additives than bottled beer and must be consumed quickly, within four weeks compared to nine months for traditional bottled beer).
- Lifting restrictions on takeaway alcohol so that bars could still operate at a reduced level.

Businesses reinvented themselves. And did so quickly. A fashion school that teaches clothing design to migrants and refugees adopted a different business model and new strategy to "survive and thrive," switching from a fashion focus to sewing scrubs for healthcare workers in the fight against COVID-19.

The medicos had been grappling with the idea of introducing telehealth consultations for some time, but had never progressed past the concept stage due to differing opinions on the advantages and disadvantages. Telehealth consultations were implemented swiftly when the global pandemic COVID-19 social-distancing and isolation restrictions came into force in 2020. The concept worked well and was well-received, and is expected to become a normal and accepted part of the health system in future (noting that some consultations will still need to be face-to-face). There are suggestions that tripartite telehealth consultations could now be viable in the future, involving the general practitioner, specialist, and patient.

*A **telehealth consultation** is a consultation where a patient and their specialist or general practitioner are not in the same room as each other and utilize technology to be able to see and hear each other. The patient sees the doctor through their computer screen.*

CONTEXT

When taken together, the key insights from this phase of my story are illustrated in **Exhibit 14.1**.

EXHIBIT 14.1 Responding to changes in the global business environment.

KEY TAKEAWAYS AND DEEP DIVES

Embrace Crisis Management

Esteemed CEO Peter Jones reflected sagely when addressing the COVID-19 pandemic, "Many companies have had crisis management plans in place, but few would have factored in a scenario of a global pandemic that effectively shuts down the economy. … (T)he COVID-19 crisis is unprecedented in its scope and the speed with which it has spread. A health crisis now triggers an economic one – an ultimate risk management scenario."[2]

> ***Crisis management*** *is a critical public relations process by which an organization deals with a sudden, unexpected, significant, and disruptive event that threatens to harm its operations and activities or its customers and other stakeholders.*

Mr Jones further highlighted, "According to PWC's Global Crisis Survey 2019, nearly seven out of 10 leaders (69 per cent) have experienced at least one corporate crisis in the last five years, and companies with over 5,000 employees are likely to have experienced more than five crises – an average of one a year."[3]

All business brands are likely to suffer from crises that create public relations challenges. Clear and effective crisis management arrangements,

[2] Peter Jones, "Internal audit needs to reboot through the pandemic crisis" (Institute of Internal Auditors Australia), 2020 https://www.iia.org.au/news-media/news/2020/04/01/internal-audit-needs-to-reboot-through-the-pandemic-crisis (sourced 13 May 2020).

[3] Ibid

including well-considered communication, will usually invoke a quick, transparent, and genuine response, whereas trying to hide, defend, or ignore the organization's gaffes will usually stall any recovery.

Reports emerged in 2017 of a couple of unrelated events concerning a US airline. Firstly, social media exploded when the company barred two teenage passengers from boarding a flight because of the leggings they wore. Secondly, a video was released onto social media of an airline customer being brutally dragged and bloodied from a flight, after he was asked to give up his seat (initially thought to be because of overbooking, but later reported that the seats were repurposed for the company's own employees). In both cases the company defended the actions of its staff, but the public's reaction was quick and decisive. The company lost $US800 million in total value within 24 hours of the second incident, and is likely to have suffered long-term damage to its brand.

Boards and audit committees should satisfy themselves that the business has a crisis management plan in place for handling a crisis after it has occurred. The plan should aim at recovering the organization's brand and reputation as best as possible from a serious event. The common features of a crisis management plan are included in **Exhibit 14.2**. The plan should be reviewed and updated periodically and refreshed after every significant crisis to incorporate improvements and lessons learned.

Boards and business leaders recognize that many widespread crises (like the COVID-19 pandemic) require extremely fluid and dynamic planning to address multi-level and complex scenarios while maintaining business-as-usual, and tackling the crisis itself. They need to be agile in adapting

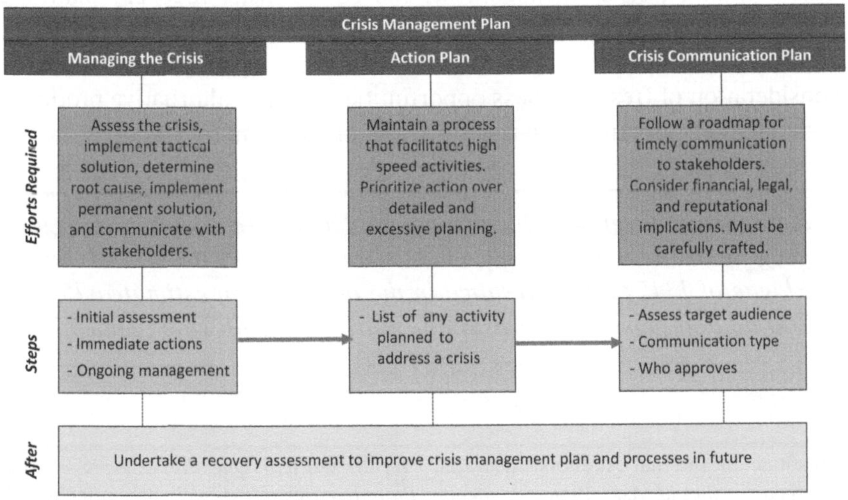

EXHIBIT 14.2 Common features of a crisis management plan.

the control environment to safeguard against the emerging and uncertain risks, including the broader effects on the economy, and its consequent impacts on supply chains, cash flows, forecasts, and staffing.

Cash sits at the heart of the fiscal health of the organization and is essential for it to stay solvent. An organization's longer-term sustainability requires it to have (or have access to) sufficient cash at all times to purchase new assets and to pay staff, rental, leases, bank loans, taxes, and other operating expenses.

Boards and audit committees should keep a close watch on the organization's solvency during an enduring crisis. This will encompass the organization's current and liquid ratios; net asset position; cash at bank and on deposit; trade debtors (and aging); bad debt write-offs in the reporting period; trade creditors (and aging); and whether taxes, compulsory retirement contributions, and insurances have been paid.

It becomes even more challenging when a crisis results in the usual business premises being closed down, requiring the business leaders and staff to function effectively in a team environment while working remotely. Well-prepared organizations are able to leverage technology as an enabler, and rely on workable secure VPN's (i.e. virtual private network, that enables users to send and receive data across shared or public networks as if their digital devices were connected directly to the private network).

Maintain a Pandemic Plan[4]

The organization's business continuity management arrangements should include pandemic planning that is integrated with the organization's business continuity, crisis management, and ICT disaster recovery planning (business continuity was discussed in Chapter 7). In addition to addressing the immediate operational needs, pandemic planning should allow for the consideration of fresh business opportunities, such as alternative products, niche markets, organization redesign, and process improvement.

> ***A pandemic*** *is an unstable disease epidemic spread across a large geographic area, including a whole country or the world. The Great Plague of 1347 to 1351 resulted in the deaths of an estimated 75 to 200 million people in Eurasia and Europe. World-wide pandemics*

[4] Institute of Internal Auditors Australia, *The 20 Critical Questions Series – What Directors Should Ask about Pandemic Planning*, https://www.iia.org.au/technical-resources/20-critical-questions-series (sourced 13 May 2020). Modified and condensed by author.

in the last century include the Spanish flu of 1918–1919 (infecting an estimated 500 million, about a third of the world's then population), HIV/AIDS, Ebola virus, swine flu, bird flu, equine influenza, Middle East Respiratory Syndrome (MERS), Severe Acute Respiratory Syndrome (SARS), and COVID-19. Each of these pandemics has had significant impact on society, countries, governments, commerce and industries, and the global, national, and regional economies. With pandemics occurring periodically, every organization should be prepared for them.

A separate pandemic plan provides guidance to the business leaders on what to do if a pandemic crisis situation occurs; these crises can be sudden and unpredicted. The pandemic plan should be sufficiently flexible to manage the unknown but not overly rigid so the organization becomes transfixed in managing the paper scenario and not the actual crisis situation. A business impact assessment should be available to identify core business functions, operations, supply chains, resources, and support services required, and expanded telecommunications capacity, and when they would be required should a crisis be called (e.g. within 4 hours, 24 hours, 3 days, 7 days, 30 days, or over 30 days).

A pandemic plan should be accessible and readily retrievable by the right people when needed. Common features include:

- Definition of a pandemic and the key risks should one occur.
- Associated strategic, operational, and telecommunications risks, including bandwidth.
- Sufficiency of ICT (information and communications technology) capacity management.
- Governance structure for managing a pandemic crisis.
- Planning for loss of staff, suppliers, customers, markets, revenue, and critical supply chains.
- Supporting policies and procedures and communication, including messaging templates.
- Information on variations to emergency purchasing and procurement arrangements, and the associated delegations and financial controls.
- List of stakeholders (e.g. government, board, investors, suppliers, customers, staff, others), how the relationship will be managed, and a communication strategy.
- Sources of professional advice and support (e.g. medical, legal, compliance, accounting, governance, insurance, business continuity).
- Monitoring government requirements and other sources of sound information, and complying with those requirements.

The pandemic plan should consider the staff and their wellbeing. Considerations include whether:

- There is a process to manage staff, such as redeployment to alternative duties, work from home, forced leave, lay-offs, or redundancy.
- The organization has the necessary set-up for staff to work from home or other locations.
- Staff have the opportunity to receive a health assessment to manage mental and physical health.
- There are clear arrangements if staff get sick or are feeling isolated because of a pandemic.

There are a range of logistical and facilities-related elements that need to be factored into the plan, for instance:

- Who needs to be informed of the situation if buildings and facilities get contaminated and/or need to be evacuated (e.g. the building manager, crisis team, insurer), and what services need to be secured to decontaminate and provide special cleaning services.
- Whether details are recorded of the supply chain for goods and services including essential goods and services, supplier contingency arrangements, supplier contingency testing, and alternative suppliers.
- Information on customers that would facilitate contact tracing by health authorities if needed.
- Requirements to maintain supplies of essential goods and identify future sourcing for these supplies such as personal protective equipment (e.g. protective clothing, masks, overalls, hand sanitizer, alcoholic wipes, cleaning equipment, bottled water).
- Whether the organization understands its obligations to continue to supply essential services (e.g. health, water, power, communications) in line with government and customer requirements and contracts where it is a supplier of essential services.
- Details of potential support to the community and other industry sectors if the organization has a niche, the required capability, or an ability to pivot into new product delivery.

The pandemic plan should provide for activities after the crisis has been brought under control, including a post-pandemic version of what that will likely be, a debrief, identification of lessons learned to help refine the plan, and identification of revised operational processes successfully used during the crisis that can be transitioned to business-as-usual.

The board and/or audit committee should ensure that there is a pandemic plan, that it is tested periodically to provide assurance that the plan will work if activated and aid operational staff, and that internal audit conducts periodic reviews of business continuity management arrangements and reports the results to the audit committee and business leaders.

Pursue Red Tape Reduction

The events of early in the 2020 decade have provided once in a generation chance to reshape business and the economy. Governments have demonstrated a capacity for agility in reducing red tape when motivated to do so in response to crisis situations. This will hopefully translate into a continued focus on eliminating or softening unnecessary red tape that is holding business back while generating little tangible benefits for society. Boards and business leaders have an opportunity to lobby governments and public servants to achieve a philosophical change and speedier responsiveness to much-needed transformation.

> ***Red tape*** *refers to the control requirements for a business that are excessive, overly bureaucratic, cumbersome, or redundant. They inhibit strategic initiatives, customer-centric outcomes, and decision-making and occur in organizations of all types usually as a consequence of excessive government regulation, or formal organizational policies, procedures, and rules.*

Unchallenged and unmanaged red tape is bad for business. It consumes capital and diverts senior management attention away from strategies that grow the business and deliver services to customers; in the public sector it has a similar effect by consuming limited funding. In some situations, red tape is imposed by business operatives and then gets passed along. It could well be that the control was established by "custom and practice" rather than risk-based design.

Likewise, it can also be hugely beneficial to take a proactive stance with regulators to truly understand their requirements. One business leader reflected on how he cut back by almost two-thirds of what was previously submitted to the regulator and received a glowing report on what was delivered. The outcome was achieved by simply meeting with the regulator to understand their actual needs.

Boards, audit committees, and business leaders have an opportunity to drive improvements to the organization's operations by challenging unnecessary red tape imposed by the business, or by better managing red tape imposed by regulators and other external parties. Their appetite for red tape reduction will usually be consistent with the organization's strategies, objectives, and risks. The chief audit executive, chief finance officer, chief risk officer, and compliance managers can aid in this exercise by being mandated (individually and collectively) to pursue red tape reduction through a considered, collaborative, and lawful approach.

When business leaders focus on reducing red tape (or managing it better if it is an externally imposed requirement), they will save the organization money and effort. They will also:

- Help to increase productivity and efficiency.
- Sharpen the business model to drive customer-centric results.
- Empower management to focus on the core activities of the business.
- Boost the staff's ability to achieve business objectives and maintain operational processes.
- Improve productivity.
- Eliminate unnecessary compliance paperwork or controls.
- Remove compliance-created frustrations that can adversely affect employees' job satisfaction.

The theory of constraints *has the premise that where a business process has a bottleneck or weak link (i.e. constraint), it diminishes the output and throughput of the process and, ultimately, impacts adversely on sales, customer satisfaction, and profit. It identifies the weakest area of a process or system and focuses improvement efforts on that area. Constraints can be physical (e.g. machine capacity, resources working on a task, weather conditions, or availability of materials) or non-physical (e.g. company policies and procedures, employee engagement, or low product demand). Eliminating unnecessary, uncompromising, and costly red tape has the potential to address some of these business constraints.*

Business leaders can use a systematic and collaborative approach for reducing or better managing red tape by following five key steps:

1. Identify processes or systems that could be improved or eliminated, and prioritize them based on risk and potential benefits to the organization.
2. Map the process to understand how it works in practice, including the risks and controls, the steps, the participants, the goals, and any connections or interfaces with other areas, then model the process to determine how it could work more efficiently and effectively.
3. Attribute a cost saving or customer benefit that would be delivered through the change and recommend the revised process to the

appropriate decision-makers, then have the responsible management execute it with all its improvements.

4. Review the revised process once it has been in operation to confirm improvements have been optimized. Consider what worked well and what didn't to identify any further improvement points.
5. Report the outcomes of red tape initiatives to the audit committee and CEO progressively (as part of the regular reporting approach), and periodically consolidate the overall outcomes (e.g. cost savings and customer benefits) and provide these in a high-level themes-based report to board and C-suite.

Sustain the Supply Chain Long-Term

Notwithstanding the downside, every crisis provides an opportunity. The COVID-19 pandemic has exposed the gaps in manufacturing supply chains across the world, and has demonstrated the vulnerability of commodity-based economies to external shocks and the need to address the hollowing out of manufacturing capability. There has been a consequent shift in attitudes and the opportunities with regard to supply chains and local manufacturing that are likely to play out over the next decade.

There have been stories of sudden restrictions in overseas markets coupled with the unprecedented global demand for products such as medical supplies that have shone the light on an over-reliance on supply chains out of certain regions. Some manufacturing companies have "pivoted" out of their normal production into critical ventilator production, while others producing personal protective equipment (PPE) have boosted resourcing to ramp-up production.

Nations are likely to consider a targeted industry strategy which will include a reevaluation of supply chains, diversity of production, and a fresh focus on niche manufacturing where there are comparative advantages to do so. As an example, Australia has an abundance of lithium, but it exports the raw product overseas where batteries are created for use in electronic devices (e.g. the iPhone) and electric car batteries. As a nation, Australia was digging the lithium out of the ground, sending it overseas and then buying the batteries back at a substantially inflated price. A new lithium battery research center will help to shape an Australian lithium manufacturing sector.

While nations with higher wages and salaries will not necessarily be able to manufacture everything they *want*, there is likely to be a shift so they are better-placed to manufacture everything they *need*. Given the reliance on computers and other electronics, it is not surprising that the United States stepped up efforts in 2020 to build new semi-conductor plants within its borders rather than rely on overseas suppliers for chips used in electronics. It is part of a wider solution to improve domestic technology sources.

Boards, audit committees, and business leaders should be refreshing their supply change risk assessments and identifying practical and cost-effective solutions to firm-up more robust supply arrangements in the future. These risk assessments should factor in the broader risks to the nation's sovereignty (discussed in the next section).

Modern slavery reflects another heightened area of risk within the supply chain.

Modern slavery *refers to the condition of being forced, deceived, or coerced by threats or violence to work for little or no pay, and of having no power to control what work you do or where you do it. It is exploitation of people, and often subjects its victims to abuse, inhumane, and degrading treatment. It is also referred to as trafficking in persons, human trafficking, and neo-slavery.*

Trafficking and slavery are common denominators undermining the United Nations' 17 Sustainable Development Goals. As a consequence, modern slavery legislation is being introduced in many developed nations. Regardless of whether legislation is in place, the community is becoming more attuned to responsible consumption, with their purchasing decisions influenced by supply chain safeguards established to address human trafficking, child labor, forced labor, slavery, and human rights crimes.

Where the organization's supply chain extends into other jurisdictions, boards, audit committees, and business leaders need to determine the organization's arrangements for addressing modern slavery. This includes:

1. The risk of human trafficking and slavery in the organization's supply chains and in any part of its own business, including the highest areas of risk and the steps being taken to reduce these risks.
2. The approach used to monitor and measure the effectiveness of removing human trafficking and slavery from the organization's supply chain (including details of any performance indicators established to measure this).
3. Any statements made by the organization about its commitment to addressing modern slavery and how this translates to the organization's values, strategies, objectives, and risks.
4. The human trafficking and slavery policies of the organization, including its due diligence procedures covering human trafficking

and slavery in its business and supply chains (including instances where multiple suppliers and subcontractors are used).
5. The training available to the organization's employees on human trafficking and slavery.

Consider Risks to Sovereignty

Sovereignty is an important concept for any nation. It relates to a state's full right to exercise its power without interference from outside sources or bodies.

An example of risk to sovereignty occurred in 2016 when an eastern-European government was alleged to have interfered in the US presidential election, with the goal of increasing political and social discord and harming the campaign of one of the candidates. Should this have occurred (and that is up to others to determine), then it would undermine the democratic foundations of the United States, which allow the people to choose their government by voting for it.

As we move through the 2020s we are seeing a rise of nationalism across the world. The most notable example is the UK leaving the European Union (EU), with the change known colloquially as Brexit. Some of the apparent drivers for Brexit include a growing distrust of multinational financial, trade, and defense organizations, coupled with the concern of the British people that the EU deprives individual nations (such as theirs) of the power to make many decisions.

A key principle of the UK constitution (some people regard it as the most important part) is parliamentary sovereignty, which makes parliament the supreme legal authority in the UK which can create or end any law. Generally, the courts cannot overrule its legislation and no parliament can pass laws that future parliaments cannot change.[5] To some people, the UK's sovereign law-making powers were challenged by its membership of the EU because the UK was constrained in its actions by the agreements it entered into and laws made under the EU treaties.

Globalization has emerged over recent decades to achieve integration across the world in areas such as transportation, communication, education, trade, and other practices. It has been embraced by different societies, cultures, and regional economies. Global integration has increased the interdependence of various nations and shaped world affairs by driving economic, political, cultural, security, consumption, environmental, and social impacts. It has also boosted the exchange of ideas across different nations.

[5] https://www.parliament.uk/site-information/glossary/parliamentary-sovereignty/ (sourced 12 May 2020).

Global pandemics and economic downturns have highlighted the risks arising from global integration, including:

- Trade integration results in greater exposure to the economies and policies of other countries (e.g., in 2021 the trade sanctions and increased tariffs imposed unfairly on the goods of another country by a major economic powerhouse as a perceived act of punishment for speaking out, threatened whole industries, a national economy and its sovereignty).
- Financial integration can result in more severe financial crises.
- People-to-people links means the disease in one nation can quickly become a global pandemic.

Conversely, the continuation of international trade is vital to innovation and competition, and some experts caution that any move to increase economic independence nationally is likely to result in reduced living standards. In any event, many nations will consider the potential for stronger domestic capacity to manufacture medical equipment as part of their response to the COVID-19 pandemic. Some rebalancing is likely to occur, as discussed in the previous section on supply chains.

Boards and business leaders have an opportunity to consider the risks to their nation's sovereignty when making far-reaching business decisions. For example, if competitors in the same industry are outsourcing to the same jurisdiction, or are reliant on similar supply chains, or have the majority of exports to the same market, does this present a national (rather than business) risk that should be diversified? The Australian Cyber Security Centre has reflected, "understanding if another country's laws and intent pose a specific threat to an Australian interest requires understanding the specific country's likely interest in the system and their historical relationship with Australia."[6] Guidance issued by the Centre reflects the importance of organizations in understanding the cyber risk posed by the interaction of a nation and a vendor. There are five key points to consider:[7]

1. What country has primary influence over that vendor, and to what extent the vendor is influenced by the state? This is usually determined by the primary nationality of the vendor, though this may even differ for different companies in the same country.

[6] https://www.cyber.gov.au/publications/cyber-supply-chain-risk-management-practitioner-guide (sourced 12 May 2020).

[7] Ibid

2. What other nations influence the vendor? This occurs if the vendor provides services to, or manufactures its product in another country. It may be of particular interest if your data is located in a country considered high risk through a service used or provided by the vendor.
3. What significant dependencies does a vendor have for the delivery of their product or service? Sub-contracting is very common, and an organization may find its data being stored or accessed by another vendor it did not expect to be involved.
4. The broader perspective of a specific vendor's activity in your nation. For large vendors, nation-wide influence is feasible. Look at other activity undertaken by that vendor in your region to determine if there is any unexpected influence to your system.
5. Where there is a nationally critical system, it is useful to know the experience of others with that vendor, including whether it has successfully positioned itself in another aspect of your cyber supply chain or influencers. Also consider what their internal cyber security practices are like. If a vendor cannot secure itself, it is open to exploitation by any actor interested in exploiting an organization through the trust given to a vendor.

Maintain Professional Connections

As a chief audit executive, I used to monitor the performance of the internal audit activity through a series of key performance indicators (KPIs) presented in a quarterly balanced scorecard report. One of the key measures was "professional outreach," as I wanted to encourage senior members of the team to maintain high-level interactions with practitioners outside the company. The key drivers were to maintain environmental awareness of emerging trends and issues, boost professionalism, and avoid becoming too inward-looking.

> *A **balanced scorecard** is a well-established approach to structuring qualitative and quantitative performance measures for an activity and reporting the results in a balanced way.*

We also established a stakeholder-relationship management program with the objective of identifying our stakeholders, then determining strategies and approaches to build and maintain effective relationships. (Stakeholder management and communications were discussed in Chapters 3 and 8). There are formal stakeholder relationships within the organization (i.e.

persons, groups or organizations that can affect, or be affected by, your activity) and these include the board, CEO, business leaders, auditors, managers, service providers, and staff.

Within a stakeholder-relationship program, professional connections are likely to have "low influence" and "high impact" on the priority quadrant. While professional liaison has a low degree of influence within the organization, it has a high impact on the professionalism of a service area. These contacts encompass governance, risk management, compliance, accounting, audit. and other professional bodies that set standards and provide guidance.

Outside of the formal stakeholder relationships, there are many professional connections that help you to stay afloat and remain connected with the outside world.

Once you have recognized a professional connection that shares similar values and is likely to be interested in sharing ideas, then log their details in a running list you have made. You can record the list in your planner, create an Excel spreadsheet, use a sophisticated application, or maintain another repository. Whichever form your list takes, record relevant information for each contact including their name, place of employment, date and location of your first meeting, the last time you connected with them, the reason for the contact, notes from your last conversation, and any other noteworthy information. Keep your contacts list updated, noting changes as they occur.

When you meet someone new, record key details on the reverse of their business card, then transcribe the information onto your running list if it is a connection you wish to maintain. Follow up with them within 24 hours (for instance send a quick email on the morning after the meeting or event) as this will encourage relationship-building.

Reach out to your professional connections periodically. Don't just wait until you need something. Drop them a letter or an email periodically, send them a card on special occasions, connect through social media like Facebook or LinkedIn. Plan regular check-ins or arrange occasional get-togethers.

If one of your professional connections reaches out to you for help, act quickly and effectively as this can strengthen your relationship in general.

Things do change over time, and it is entirely possible that your professional connection drops you from their network. So, if they ignore three of your messages over a reasonable period of time, then assume they don't want to keep up with you. Don't be put off by it, just move on.

Watch Out for Others in Need

When pandemics and other crises arise, it is important to keep abreast of changes in the economic, health, and professional landscapes through national and state government websites, media reports, and other occasional updates. These updates will equip you with information on your personal health risk factors, and the knowledge to address any concerns that might arise quickly in a well-informed manner.

Business leaders, HR practitioners, and GRC specialists can also watch out for others during a crisis through ten key steps:

1. Establish a new routine with your manager, peers, and other work colleagues to maintain regular contact daily or at least several times a week (e.g. through video-conferencing, teleconferencing, emails, social media, or personal phone contact).
2. Maintain effective networking, including reaching out to key stakeholders, customers, regulators, and scrutineers (e.g. external auditors) to keep them informed of the impacts on your services and completion of the work plan, and what it means for them.
3. If you are offering advisory and consulting expertise to external or internal clients, let them know who to call to discuss difficult operational issues, business changes, new products or services, or proposed/enforced changes to the internal control environment.
4. Maintain contact with others who are in higher-risk health or vulnerability categories, such as immediate family members, relatives, friends, professional colleagues, and neighbors; similarly, consider reaching out to former professional colleagues that you might wish to reconnect with while the opportunity is there.
5. Look out for the anxiety levels of your colleagues, and, where needed, offer yourself as someone who they can talk to openly, frankly, and meaningfully to put their mind at ease.
6. Watch for potential instances of domestic or family violence, as these can spike at times of crisis, and be aware of "help and support hotlines" that could be used.
7. Encourage colleagues to keep abreast of any changes to their personal financial circumstances, maintain an adequate cash flow, seek government benefits that may be on offer, inform their bank of any liquidity challenges, maintain their taxation obligations, and pay their bills and other commitments on time.
8. Ensure colleagues are maintaining a "normal" routine as much as possible, including keeping on top of household tasks (e.g. mowing, gardening, home maintenance, home cleaning, washing, shopping, etc.), maintaining a healthy well-balanced diet, following their faith, and sustaining personal hygiene and grooming. (Lapses in these areas can be detrimental to a person's mental health and wellbeing).

9. Where a lockdown occurs, encourage people to catch up on things they normally put off because they are "time poor" (such as reading, catching the latest movie, watching favorite reruns, playing board games and cards, volunteering/charity work, or taking up a new hobby like painting), and maintain regular exercise within the confines of their own home or within the local community (while keeping recommended distances from others).
10. Ensure someone (e.g. a partner, family member or friend) has details of professional contacts (e.g. your manager, the chief executive, the audit committee secretariat, the chair of the audit committee, a critical stakeholder or supplier etc.) that they can use to inform them of your situation if you are suddenly unavailable due to unanticipated illness or hospitalization.

Position Yourself to Step from One Level of Leadership to Another

Boards should always maintain one eye on CEO succession (discussed in Chapter 12). In turn, the CEO and other business leaders need to identify and invest in the "stars" within the organization at several rungs below the C-suite so that these people can be tested in more senior roles should opportunities arise (the importance of identifying talent is discussed in Chapter 4).

Boards, audit committees, and business leaders are expecting more from those who report to them. As an example, with the responsibilities of audit committees expanding, they need better and more timely insights from the chief audit executive, chief finance officer, chief risk officer, compliance managers, and others. At the same time, it is now more common for the chief audit executive to sit within the C-suite as a trusted partner of the board and CEO. It follows that there are greater opportunities for the people sitting below the C-suite.

Individuals need to initially focus on mastering their current role. Once they have done so, they should gradually learn about the roles that sit above them. This can be achieved by shadowing the leaders, observing how they operate, offering to handle some of their tasks, managing stakeholder relationships effectively, demonstrating an innovative mindset and a capability for leading others, and perhaps undertaking further relevant tertiary studies.

Just prior to retiring from the Australian Tax Office I was asked to speak to a group of emerging leaders about how they could improve the likelihood of them achieving success in their careers. Football was a "common language" amongst the group, so I developed an acronym based on my

EXHIBIT 14.3
PANTHERS planks for achieving career success

People	Recognize leadership is not about what you can do by yourself, rather it's about what you can inspire your team to do. People truly are the entity's most valuable assets and their growth and wellbeing are entrusted to you. If you are not interested in the development of others, then avoid leadership responsibilities and stick to lower-level roles. If you find leading others to be energizing then you are likely to excel in a leadership role.
Aspiration	Understand your personal aspirations, so you can move towards your hopes and dreams with a view to reaching something that you would truly like to attain in your life. Clarity of your aspiration will help you to achieve your future vision, and it can be short-term or long-term. Your aspirations will usually dovetail with your career or life goals, which reflect the path you expect to take as part of your career or life trajectory.
Never-ending search for excellence	Recognize that what you do today will not be good enough tomorrow as the goal-posts keep changing. The needs and expectations of your board and business leaders will be ever-expanding. You and your team must constantly evolve to deliver the level of excellence stakeholders' demand. You will need to maintain an innovative mindset and strive to deliver outcomes that meet or exceed the needs of stakeholders.
Tone at the top	Ensure your personal values align with the corporate values and culture nurtured by the board and business leaders. You need to be comfortable with the tone at the top reflected by the organization's leadership, which will be evident through the ethical atmosphere that cascades throughout the organization. If your values are at odds with the tone at the top, and you have little chance of influencing a change, then leave the organization.
Happy workplace	Strive to nurture happy employees to achieve optimal teamwork, more trusting relationships, and stronger employee retention. The benefits of inspiring a sense of fun at work are illustrated in **Exhibit 1.5**. If you're not happy at work, then this will show through and impact your legitimacy, influence, and outcomes. If you can't engender a sense of fun in the workplace, then you need to consider working elsewhere.

(*Continued*)

EXHIBIT 14.3 (*Continued*)
PANTHERS planks for achieving career success

External focus/ internal alignment	Ensure the needs and expectations of customers and other stakeholders external to the organization are delivered through seamless, focused, and aligned internal service providers who are guided by the overarching business strategies, values, objectives, and goals, customer service charter commitments (see Chapter 2), and the brand promise. The concept of external focus and internal alignment was explored in Chapter 4.
Relationships	Strive to establish and maintain meaningful relationships with people at all levels within the organization and externally. Effective stakeholder engagement will help you keep abreast of their strategies, objectives, risks, emerging issues, and priorities. You will then be better-placed to service their needs. Maintain a systematic approach to managing meaningful relationships, and don't allow them to drift along through an ad hoc approach.
Stability of direction/ leadership	Inspire others to achieve business objectives and goals by leaving no doubt in their minds as to what matters, and what will and won't be tolerated. Stability of direction and leadership impact positively on people by creating a credible tone at the top that shapes a lived culture that is aligned with the corporate values, boosts productivity, builds trust, and helps to retain top talent. People want a sure hand; capable, calm, steady, and believable.

favorite football team, the Penrith Panthers (my local side in the national league). The essential planks of PANTHERS are:

People
Aspiration
Never-ending search for excellence
Tone at the top
Happy workplace
External focus/internal alignment
Relationships
Stability of direction/leadership

These planks are explained in **Exhibit 14.3**, and those people who embrace them will be better positioned to step from one level of leadership to another when the opportunity arises.

CHAPTER 14 – TEN CLOSING REFLECTIONS

- Boards and audit committees should satisfy themselves that the business has an up-to-date crisis management plan that helps to recover the organization's brand and reputation from a serious incident.
- Boards and audit committees should monitor the organization's solvency during an enduring crisis, given that cash sits at the heart of the fiscal health of the organization.
- The board and/or audit committee should ensure there is a pandemic plan, and that it is tested periodically to ensure it will work if activated.
- Boards, audit committees, and business leaders can drive improvements to the organization's operations by challenging unnecessary red tape imposed by the business, or by better managing red tape imposed by regulators and other external parties.
- The chief audit executive, chief finance officer, chief risk officer, and compliance managers can aid in red tape reduction through a considered, collaborative, and lawful approach.
- Boards, audit committees, and business leaders should refresh their supply chain risk assessments, identify solutions to firm-up more robust future supply arrangements, and consider modern slavery implications where the supply chain extends into other jurisdictions.
- Boards and business leaders should consider national sovereignty and supply chain diversity risks when making far-reaching business decisions, especially where whole industries rely on similar supply chains that potentially present a national (rather than solely business) risk.
- Individuals should recognize and invest in professional connections that will help them to stay afloat and remain connected with the outside world.
- Business leaders, HR practitioners, and GRC specialists should watch out for the wellbeing of others during pandemics and other crises, and equip colleagues with information on personal health risk factors and periodic economic, health, and professional updates.
- Individuals need to recognize that building a reputation results from what you have achieved, rather from what you believe are going to do; they should master their current role, then gradually learn about the roles that sit above them.

15 A Glance into the Future ...

WE DON'T KNOW WHAT WE DON'T KNOW

During much of my career we relied heavily on staple business instruments like landline telephones, checks, and fax machines. The decline of these business instruments has been significant and dramatic:

- Landline telephone usage reached a peak in 2000 with 90 percent of households in the United States having landlines, well above cell phone usage of just 5 percent. Since then, landline phones have lost their relevance – down to little more than 40 percent of households – with smartphones and other mobile technologies becoming a "must have" companion for most people in the developed world.
- Checks were an important and reliable non-cash payment method for both businesses and consumers for several centuries. Market forces and a preference for faster payments have seen the growth of card and electronic payments. As an example, in Australia in 2016, checks represented just 1 percent of the number of non-cash payments, and about 7 percent of the value compared to 85 percent of the number and almost all of their value in 1980.
- Fax (facsimile) machines increased the speed of business transactions in the 1980s, by allowing individuals and companies to disseminate information broadly and quickly. After reaching their peak usage in 1997, reliance on fax machines has declined significantly, though some industries (e.g. law enforcement and the health system) are yet to embrace more modern communication channels and near-instantaneous messaging via text, email, and Instagram.

The technological advances experienced in a single generation even surprised American Superstar Dolly Parton who said, "I never thought, in my lifetime, that you'd be able to watch movies, read books and listen to music from a phone, but I guess the technology of tomorrow is here today."

When I bought my first cell phone about 20 years ago, I could never have imagined the potential power of the device or the innovations to be unleashed through the 2000s in the form of even more advanced smartphones. Global sales of smartphones accelerated from 122.3 million in 2007, to 680.1 million within 5 years (2012), and ultimately hit 1,536.5 million in 2017; the numbers have since stabilized.[1]

And of course, the technological convergence that is now occurring with computers, television sets, and set-top boxes through "Smart TVs" (or a "Connected TV" – TVC) was beyond my wildest imagination. Who would have thought that a traditional television set would evolve to provide integrated internet and interactive web features that equip users to stream music and videos, browse the internet, view photos, watch online interactive media, and access on-demand streaming media at one's fingertips? The global smart TV market is expected to grow by over 293 million units during 2020–2024 with a 21 percent compound annual growth rate (CAGR) during the forecast period.[2]

CONTEXT

There are many new technological developments that will reshape the way businesses operate in the future through innovative methods, systems, and devices.

Exhibit 15.1 includes examples of communication channels and technologies of the future as we know it today. The black boxes in the center of **Exhibit 15.1** reflect examples of staple business instruments that have been substantially transformed (discussed earlier); the dark gray inner boxes reflect examples of changes to digital landscape that have been embraced or gained momentum over recent years; and the light gray outer boxes reflect disruptive innovations and technology that are emerging.

It is hard to comprehend the future of technology by the year 2050. But if the predictions in the media reports are correct, we will expect by 2050:

- The internet to be free for everybody.
- Intercontinental rail travel will be a reality.
- There will be personal aircraft for short trips.
- AI-powered devices will used for routine tasks.
- Self-driving cars will be more common.
- Robots will have taken on half of human's work.
- Cancer mortality will be reduced substantially.
- And perhaps humans will live on mars!

1 "Number of smartphones sold to end users worldwide from 2007 to 2020," https://www.statista.com/statistics/263437/global-smartphone-sales-to-end-users-since-2007/ (sourced 1 September 2020). Intended to be illustrative.

2 "Largest TV manufacturers in the world by market share 2020," blog 21 May 2020. https://blog.technavio.com/blog/largest-tv-manufacturers-by-market-share (sourced 11 September 2020). Intended to be illustrative.

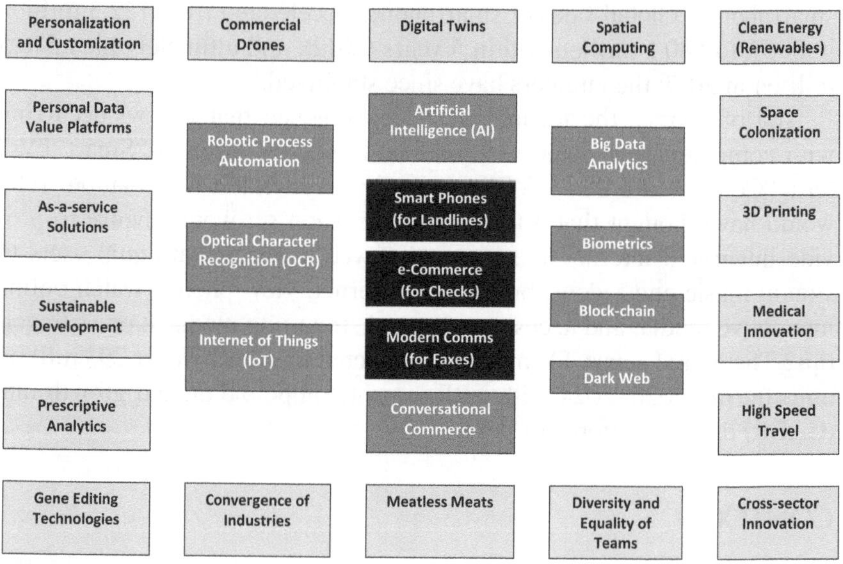

EXHIBIT 15.1 Technologies of the future.[3]

Note: These examples are intended to be illustrative. More technical insights and descriptions are available in other contemporary technical publications.

And one of the scariest predictions is that, by 2050 there will be also a huge increase in the number of cyber-crimes and hackers, commensurate with the increase of internet usage. Data privacy and security will be a primary concern for most people, with cyber-security training to be provided by educators to guide primary school children through to technology users within business.

Quantum computers will also shake up the encryption and authentication protections that organizations rely on today, so business leaders need to be proactive in strengthening the security arrangements that protect their data and systems. Quantum computers have the capability to break the cryptography underlying public key infrastructure (PKI) by 2030, so replacement algorithms capable of securing against quantum computer-based technologies are needed. This is crucial for business segments that need to secure devices or maintain confidentiality of information beyond 2030, especially those with high-level security requirements such as critical infrastructure (e.g. water, energy, and satellites), the military, law

[3] Bruce R. Turner, *Team Leaders Guide to Internal Audit Leadership* (Lake Mary, FL: Internal Audit Foundation, 2020), 39.

enforcement, fire-fighters, automotive industry, airline industry, financial services, and health services.[4]

Quantum computers *harness the wonders of quantum mechanics to deliver greater processing power. They are expected to solve computational problems, such as integer factorization, much faster than classical computers. Quantum computers have the capability to break the cryptography underlying public key infrastructure (PKI).*

With the pending introduction of quantum computers, business leaders should already be planning for the replacement of hardware, software, and services that use public-key algorithms, so that the information is protected from future attacks. With cryptography being the foundation of digital trust, any threat to cryptography can result in unauthorized access to sensitive information, lack of control over connected devices and, potentially, significant dangers to organizational integrity.

KEY TAKEAWAY AND DEEP DIVE

Leverage the Insights of IT Auditors

Information technology (IT) auditing has been a critical element of internal auditing for several decades. Traditionally, IT auditors examine and evaluate an organization's information technology infrastructure, applications, policies, and operations (and this remains important). The primary aim of IT auditing is usually to establish whether established IT controls protect corporate assets, ensure data integrity, and technology solutions are aligned with the organization's overall objectives and goals. IT auditors examine not only physical security controls, but also overall business and financial controls that involve information technology systems.

As operations at modern organizations are increasingly computerized, the breadth of IT auditing has expanded to more broadly cover information and communication technology (ICT) and cloud services. Boards, audit committees, and business leaders are also looking increasingly to IT auditors to provide assurance and advice on cyber-security and controls, particularly given the recent increase (and predicted continued increase) in the number of cyber-crimes and hackers.

4 Paul Lucier, "Six steps to start readying for quantum," 10 August 2020, https://www.isaca.org/resources/news-and-trends/industry-news/2020/six-steps-to-start-readying-for-quantum (sourced 14 September 2020).

***IT auditors** should ideally be certified information systems auditors (CISA), which is a certification gained through ISACA (formerly called the Information Systems Audit and Control Association). To gain CISA certification, individuals need to undertake a course of study, successfully complete an exam, have relevant work experience in a recognized IT field, and satisfy continuing professional education requirements. IT auditors with CISA certification are recognized globally as having attained a standard of achievement in auditing, controlling, monitoring, and assessing an organization's information technology and business systems. CISAs are required to follow ISACA's Information Technology Assurance Framework (ITAF), which includes IT auditing standards and a code of professional ethics.*

The proposed IT audit program of work is usually considered by the audit committee when the chief audit executive presents the forward audit plan. Common considerations in IT audit planning are information systems auditing processes; governance and management of IT; information systems acquisition, development and implementation; information systems operations and business resilience; and, protection of information assets.

The audit committee needs to consider the value they expect to gain from the insights of the IT auditors, with an example of IT audit coverage shown in **Exhibit 15.2**. This coverage could result in:

- Input to the IT/ICT development plan and budget which is usually a subset of the organization's broader strategic and business planning.
- Insights on the best use of existing information technology within and across the organization, and the external interfaces.
- Assurance on ownership, accessibility, and protection of the technology available to the organization.
- Identification of specific training and development needs of the ICT resources relied upon by the business leaders.

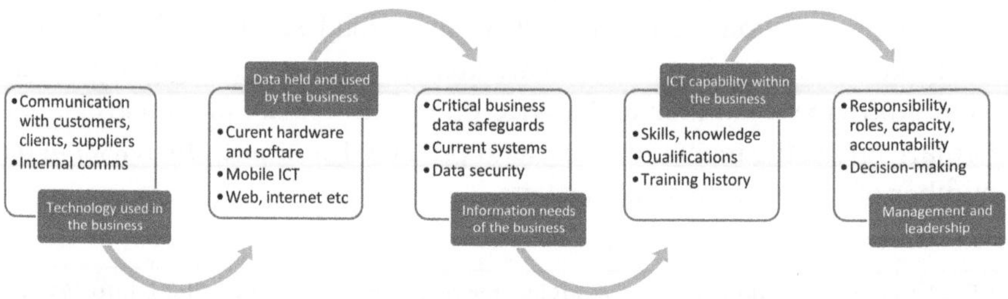

EXHIBIT 15.2 Example of IT auditing coverage.

- Clarity of the current and future positioning of the organization, including inherent risks associated with any proposed ICT development pathways.
- Positioning business leaders to make informed decision-making.

As IT auditing keeps growing in significance, audit committees should be expected to take an interest in ensuring the digital capabilities of IT auditors and those charged with ICT delivery are keeping up with (or ahead of) the broader business environment.

Chapter 6 discusses the importance of stepping-up the internal audit vision, which includes the need for the chief audit executive to develop a strategic roadmap that the audit committee should review, approve, and then monitor through quarterly or half-yearly progress reporting. Internal audit's strategic roadmap should shine the light on the IT audit capability necessary to support the future internal audit work profile, future use of technology for auditing, and, professional development, and advanced technology audit skills needed to transition to new ways of working in the digital-age.

CHAPTER 15 – FIVE CLOSING REFLECTIONS

- Chief audit executives should monitor the new technology developments that are reshaping how businesses operate in the future, and keep abreast of the innovative methods, systems, and devices.
- Business leaders should be planning for the replacement of hardware, software, and services that use public-key algorithms, so that the information is protected from future attacks once advanced technologies like quantum computers are introduced.
- Boards, audit committees, and business leaders should seek assurance and advice from IT auditors on cyber-security and controls, particularly given the recent increase (and predicted continued increase) in the number of cyber-crimes and hackers.
- Audit committees should ensure the digital capabilities of IT auditors and those charged with ICT delivery are keeping up with (or ahead of) the broader business environment.
- Chief audit executives need to inform the audit committee of the IT audit capability and its capacity to support the future internal audit work profile, future use of technology for auditing, and skills needed to transition to new ways of working in the digital-age.

Bruce's great grandmother Elizabeth Jackson 1866–1939. Only in later life did the family find out about its roots with the Gamilaroi people, one of the four largest Indigenous nations in Australia. (Photo: Family's genealogy collection (maintained by Bruce).)

Bruce (front left) with parents Bonnie and Alan and siblings Jen and Jon. (Photo: Personal collection.)

Bruce's childhood home in Penrith where he lived until he married and moved two miles west across the majestic Nepean River to Emu Plains. (Photo: Personal collection.)

Bruce as a toddler with sister Jen. (Photo: Personal collection.)

Bruce as a wedding "page boy." (Photo: Personal collection.)

Bruce second row from front, third from left in middle school class 5A. (Photo: Personal collection.)

Bruce and Bea on their wedding day in 1978. (Photo: Personal collection.)

Visiting his former middle school in Penrith in 2015 for its sesquicentenary. (Photo: Personal collection.)

Bruce has an impressive civic-minded lineage! The Ausburn family's contribution to Penrith across seven generations was recognized in 2017 with the naming of the Ausburn Reserve in Emu Plains in their honor. Bruce's mother, Winsome (Bonnie) Turner nee Ausburn, is pictured sitting on the right with local dignitaries and members of the Ausburn family, including many who travelled from interstate and overseas. (Photo: Penrith City Council (used with permission).)

The ATO Penrith established the Bruce Turner Citizenship Award in 2012 to recognise people who truly make a difference to the business. With the tenth recipient Carol Pinkerton in late-2019. (Photo: Personal collection.)

With siblings Cherylynne, Jonathan (Jon), Leisha, and Jennifer (Jen) in mid-2017 for the funeral of their mother Bonnie. (Photo: Personal collection.)

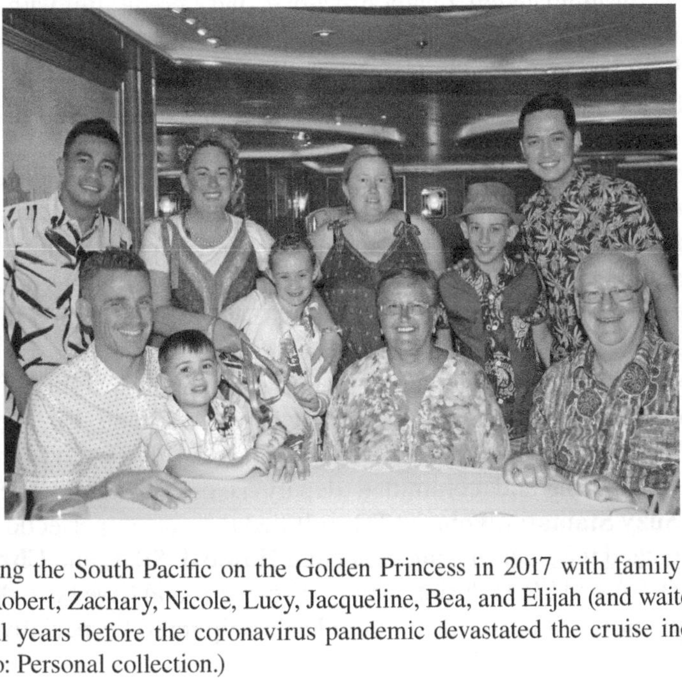

Cruising the South Pacific on the Golden Princess in 2017 with family members Robert, Zachary, Nicole, Lucy, Jacqueline, Bea, and Elijah (and waiters) ... several years before the coronavirus pandemic devastated the cruise industry. (Photo: Personal collection.)

Appendices

ACKNOWLEDGEMENT OF TWENTY-FOUR LEGENDS WHO INSPIRED ME

You cannot craft a successful career on your own. You are really only as good as the 360° support you receive. Having worked with thousands of people throughout the last five decades, I wanted to acknowledge a handful of people who really stood out in terms of their impact on my career. Everyone has been important, and I am sorry if I missed naming anyone who felt they should have been recognized.

In the end, 50% of the people directly acknowledged held senior roles (i.e. audit committee, company secretary, chief executive, and peers) and the remaining 50% were in roles that supported me directly; I also achieved an equal gender representation of 50% males and 50% females. And I was keen to include people representing each of the organizations that I'd worked for prior to my retirement from fulltime work.

I excluded people with whom I have worked for less than two years, and those that I have been involved with solely through my roles on boards and audit committees as they are still active.

One person, **Nihal Fernandopulle** (SBN and RBA), stands out as being the consummate chief audit executive, and I credit him with teaching me about professional internal auditing and how professional auditing standards underpin our work. He also challenged me to think beyond the norm. His exemplary foundations were maintained and driven further by his successor **Clarita Imperial** (RBA).

Internal auditors undertake considerable travel, and it is essential that you travel with people who deliver upon the audit objectives to a high standard and are good travel companions, as were **Valeria Dennis** (RBA), **Brad Harkins** (RBA), and **Leonard Yong** (SBN); Leonard has also written books on foreign exchange and corporate governance which inspired me to take on the challenge of writing books.

All executives rely heavily on the commitment and capability of those who support them directly, as did my Executive Assistants **Liz Memory** (ATO), **Nicole Rapp** (ATO), and **Belinda Hewitt** (SRA). And having a capable, competent and committed deputy is essential, and executive director **Suzy Stamatonikolos** (ATO) fulfilled this role to perfection.

I recognized the emerging talent in **Glen Howard** (SRA) and **Christina Phillips** (RBA and SRA) during their early careers, and have been thrilled to see them progress into critical senior leadership roles. I especially loved the way that experienced risk and audit specialists like **Siri Thongsiri** leveraged their unique ability to 'think outside the box', using techniques that were fresh, creative and inventive.

I reflected on the importance of maintaining a fun business environment in chapter 1, and **Steve Dardo** (ATO) and **Nicole Preissl** (ATO) helped enormously through their passion and energy to nurture the 'joy of life' at the ATO's Penrith site. In my early banking days **Bea Waayer** (now Turner) (RBN) was a delight to work with and she has since proven to be the rock throughout my career and the catalyst for any success I have achieved (we married in 1978).

Andrew Cox (IIA) is a governance, risk management and internal auditing guru who warrants particular recognition as he has had the greatest influence on my professional pursuits over the last fifteen years, always identifying fresh challenges that have helped to keep my mind energized. A rare gem!

When I was a chief audit executive, my audit committee chairs **Bruce Quigley** (ATO) initially and then **Jennie Granger** (ATO) empowered, inspired and stretched me well beyond my 'day job' through their trust, support and encouragement. And independent audit committee member **Peter Kennedy** (ATO) helped me to transition to my first true role as a public servant in a central government agency during the twilight of my career, going above and beyond to aid in my successful transition.

I have worked with some excellent chief executives throughout my career, and three of them stand out because of the values and vision they promoted and the energy, passion and expertise they consistently displayed, **Michael D'Ascenzo** (ATO), **Howard Lacey** (SRA) and **Danny O'Connor** (WSLHD). They were all highly professional and inspirational leaders who got in and got the job done, and provided strong support for my independent audit and oversight roles.

The Company Secretary provides the thread that holds together an effective board and audit committee, and **Irina White** (SRA and IEA) and **Julie Young** (IIA) were exemplars.

Abbreviations:

ATO = Australian Taxation Office
IEA = Integral Energy Australia
IIA = Institute of Internal Auditors
RBA = Reserve Bank of Australia
RBN = Rural Bank of NSW
SBN = State Bank of NSW
SRA = State Rail Authority of NSW
WSLHD = Western Sydney Local Health District

Photographic and Information Repository

Most organizations have someone who flutters around and records their team's memories through photographs and videos. We usually don't value the role they fulfill until we need something. A special call-out to **Simon Woo** (ATO) who has maintained an excellent photographic collection and information repository that has proven to be a savior for me on many occasions, including for this book.

Support Material

Various ancillary/supporting materials can be viewed online at https://www.routledge.com/Rising-from-the-Mailroom-to-the-Boardroom-Unique-Insights-for-Governance/Turner/p/book/9780367559991 or by using the adjoining QR code that will link the reader straight to the download.

These supporting materials include:

- Summary of the 101 Key Insights (the building blocks)
- Detailed steps for reporting to the Audit Committee on the Organization's Values of Integrity
- Further Reading - Twenty-four Books that Helped to Guide Me
- Listing of Exhibits

Index

C

Q

R

S

Y